JOHN CARPENTER'S
ASYLUM

Created by

**John Carpenter,
Thomas Ian Griffith and Sandy King**

VOLUME 2

KING   OLSEN   MANCO   MANDRAKE

A Storm King Comics Publication

STORM KING
COMICS

JOHN CARPENTER'S
ASYLUM
Volume 2

Created by
John Carpenter,
Thomas Ian Griffith and Sandy King

THE BARRENS: Issues 7-8
Written by **Sandy King** and **Trent Olsen**   Art by **Tom Mandrake**
Colors by **Sian Mandrake**   Letter Artist **Janice Chiang**
Covers by **Tom Mandrake**   Edited by **Sandy King**

WELCOME TO ARLINGTON: Issues 9-14
Written by **Sandy King** and **Trent Olsen**   Art by **Leonardo Manco**
Colors by **Mariana Sanzone**   Letter Artist **Janice Chiang**
Covers by **Nick Percival**   Edited by **Sandy King**

Cover Art by **Tim Bradstreet**

Story and characters created by
John Carpenter,
Thomas Ian Griffith and Sandy King

Book Design By **John J. Hill**
Storm King Projects Manager **Ross Sauriol**
Graphic Designer/Onboarding **Sophie Gransard Davies**
Office Co-ordinator **Sean Sobczak**
Sales and Marketing **Rich Johnson**
Publicity by **Sphinx Group — Elysabeth Galati**

Previously published as Issues 7-14 of the Storm King Comics series John Carpenter's Asylum
John Carpenter's Asylum Volume Two, October 2016
Published by Storm King Comics, a division of Storm King Productions, Inc.

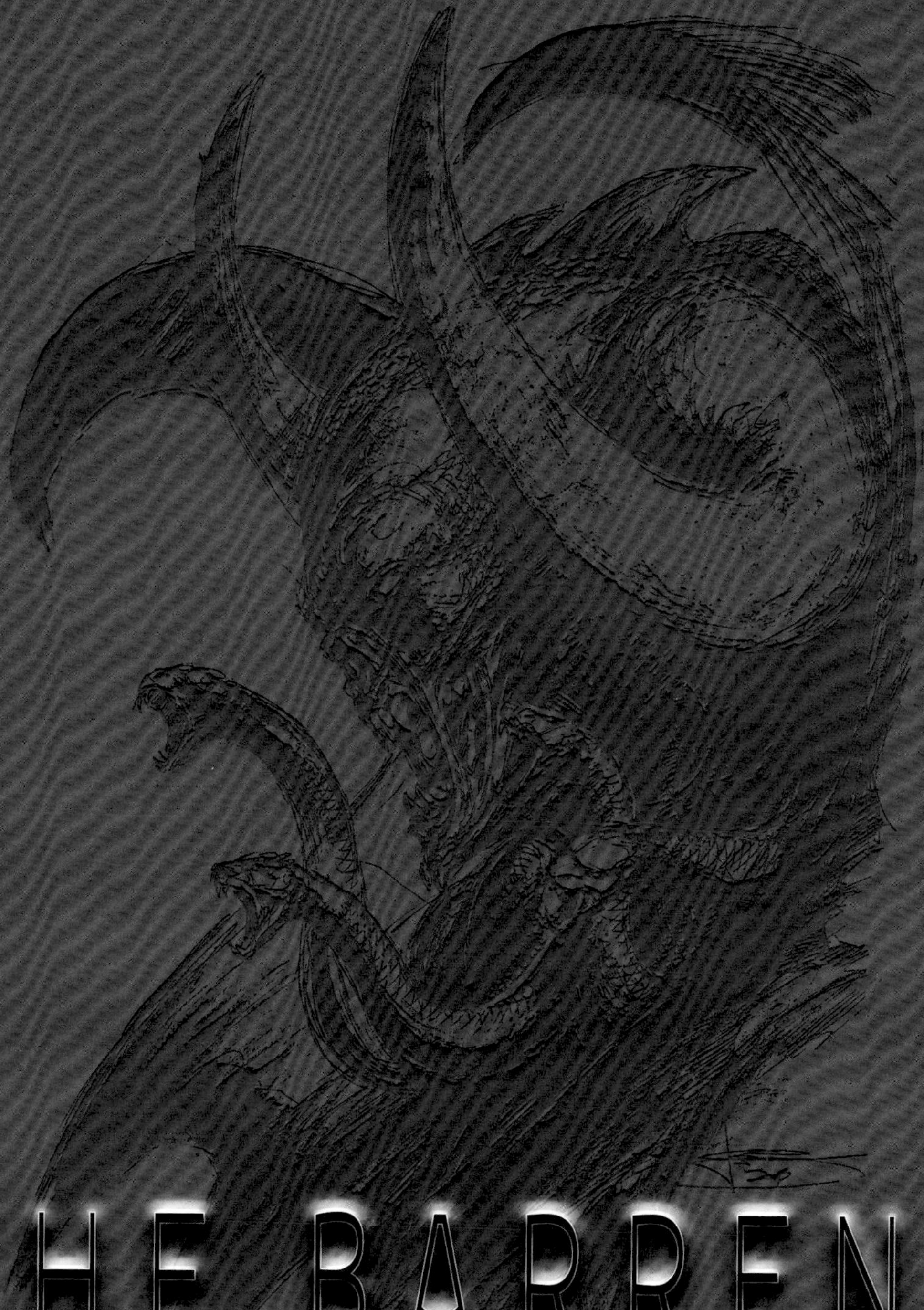

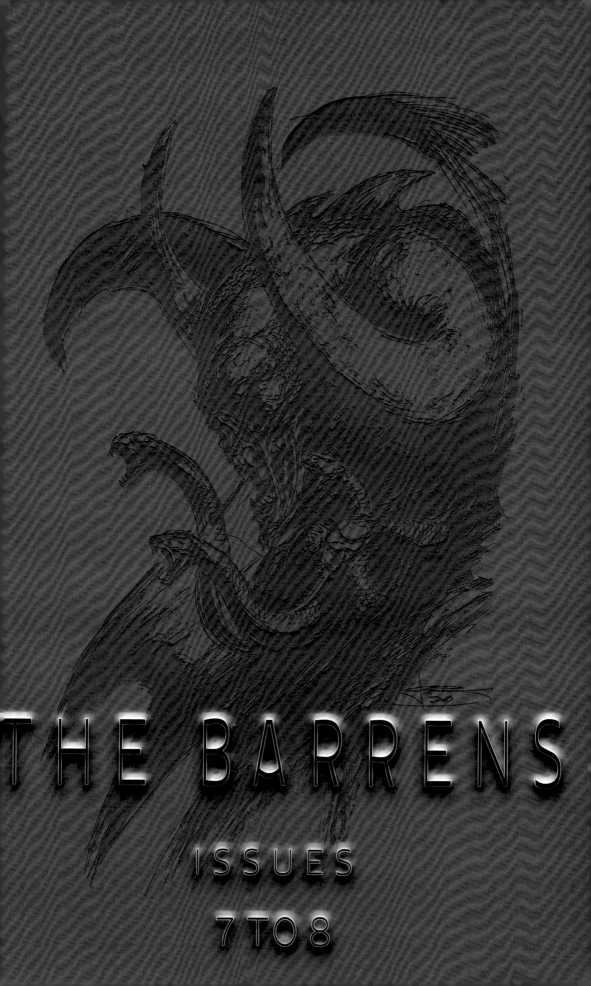

THE BARRENS

ISSUES

7 TO 8

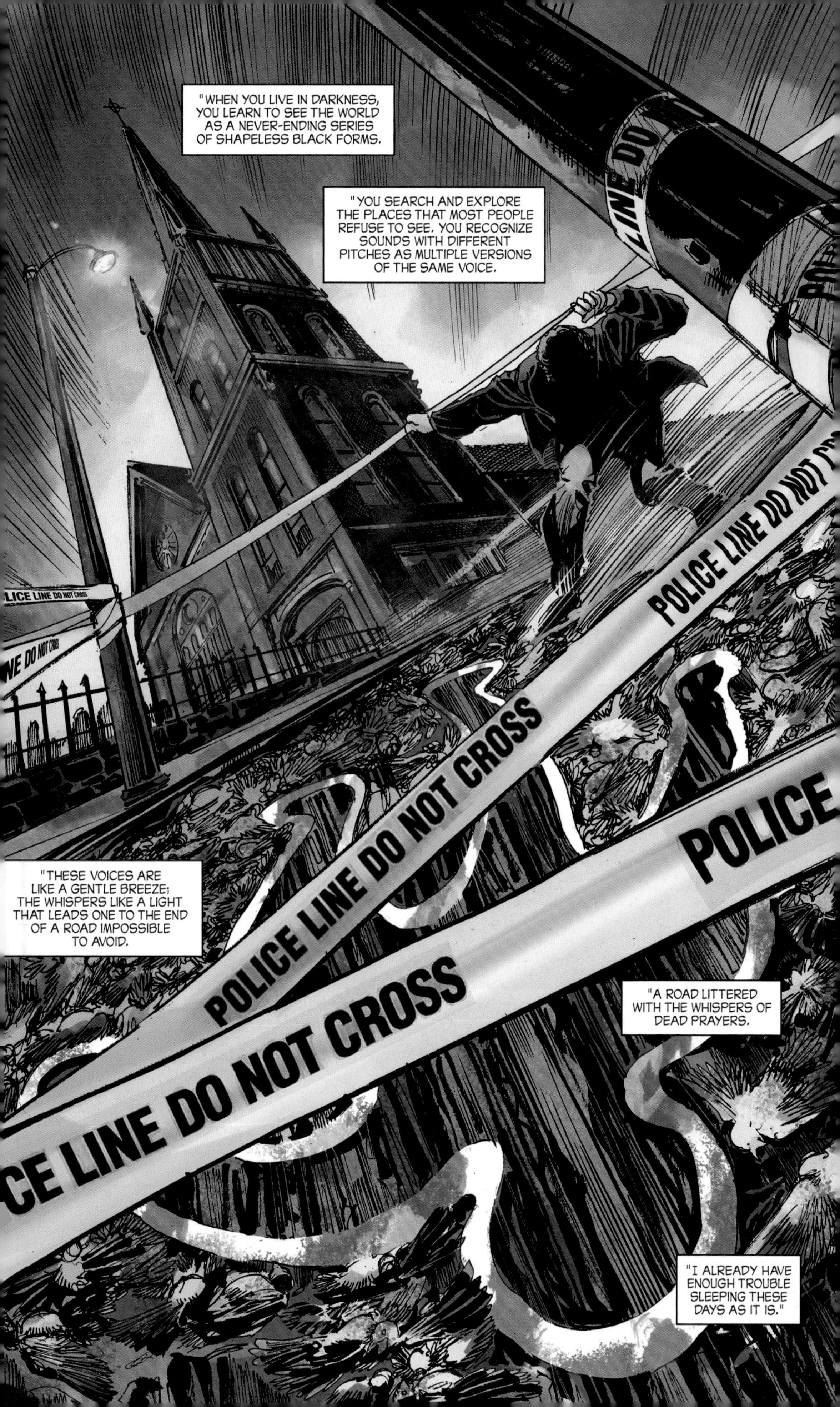
"WHEN YOU LIVE IN DARKNESS, YOU LEARN TO SEE THE WORLD AS A NEVER-ENDING SERIES OF SHAPELESS BLACK FORMS.
"YOU SEARCH AND EXPLORE THE PLACES THAT MOST PEOPLE REFUSE TO SEE. YOU RECOGNIZE SOUNDS WITH DIFFERENT PITCHES AS MULTIPLE VERSIONS OF THE SAME VOICE.
POLICE LINE DO NOT CROSS
POLICE LINE DO NOT
POLICE LINE DO NOT CROSS
POLICE
"THESE VOICES ARE LIKE A GENTLE BREEZE; THE WHISPERS LIKE A LIGHT THAT LEADS ONE TO THE END OF A ROAD IMPOSSIBLE TO AVOID.
CE LINE DO NOT CROSS
"A ROAD LITTERED WITH THE WHISPERS OF DEAD PRAYERS.
"I ALREADY HAVE ENOUGH TROUBLE SLEEPING THESE DAYS AS IT IS."

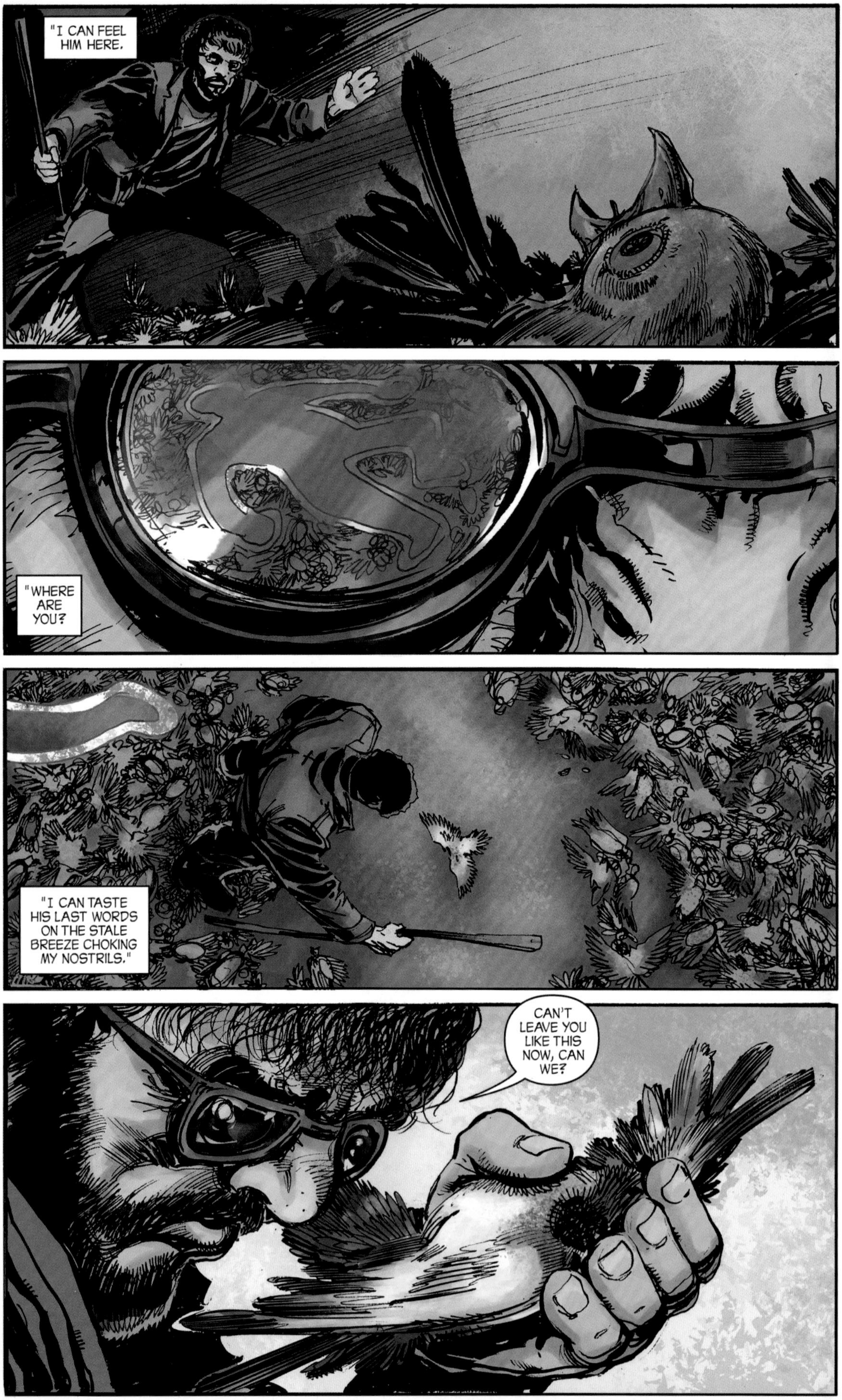
"I CAN FEEL HIM HERE.
"WHERE ARE YOU?
"I CAN TASTE HIS LAST WORDS ON THE STALE BREEZE CHOKING MY NOSTRILS."
CAN'T LEAVE YOU LIKE THIS NOW, CAN WE?

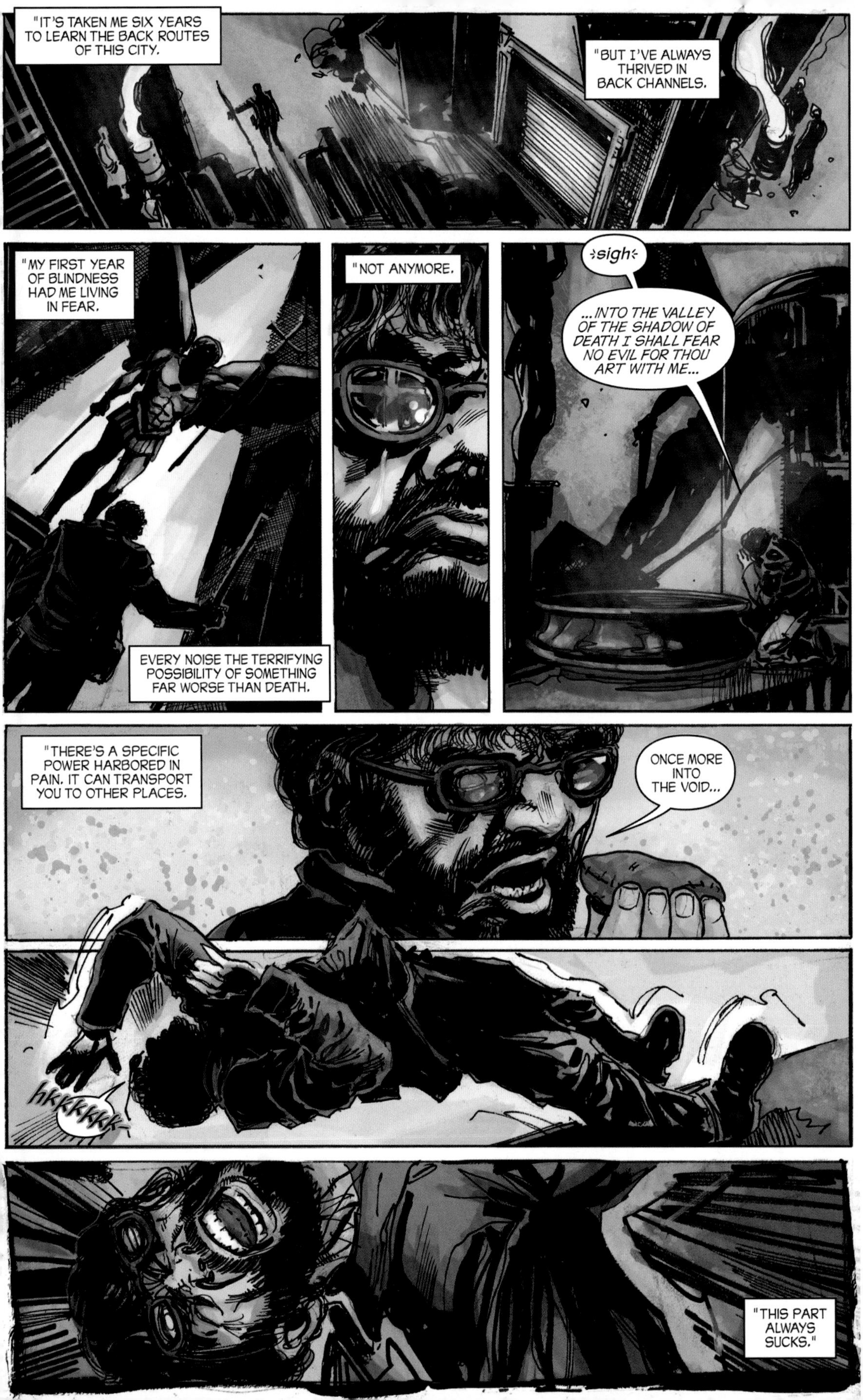
"IT'S TAKEN ME SIX YEARS TO LEARN THE BACK ROUTES OF THIS CITY.
"BUT I'VE ALWAYS THRIVED IN BACK CHANNELS.
"MY FIRST YEAR OF BLINDNESS HAD ME LIVING IN FEAR.
EVERY NOISE THE TERRIFYING POSSIBILITY OF SOMETHING FAR WORSE THAN DEATH.
"NOT ANYMORE.
sigh
...INTO THE VALLEY OF THE SHADOW OF DEATH I SHALL FEAR NO EVIL FOR THOU ART WITH ME...
"THERE'S A SPECIFIC POWER HARBORED IN PAIN. IT CAN TRANSPORT YOU TO OTHER PLACES.
ONCE MORE INTO THE VOID...
hkkkkkk
"THIS PART ALWAYS SUCKS."

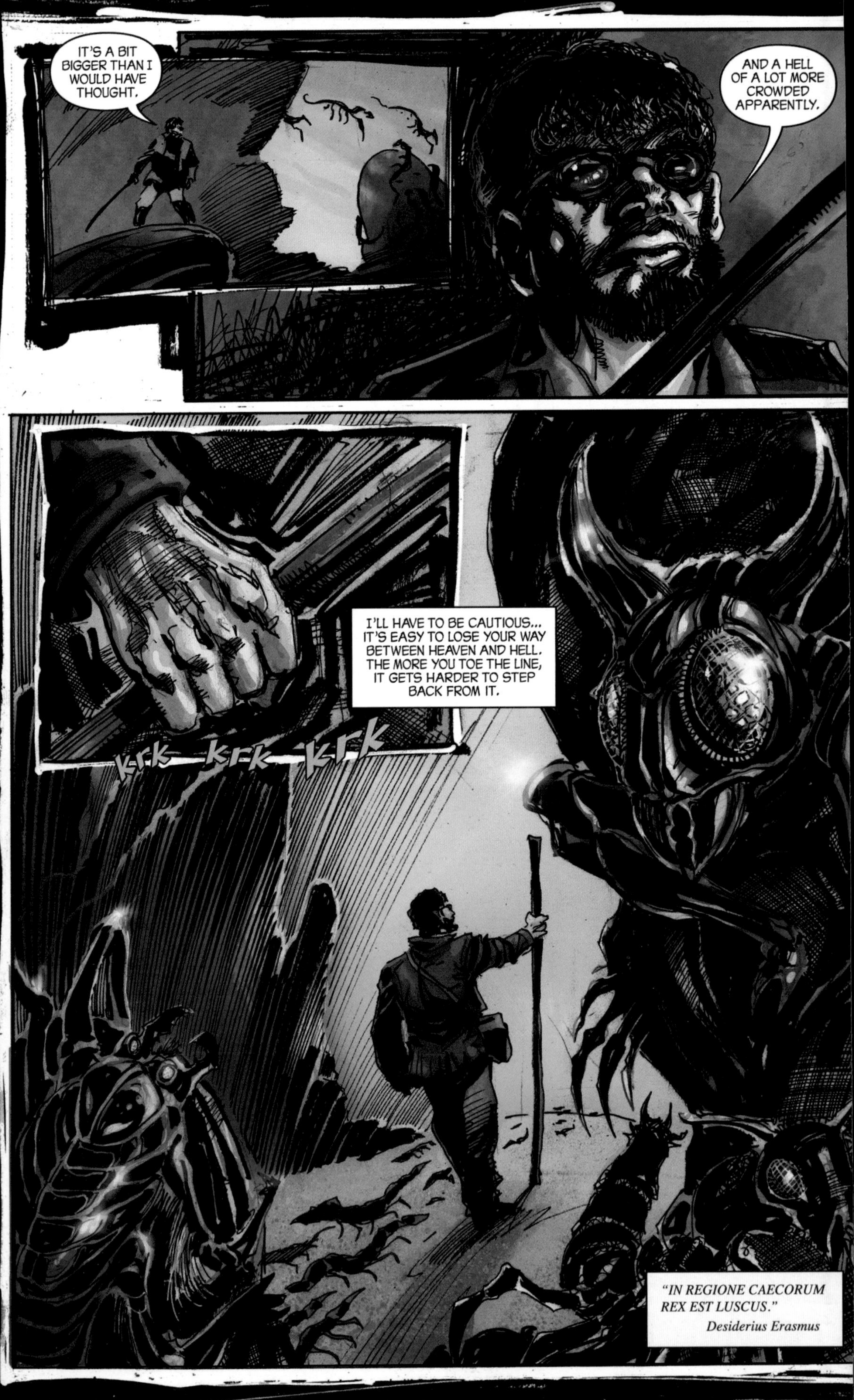
IT'S A BIT BIGGER THAN I WOULD HAVE THOUGHT.
AND A HELL OF A LOT MORE CROWDED APPARENTLY.
I'LL HAVE TO BE CAUTIOUS... IT'S EASY TO LOSE YOUR WAY BETWEEN HEAVEN AND HELL. THE MORE YOU TOE THE LINE, IT GETS HARDER TO STEP BACK FROM IT.
KRK KRK KRK
"IN REGIONE CAECORUM REX EST LUSCUS."
Desiderius Erasmus

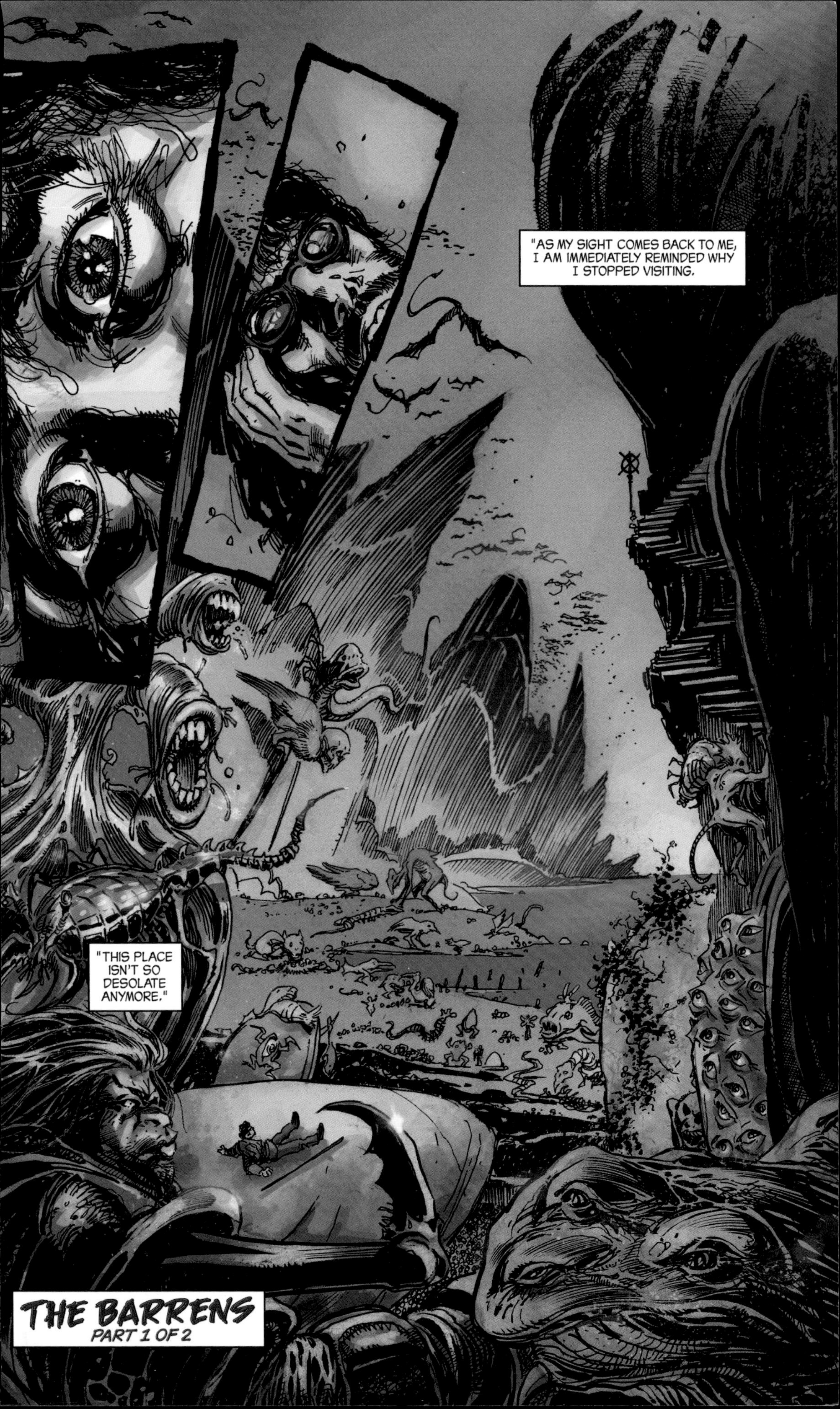
"AS MY SIGHT COMES BACK TO ME, I AM IMMEDIATELY REMINDED WHY I STOPPED VISITING.
"THIS PLACE ISN'T SO DESOLATE ANYMORE."
THE BARRENS
PART 1 OF 2

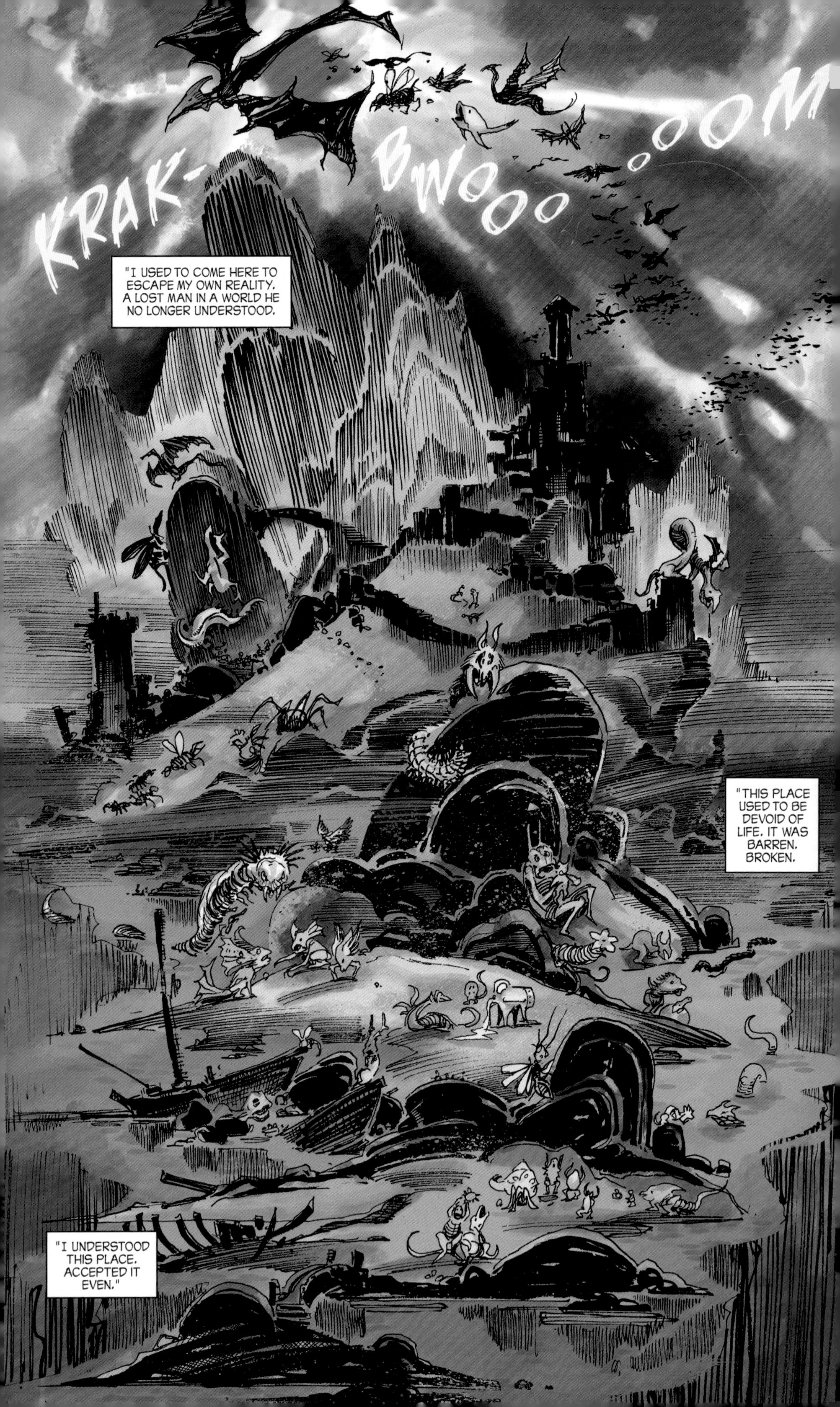
KRAK-BWOOO...OOOM
"I USED TO COME HERE TO ESCAPE MY OWN REALITY. A LOST MAN IN A WORLD HE NO LONGER UNDERSTOOD.
"THIS PLACE USED TO BE DEVOID OF LIFE. IT WAS BARREN. BROKEN.
"I UNDERSTOOD THIS PLACE. ACCEPTED IT EVEN."

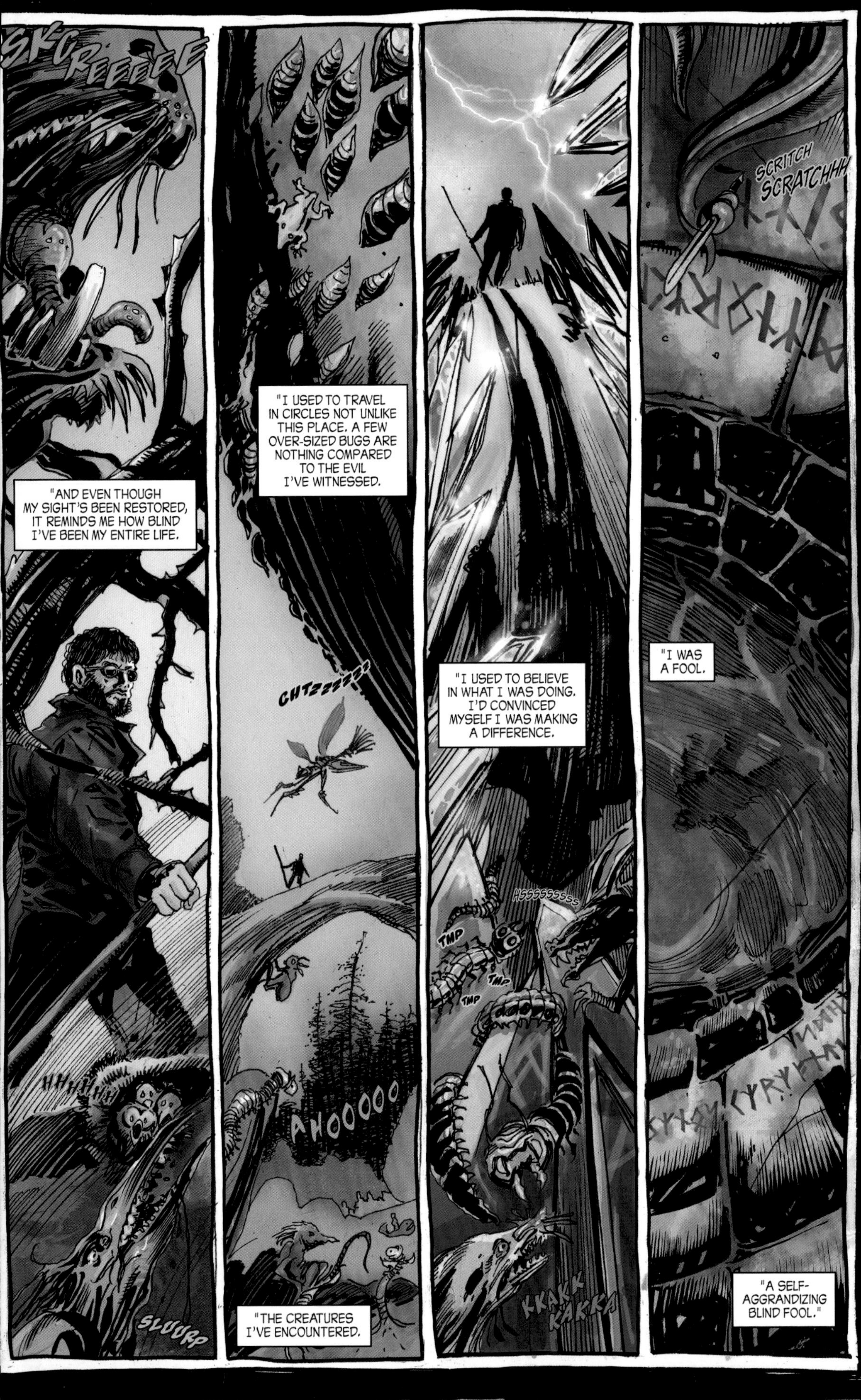
SKCREEEEEE
"AND EVEN THOUGH MY SIGHT'S BEEN RESTORED, IT REMINDS ME HOW BLIND I'VE BEEN MY ENTIRE LIFE.
SLUURP
"I USED TO TRAVEL IN CIRCLES NOT UNLIKE THIS PLACE. A FEW OVER-SIZED BUGS ARE NOTHING COMPARED TO THE EVIL I'VE WITNESSED.
CHTZZZZZZ
AHOOOOO
"THE CREATURES I'VE ENCOUNTERED.
"I USED TO BELIEVE IN WHAT I WAS DOING. I'D CONVINCED MYSELF I WAS MAKING A DIFFERENCE.
HSSSSSSSSS
TMP
TMP
TMP
KKAKK KAKKA
SCRITCH SCRATCHHH
"I WAS A FOOL.
"A SELF-AGGRANDIZING BLIND FOOL."

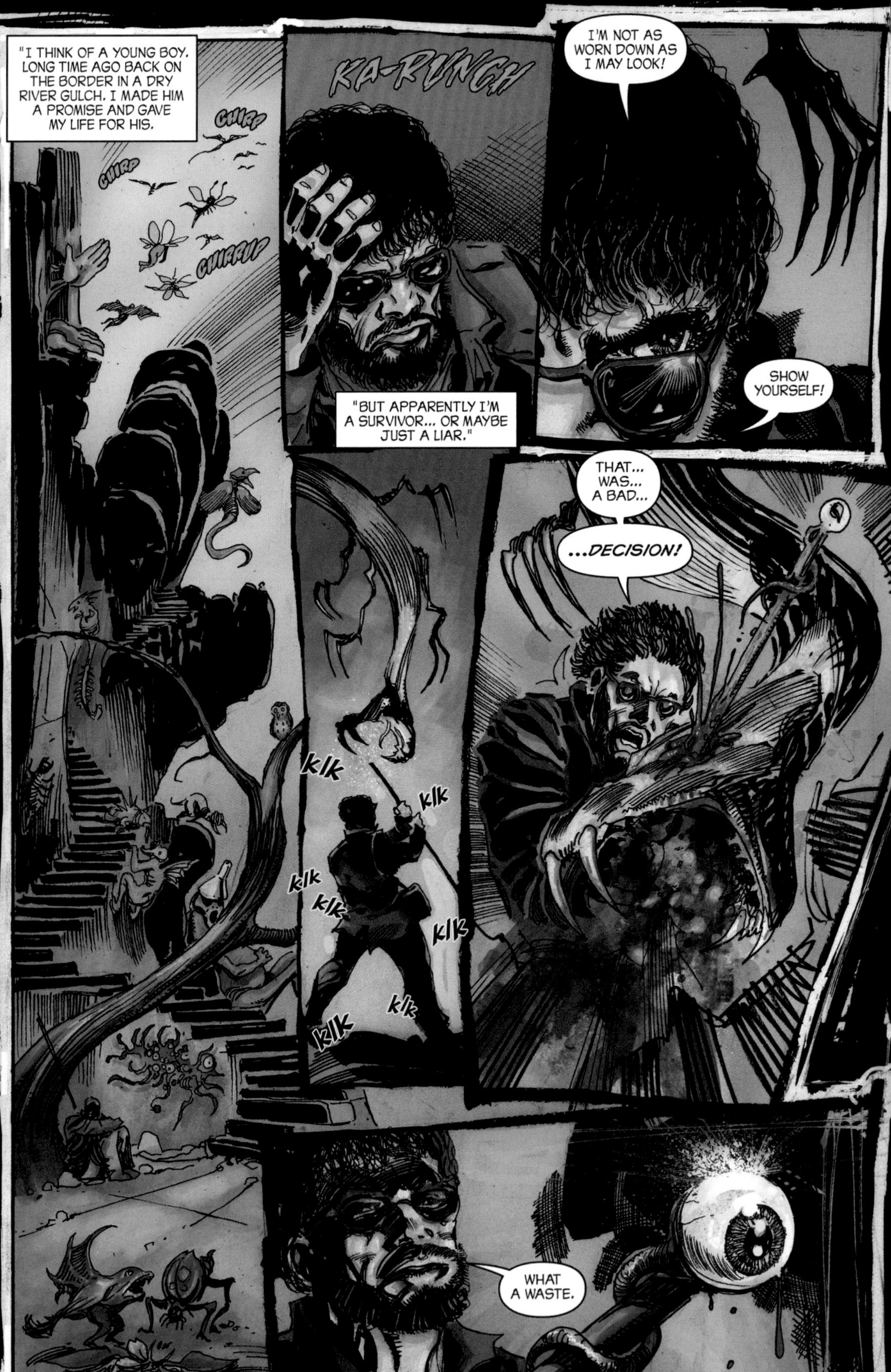
"I THINK OF A YOUNG BOY. LONG TIME AGO BACK ON THE BORDER IN A DRY RIVER GULCH. I MADE HIM A PROMISE AND GAVE MY LIFE FOR HIS.
CHIRP
CHIRP
CHIRRUP
KA-RUNCH
"BUT APPARENTLY I'M A SURVIVOR... OR MAYBE JUST A LIAR."
I'M NOT AS WORN DOWN AS I MAY LOOK!
SHOW YOURSELF!
KLK
KLK
KLK
KLK
KLK
KLK
KLK
THAT... WAS... A BAD...
...DECISION!
WHAT A WASTE.

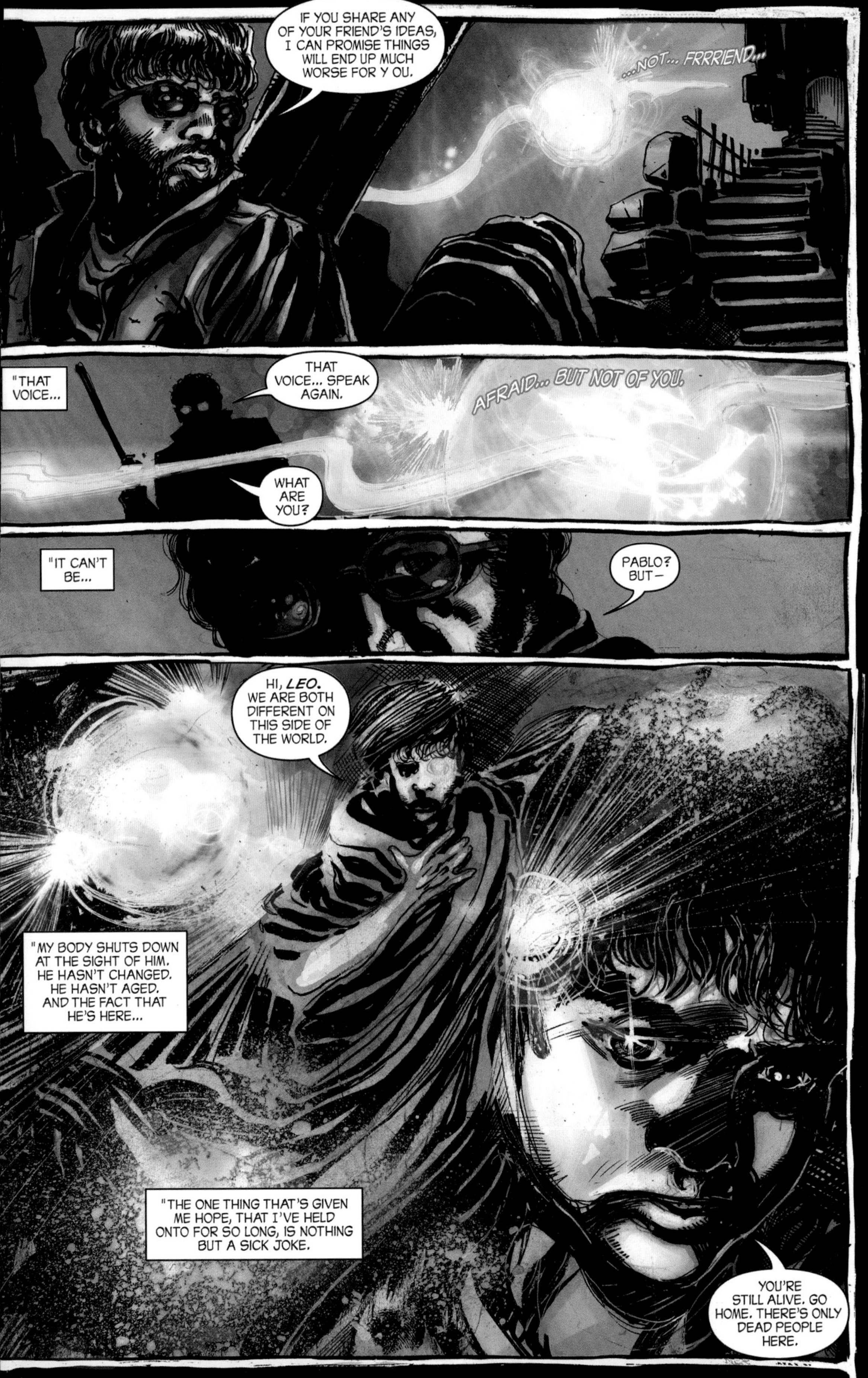
IF YOU SHARE ANY OF YOUR FRIEND'S IDEAS, I CAN PROMISE THINGS WILL END UP MUCH WORSE FOR Y OU.
...NOT... FRRRIEND...
"THAT VOICE...
THAT VOICE... SPEAK AGAIN.
AFRAID... BUT NOT OF YOU.
WHAT ARE YOU?
"IT CAN'T BE...
PABLO? BUT—
HI, *LEO.* WE ARE BOTH DIFFERENT ON THIS SIDE OF THE WORLD.
"MY BODY SHUTS DOWN AT THE SIGHT OF HIM. HE HASN'T CHANGED. HE HASN'T AGED. AND THE FACT THAT HE'S HERE...
"THE ONE THING THAT'S GIVEN ME HOPE, THAT I'VE HELD ONTO FOR SO LONG, IS NOTHING BUT A SICK JOKE.
YOU'RE STILL ALIVE. GO HOME. THERE'S ONLY DEAD PEOPLE HERE.

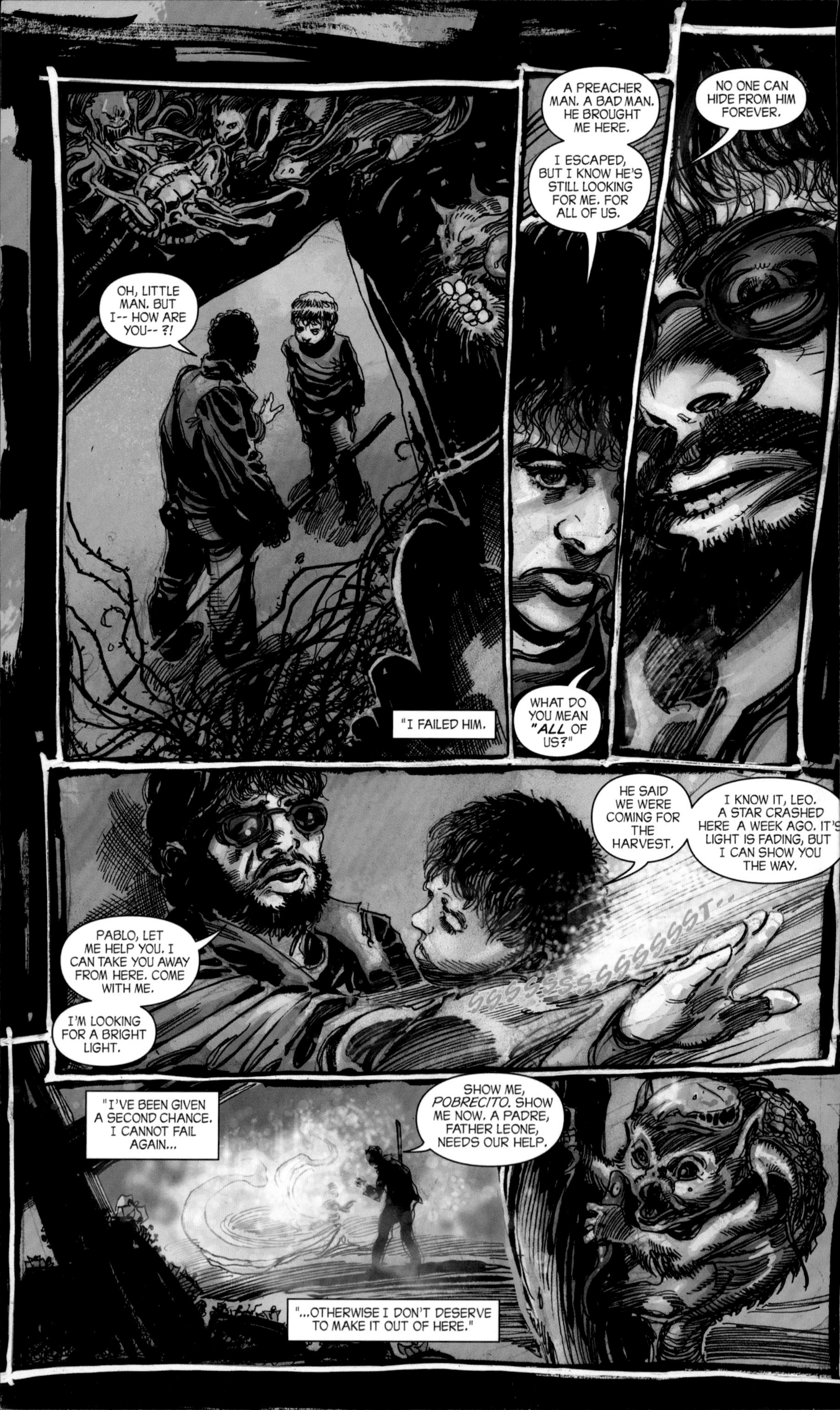
OH, LITTLE MAN. BUT I-- HOW ARE YOU-- ?!
"I FAILED HIM.
A PREACHER MAN. A BAD MAN. HE BROUGHT ME HERE.
I ESCAPED, BUT I KNOW HE'S STILL LOOKING FOR ME. FOR ALL OF US.
WHAT DO YOU MEAN "ALL OF US?"
NO ONE CAN HIDE FROM HIM FOREVER.
PABLO, LET ME HELP YOU. I CAN TAKE YOU AWAY FROM HERE. COME WITH ME.
I'M LOOKING FOR A BRIGHT LIGHT.
HE SAID WE WERE COMING FOR THE HARVEST.
I KNOW IT, LEO. A STAR CRASHED HERE A WEEK AGO. IT'S LIGHT IS FADING, BUT I CAN SHOW YOU THE WAY.
SSSSSSSSSSSSSSST--
"I'VE BEEN GIVEN A SECOND CHANCE. I CANNOT FAIL AGAIN...
SHOW ME, *POBRECITO*. SHOW ME NOW. A PADRE, FATHER LEONE, NEEDS OUR HELP.
"...OTHERWISE I DON'T DESERVE TO MAKE IT OUT OF HERE."

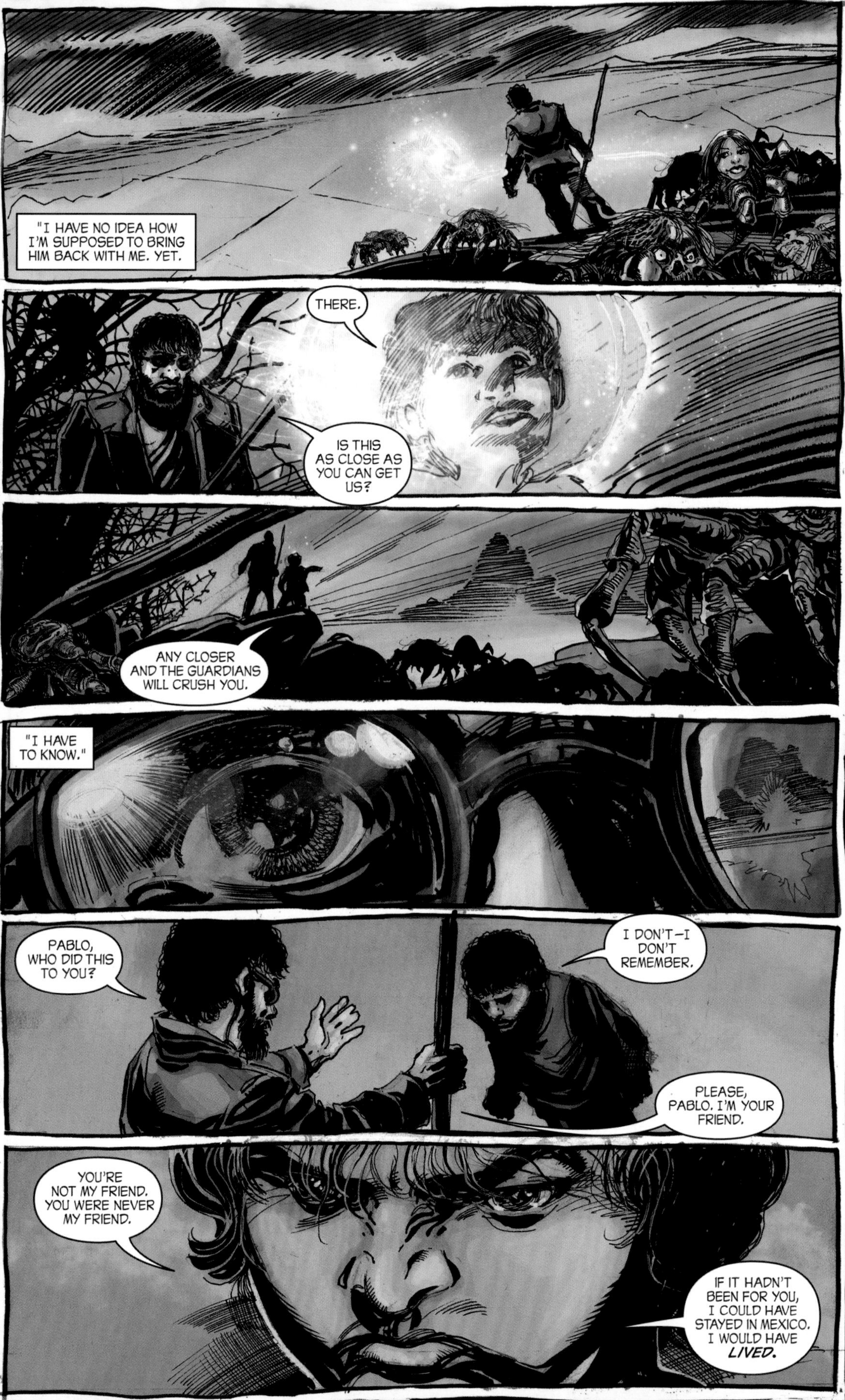
"I HAVE NO IDEA HOW I'M SUPPOSED TO BRING HIM BACK WITH ME. YET.
THERE.
IS THIS AS CLOSE AS YOU CAN GET US?
ANY CLOSER AND THE GUARDIANS WILL CRUSH YOU.
"I HAVE TO KNOW."
PABLO, WHO DID THIS TO YOU?
I DON'T—I DON'T REMEMBER.
PLEASE, PABLO. I'M YOUR FRIEND.
YOU'RE NOT MY FRIEND. YOU WERE NEVER MY FRIEND.
IF IT HADN'T BEEN FOR YOU, I COULD HAVE STAYED IN MEXICO. I WOULD HAVE *LIVED*.

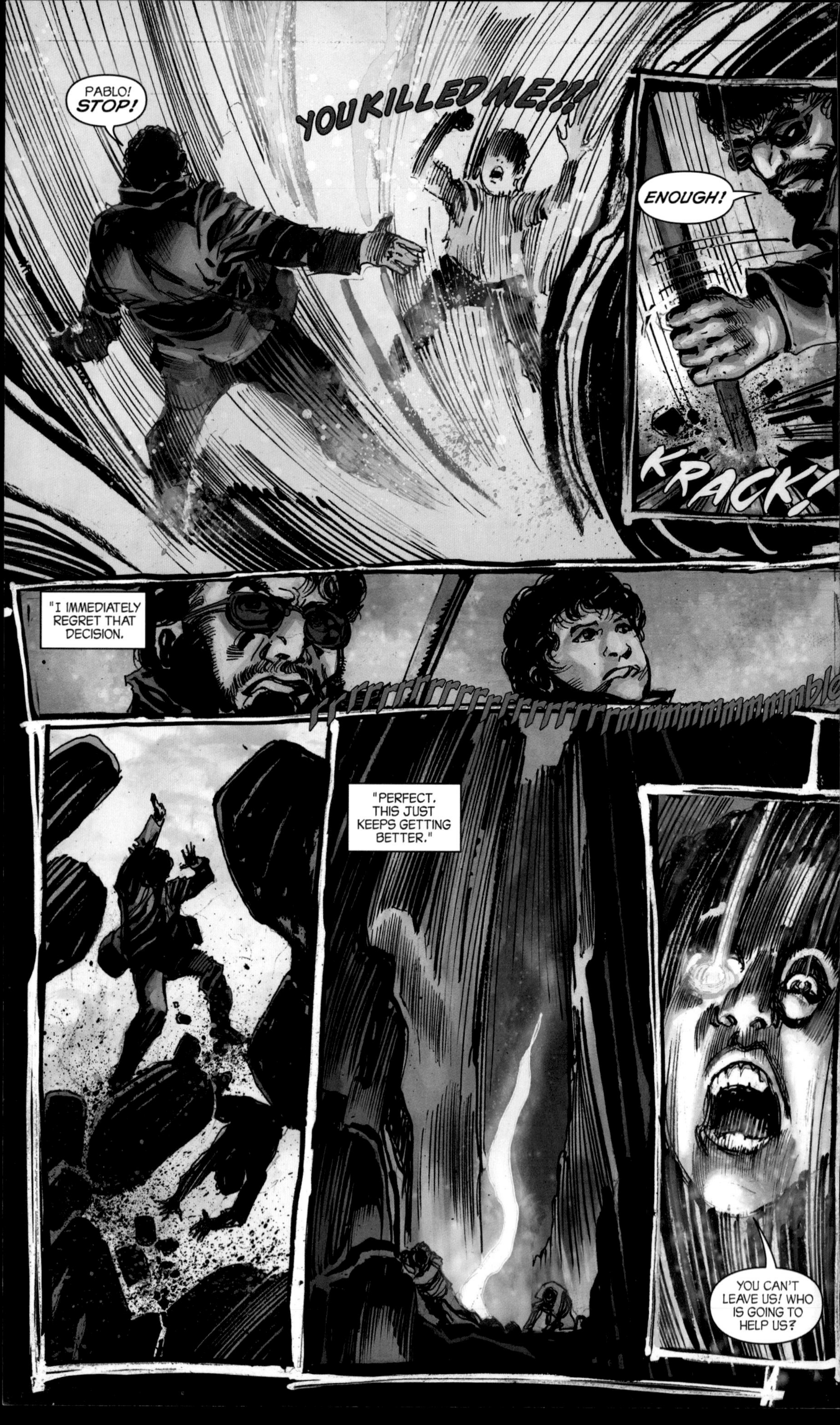
PABLO! STOP!
YOUKILLEDME!!!
ENOUGH!
KRACK!
"I IMMEDIATELY REGRET THAT DECISION.
rrrrrrrrrrrrrrrrrrrrrrrrrrrrrrrmmmmmmmmmmmmmmble
"PERFECT. THIS JUST KEEPS GETTING BETTER."
YOU CAN'T LEAVE US! WHO IS GOING TO HELP US?

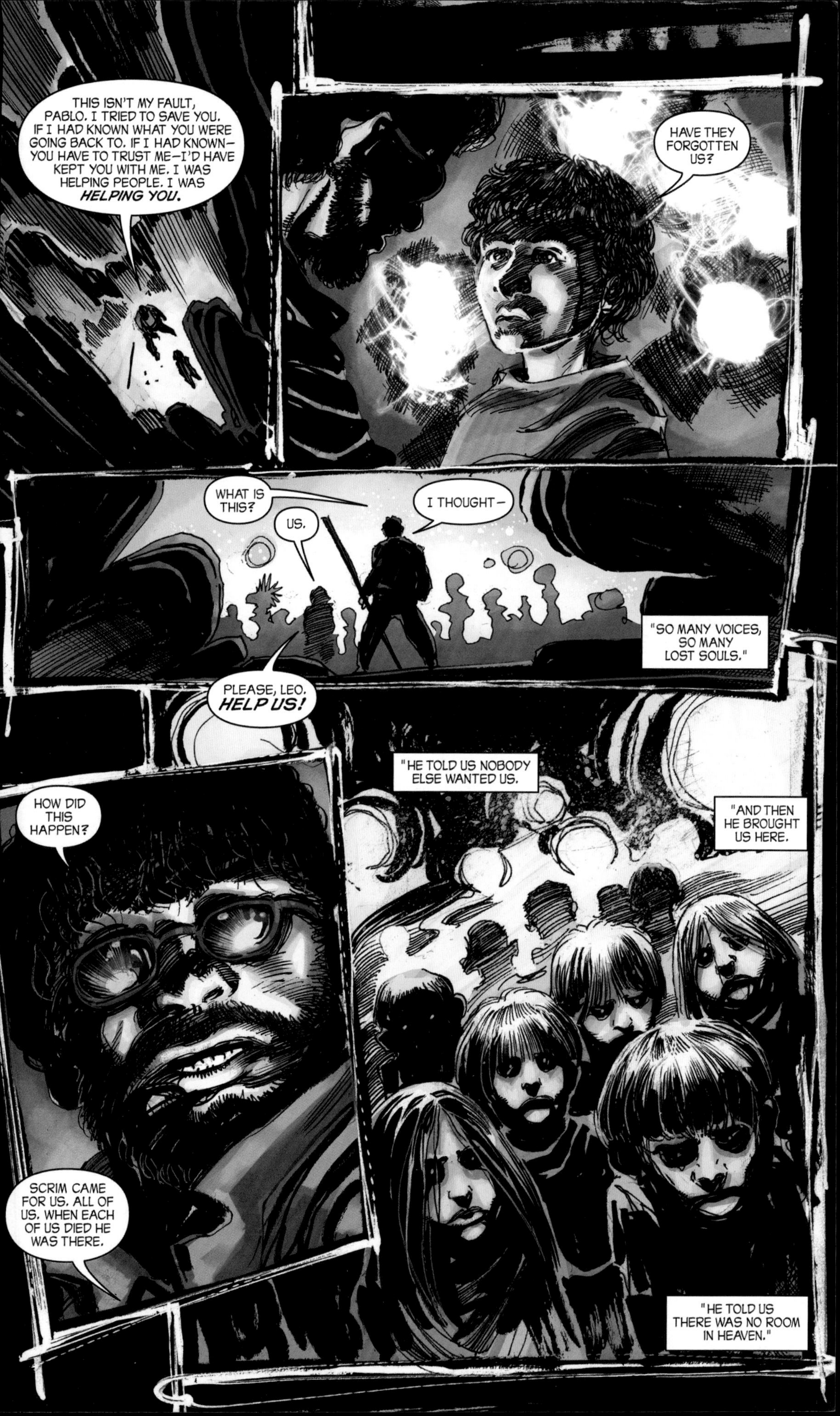
THIS ISN'T MY FAULT, PABLO. I TRIED TO SAVE YOU. IF I HAD KNOWN WHAT YOU WERE GOING BACK TO. IF I HAD KNOWN— YOU HAVE TO TRUST ME—I'D HAVE KEPT YOU WITH ME. I WAS HELPING PEOPLE. I WAS *HELPING YOU.*
HAVE THEY FORGOTTEN US?
WHAT IS THIS?
US.
I THOUGHT—
"SO MANY VOICES, SO MANY LOST SOULS."
PLEASE, LEO. *HELP US!*
HOW DID THIS HAPPEN?
SCRIM CAME FOR US. ALL OF US. WHEN EACH OF US DIED HE WAS THERE.
"HE TOLD US NOBODY ELSE WANTED US.
"AND THEN HE BROUGHT US HERE.
"HE TOLD US THERE WAS NO ROOM IN HEAVEN."

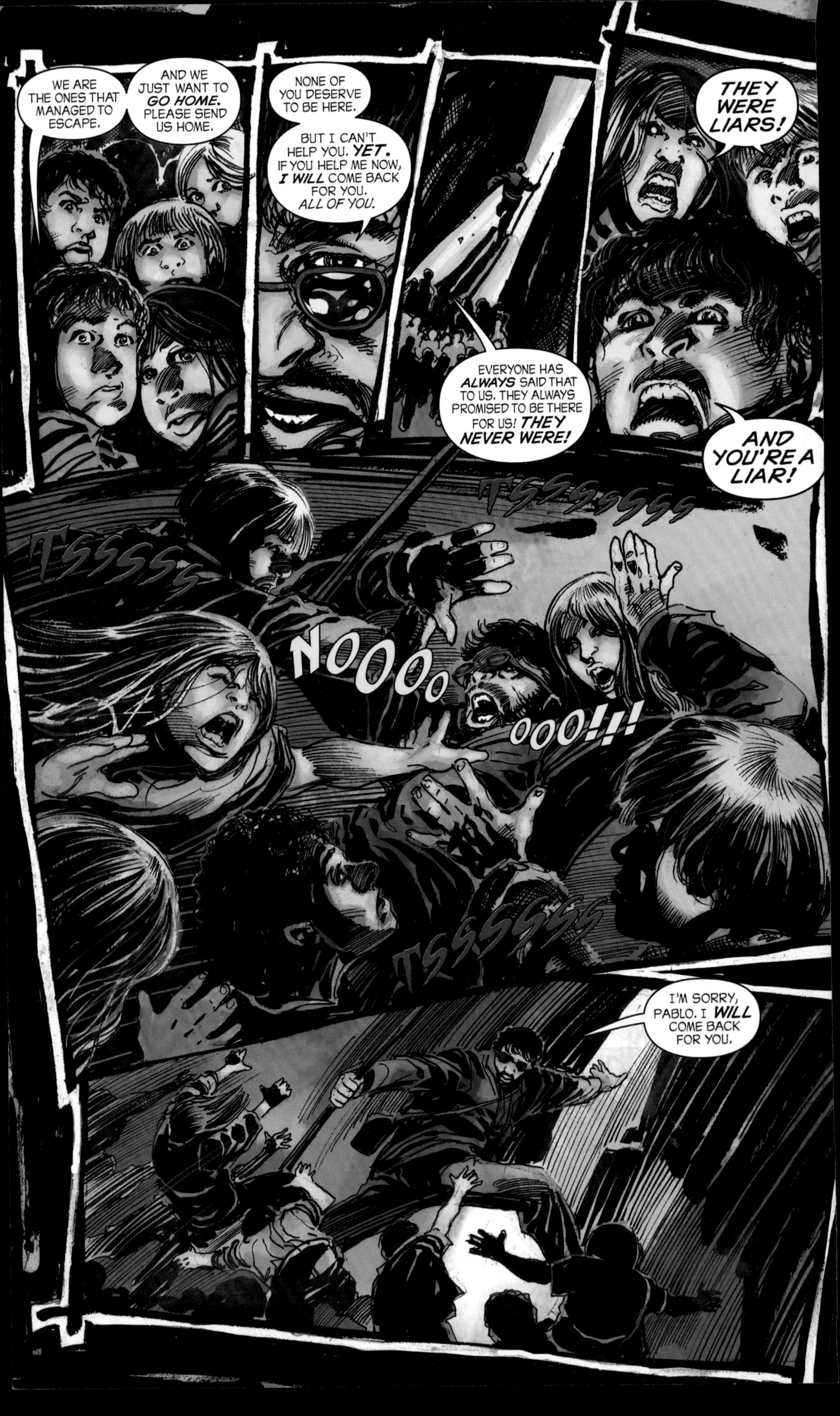
WE ARE THE ONES THAT MANAGED TO ESCAPE.
AND WE JUST WANT TO GO HOME. PLEASE SEND US HOME.
NONE OF YOU DESERVE TO BE HERE.
BUT I CAN'T HELP YOU. YET. IF YOU HELP ME NOW, I WILL COME BACK FOR YOU. ALL OF YOU.
EVERYONE HAS ALWAYS SAID THAT TO US. THEY ALWAYS PROMISED TO BE THERE FOR US! THEY NEVER WERE!
THEY WERE LIARS!
AND YOU'RE A LIAR!
TSSSSSSSS
TSSSSS
NOOOOoooo!!!
TSSSSSSS
I'M SORRY, PABLO. I WILL COME BACK FOR YOU.

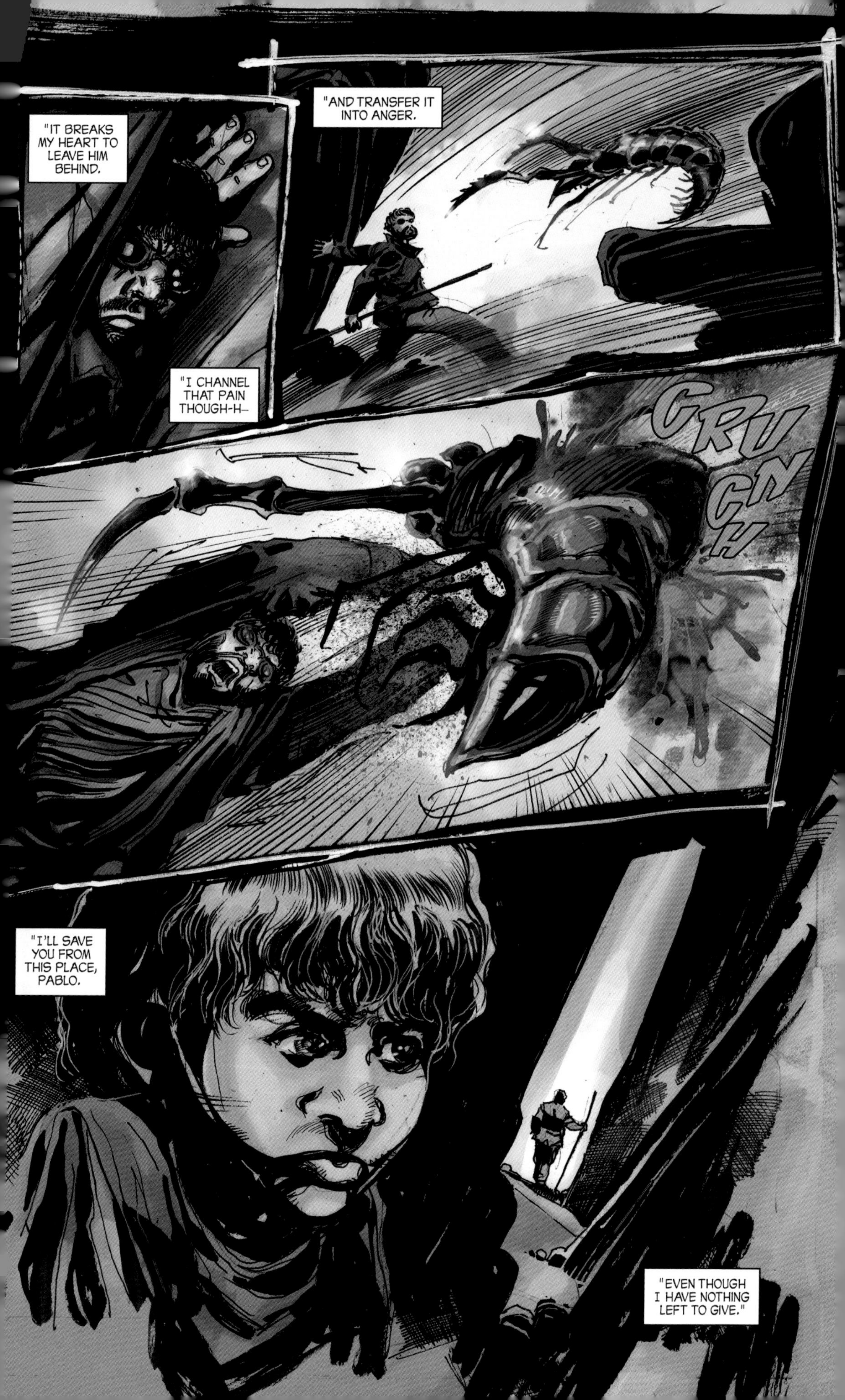
"IT BREAKS MY HEART TO LEAVE HIM BEHIND.
"I CHANNEL THAT PAIN THOUGH-H–
"AND TRANSFER IT INTO ANGER.
CRUNCH
"I'LL SAVE YOU FROM THIS PLACE, PABLO.
"EVEN THOUGH I HAVE NOTHING LEFT TO GIVE."

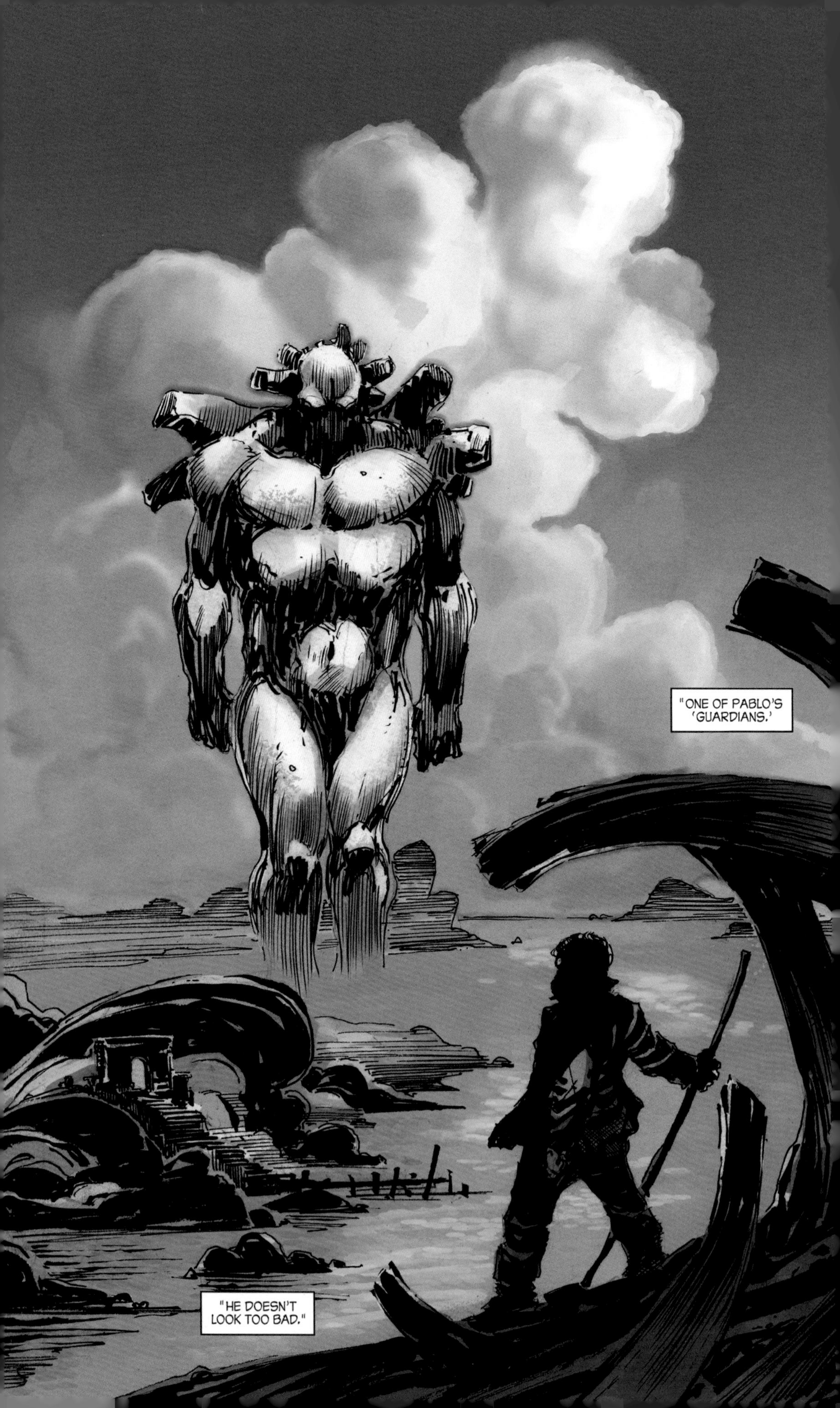
"ONE OF PABLO'S 'GUARDIANS.'
"HE DOESN'T LOOK TOO BAD."

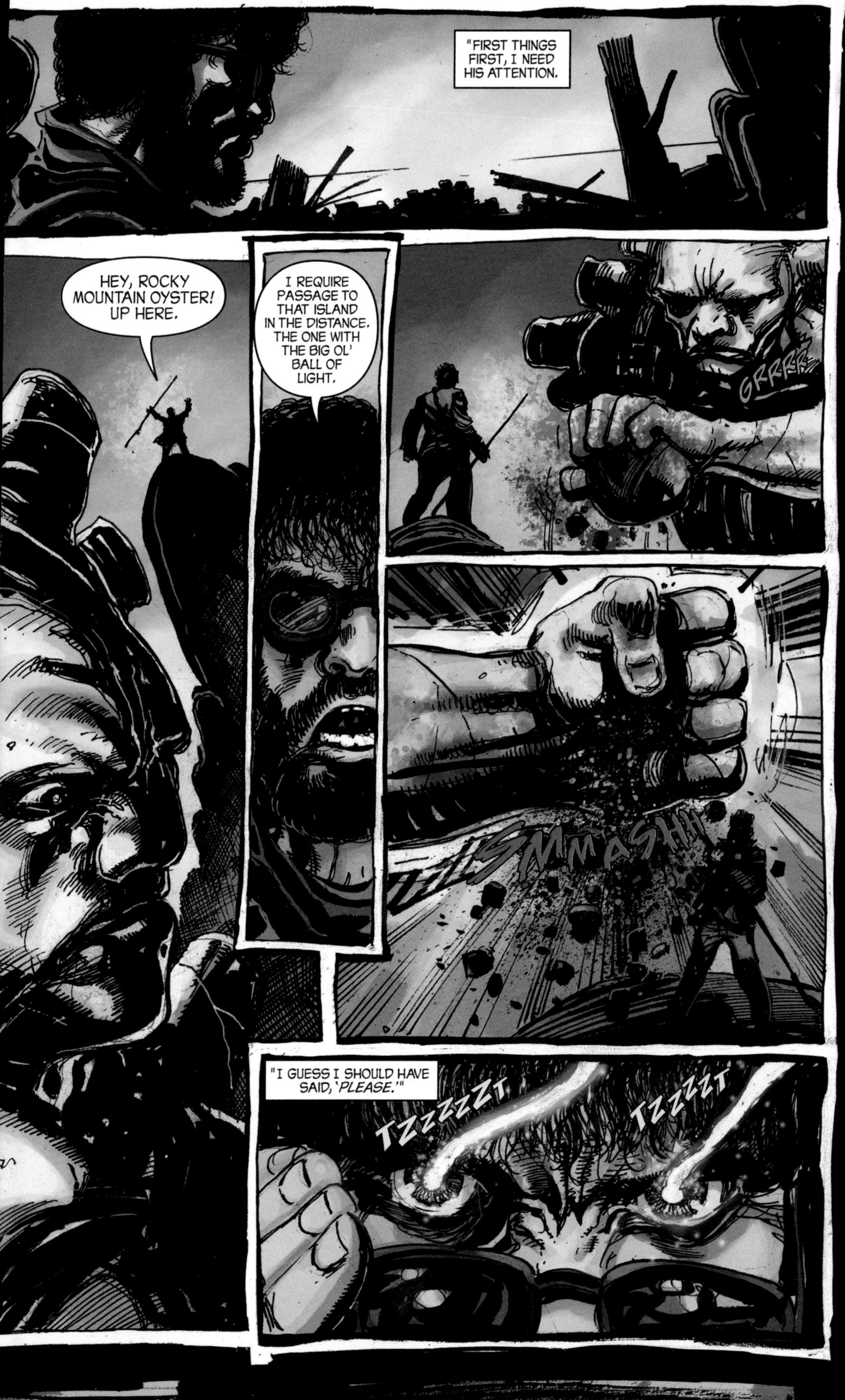
"FIRST THINGS FIRST, I NEED HIS ATTENTION.
HEY, ROCKY MOUNTAIN OYSTER! UP HERE.
I REQUIRE PASSAGE TO THAT ISLAND IN THE DISTANCE. THE ONE WITH THE BIG OL' BALL OF LIGHT.
GRRRR
SMMASHH
"I GUESS I SHOULD HAVE SAID, '*PLEASE.*'"
TZZZZZT
TZZZZT

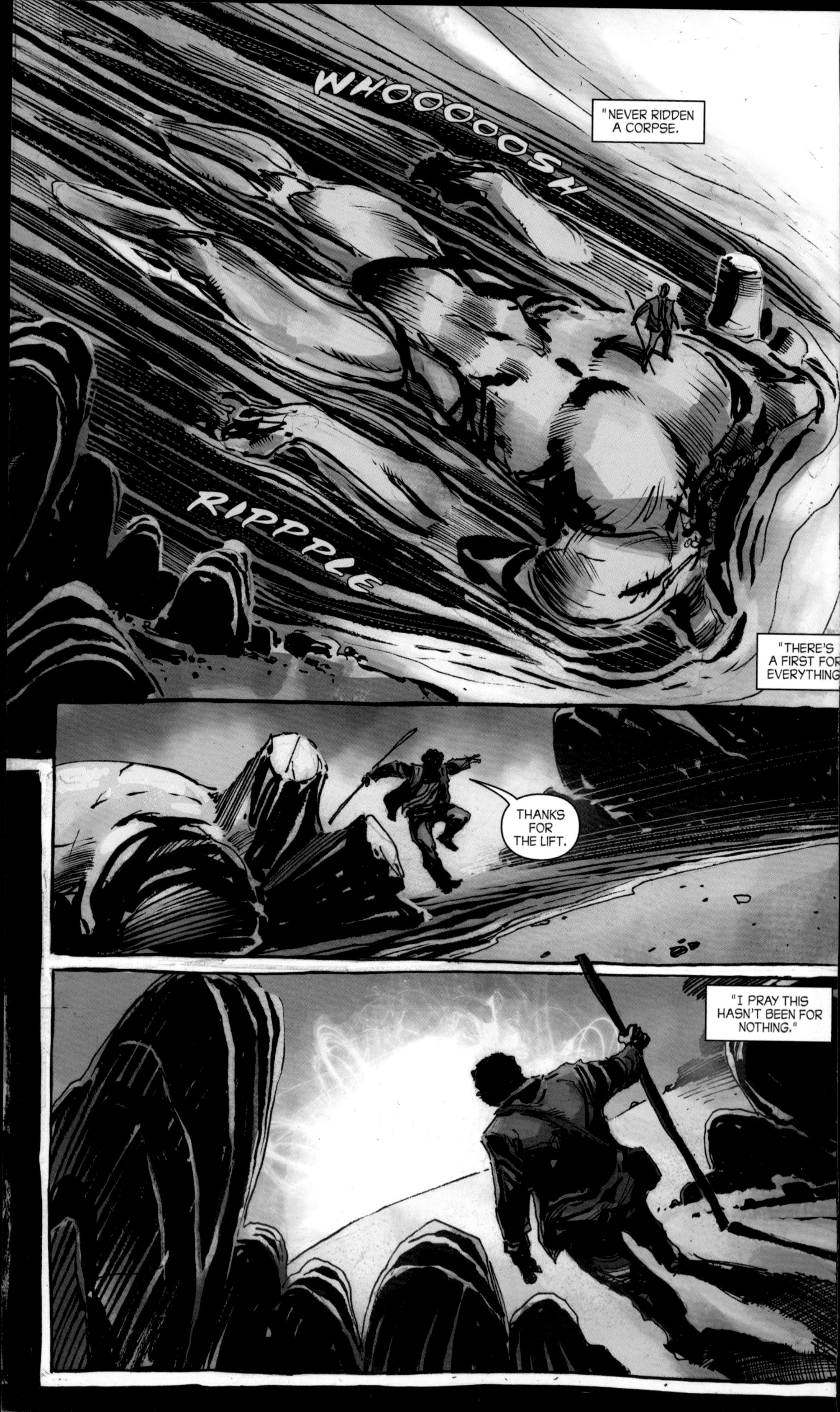
WHOOOOOOSH
"NEVER RIDDEN A CORPSE.
RIPPPLE
"THERE'S A FIRST FOR EVERYTHING
THANKS FOR THE LIFT.
"I PRAY THIS HASN'T BEEN FOR NOTHING."

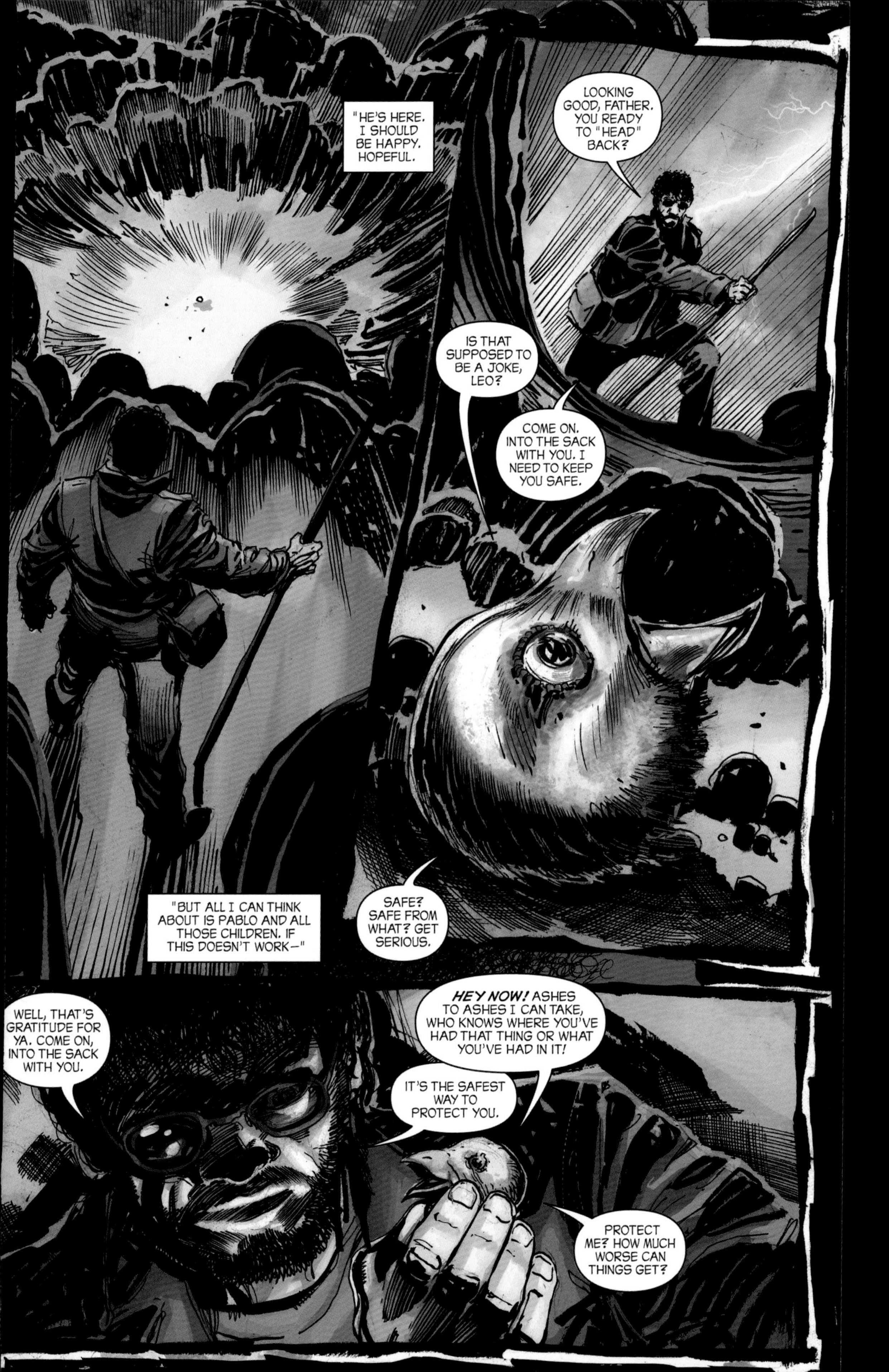

"HE'S HERE. I SHOULD BE HAPPY. HOPEFUL.
"BUT ALL I CAN THINK ABOUT IS PABLO AND ALL THOSE CHILDREN. IF THIS DOESN'T WORK—"
LOOKING GOOD, FATHER. YOU READY TO "HEAD" BACK?
IS THAT SUPPOSED TO BE A JOKE, LEO?
COME ON. INTO THE SACK WITH YOU. I NEED TO KEEP YOU SAFE.
SAFE? SAFE FROM WHAT? GET SERIOUS.
WELL, THAT'S GRATITUDE FOR YA. COME ON, INTO THE SACK WITH YOU.
HEY NOW! ASHES TO ASHES I CAN TAKE, WHO KNOWS WHERE YOU'VE HAD THAT THING OR WHAT YOU'VE HAD IN IT!
IT'S THE SAFEST WAY TO PROTECT YOU.
PROTECT ME? HOW MUCH WORSE CAN THINGS GET?

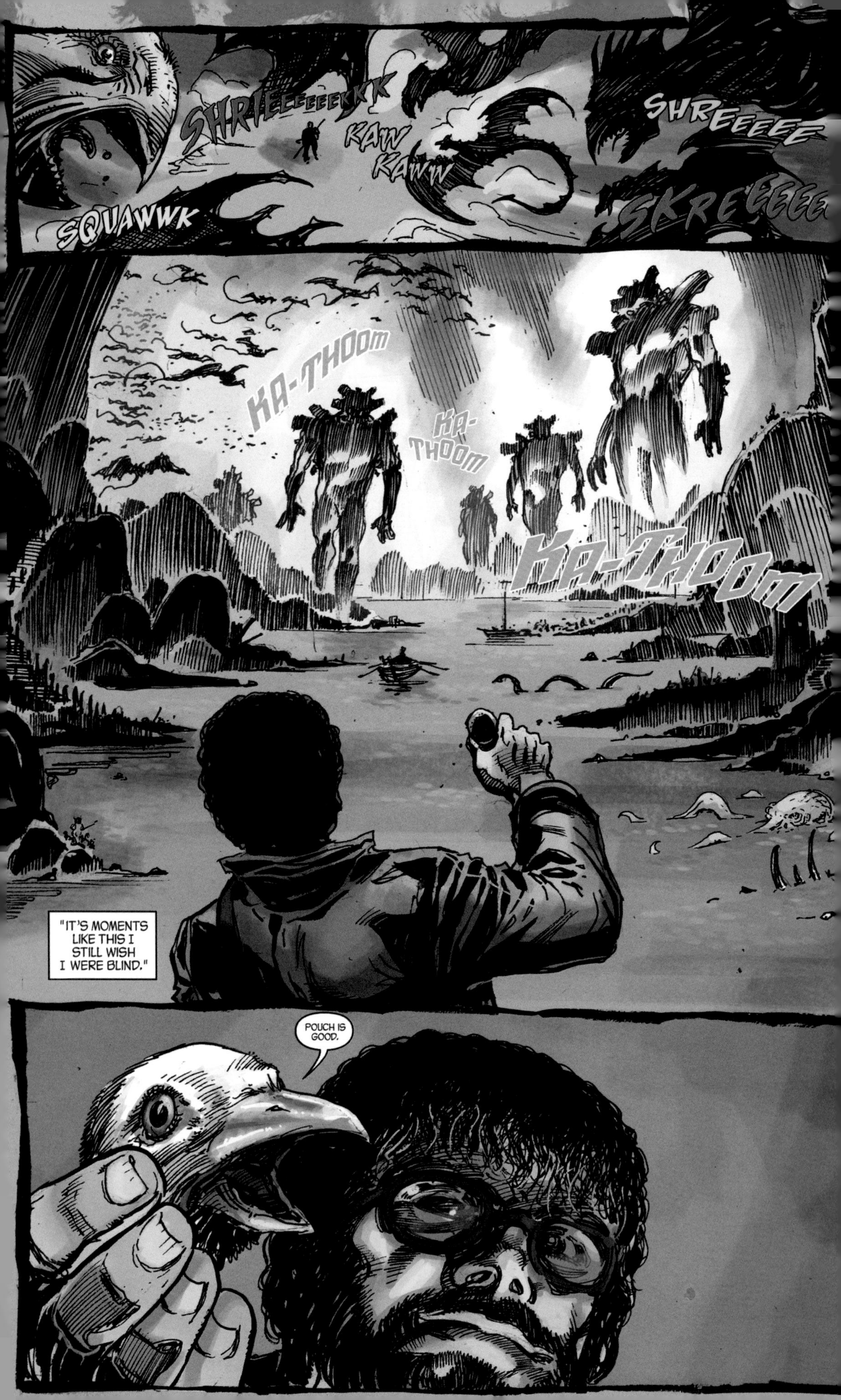
SHRIEEEEEEKKK
KAW KAWW
SQUAWWK
SHREEEEE
SKREEEEEE
KA-THOOM
KA-THOOM
KA-THOOM
"IT'S MOMENTS LIKE THIS I STILL WISH I WERE BLIND."
POUCH IS GOOD.

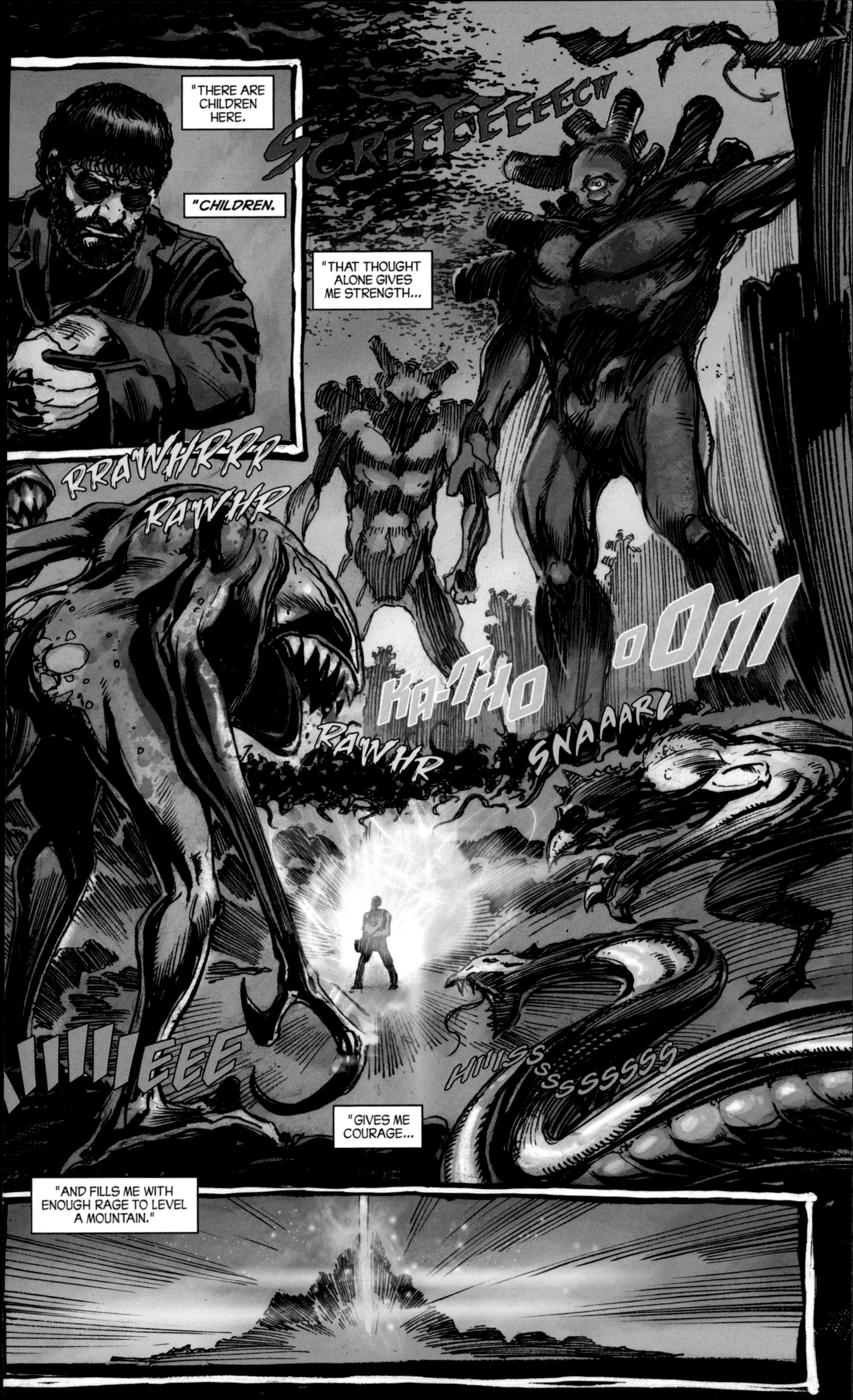
"THERE ARE CHILDREN HERE.
"CHILDREN.
SCREEEEEEECH
"THAT THOUGHT ALONE GIVES ME STRENGTH...
RRAWHRRR
RAWHR
KA-THOoOM
RAWHR
SNAAARL
IIIIIIEEE
HIIISSSSSSSSSS
"GIVES ME COURAGE...
"AND FILLS ME WITH ENOUGH RAGE TO LEVEL A MOUNTAIN."

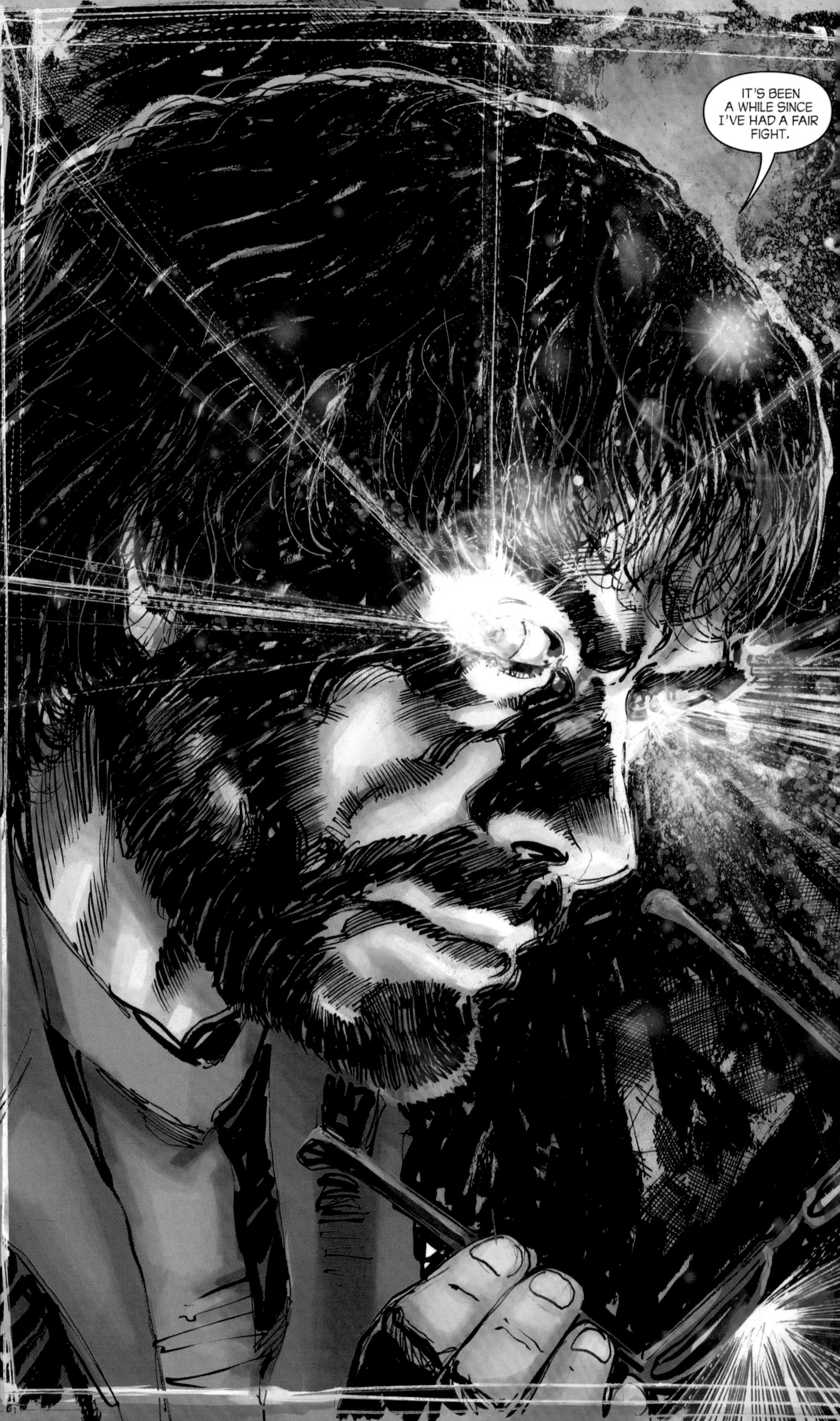
IT'S BEEN A WHILE SINCE I'VE HAD A FAIR FIGHT.

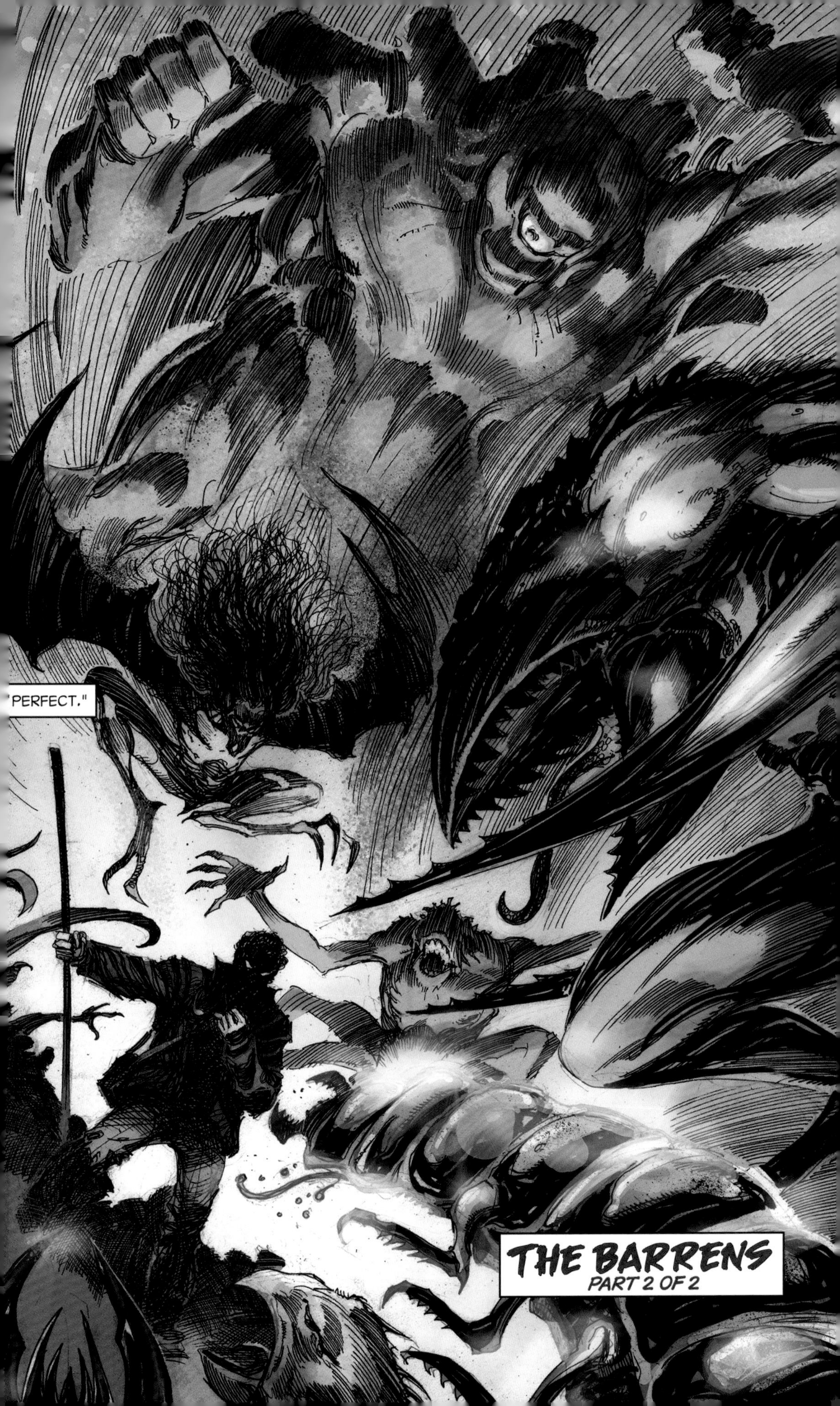
"PERFECT."
THE BARRENS
PART 2 OF 2

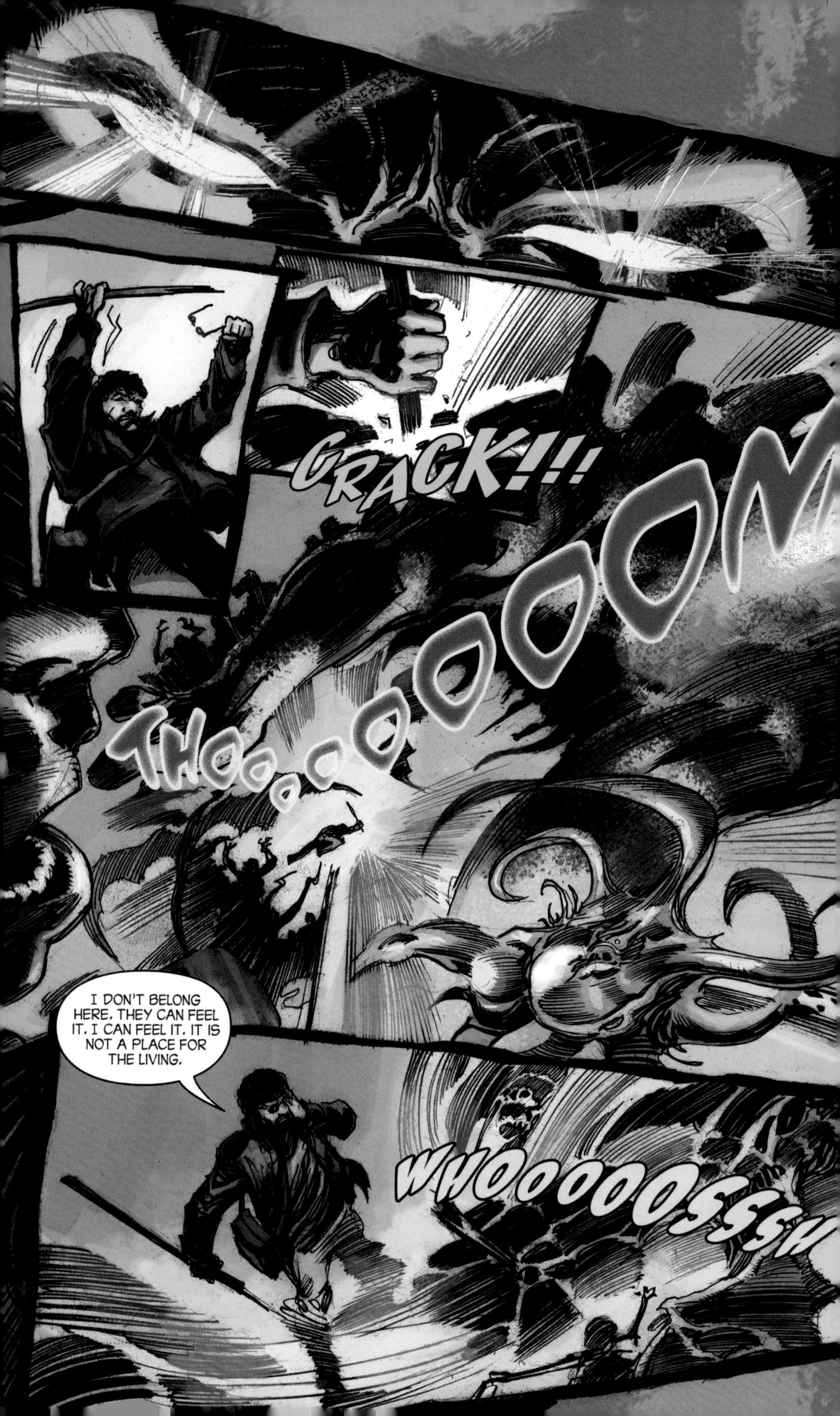
CRACK!!!
THOOOOOOOOOM
I DON'T BELONG HERE. THEY CAN FEEL IT. I CAN FEEL IT. IT IS NOT A PLACE FOR THE LIVING.
WHOOOOOOSSSH

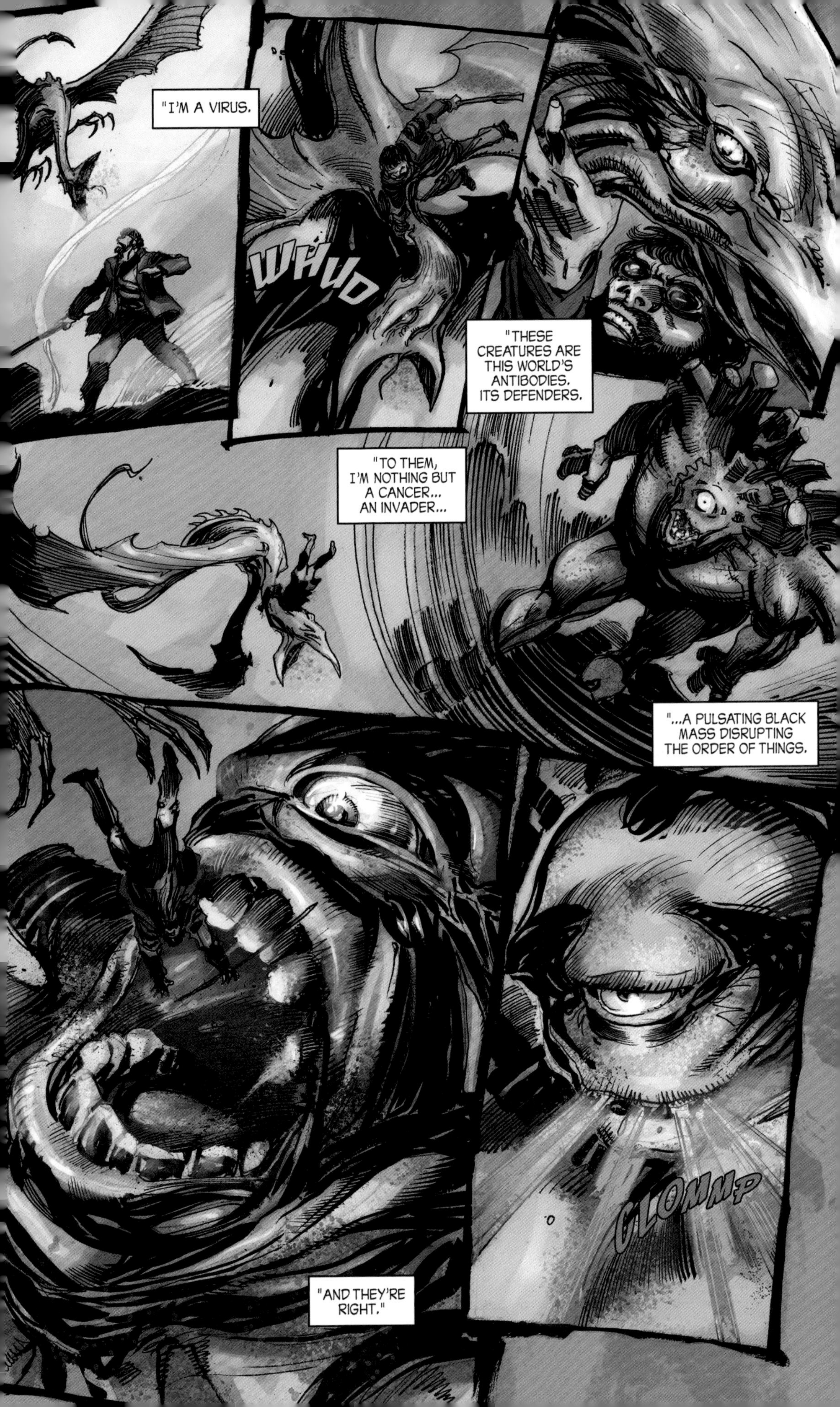
"I'M A VIRUS.
WHUD
"THESE CREATURES ARE THIS WORLD'S ANTIBODIES. ITS DEFENDERS.
"TO THEM, I'M NOTHING BUT A CANCER... AN INVADER...
"...A PULSATING BLACK MASS DISRUPTING THE ORDER OF THINGS.
GLOMMP
"AND THEY'RE RIGHT."

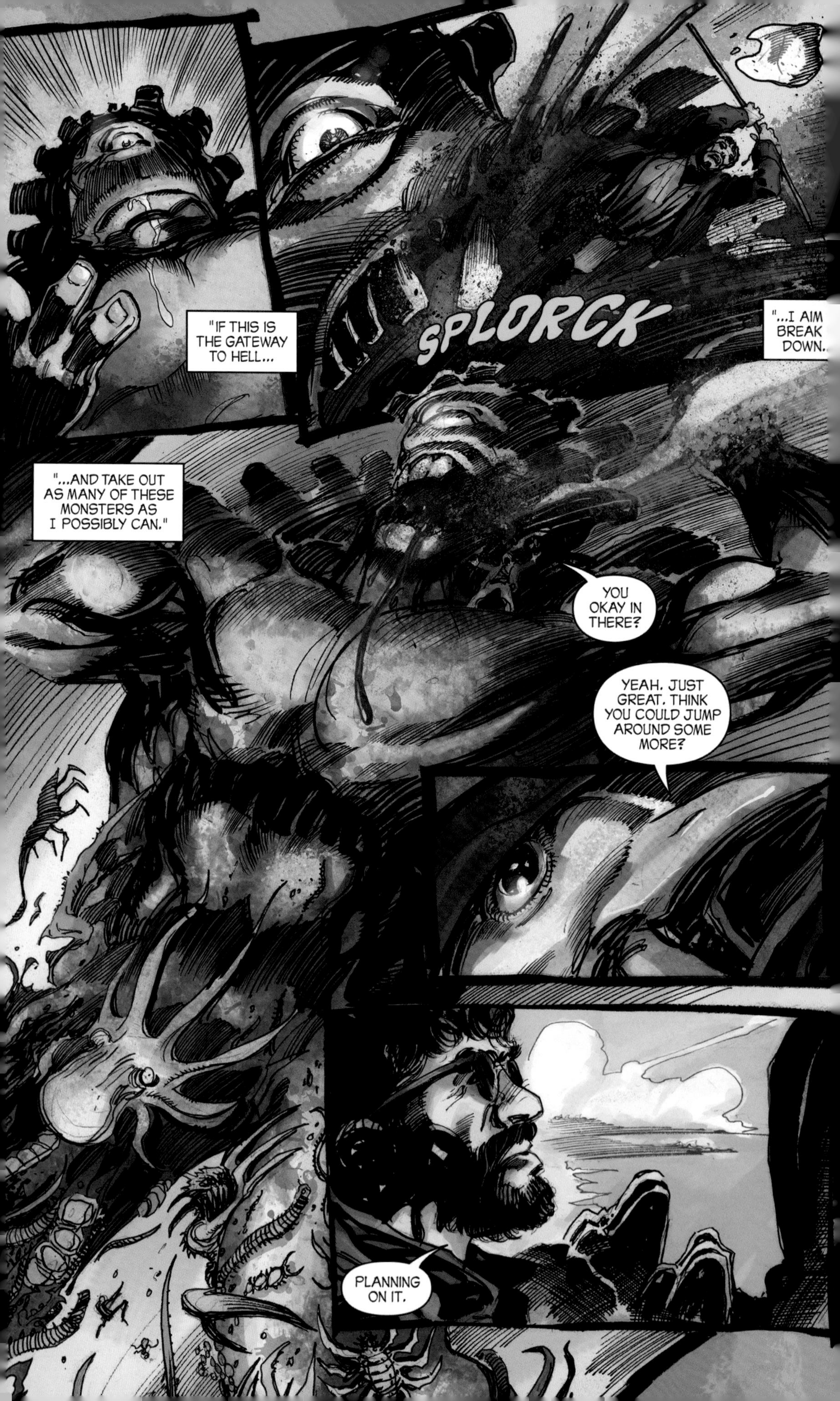
"IF THIS IS THE GATEWAY TO HELL...
SPLORCK
"...I AIM BREAK DOWN.
"...AND TAKE OUT AS MANY OF THESE MONSTERS AS I POSSIBLY CAN."
YOU OKAY IN THERE?
YEAH. JUST GREAT. THINK YOU COULD JUMP AROUND SOME MORE?
PLANNING ON IT.

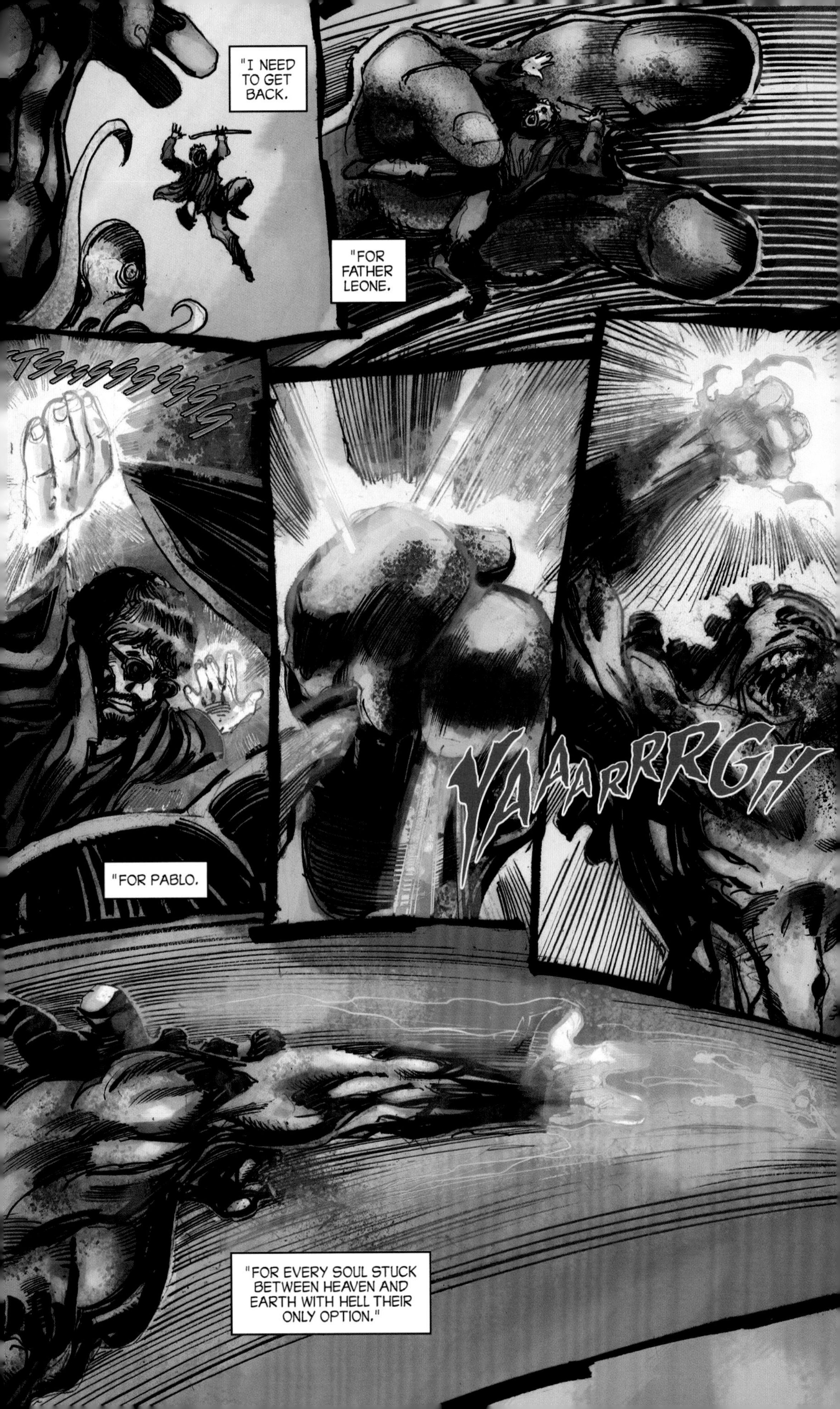
"I NEED TO GET BACK.
"FOR FATHER LEONE.
TSSSSSSSSSSS
"FOR PABLO.
YAAARRRGH
"FOR EVERY SOUL STUCK BETWEEN HEAVEN AND EARTH WITH HELL THEIR ONLY OPTION."

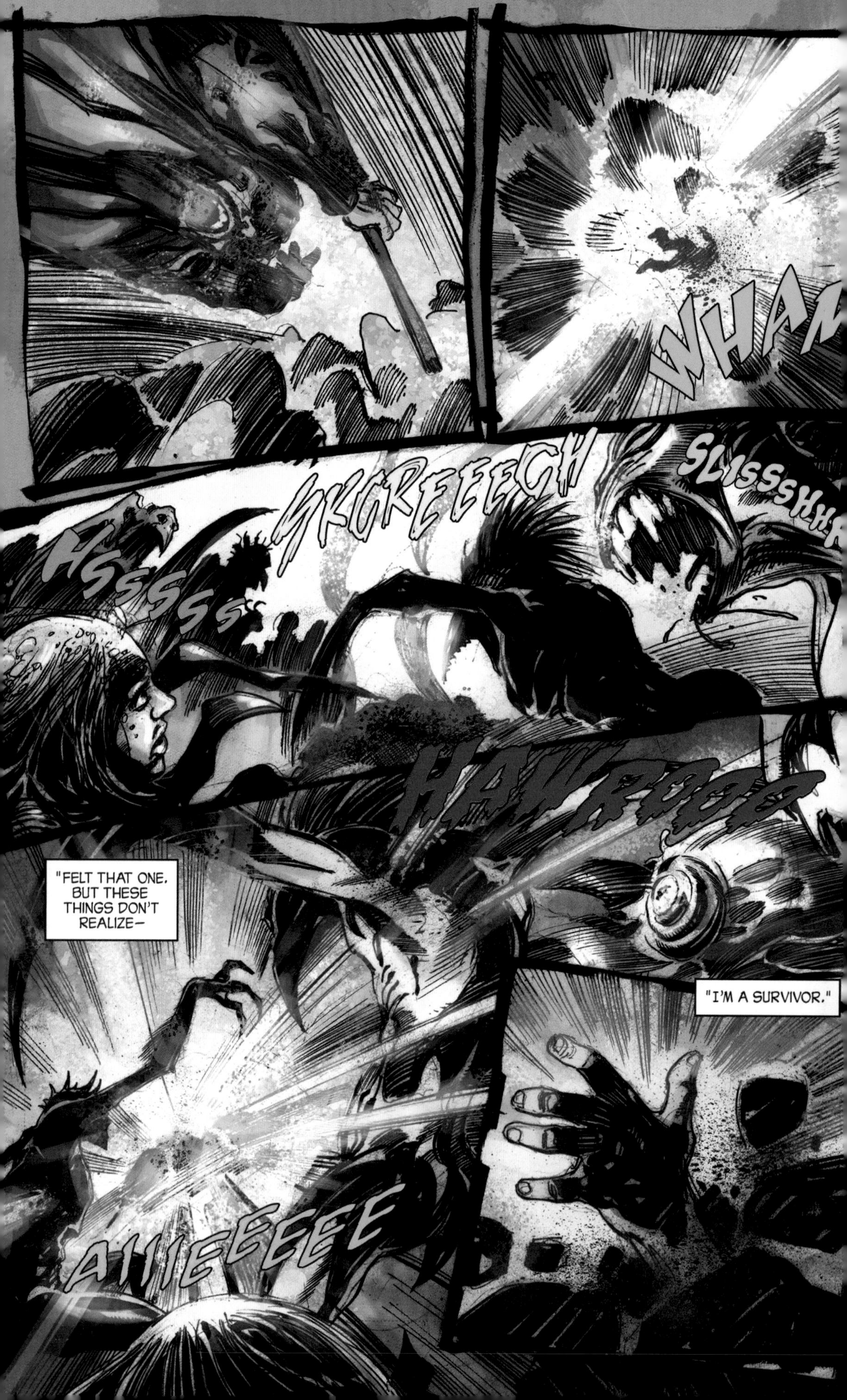

WHAM
SKCREEECH
SLISSSHHH
HSSSSSS
HAWROOO
"FELT THAT ONE, BUT THESE THINGS DON'T REALIZE–
"I'M A SURVIVOR."
AIIIEEEEE

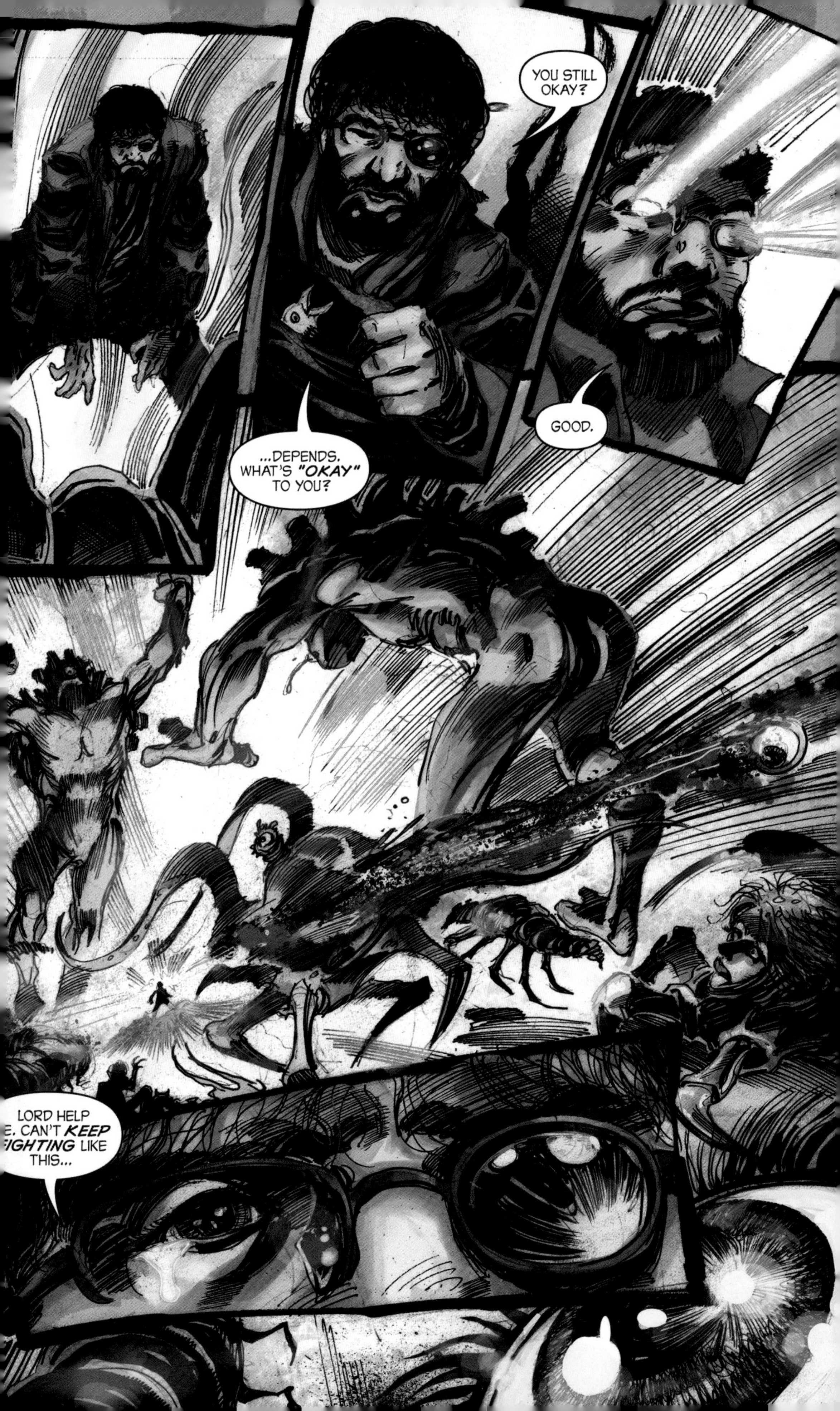
YOU STILL OKAY?
...DEPENDS. WHAT'S "OKAY" TO YOU?
GOOD.
LORD HELP
E. CAN'T KEEP
IGHTING LIKE
THIS...

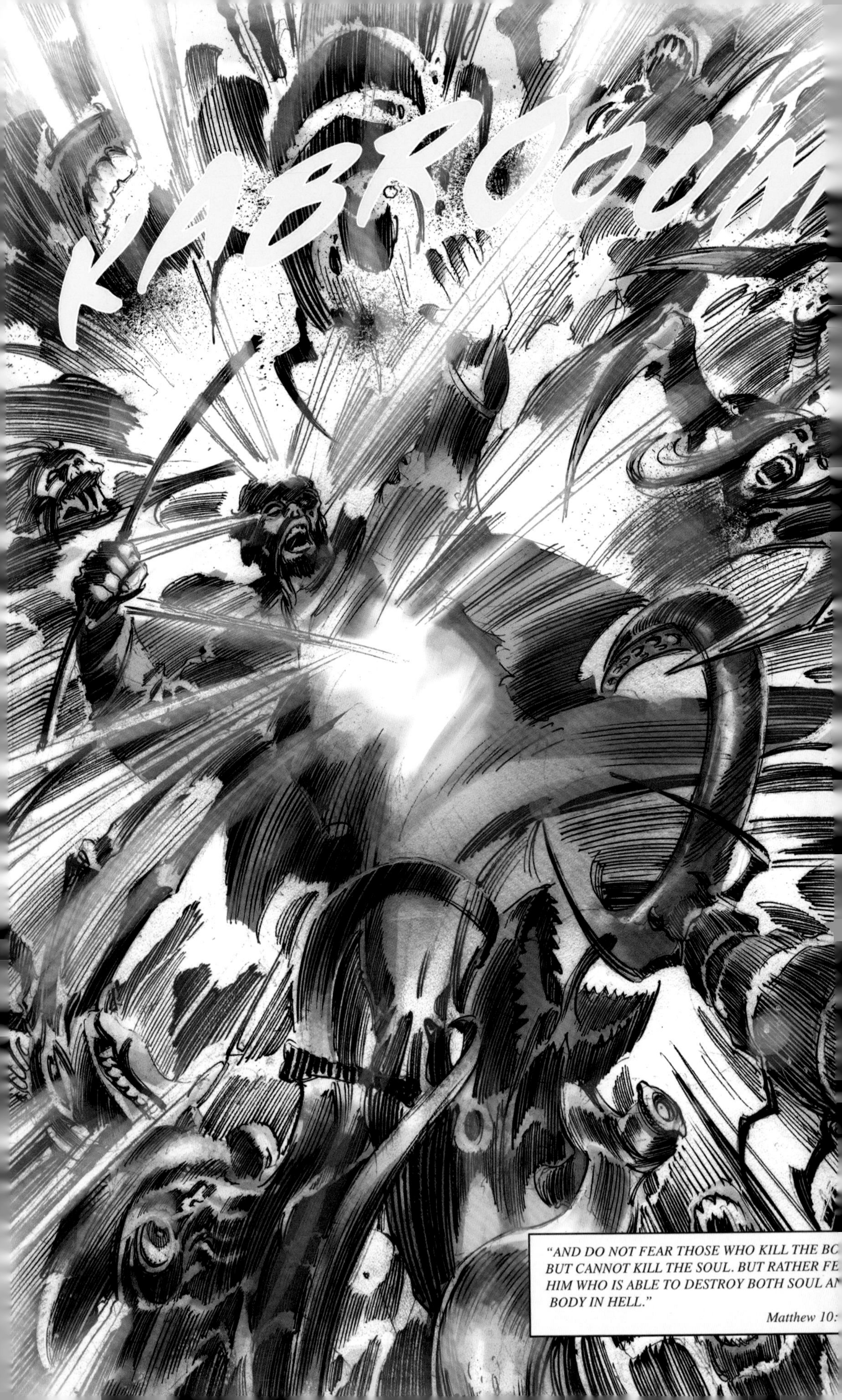
KABROOUM
"AND DO NOT FEAR THOSE WHO KILL THE BO
BUT CANNOT KILL THE SOUL. BUT RATHER FE
HIM WHO IS ABLE TO DESTROY BOTH SOUL AN
BODY IN HELL."
Matthew 10:

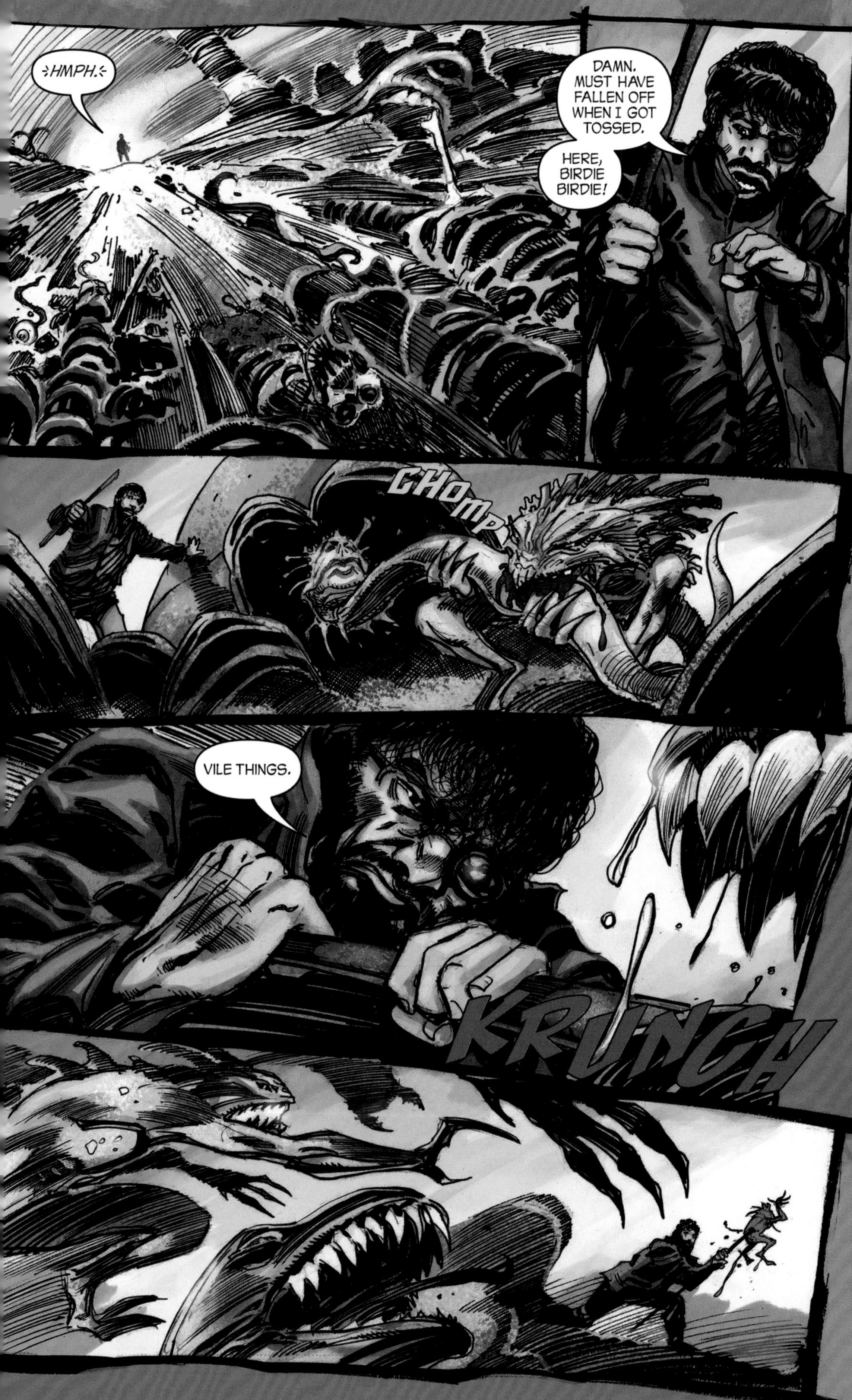
HMPH.
DAMN. MUST HAVE FALLEN OFF WHEN I GOT TOSSED.
HERE, BIRDIE BIRDIE!
CHOMP
VILE THINGS.
KRUNCH

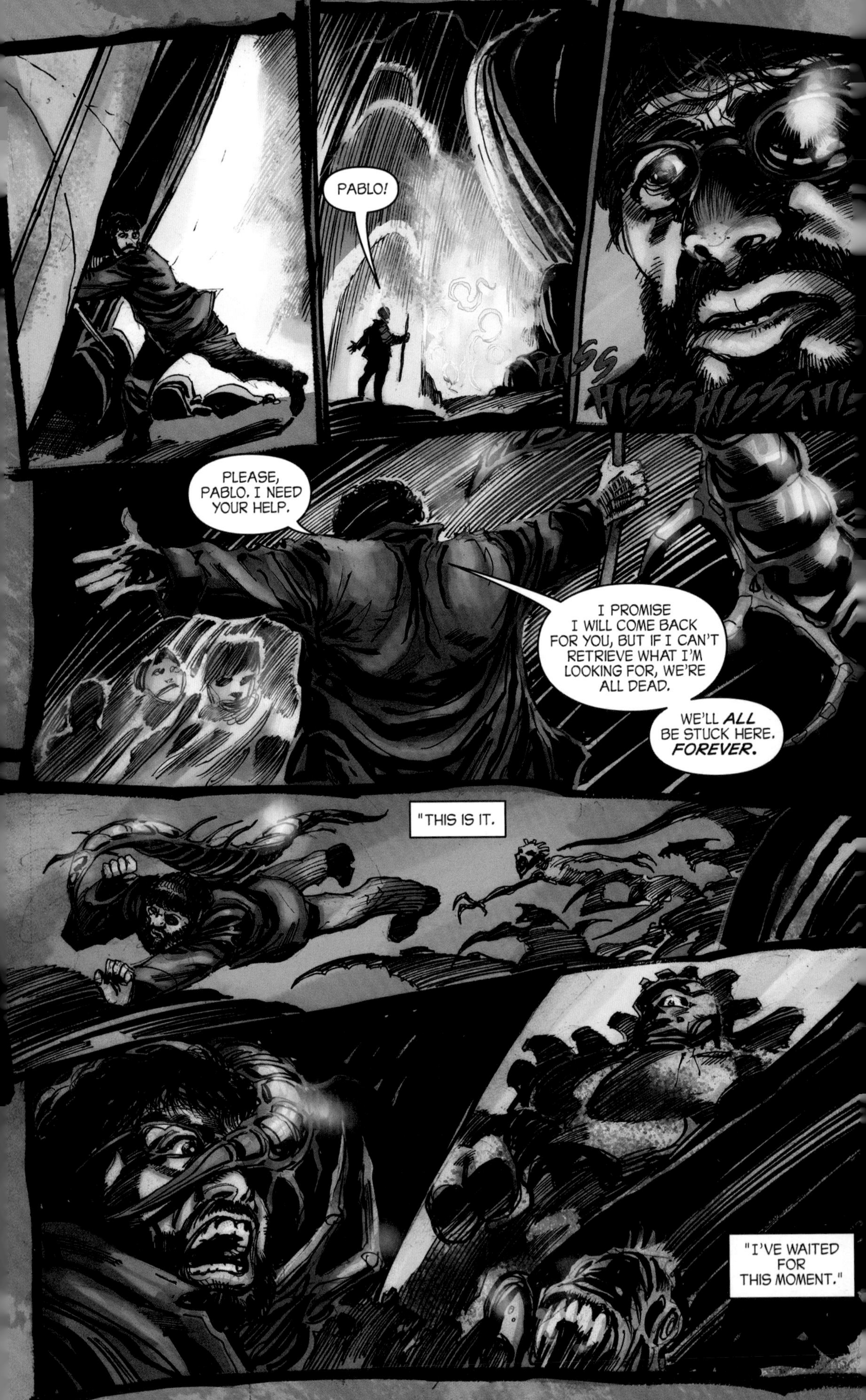
PABLO!
HISS HISSS HISSS HI
PLEASE, PABLO. I NEED YOUR HELP.
I PROMISE I WILL COME BACK FOR YOU, BUT IF I CAN'T RETRIEVE WHAT I'M LOOKING FOR, WE'RE ALL DEAD.
WE'LL ALL BE STUCK HERE. FOREVER.
"THIS IS IT.
"I'VE WAITED FOR THIS MOMENT."

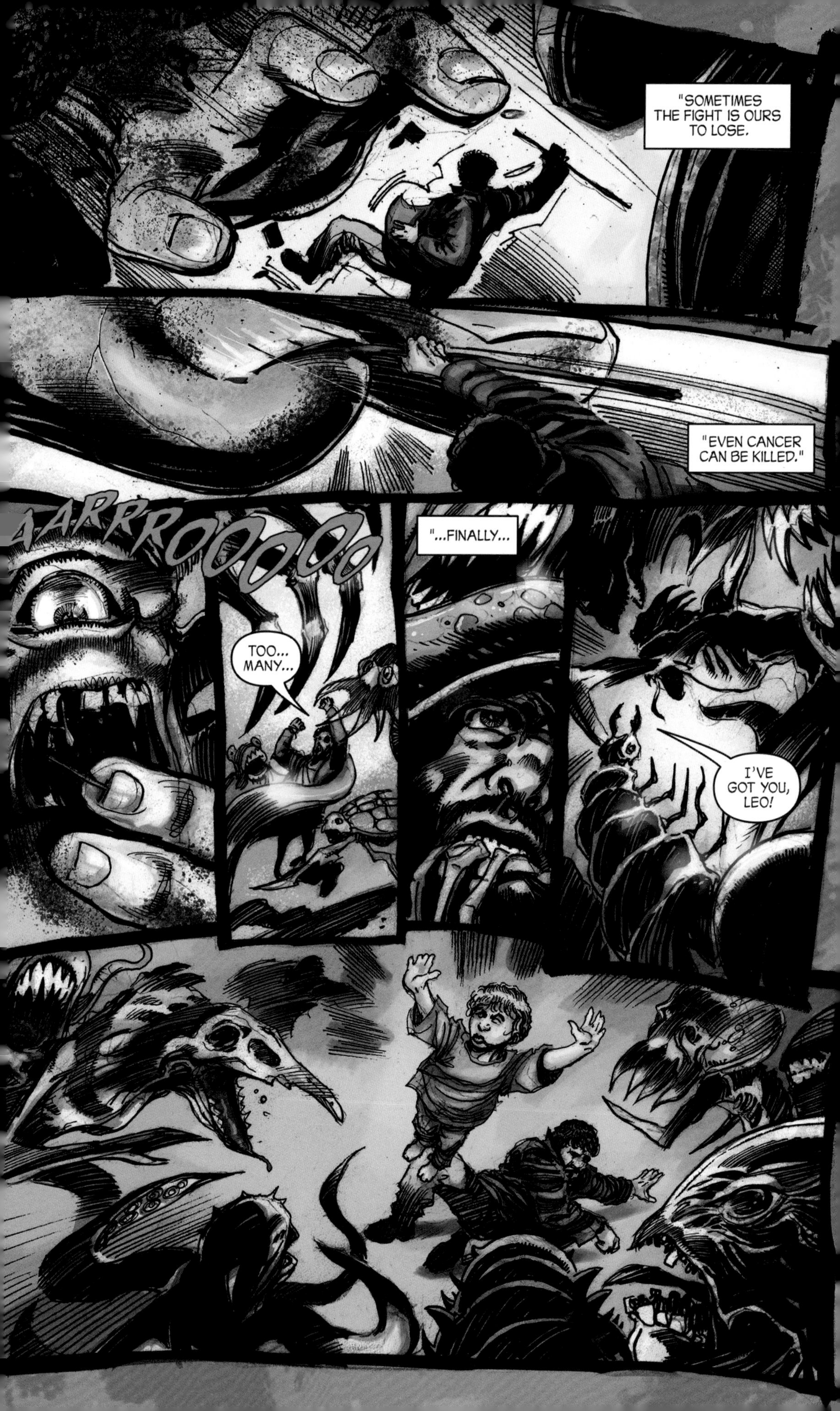
"SOMETIMES THE FIGHT IS OURS TO LOSE.
"EVEN CANCER CAN BE KILLED."
AARRROOOOOO
TOO... MANY...
"...FINALLY...
I'VE GOT YOU, LEO!

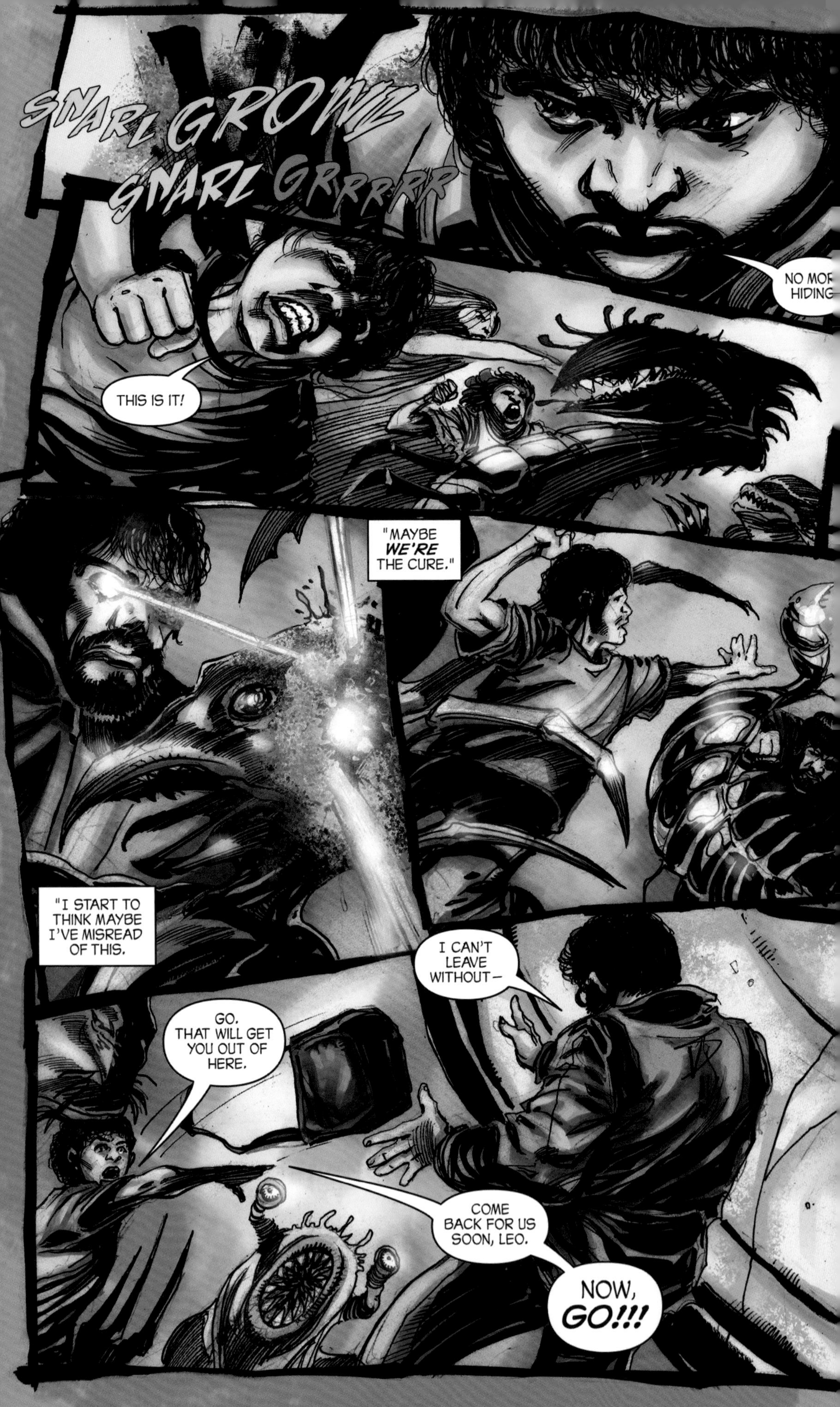
SNARL GROWL
SNARL GRRRRRR
NO MOR HIDING
THIS IS IT!
"I START TO THINK MAYBE I'VE MISREAD OF THIS.
"MAYBE **WE'RE** THE CURE."
I CAN'T LEAVE WITHOUT—
GO. THAT WILL GET YOU OUT OF HERE.
COME BACK FOR US SOON, LEO.
NOW, **GO!!!**

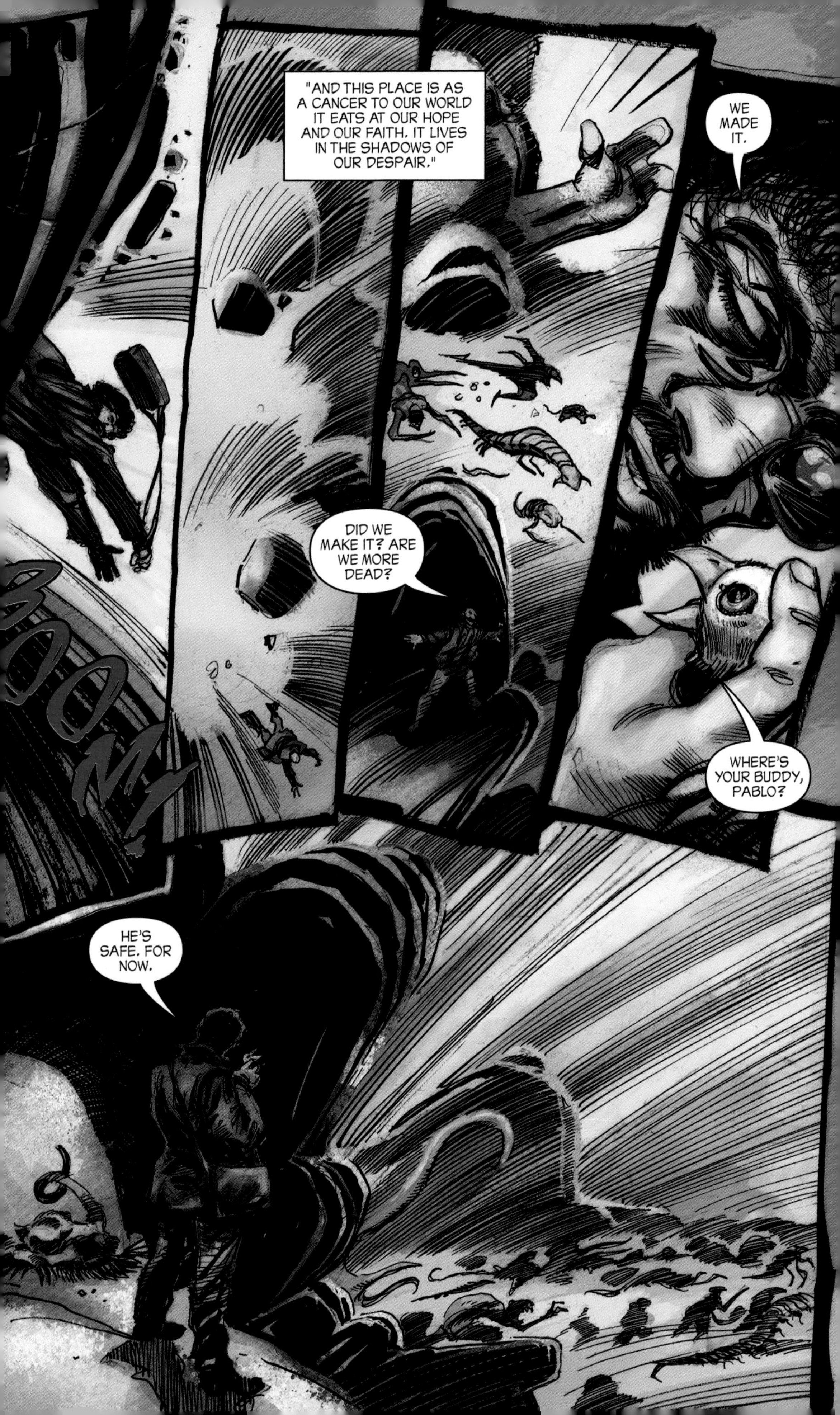
BOOM!
"AND THIS PLACE IS AS A CANCER TO OUR WORLD IT EATS AT OUR HOPE AND OUR FAITH. IT LIVES IN THE SHADOWS OF OUR DESPAIR."
DID WE MAKE IT? ARE WE MORE DEAD?
WE MADE IT.
WHERE'S YOUR BUDDY, PABLO?
HE'S SAFE. FOR NOW.

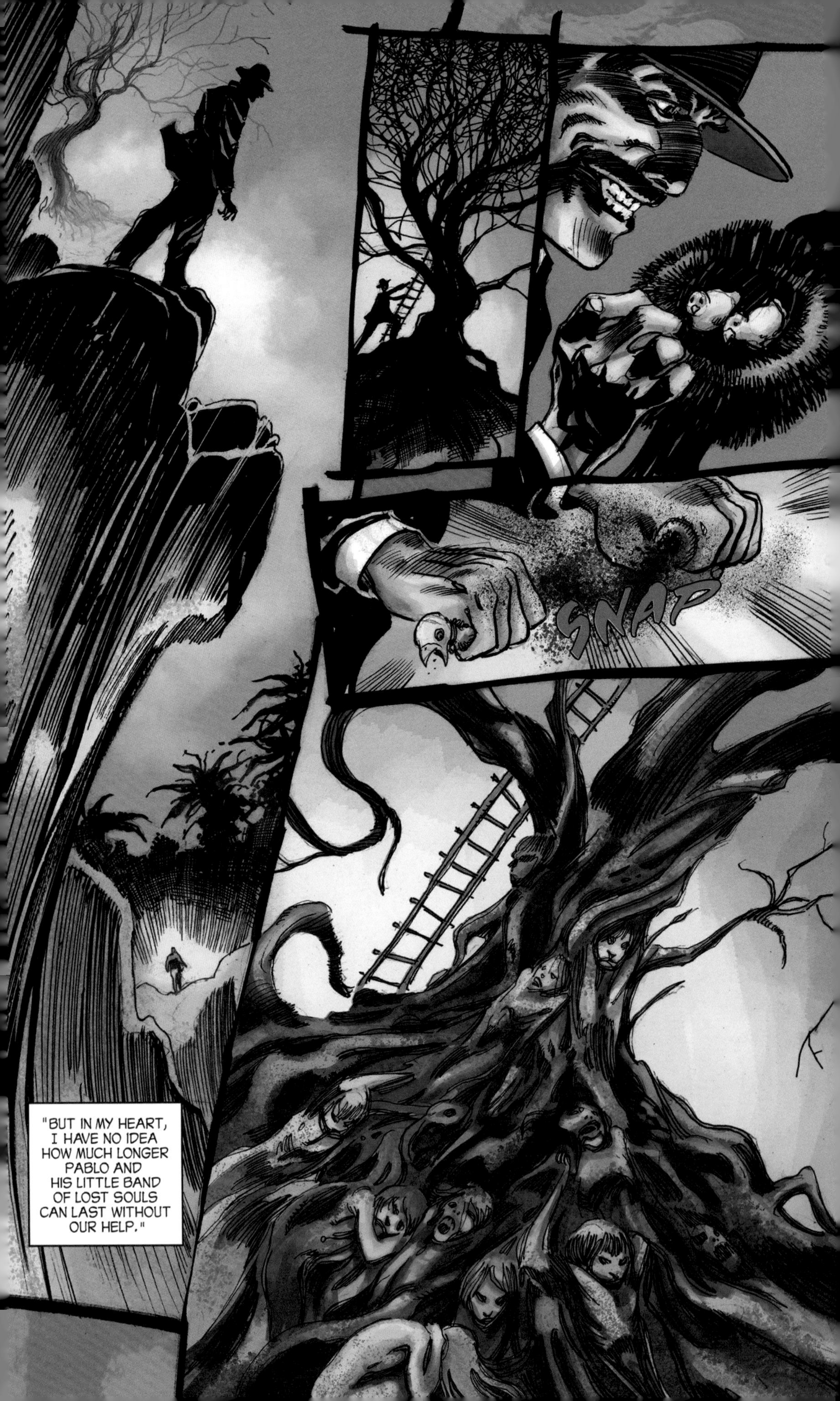
SNAP
"BUT IN MY HEART, I HAVE NO IDEA HOW MUCH LONGER PABLO AND HIS LITTLE BAND OF LOST SOULS CAN LAST WITHOUT OUR HELP."

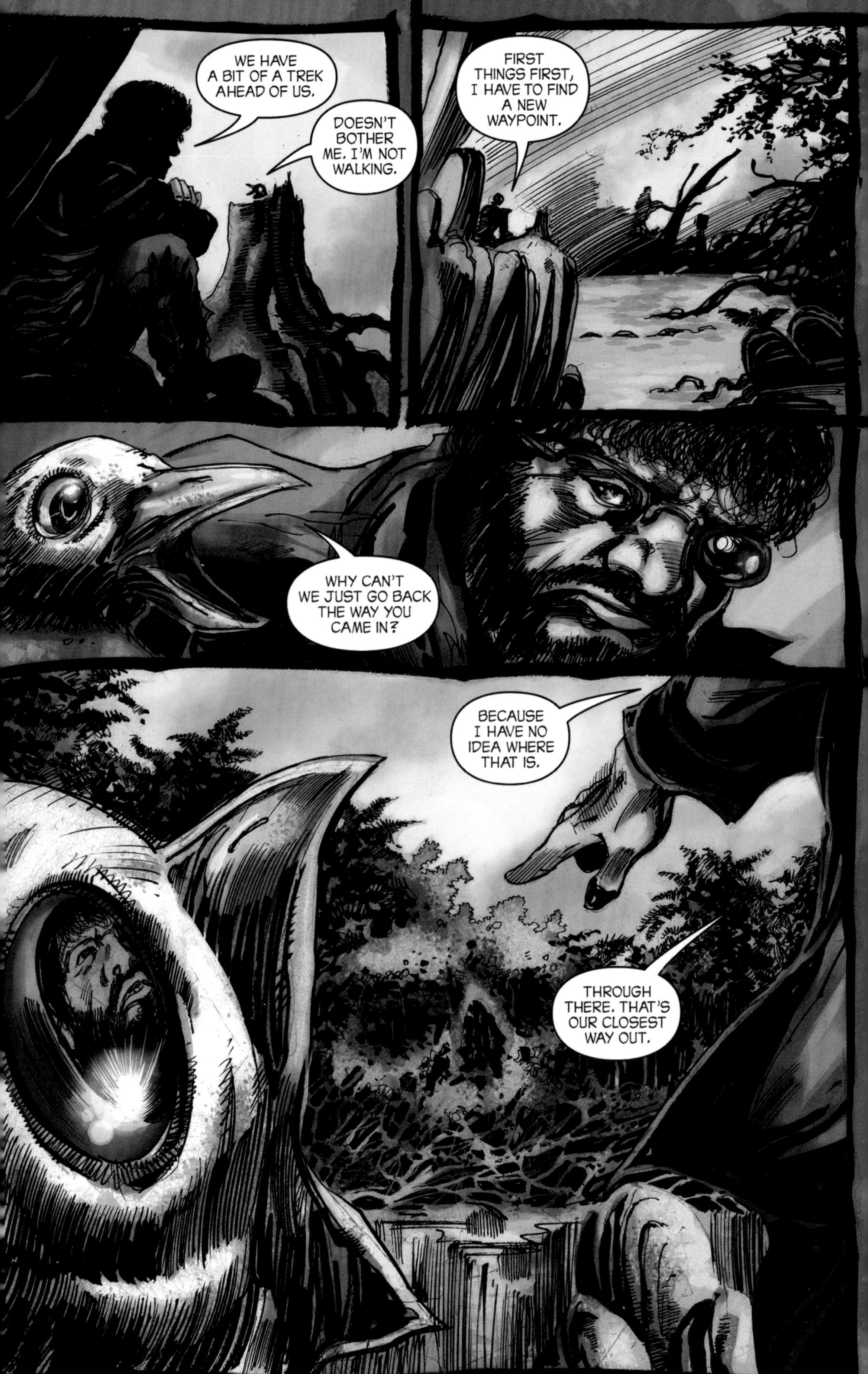
WE HAVE A BIT OF A TREK AHEAD OF US.
DOESN'T BOTHER ME. I'M NOT WALKING.
FIRST THINGS FIRST, I HAVE TO FIND A NEW WAYPOINT.
WHY CAN'T WE JUST GO BACK THE WAY YOU CAME IN?
BECAUSE I HAVE NO IDEA WHERE THAT IS.
THROUGH THERE. THAT'S OUR CLOSEST WAY OUT.

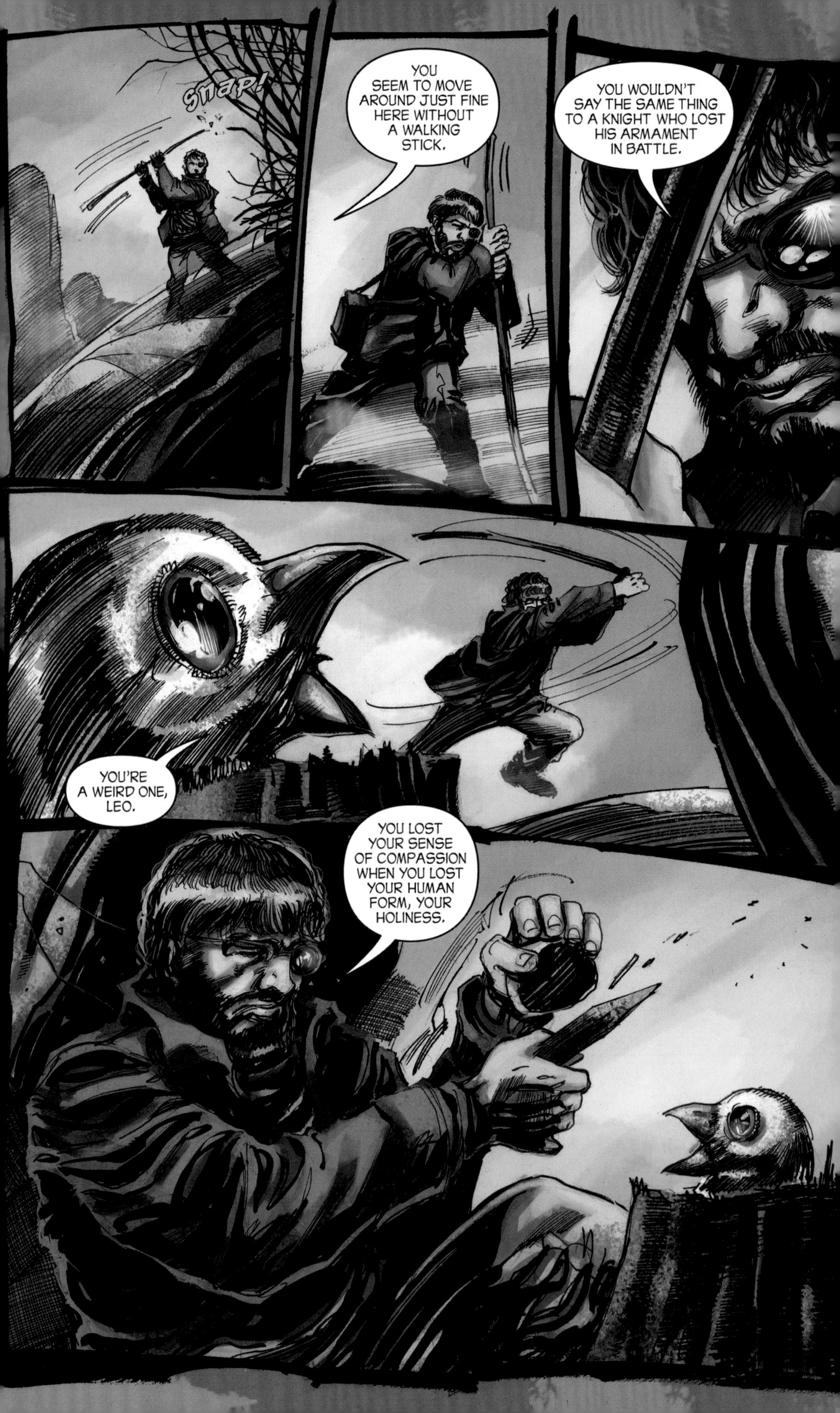
SNAP!
YOU SEEM TO MOVE AROUND JUST FINE HERE WITHOUT A WALKING STICK.
YOU WOULDN'T SAY THE SAME THING TO A KNIGHT WHO LOST HIS ARMAMENT IN BATTLE.
YOU'RE A WEIRD ONE, LEO.
YOU LOST YOUR SENSE OF COMPASSION WHEN YOU LOST YOUR HUMAN FORM, YOUR HOLINESS.

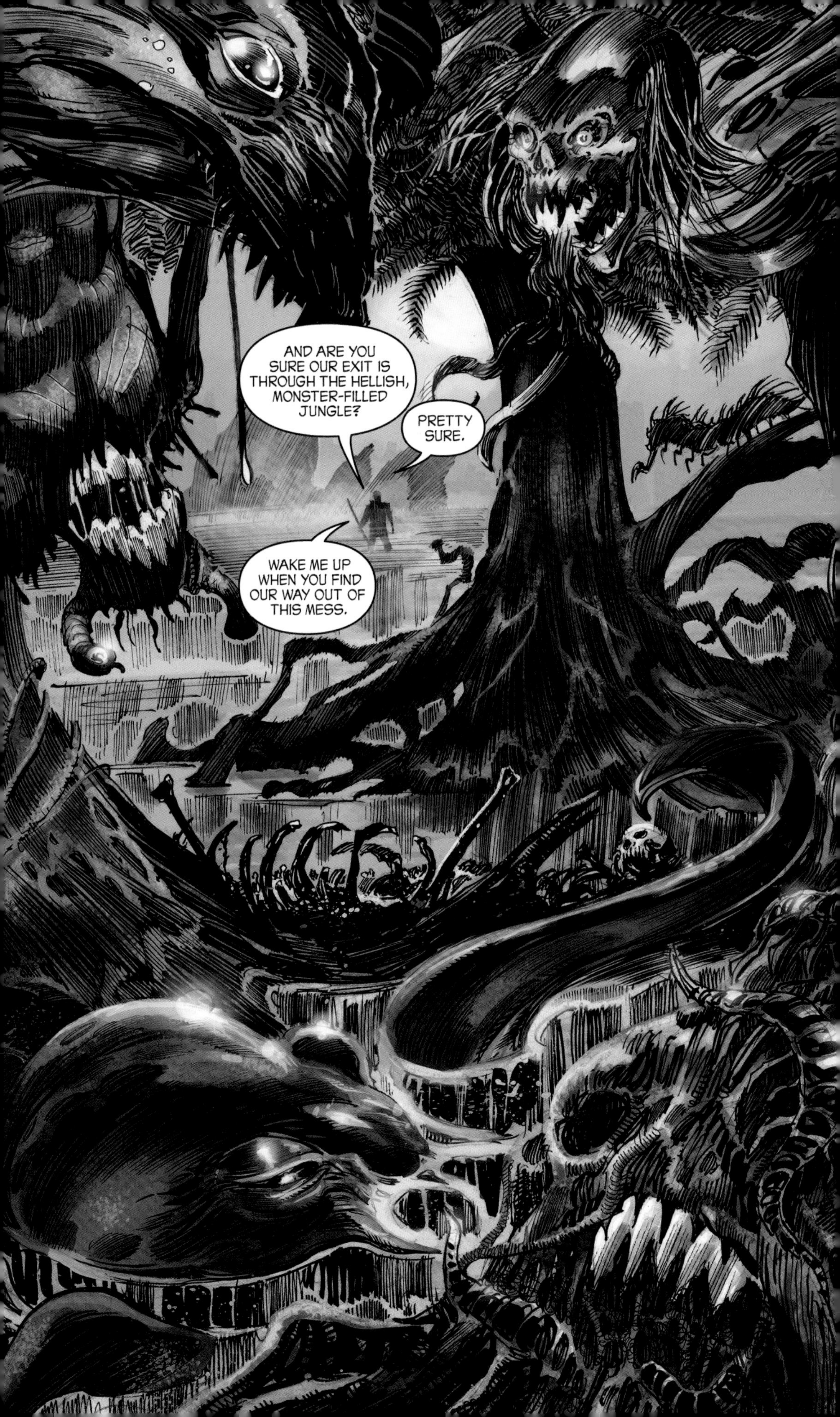
AND ARE YOU SURE OUR EXIT IS THROUGH THE HELLISH, MONSTER-FILLED JUNGLE?
PRETTY SURE.
WAKE ME UP WHEN YOU FIND OUR WAY OUT OF THIS MESS.

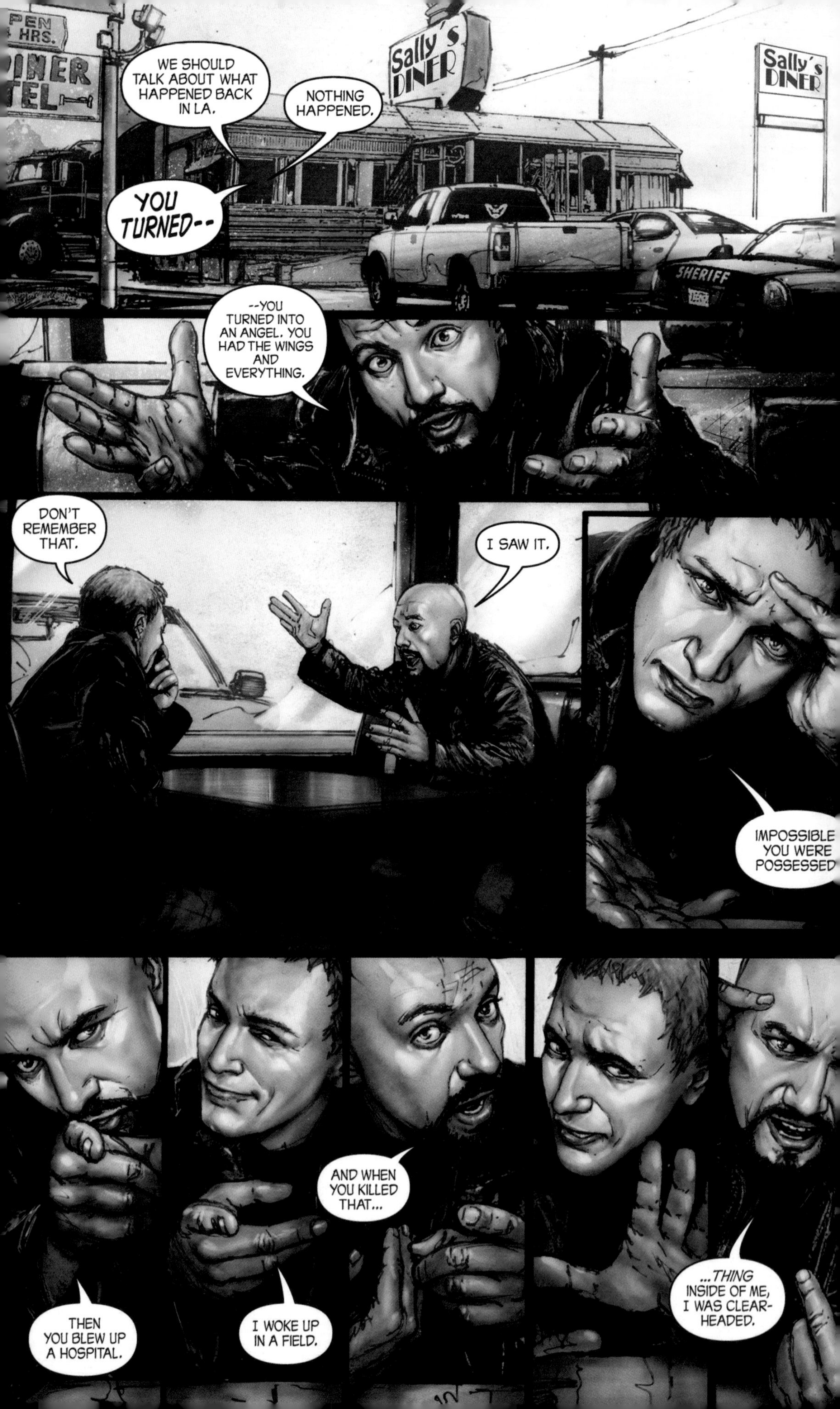

Sally's DINER
Sally's DINER
WE SHOULD TALK ABOUT WHAT HAPPENED BACK IN LA.
NOTHING HAPPENED.
YOU TURNED--
SHERIFF
--YOU TURNED INTO AN ANGEL. YOU HAD THE WINGS AND EVERYTHING.
DON'T REMEMBER THAT.
I SAW IT.
IMPOSSIBLE YOU WERE POSSESSED
THEN YOU BLEW UP A HOSPITAL.
I WOKE UP IN A FIELD.
AND WHEN YOU KILLED THAT...
...THING INSIDE OF ME, I WAS CLEAR-HEADED.

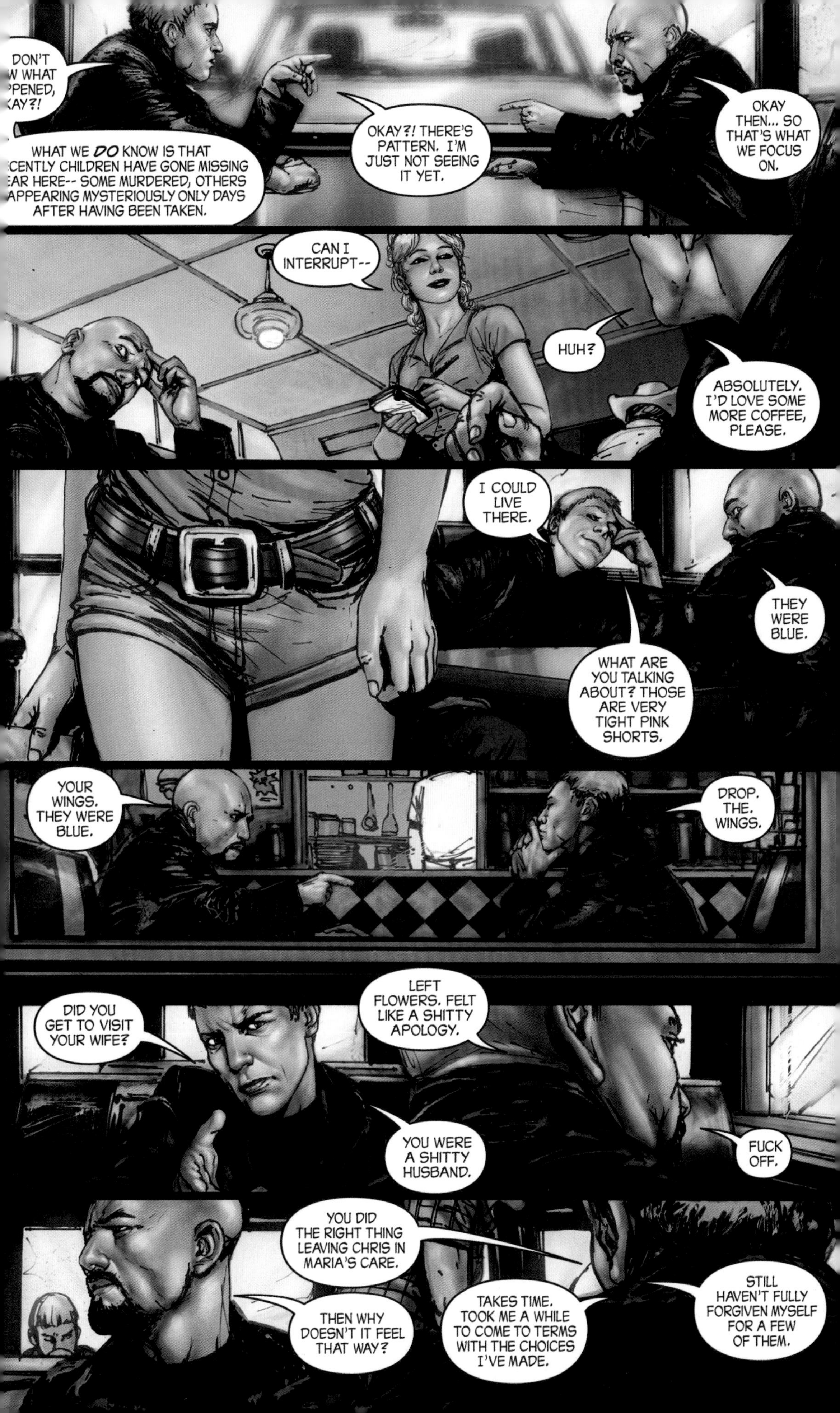
DON'T
W WHAT
PPENED,
KAY?!
WHAT WE DO KNOW IS THAT
CENTLY CHILDREN HAVE GONE MISSING
EAR HERE-- SOME MURDERED, OTHERS
APPEARING MYSTERIOUSLY ONLY DAYS
AFTER HAVING BEEN TAKEN.
OKAY?! THERE'S PATTERN. I'M JUST NOT SEEING IT YET.
OKAY THEN... SO THAT'S WHAT WE FOCUS ON.
CAN I INTERRUPT--
HUH?
ABSOLUTELY. I'D LOVE SOME MORE COFFEE, PLEASE.
I COULD LIVE THERE.
WHAT ARE YOU TALKING ABOUT? THOSE ARE VERY TIGHT PINK SHORTS.
THEY WERE BLUE.
YOUR WINGS. THEY WERE BLUE.
DROP. THE. WINGS.
DID YOU GET TO VISIT YOUR WIFE?
LEFT FLOWERS. FELT LIKE A SHITTY APOLOGY.
YOU WERE A SHITTY HUSBAND.
FUCK OFF.
YOU DID THE RIGHT THING LEAVING CHRIS IN MARIA'S CARE.
THEN WHY DOESN'T IT FEEL THAT WAY?
TAKES TIME. TOOK ME A WHILE TO COME TO TERMS WITH THE CHOICES I'VE MADE.
STILL HAVEN'T FULLY FORGIVEN MYSELF FOR A FEW OF THEM.

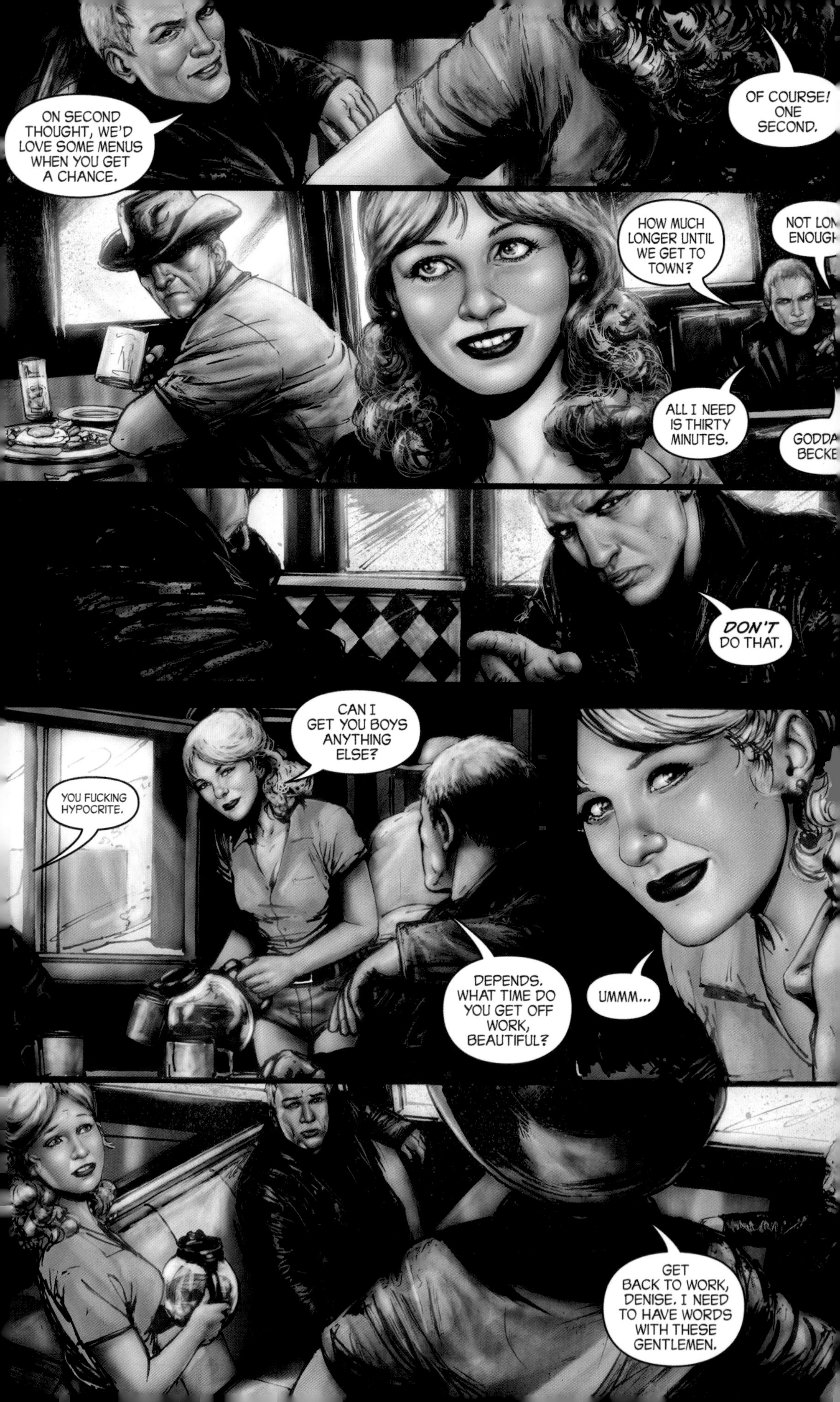
ON SECOND THOUGHT, WE'D LOVE SOME MENUS WHEN YOU GET A CHANCE.
OF COURSE! ONE SECOND.
HOW MUCH LONGER UNTIL WE GET TO TOWN?
NOT LON ENOUGH
ALL I NEED IS THIRTY MINUTES.
GODDA BECKE
DON'T DO THAT.
YOU FUCKING HYPOCRITE.
CAN I GET YOU BOYS ANYTHING ELSE?
DEPENDS. WHAT TIME DO YOU GET OFF WORK, BEAUTIFUL?
UMMM...
GET BACK TO WORK, DENISE. I NEED TO HAVE WORDS WITH THESE GENTLEMEN.

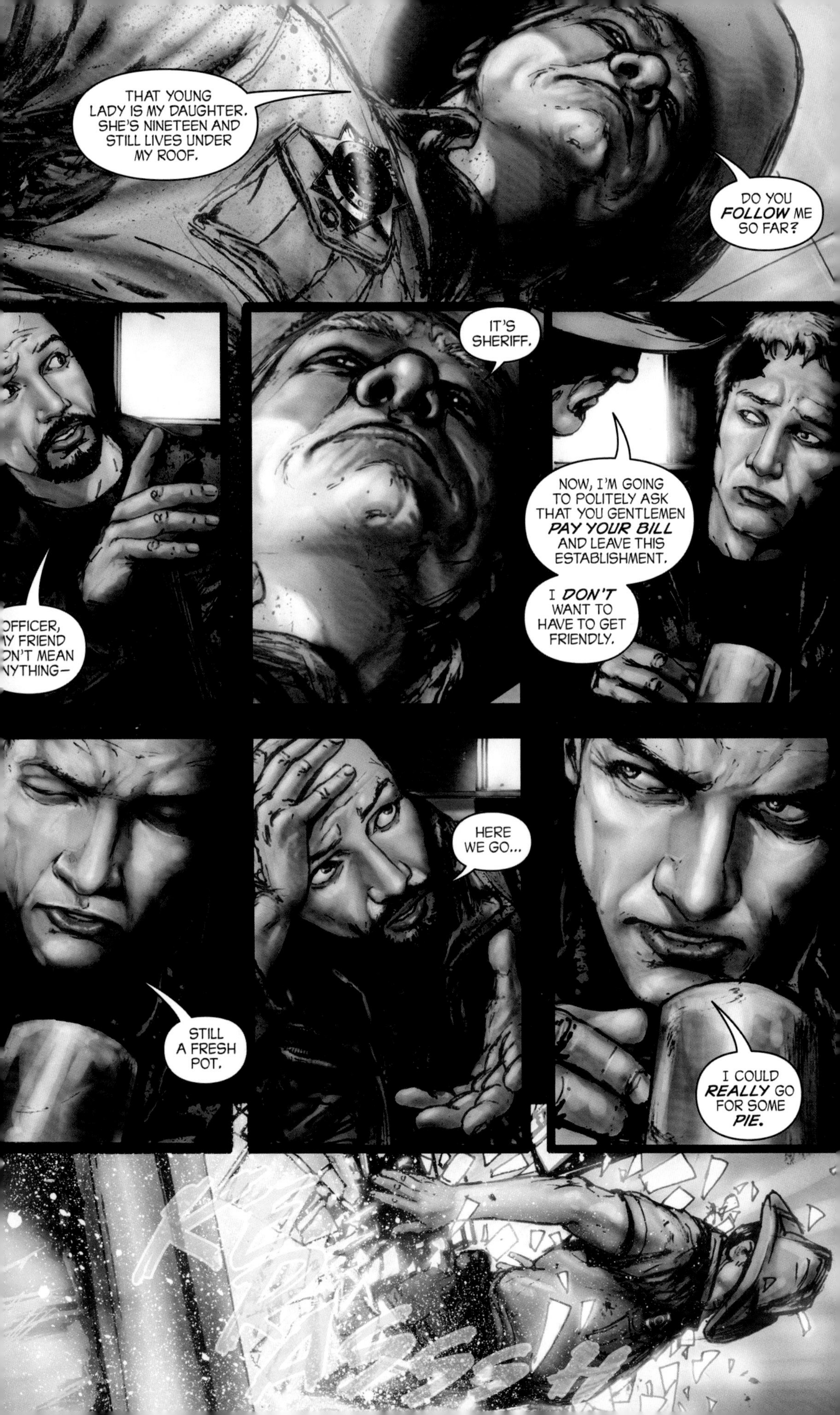
THAT YOUNG LADY IS MY DAUGHTER. SHE'S NINETEEN AND STILL LIVES UNDER MY ROOF.
DO YOU **FOLLOW** ME SO FAR?
OFFICER, Y FRIEND ON'T MEAN NYTHING—
IT'S SHERIFF.
NOW, I'M GOING TO POLITELY ASK THAT YOU GENTLEMEN **PAY YOUR BILL** AND LEAVE THIS ESTABLISHMENT.
I **DON'T** WANT TO HAVE TO GET FRIENDLY.
STILL A FRESH POT.
HERE WE GO...
I COULD **REALLY** GO FOR SOME **PIE.**

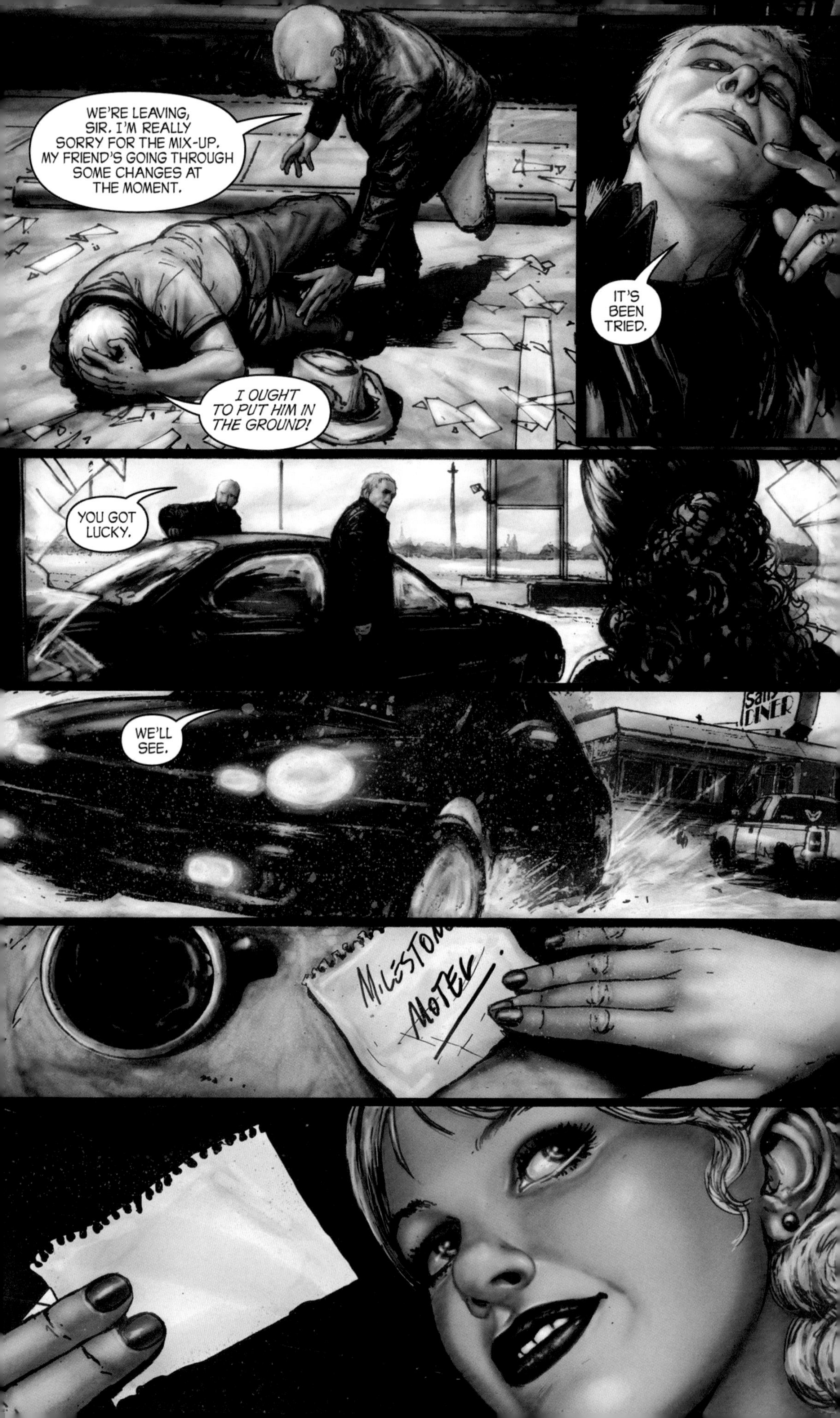
WE'RE LEAVING, SIR. I'M REALLY SORRY FOR THE MIX-UP. MY FRIEND'S GOING THROUGH SOME CHANGES AT THE MOMENT.
I OUGHT TO PUT HIM IN THE GROUND!
IT'S BEEN TRIED.
YOU GOT LUCKY.
WE'LL SEE.
DINER
MOTEL

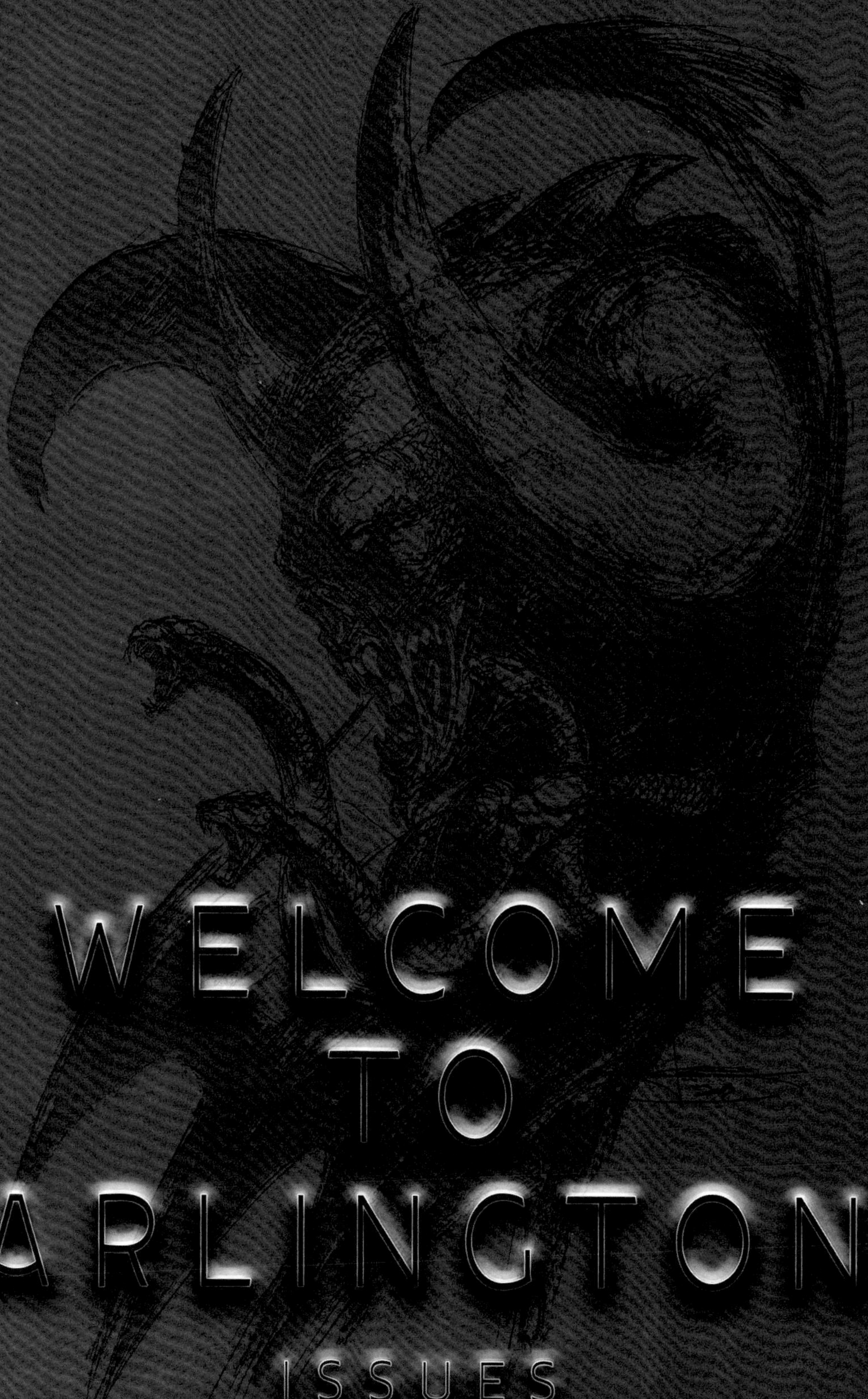

WELCOME TO ARLINGTON

ISSUES

9 TO 14

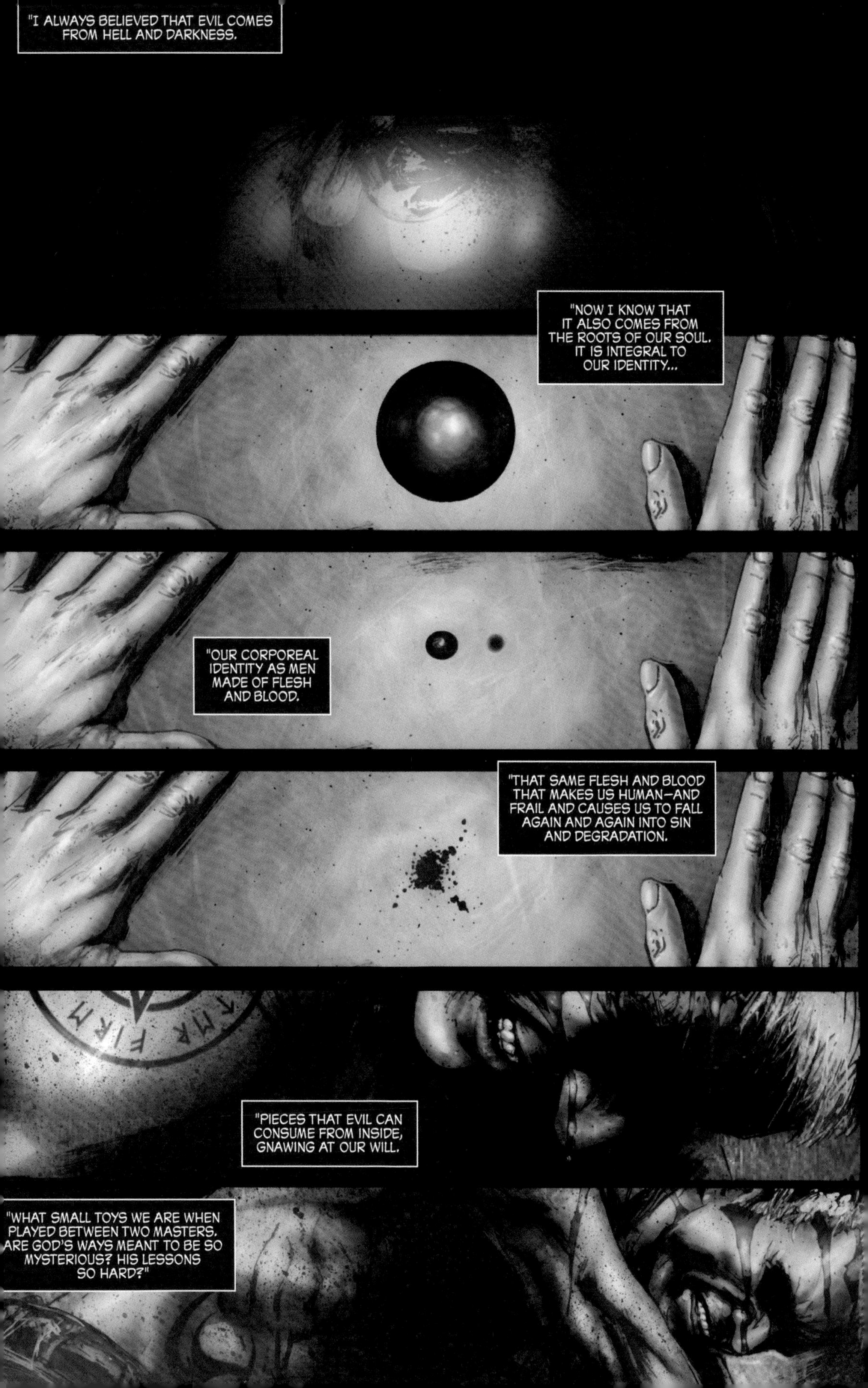
"I ALWAYS BELIEVED THAT EVIL COMES FROM HELL AND DARKNESS.
"NOW I KNOW THAT IT ALSO COMES FROM THE ROOTS OF OUR SOUL. IT IS INTEGRAL TO OUR IDENTITY...
"OUR CORPOREAL IDENTITY AS MEN MADE OF FLESH AND BLOOD.
"THAT SAME FLESH AND BLOOD THAT MAKES US HUMAN—AND FRAIL AND CAUSES US TO FALL AGAIN AND AGAIN INTO SIN AND DEGRADATION.
"PIECES THAT EVIL CAN CONSUME FROM INSIDE, GNAWING AT OUR WILL.
"WHAT SMALL TOYS WE ARE WHEN PLAYED BETWEEN TWO MASTERS. ARE GOD'S WAYS MEANT TO BE SO MYSTERIOUS? HIS LESSONS SO HARD?"

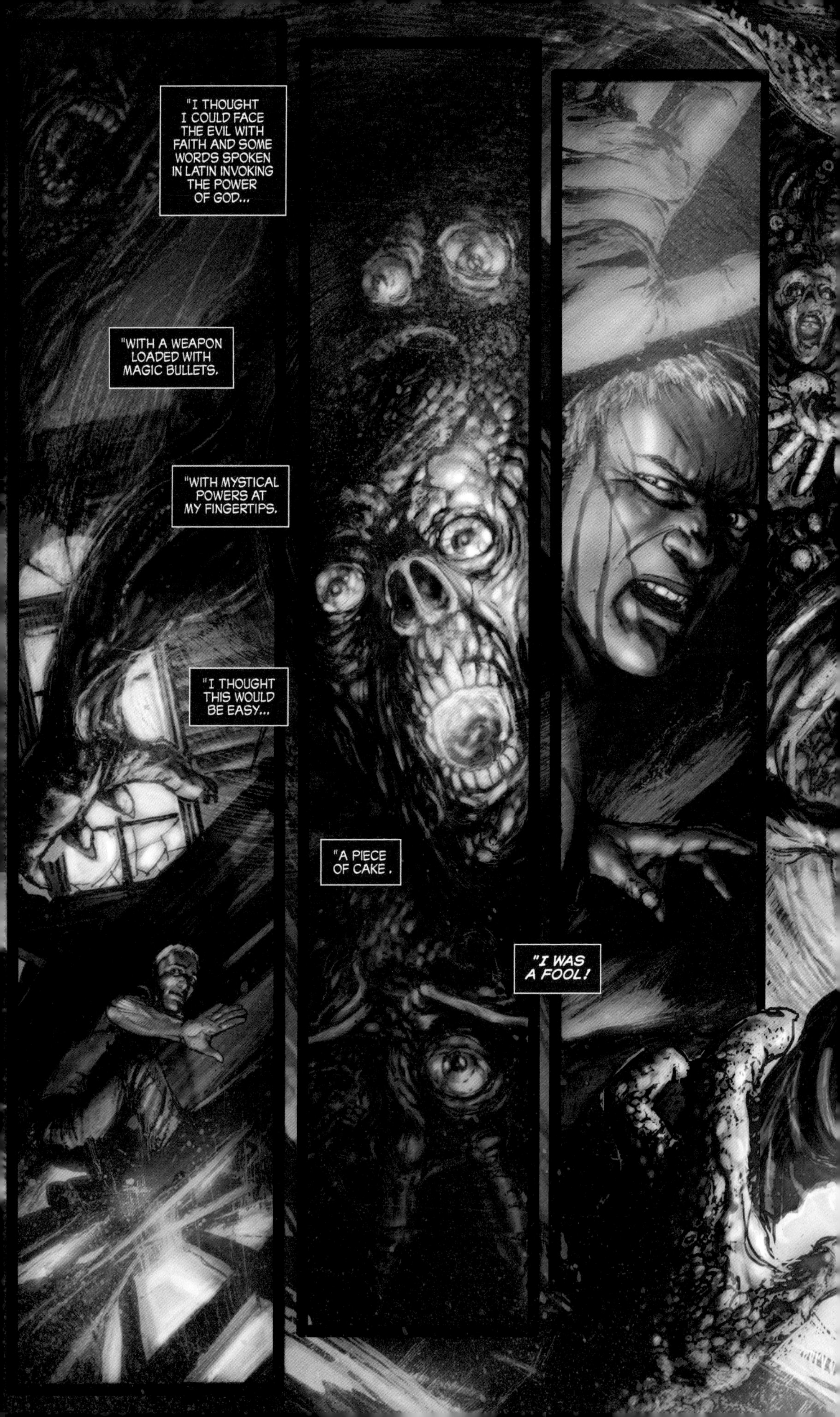
"I THOUGHT I COULD FACE THE EVIL WITH FAITH AND SOME WORDS SPOKEN IN LATIN INVOKING THE POWER OF GOD...
"WITH A WEAPON LOADED WITH MAGIC BULLETS.
"WITH MYSTICAL POWERS AT MY FINGERTIPS.
"I THOUGHT THIS WOULD BE EASY...
"A PIECE OF CAKE.
"I WAS A FOOL!

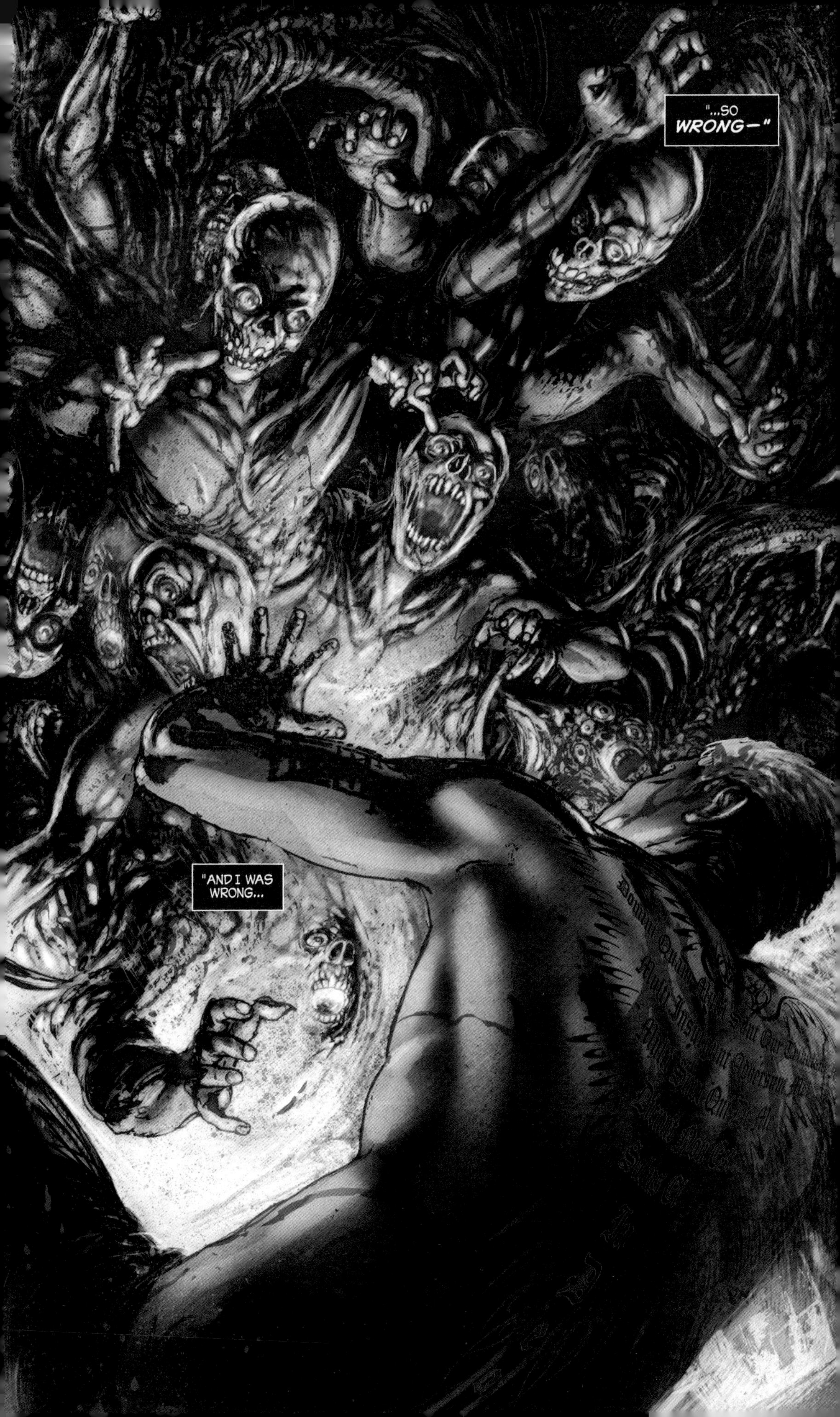
"AND I WAS WRONG...
"...SO WRONG—"

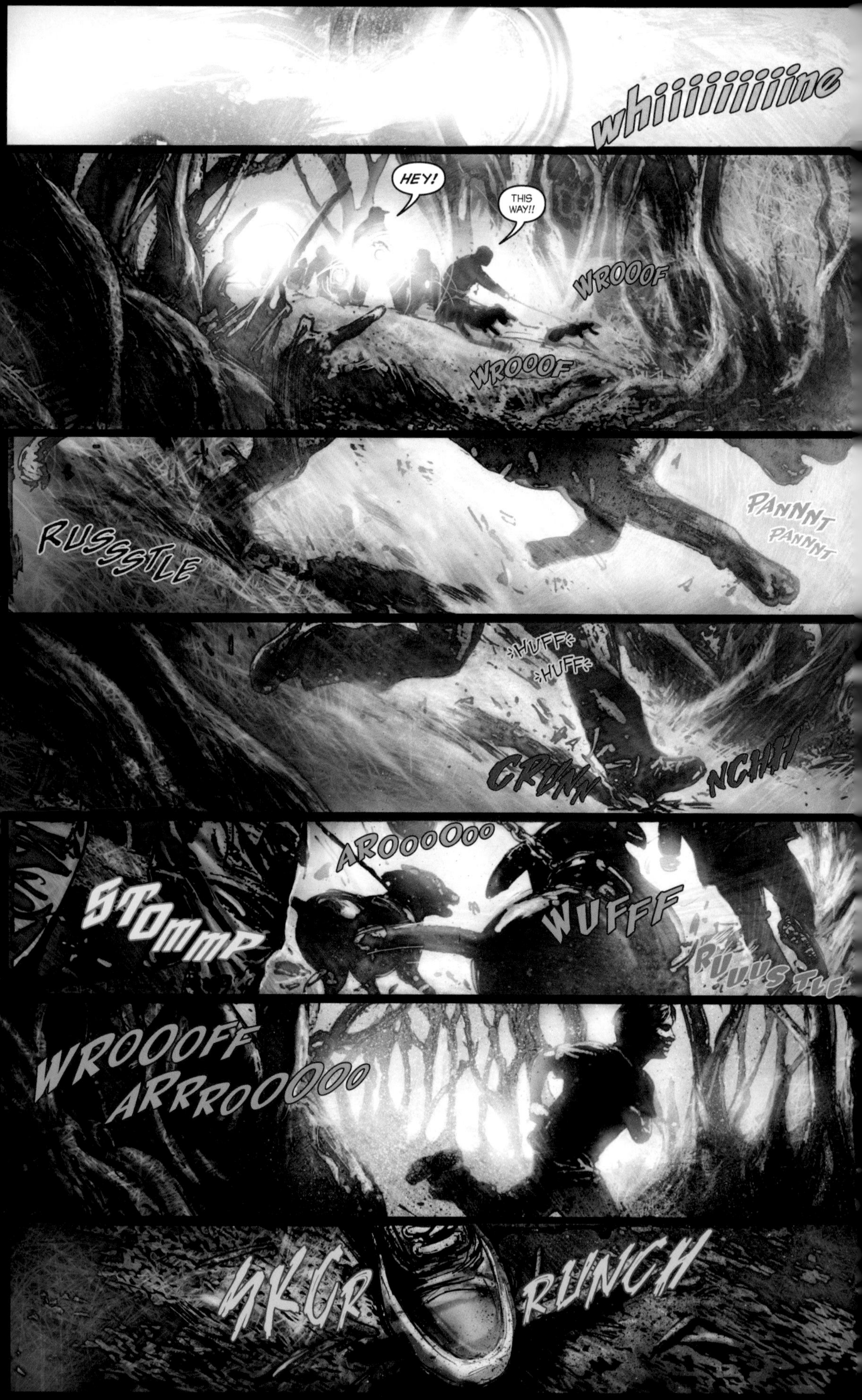
whiiiiiiiine
HEY!
THIS WAY!!
WROOOF
WROOOF
RUSSSTLE
PANNNT PANNNT
HUFF HUFF
CRUNN NCHH
STOMMP
AROOOOOO
WUFFF
RUUUSTLE
WROOOFF ARRROOOOOO
KKCR RUNCH

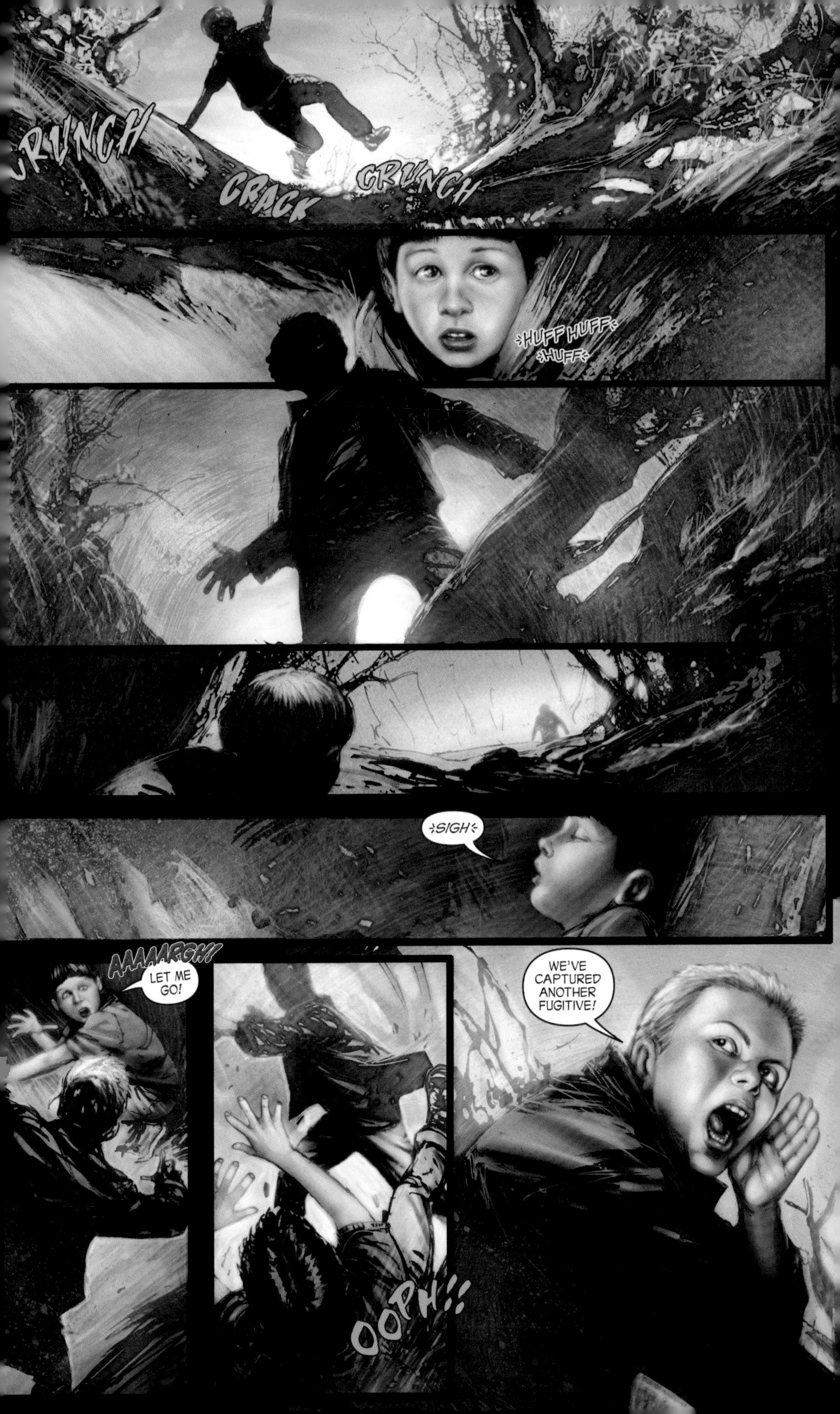

CRUNCH
CRACK
CRUNCH
HUFF HUFF
HUFF
SIGH
AAAAARGH!
LET ME GO!
OOPH!!
WE'VE CAPTURED ANOTHER FUGITIVE!

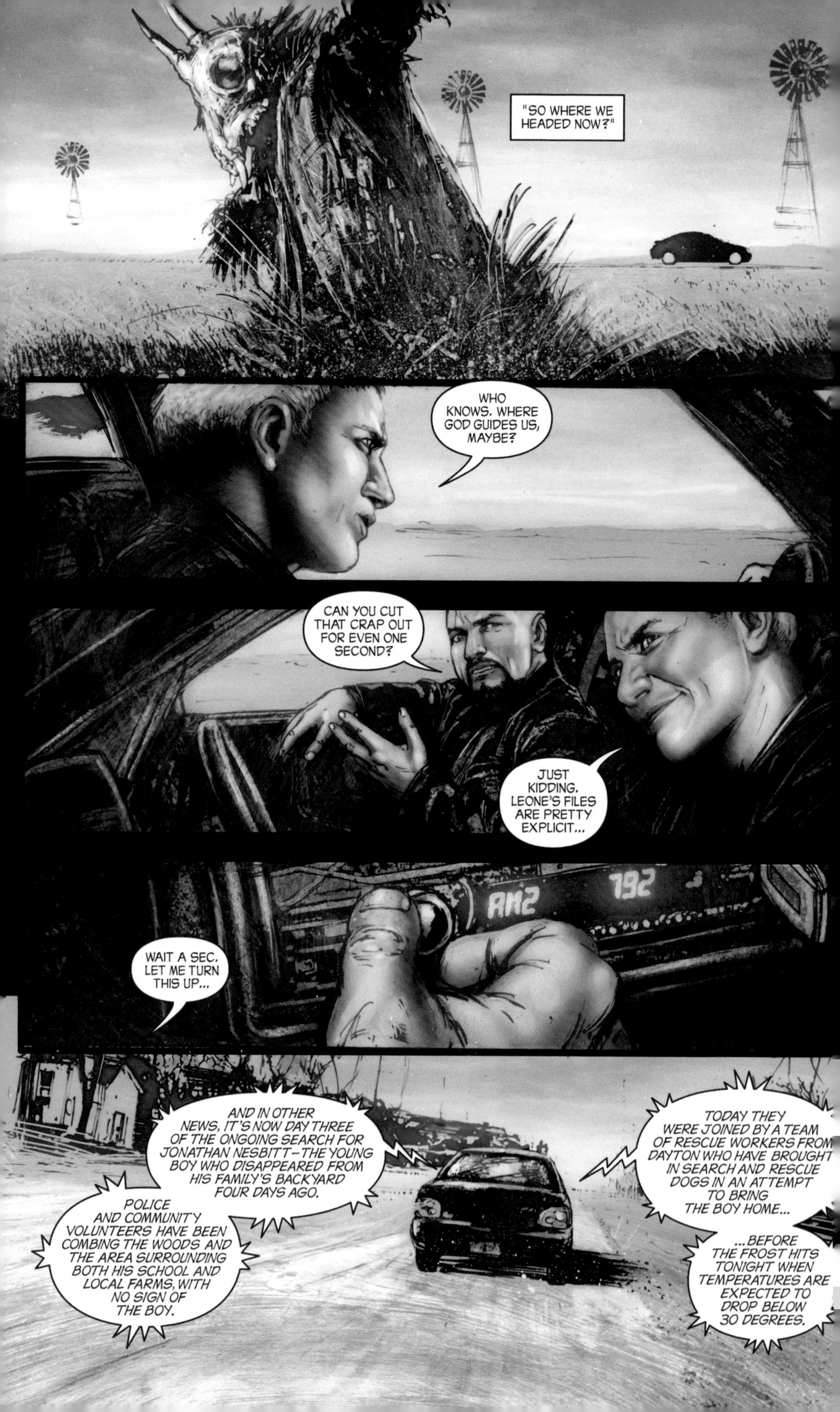
"SO WHERE WE HEADED NOW?"
WHO KNOWS. WHERE GOD GUIDES US, MAYBE?
CAN YOU CUT THAT CRAP OUT FOR EVEN ONE SECOND?
JUST KIDDING. LEONE'S FILES ARE PRETTY EXPLICIT...
AM2
792
WAIT A SEC. LET ME TURN THIS UP...
AND IN OTHER NEWS, IT'S NOW DAY THREE OF THE ONGOING SEARCH FOR JONATHAN NESBITT—THE YOUNG BOY WHO DISAPPEARED FROM HIS FAMILY'S BACKYARD FOUR DAYS AGO.
POLICE AND COMMUNITY VOLUNTEERS HAVE BEEN COMBING THE WOODS AND THE AREA SURROUNDING BOTH HIS SCHOOL AND LOCAL FARMS, WITH NO SIGN OF THE BOY.
TODAY THEY WERE JOINED BY A TEAM OF RESCUE WORKERS FROM DAYTON WHO HAVE BROUGHT IN SEARCH AND RESCUE DOGS IN AN ATTEMPT TO BRING THE BOY HOME...
...BEFORE THE FROST HITS TONIGHT WHEN TEMPERATURES ARE EXPECTED TO DROP BELOW 30 DEGREES.

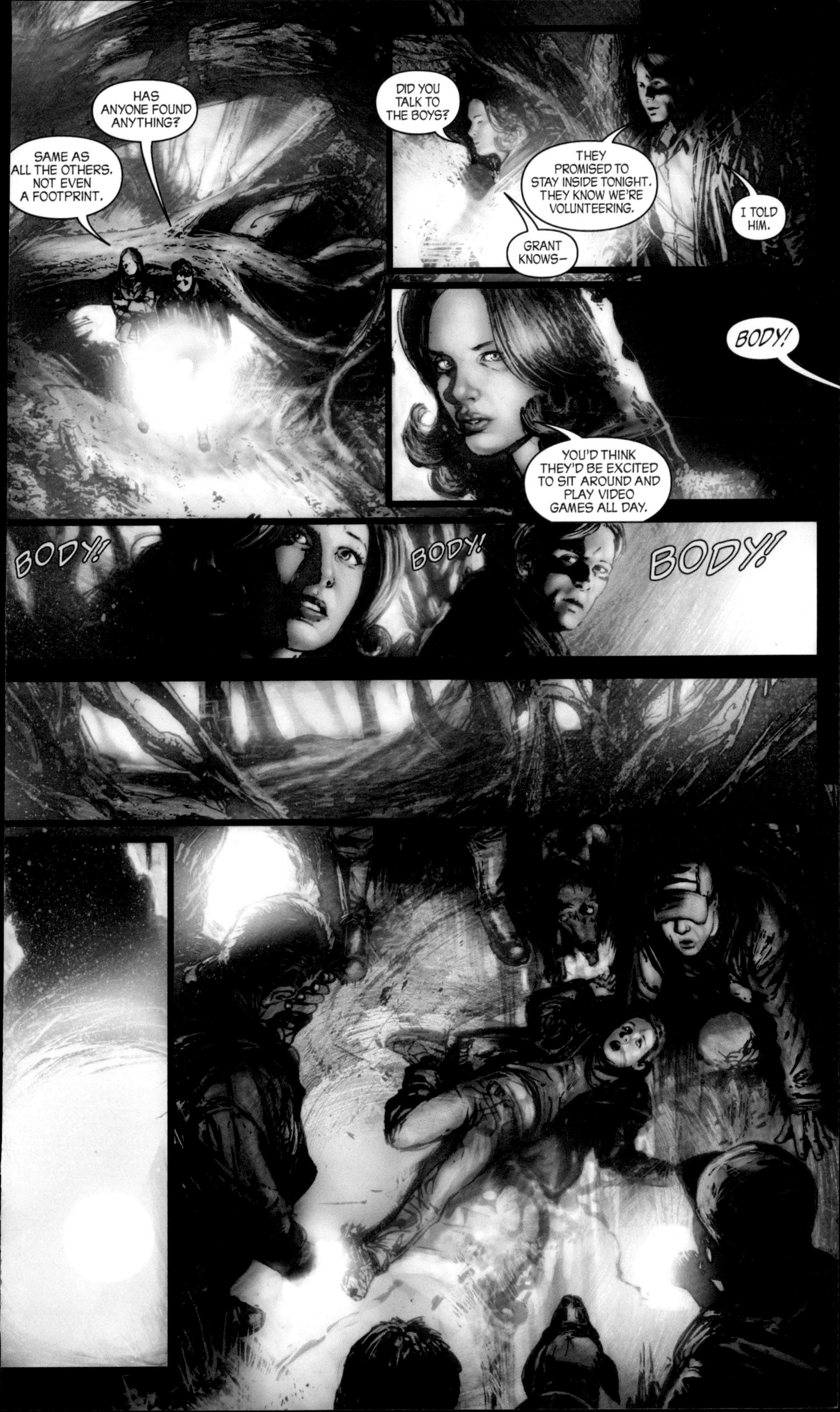
HAS ANYONE FOUND ANYTHING?
SAME AS ALL THE OTHERS. NOT EVEN A FOOTPRINT.
DID YOU TALK TO THE BOYS?
THEY PROMISED TO STAY INSIDE TONIGHT. THEY KNOW WE'RE VOLUNTEERING.
GRANT KNOWS—
I TOLD HIM.
BODY!
YOU'D THINK THEY'D BE EXCITED TO SIT AROUND AND PLAY VIDEO GAMES ALL DAY.
BODY!
BODY!
BODY!

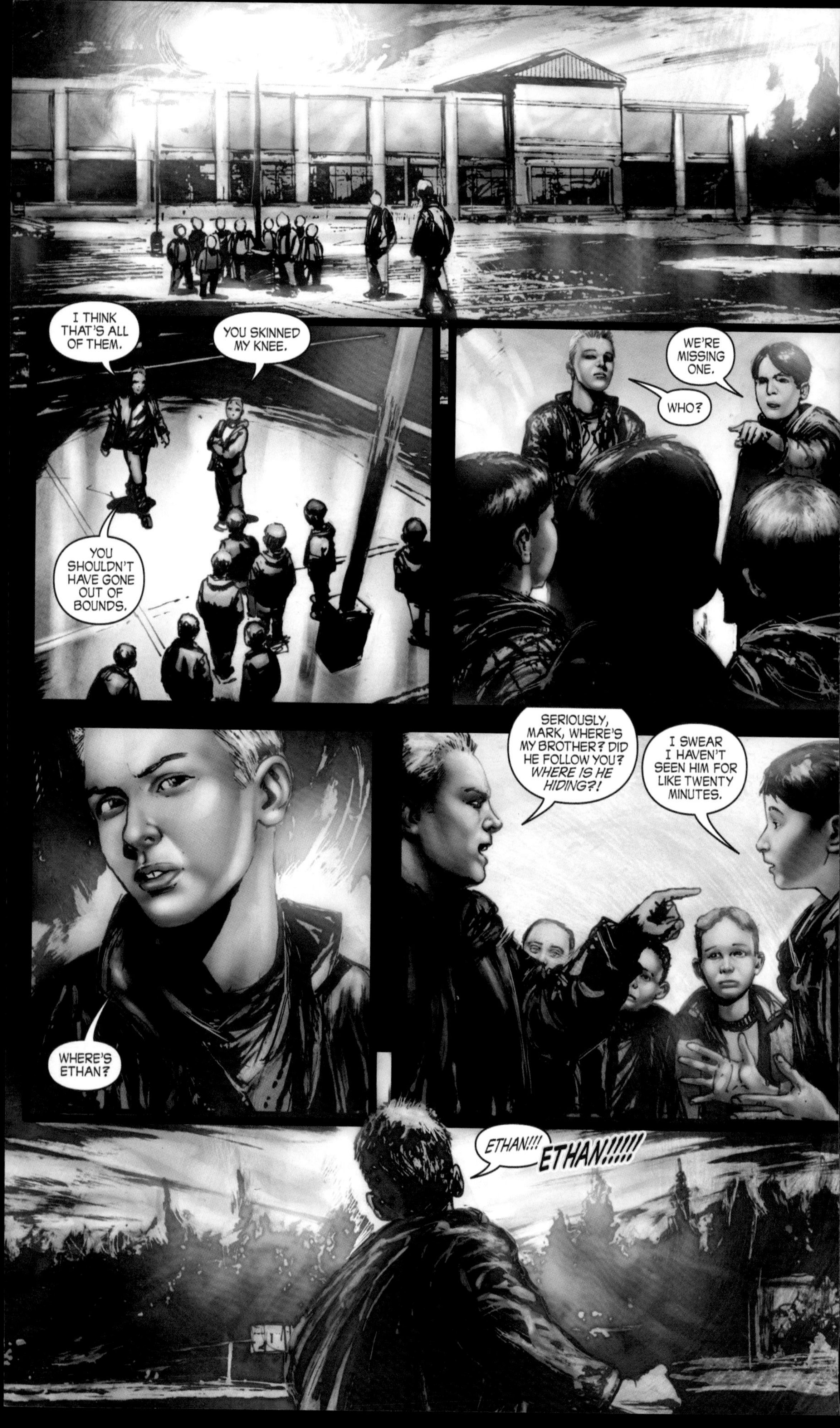
I THINK THAT'S ALL OF THEM.
YOU SKINNED MY KNEE.
YOU SHOULDN'T HAVE GONE OUT OF BOUNDS.
WE'RE MISSING ONE.
WHO?
WHERE'S ETHAN?
SERIOUSLY, MARK, WHERE'S MY BROTHER? DID HE FOLLOW YOU? *WHERE IS HE HIDING?!*
I SWEAR I HAVEN'T SEEN HIM FOR LIKE TWENTY MINUTES.
ETHAN!!! **ETHAN!!!!!**

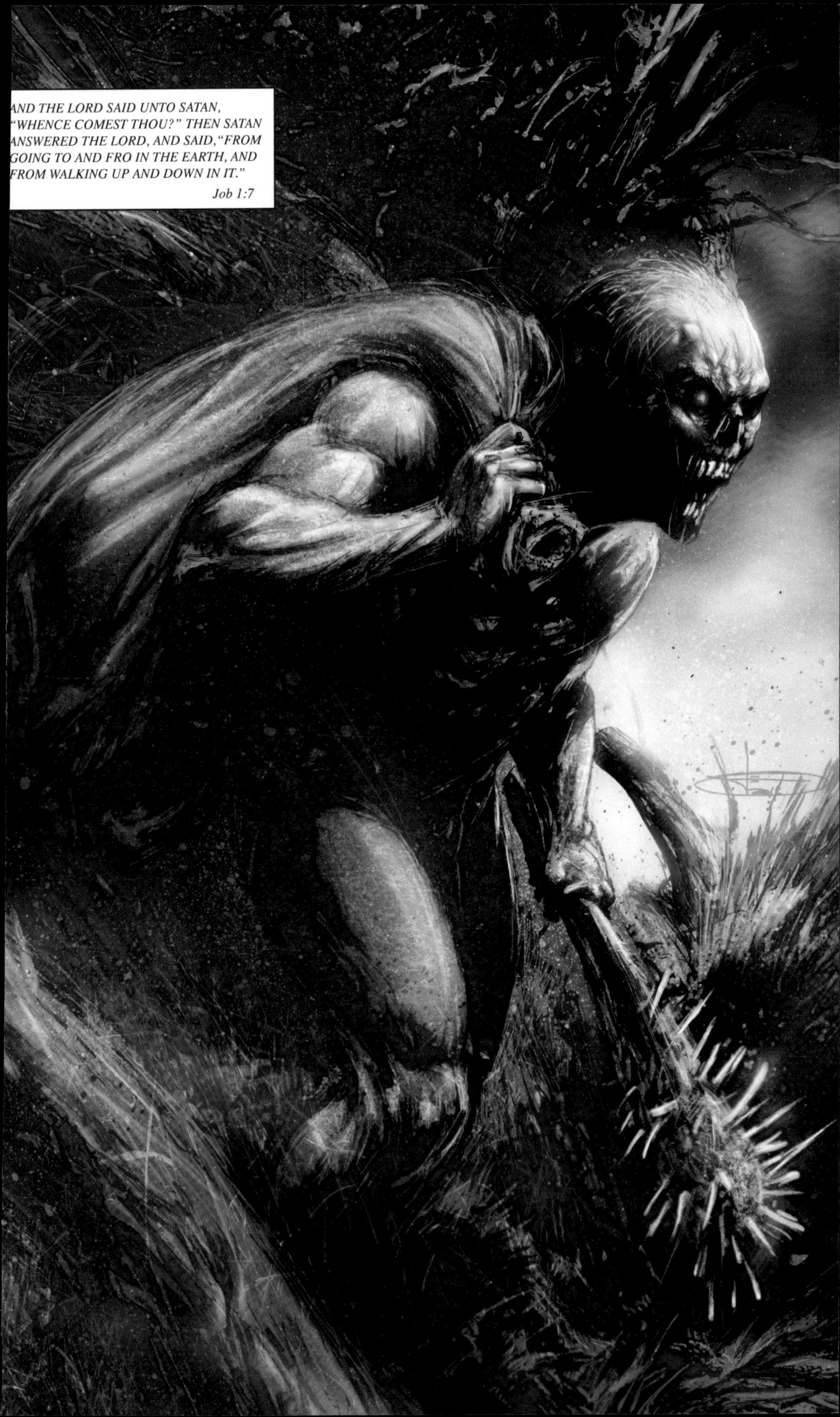
AND THE LORD SAID UNTO SATAN, "WHENCE COMEST THOU?" THEN SATAN ANSWERED THE LORD, AND SAID, "FROM GOING TO AND FRO IN THE EARTH, AND FROM WALKING UP AND DOWN IN IT."
Job 1:7

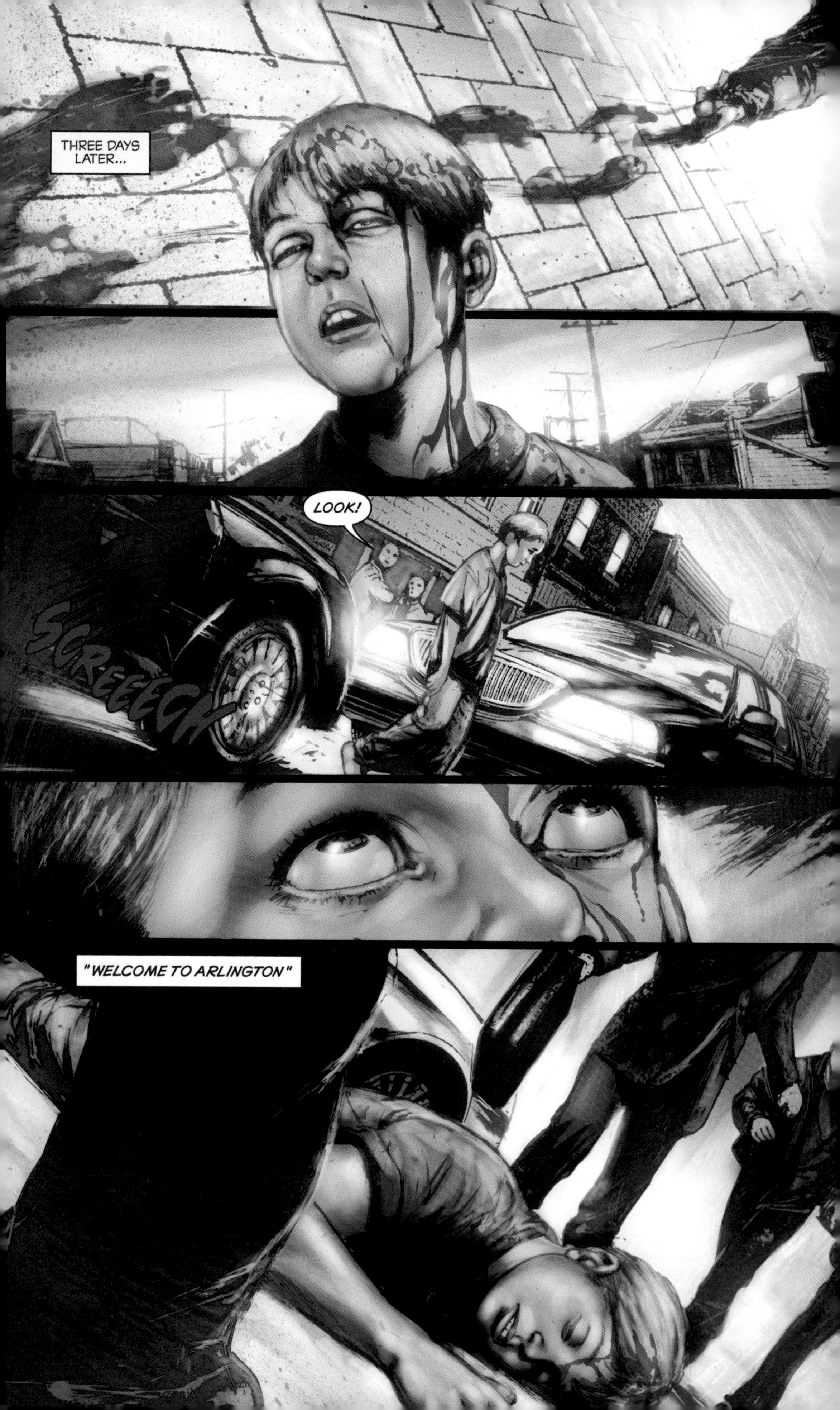
THREE DAYS LATER...
LOOK!
SCREEECH
"WELCOME TO ARLINGTON"

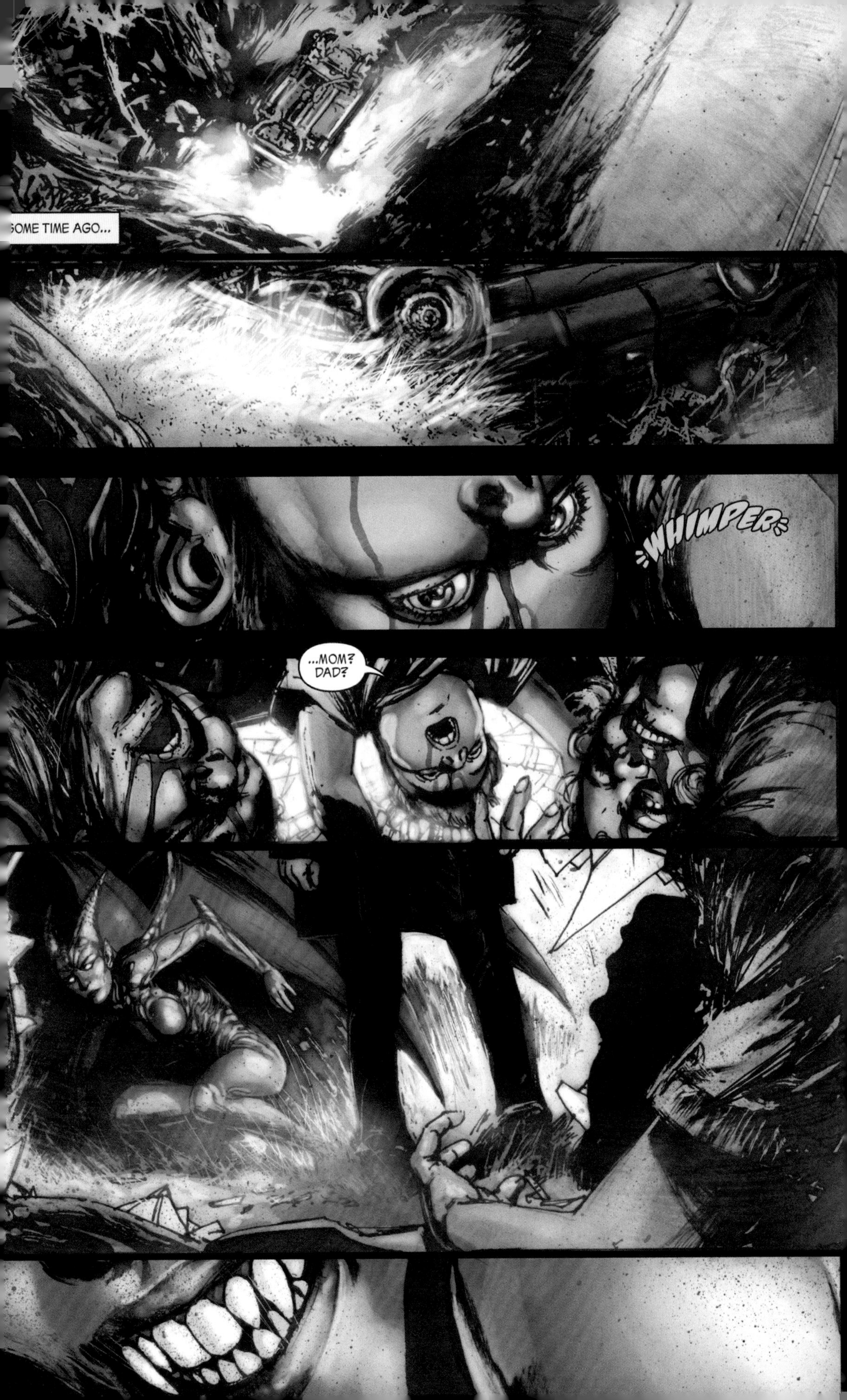
SOME TIME AGO...
WHIMPER
...MOM? DAD?

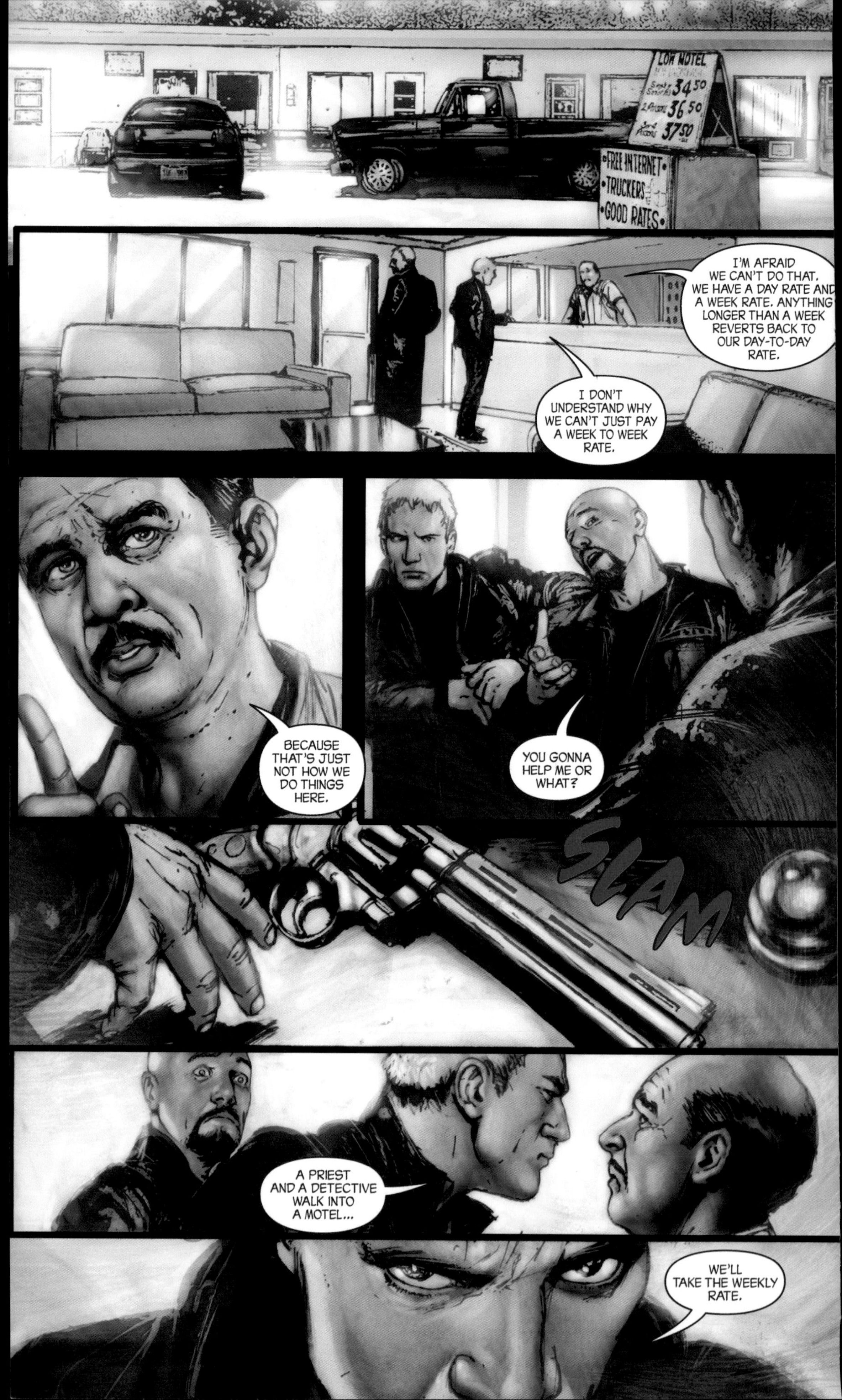
LOW MOTEL
34.50
36.50
37.50
FREE INTERNET
TRUCKERS
GOOD RATES
I'M AFRAID WE CAN'T DO THAT. WE HAVE A DAY RATE AND A WEEK RATE. ANYTHING LONGER THAN A WEEK REVERTS BACK TO OUR DAY-TO-DAY RATE.
I DON'T UNDERSTAND WHY WE CAN'T JUST PAY A WEEK TO WEEK RATE.
BECAUSE THAT'S JUST NOT HOW WE DO THINGS HERE.
YOU GONNA HELP ME OR WHAT?
SLAM
A PRIEST AND A DETECTIVE WALK INTO A MOTEL...
WE'LL TAKE THE WEEKLY RATE.

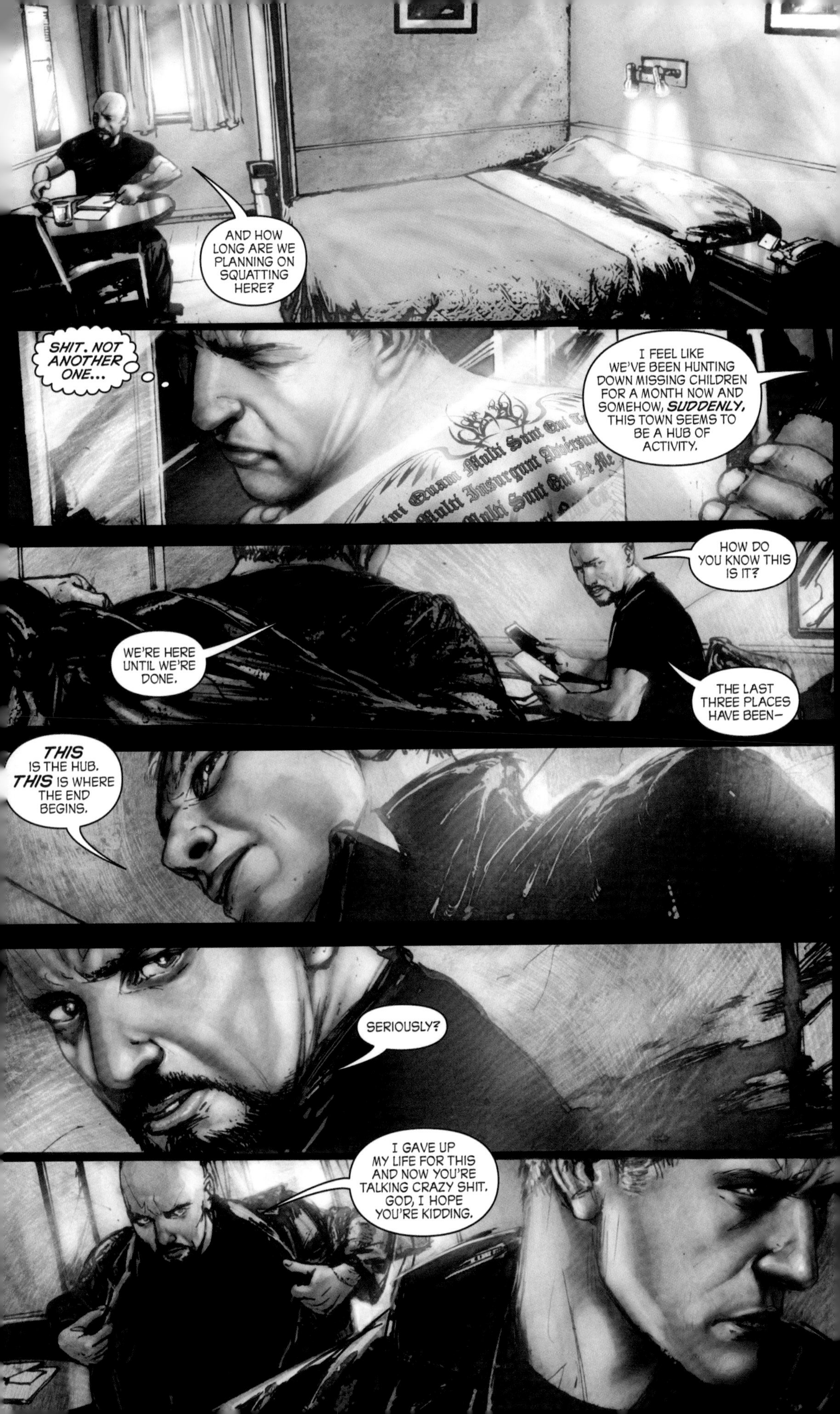
AND HOW LONG ARE WE PLANNING ON SQUATTING HERE?
SHIT. NOT ANOTHER ONE...
I FEEL LIKE WE'VE BEEN HUNTING DOWN MISSING CHILDREN FOR A MONTH NOW AND SOMEHOW, SUDDENLY, THIS TOWN SEEMS TO BE A HUB OF ACTIVITY.
WE'RE HERE UNTIL WE'RE DONE.
HOW DO YOU KNOW THIS IS IT?
THE LAST THREE PLACES HAVE BEEN—
THIS IS THE HUB. THIS IS WHERE THE END BEGINS.
SERIOUSLY?
I GAVE UP MY LIFE FOR THIS AND NOW YOU'RE TALKING CRAZY SHIT. GOD, I HOPE YOU'RE KIDDING.

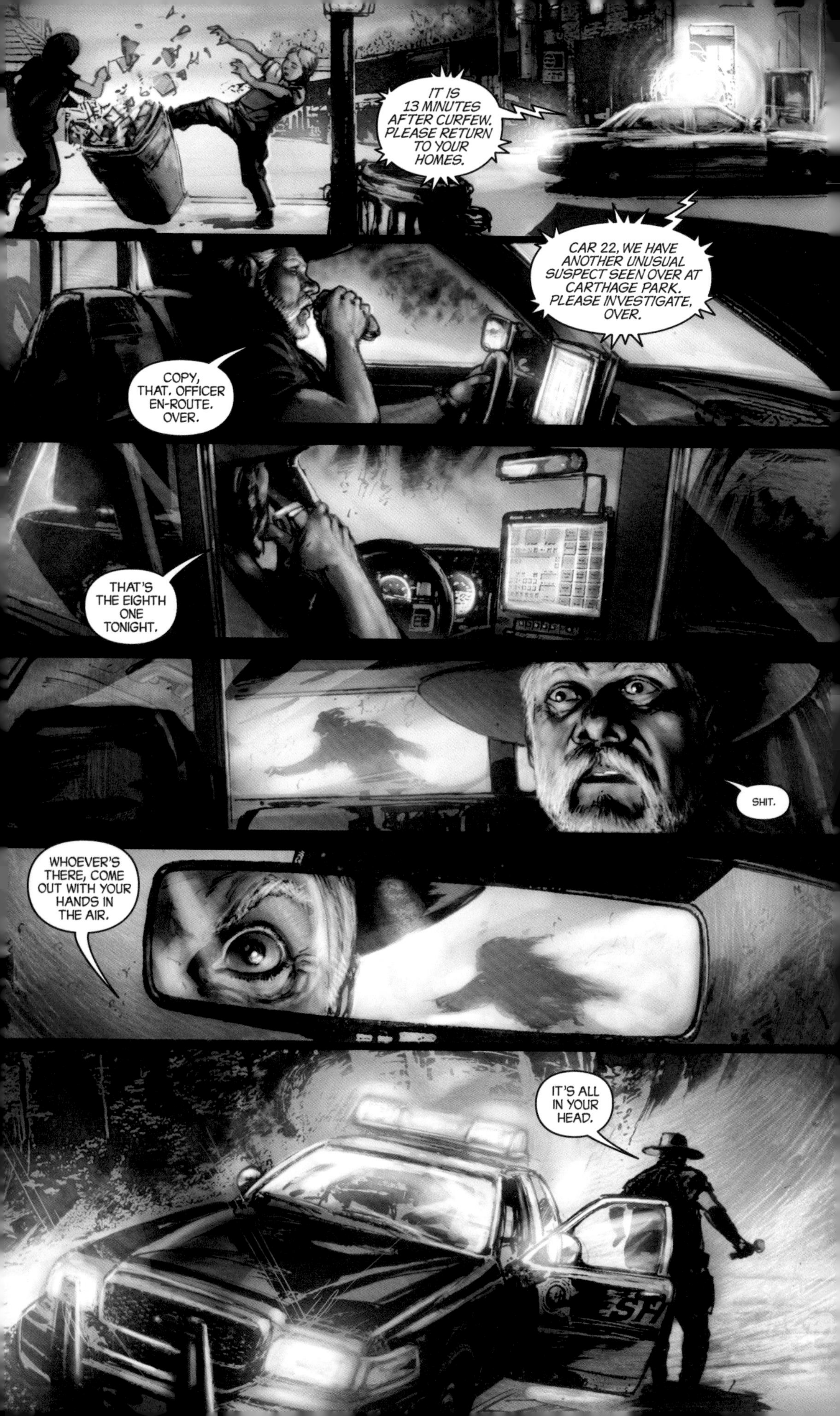
IT IS 13 MINUTES AFTER CURFEW. PLEASE RETURN TO YOUR HOMES.
CAR 22, WE HAVE ANOTHER UNUSUAL SUSPECT SEEN OVER AT CARTHAGE PARK. PLEASE INVESTIGATE, OVER.
COPY, THAT. OFFICER EN-ROUTE. OVER.
THAT'S THE EIGHTH ONE TONIGHT.
SHIT.
WHOEVER'S THERE, COME OUT WITH YOUR HANDS IN THE AIR.
IT'S ALL IN YOUR HEAD.

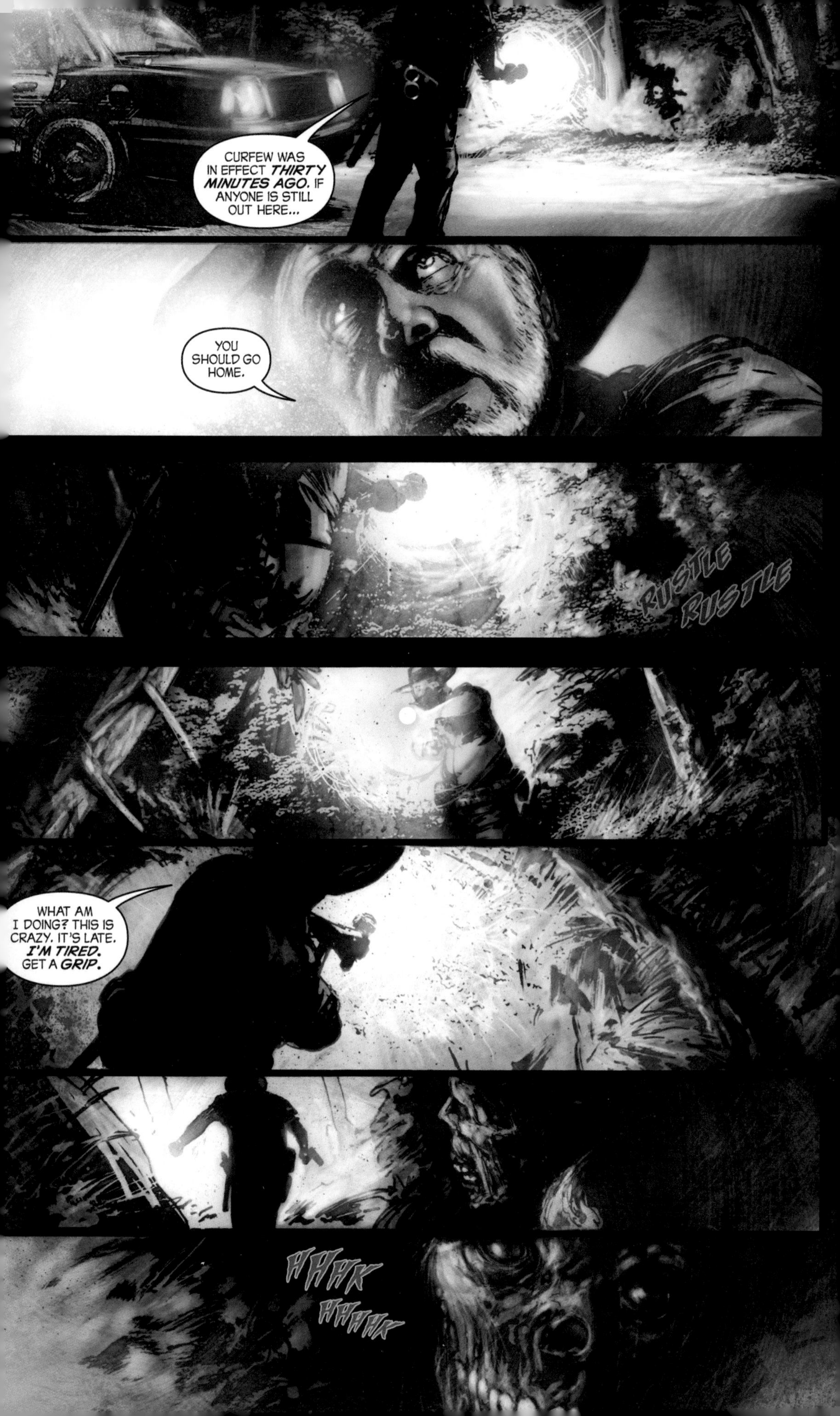
CURFEW WAS IN EFFECT *THIRTY MINUTES AGO*. IF ANYONE IS STILL OUT HERE...
YOU SHOULD GO HOME.
RUSTLE RUSTLE
WHAT AM I DOING? THIS IS CRAZY. IT'S LATE. *I'M TIRED*. GET A *GRIP*.
HHHK HHHHK

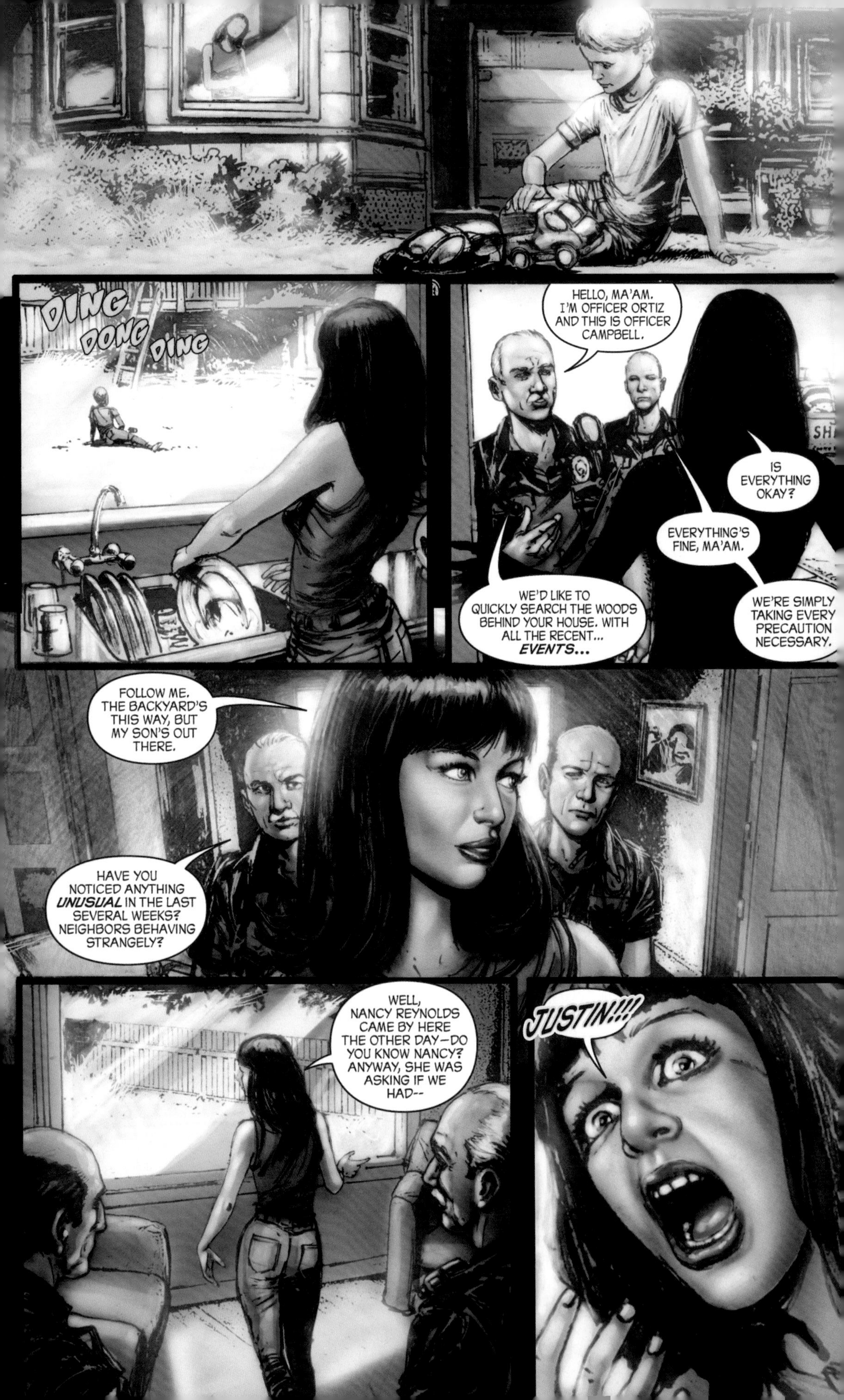
DING DONG DING
HELLO, MA'AM. I'M OFFICER ORTIZ AND THIS IS OFFICER CAMPBELL.
IS EVERYTHING OKAY?
EVERYTHING'S FINE, MA'AM.
WE'D LIKE TO QUICKLY SEARCH THE WOODS BEHIND YOUR HOUSE. WITH ALL THE RECENT... EVENTS...
WE'RE SIMPLY TAKING EVERY PRECAUTION NECESSARY.
FOLLOW ME. THE BACKYARD'S THIS WAY, BUT MY SON'S OUT THERE.
HAVE YOU NOTICED ANYTHING UNUSUAL IN THE LAST SEVERAL WEEKS? NEIGHBORS BEHAVING STRANGELY?
WELL, NANCY REYNOLDS CAME BY HERE THE OTHER DAY—DO YOU KNOW NANCY? ANYWAY, SHE WAS ASKING IF WE HAD--
JUSTIN!!!

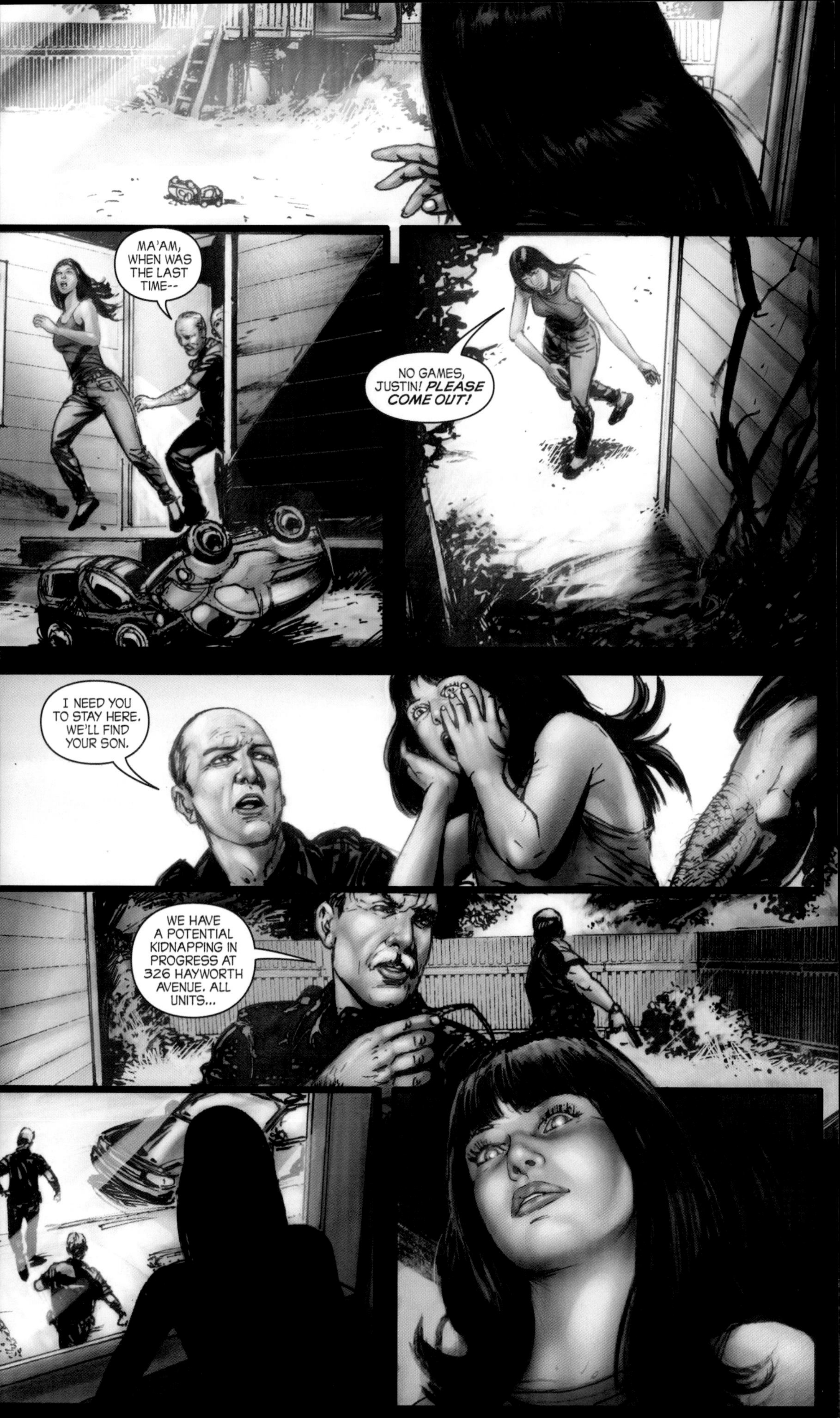
MA'AM, WHEN WAS THE LAST TIME--
NO GAMES, JUSTIN! *PLEASE COME OUT!*
I NEED YOU TO STAY HERE. WE'LL FIND YOUR SON.
WE HAVE A POTENTIAL KIDNAPPING IN PROGRESS AT 326 HAYWORTH AVENUE. ALL UNITS...

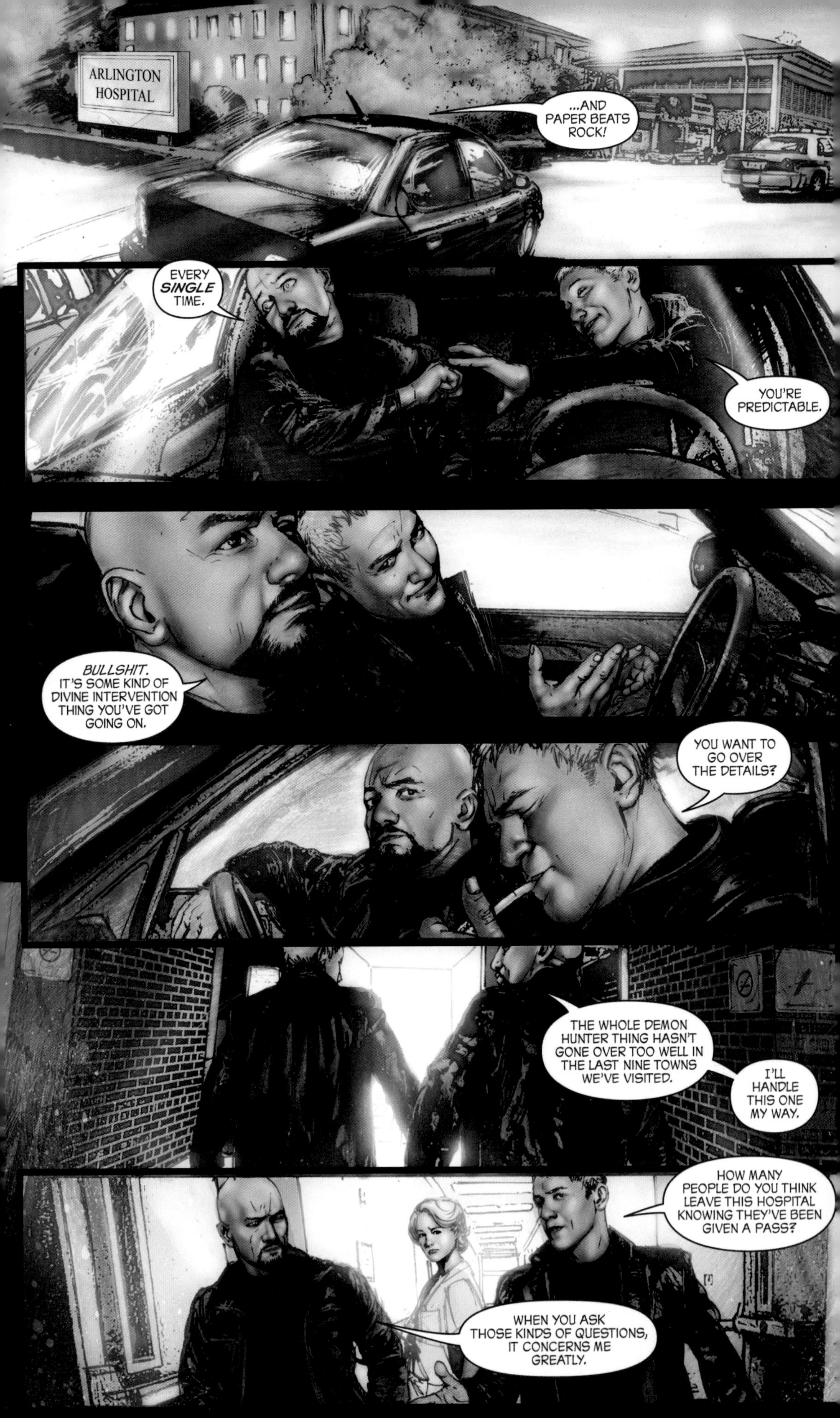
ARLINGTON HOSPITAL
...AND PAPER BEATS ROCK!
EVERY *SINGLE* TIME.
YOU'RE PREDICTABLE.
BULLSHIT. IT'S SOME KIND OF DIVINE INTERVENTION THING YOU'VE GOT GOING ON.
YOU WANT TO GO OVER THE DETAILS?
THE WHOLE DEMON HUNTER THING HASN'T GONE OVER TOO WELL IN THE LAST NINE TOWNS WE'VE VISITED.
I'LL HANDLE THIS ONE MY WAY.
HOW MANY PEOPLE DO YOU THINK LEAVE THIS HOSPITAL KNOWING THEY'VE BEEN GIVEN A PASS?
WHEN YOU ASK THOSE KINDS OF QUESTIONS, IT CONCERNS ME GREATLY.

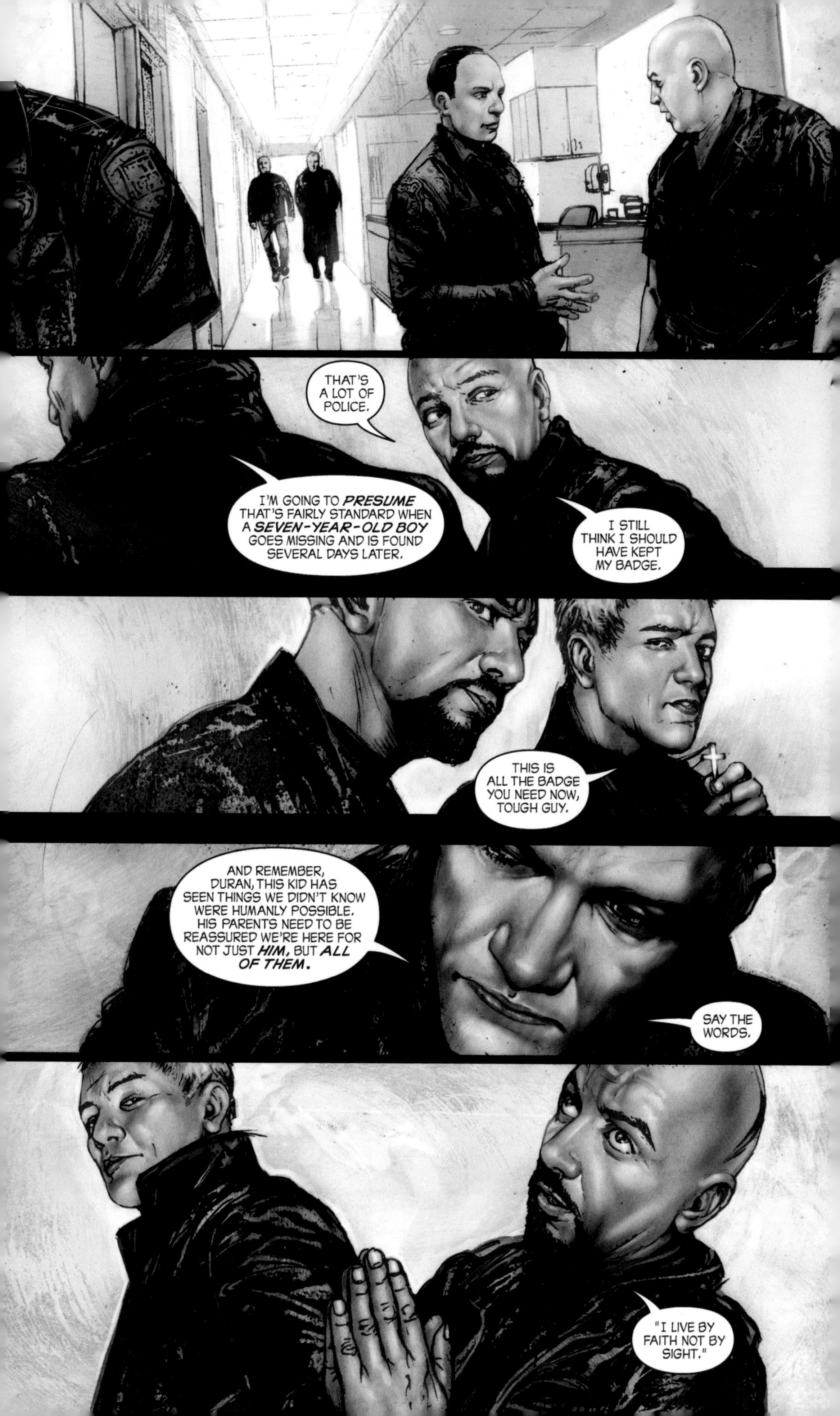
THAT'S A LOT OF POLICE.
I'M GOING TO ***PRESUME*** THAT'S FAIRLY STANDARD WHEN A ***SEVEN-YEAR-OLD BOY*** GOES MISSING AND IS FOUND SEVERAL DAYS LATER.
I STILL THINK I SHOULD HAVE KEPT MY BADGE.
THIS IS ALL THE BADGE YOU NEED NOW, TOUGH GUY.
AND REMEMBER, DURAN, THIS KID HAS SEEN THINGS WE DIDN'T KNOW WERE HUMANLY POSSIBLE. HIS PARENTS NEED TO BE REASSURED WE'RE HERE FOR NOT JUST ***HIM,*** BUT ***ALL OF THEM.***
SAY THE WORDS.
"I LIVE BY FAITH NOT BY SIGHT."

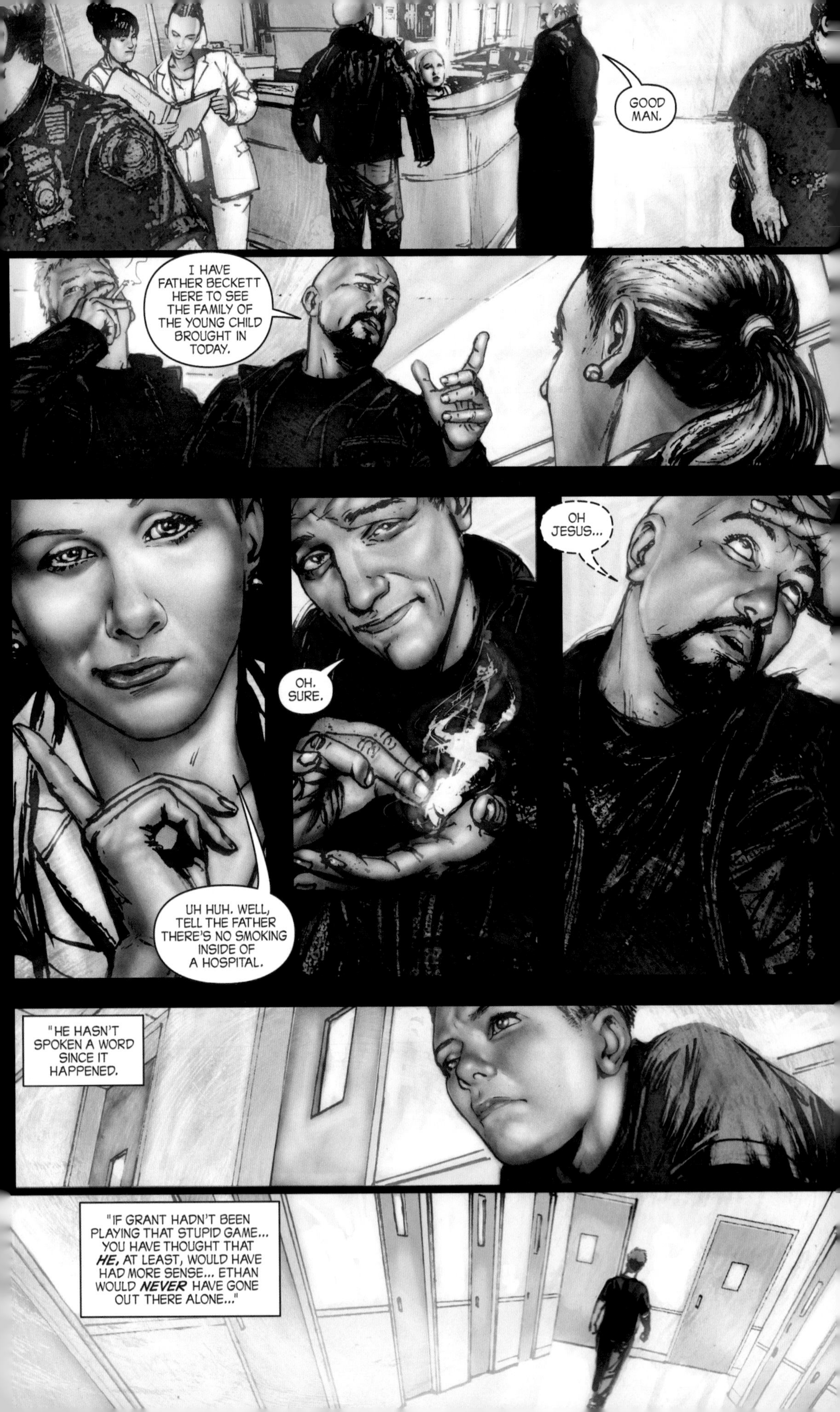
GOOD MAN.
I HAVE FATHER BECKETT HERE TO SEE THE FAMILY OF THE YOUNG CHILD BROUGHT IN TODAY.
UH HUH. WELL, TELL THE FATHER THERE'S NO SMOKING INSIDE OF A HOSPITAL.
OH. SURE.
OH JESUS...
"HE HASN'T SPOKEN A WORD SINCE IT HAPPENED.
"IF GRANT HADN'T BEEN PLAYING THAT STUPID GAME... YOU HAVE THOUGHT THAT ***HE,*** AT LEAST, WOULD HAVE HAD MORE SENSE... ETHAN WOULD ***NEVER*** HAVE GONE OUT THERE ALONE..."

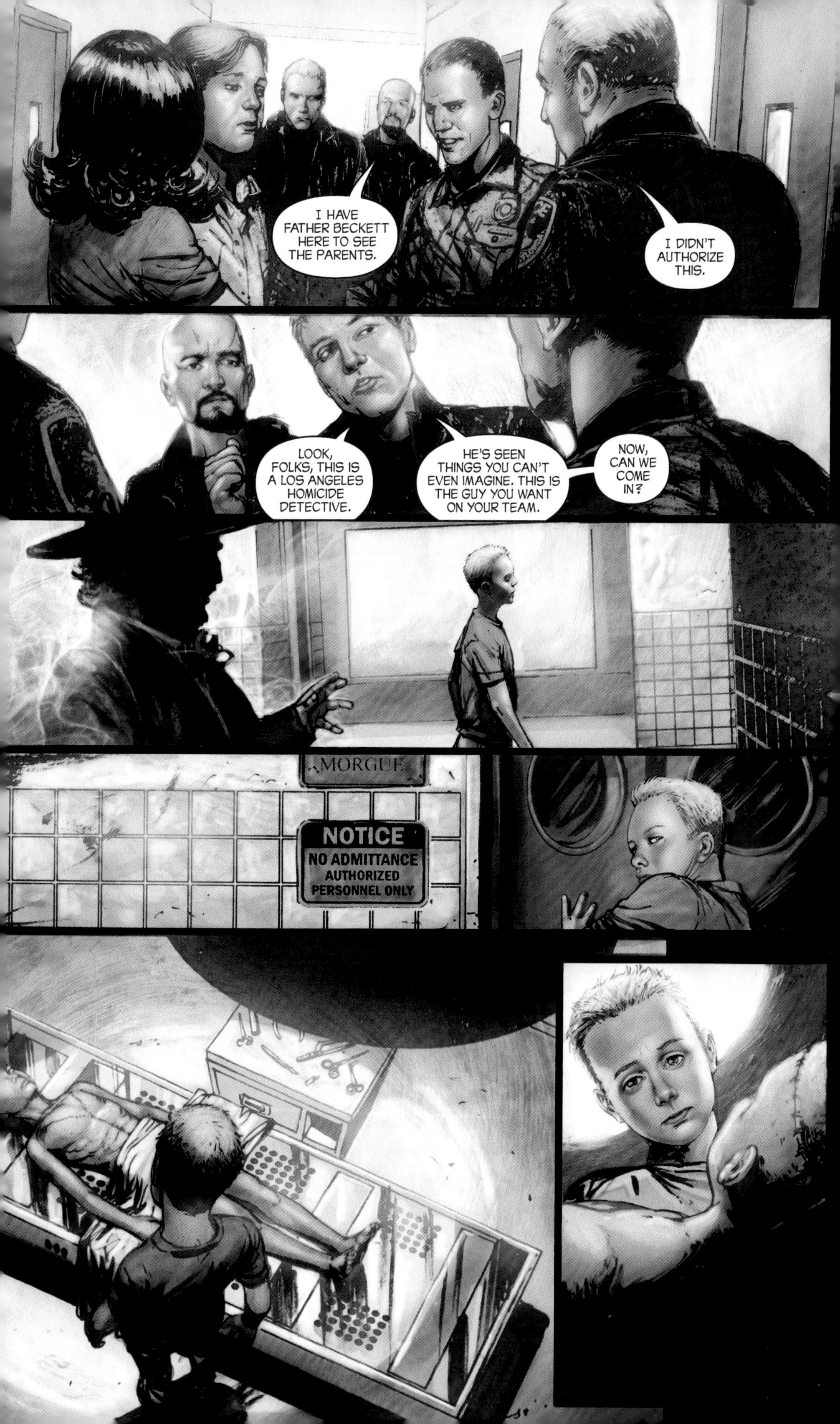
I HAVE FATHER BECKETT HERE TO SEE THE PARENTS.
I DIDN'T AUTHORIZE THIS.
LOOK, FOLKS, THIS IS A LOS ANGELES HOMICIDE DETECTIVE.
HE'S SEEN THINGS YOU CAN'T EVEN IMAGINE. THIS IS THE GUY YOU WANT ON YOUR TEAM.
NOW, CAN WE COME IN?
MORGUE
NOTICE
NO ADMITTANCE
AUTHORIZED PERSONNEL ONLY

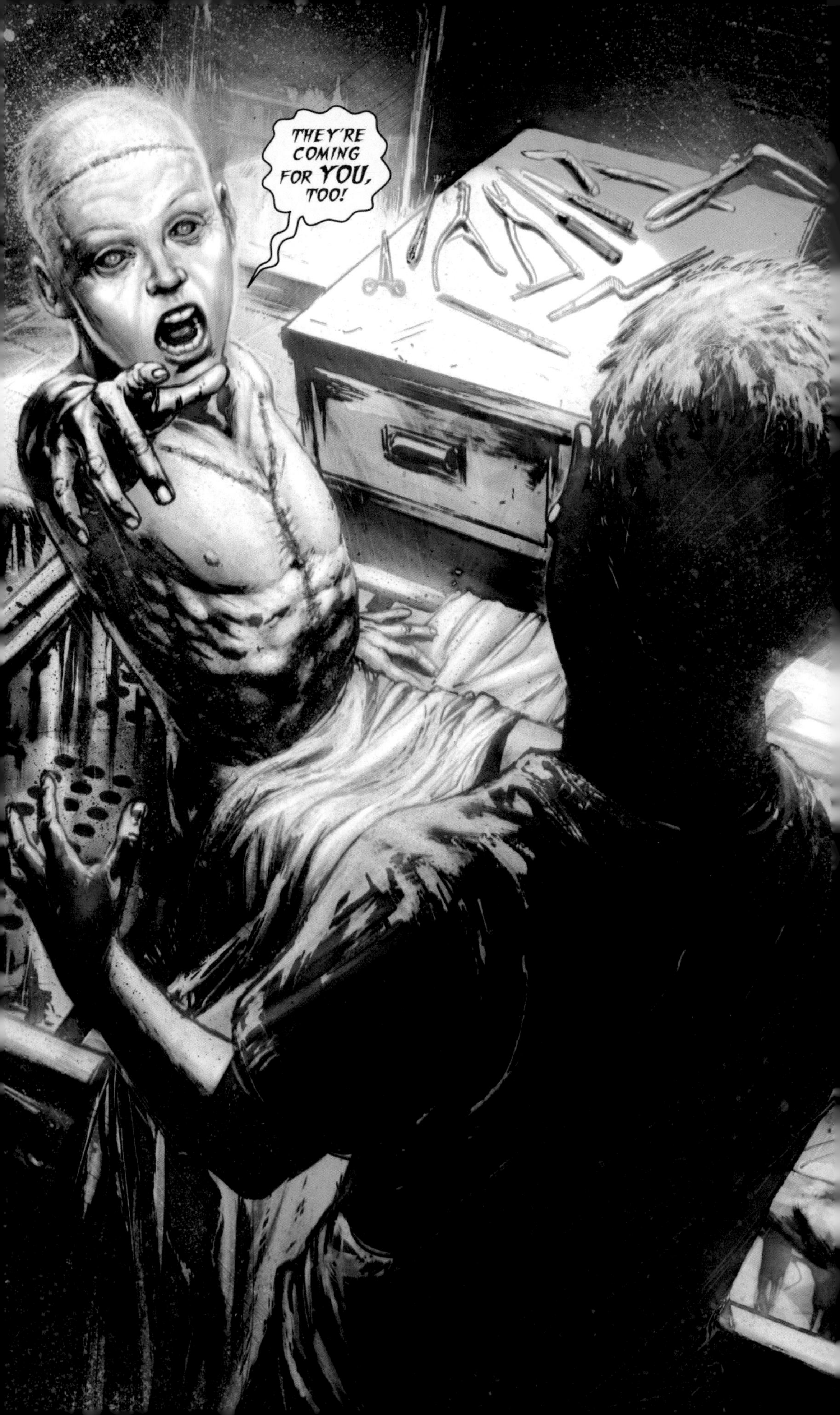
THEY'RE COMING FOR YOU, TOO!

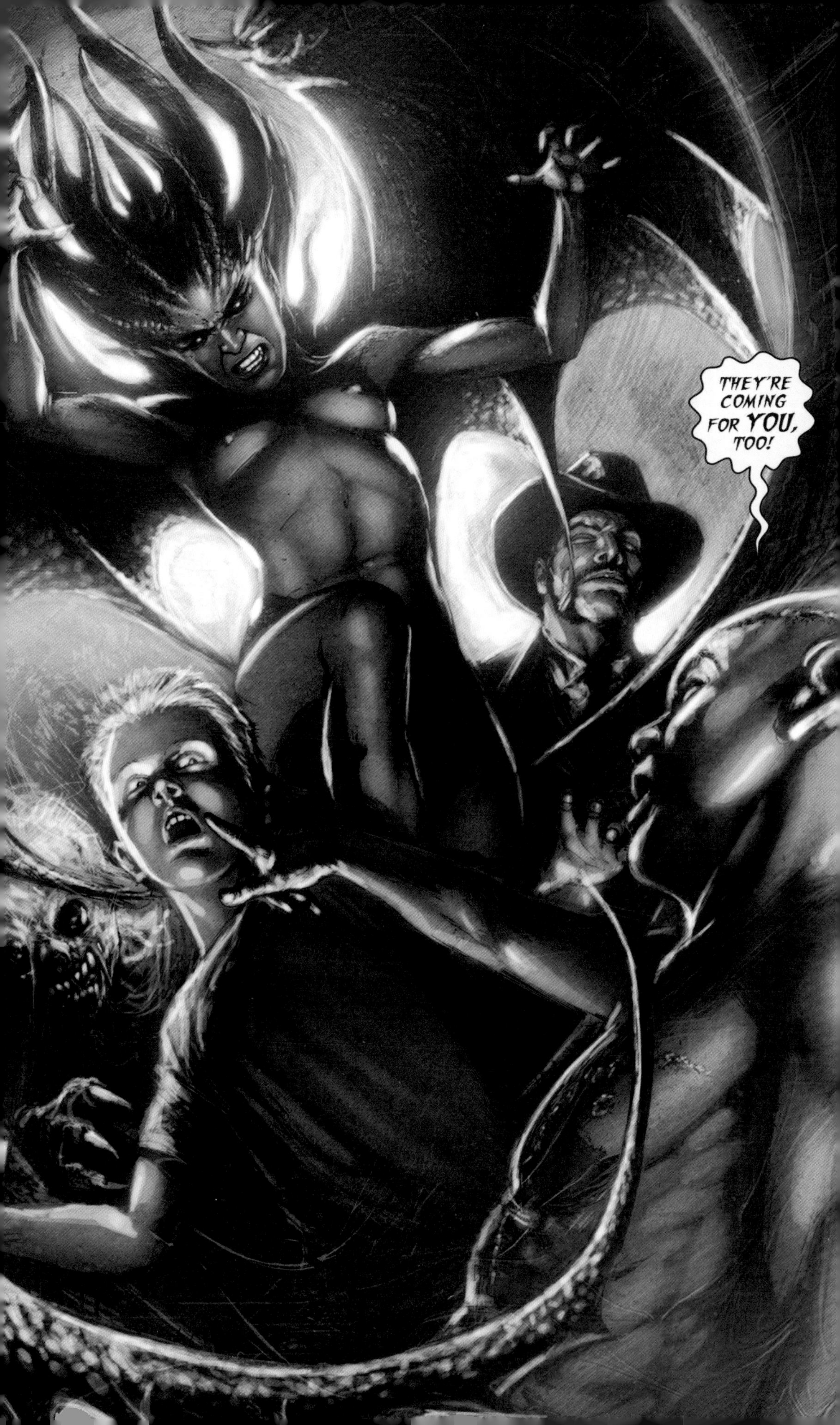
THEY'RE COMING FOR YOU, TOO!

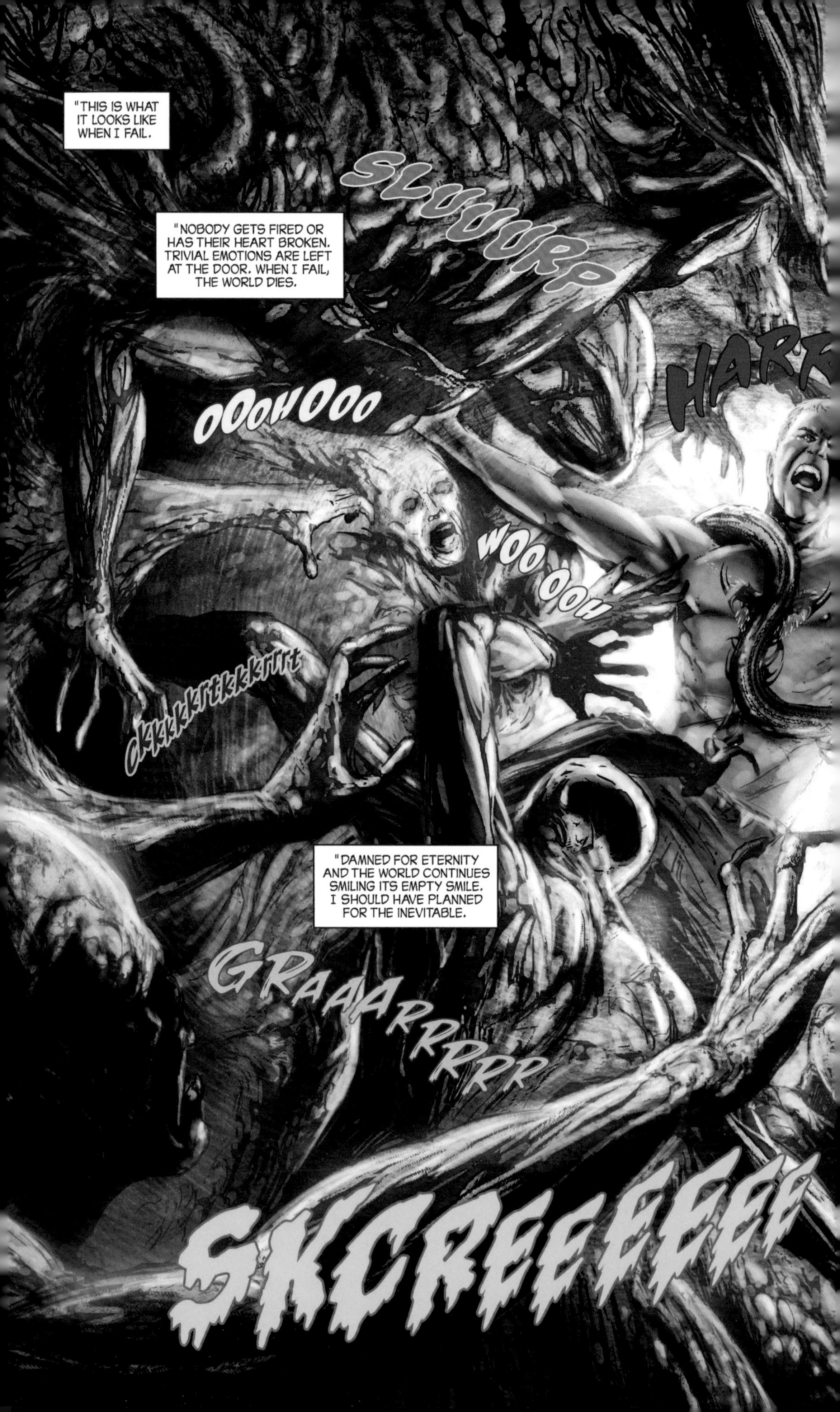
"THIS IS WHAT IT LOOKS LIKE WHEN I FAIL.
SLUUUURP
"NOBODY GETS FIRED OR HAS THEIR HEART BROKEN. TRIVIAL EMOTIONS ARE LEFT AT THE DOOR. WHEN I FAIL, THE WORLD DIES.
HARR
OOOWOOO
WOO OOOH
ckkkkkrrtkkkrrrrt
"DAMNED FOR ETERNITY AND THE WORLD CONTINUES SMILING ITS EMPTY SMILE. I SHOULD HAVE PLANNED FOR THE INEVITABLE.
GRAAARRRRR
SKCREEEEEE

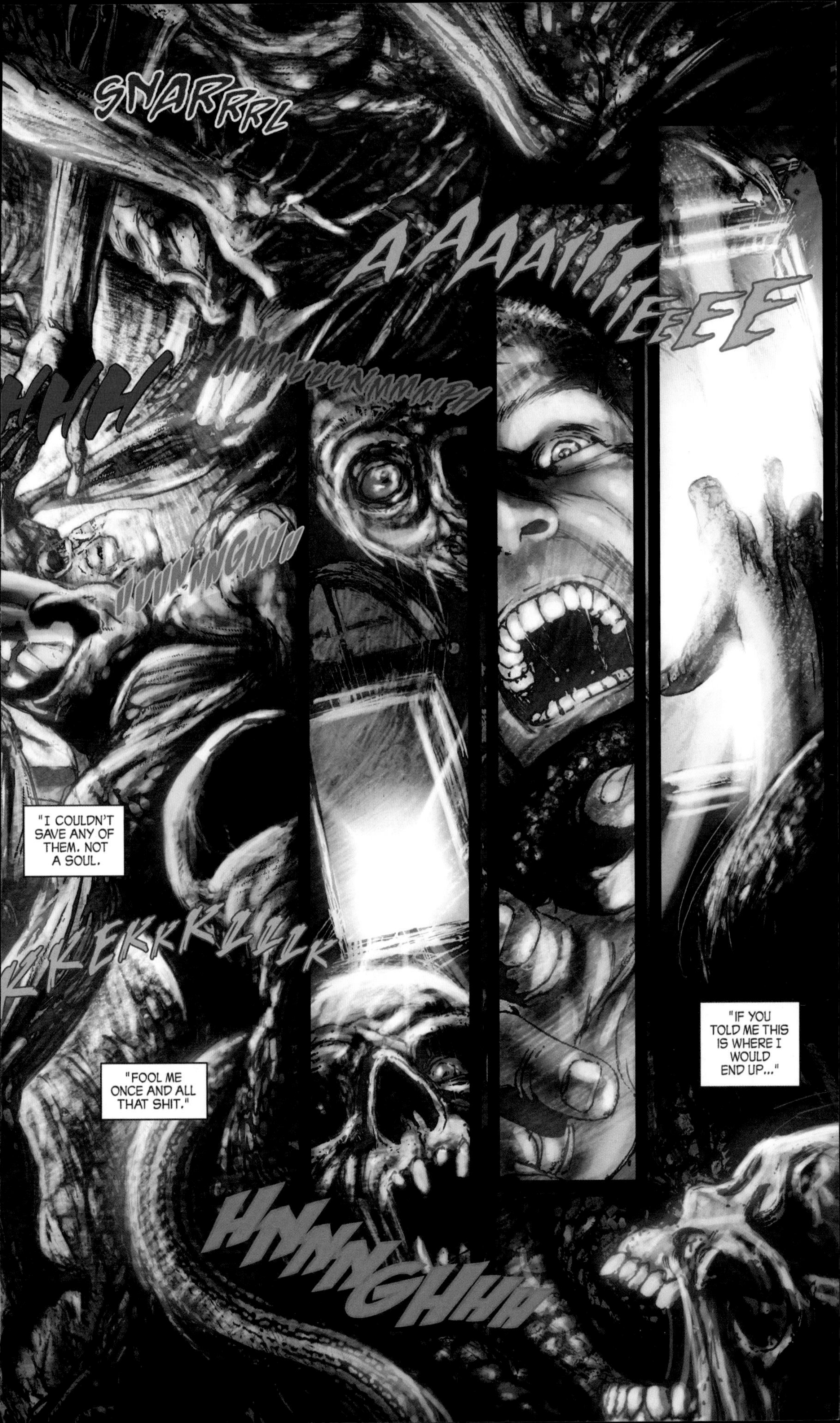
SNARRRL
AAAAIIIIEEEE
"I COULDN'T SAVE ANY OF THEM. NOT A SOUL.
"IF YOU TOLD ME THIS IS WHERE I WOULD END UP..."
"FOOL ME ONCE AND ALL THAT SHIT."

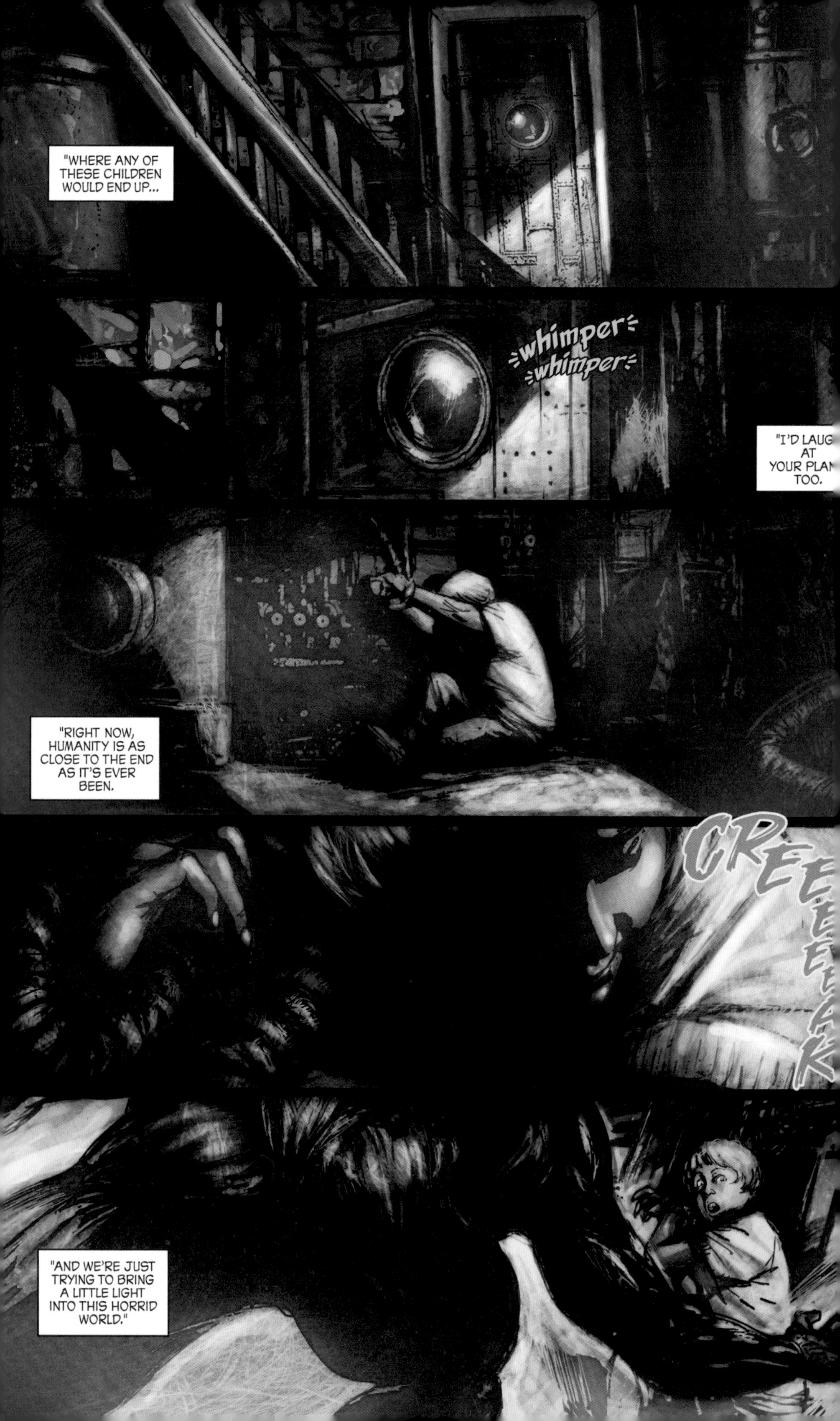
"WHERE ANY OF THESE CHILDREN WOULD END UP...
whimper whimper
"I'D LAUG AT YOUR PLA TOO.
"RIGHT NOW, HUMANITY IS AS CLOSE TO THE END AS IT'S EVER BEEN.
CREEEEEAK
"AND WE'RE JUST TRYING TO BRING A LITTLE LIGHT INTO THIS HORRID WORLD."

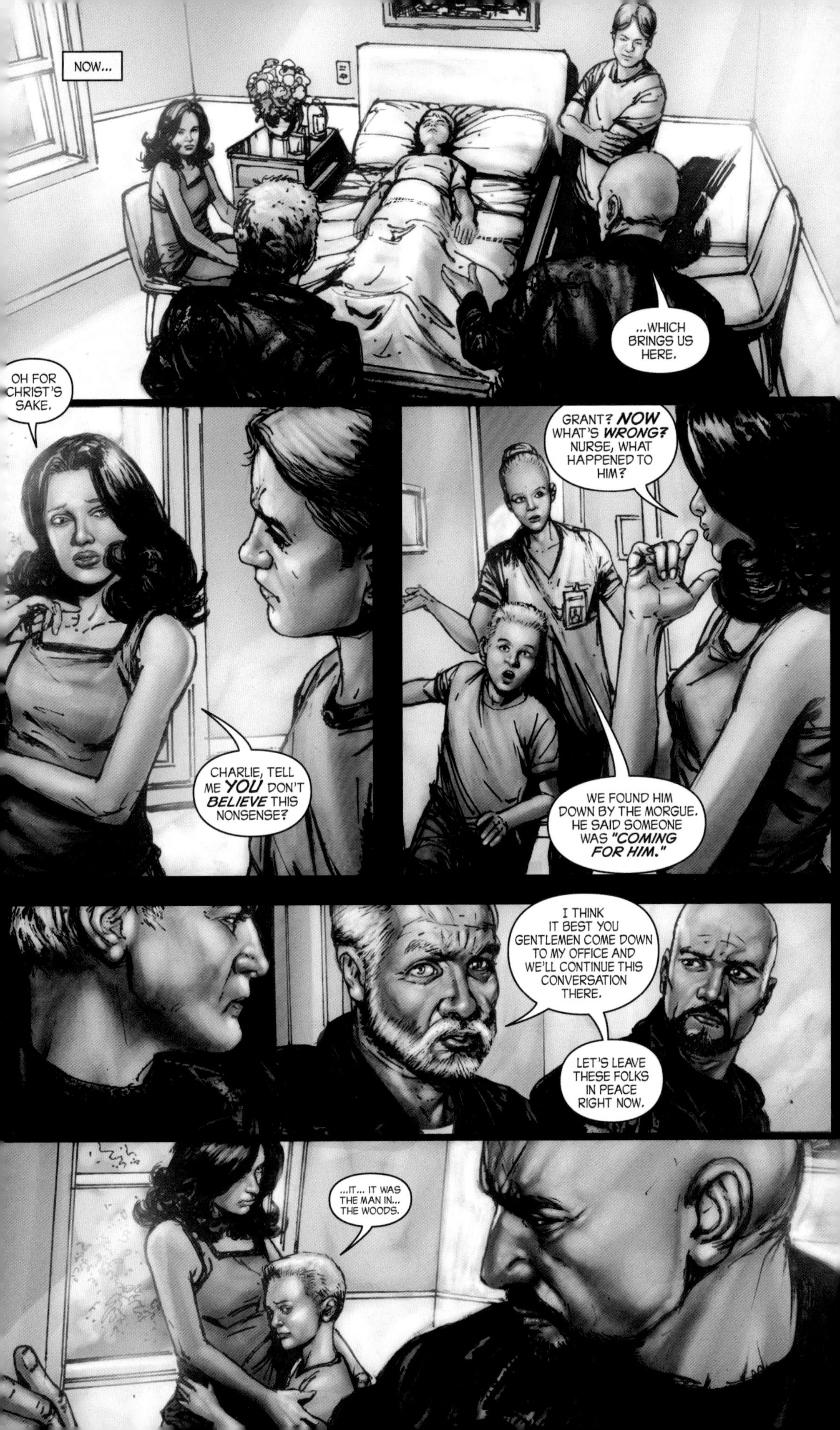
NOW...
...WHICH BRINGS US HERE.
OH FOR CHRIST'S SAKE.
CHARLIE, TELL ME **YOU** DON'T ***BELIEVE*** THIS NONSENSE?
GRANT? ***NOW*** WHAT'S ***WRONG?*** NURSE, WHAT HAPPENED TO HIM?
WE FOUND HIM DOWN BY THE MORGUE. HE SAID SOMEONE WAS ***"COMING FOR HIM."***
I THINK IT BEST YOU GENTLEMEN COME DOWN TO MY OFFICE AND WE'LL CONTINUE THIS CONVERSATION THERE.
LET'S LEAVE THESE FOLKS IN PEACE RIGHT NOW.
...IT... IT WAS THE MAN IN... THE WOODS.

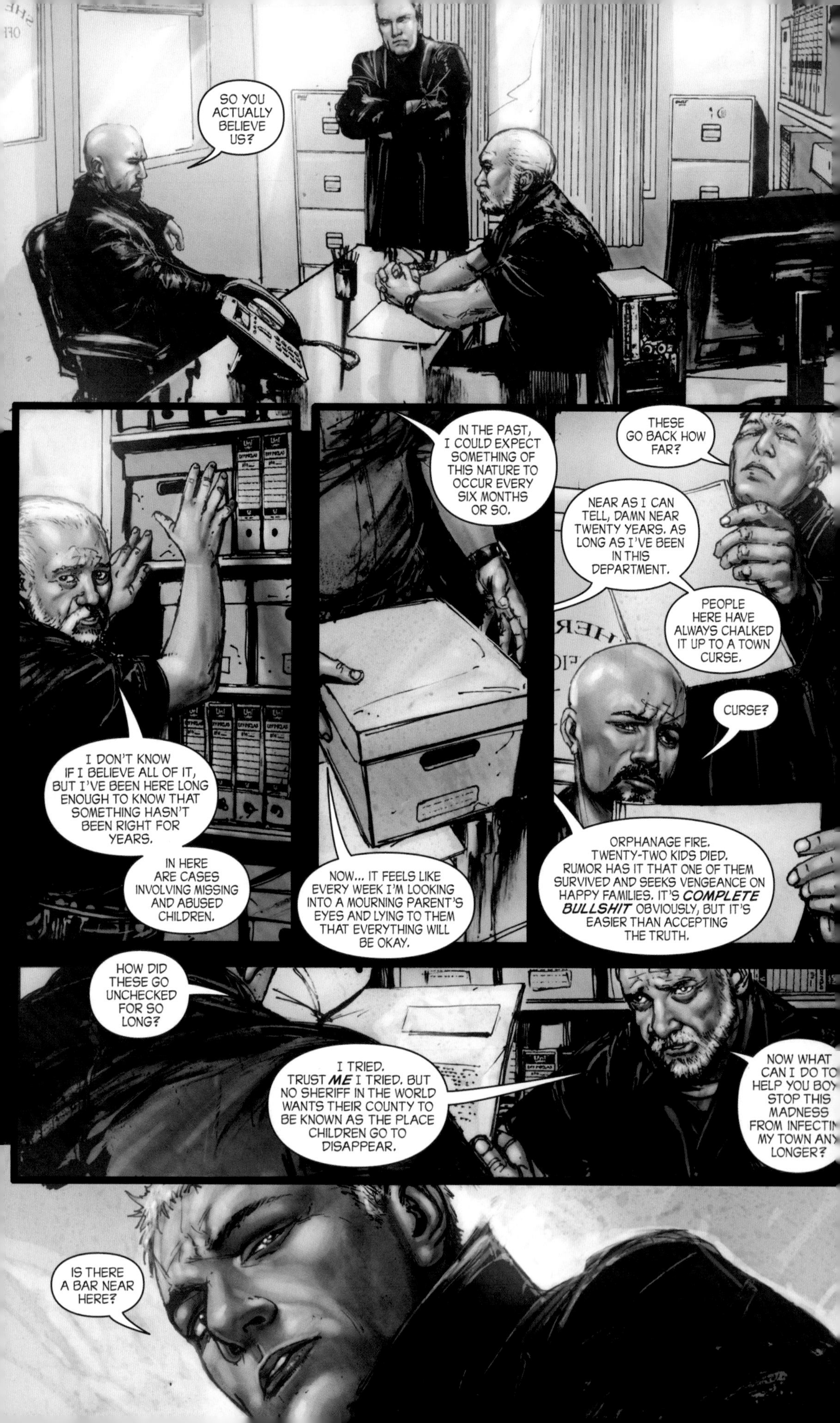

SO YOU ACTUALLY BELIEVE US?
I DON'T KNOW IF I BELIEVE ALL OF IT, BUT I'VE BEEN HERE LONG ENOUGH TO KNOW THAT SOMETHING HASN'T BEEN RIGHT FOR YEARS.
IN HERE ARE CASES INVOLVING MISSING AND ABUSED CHILDREN.
IN THE PAST, I COULD EXPECT SOMETHING OF THIS NATURE TO OCCUR EVERY SIX MONTHS OR SO.
NOW... IT FEELS LIKE EVERY WEEK I'M LOOKING INTO A MOURNING PARENT'S EYES AND LYING TO THEM THAT EVERYTHING WILL BE OKAY.
THESE GO BACK HOW FAR?
NEAR AS I CAN TELL, DAMN NEAR TWENTY YEARS. AS LONG AS I'VE BEEN IN THIS DEPARTMENT.
PEOPLE HERE HAVE ALWAYS CHALKED IT UP TO A TOWN CURSE.
CURSE?
ORPHANAGE FIRE. TWENTY-TWO KIDS DIED. RUMOR HAS IT THAT ONE OF THEM SURVIVED AND SEEKS VENGEANCE ON HAPPY FAMILIES. IT'S ***COMPLETE BULLSHIT*** OBVIOUSLY, BUT IT'S EASIER THAN ACCEPTING THE TRUTH.
HOW DID THESE GO UNCHECKED FOR SO LONG?
I TRIED. TRUST ***ME*** I TRIED. BUT NO SHERIFF IN THE WORLD WANTS THEIR COUNTY TO BE KNOWN AS THE PLACE CHILDREN GO TO DISAPPEAR.
NOW WHAT CAN I DO TO HELP YOU BOY STOP THIS MADNESS FROM INFECTIN MY TOWN ANY LONGER?
IS THERE A BAR NEAR HERE?

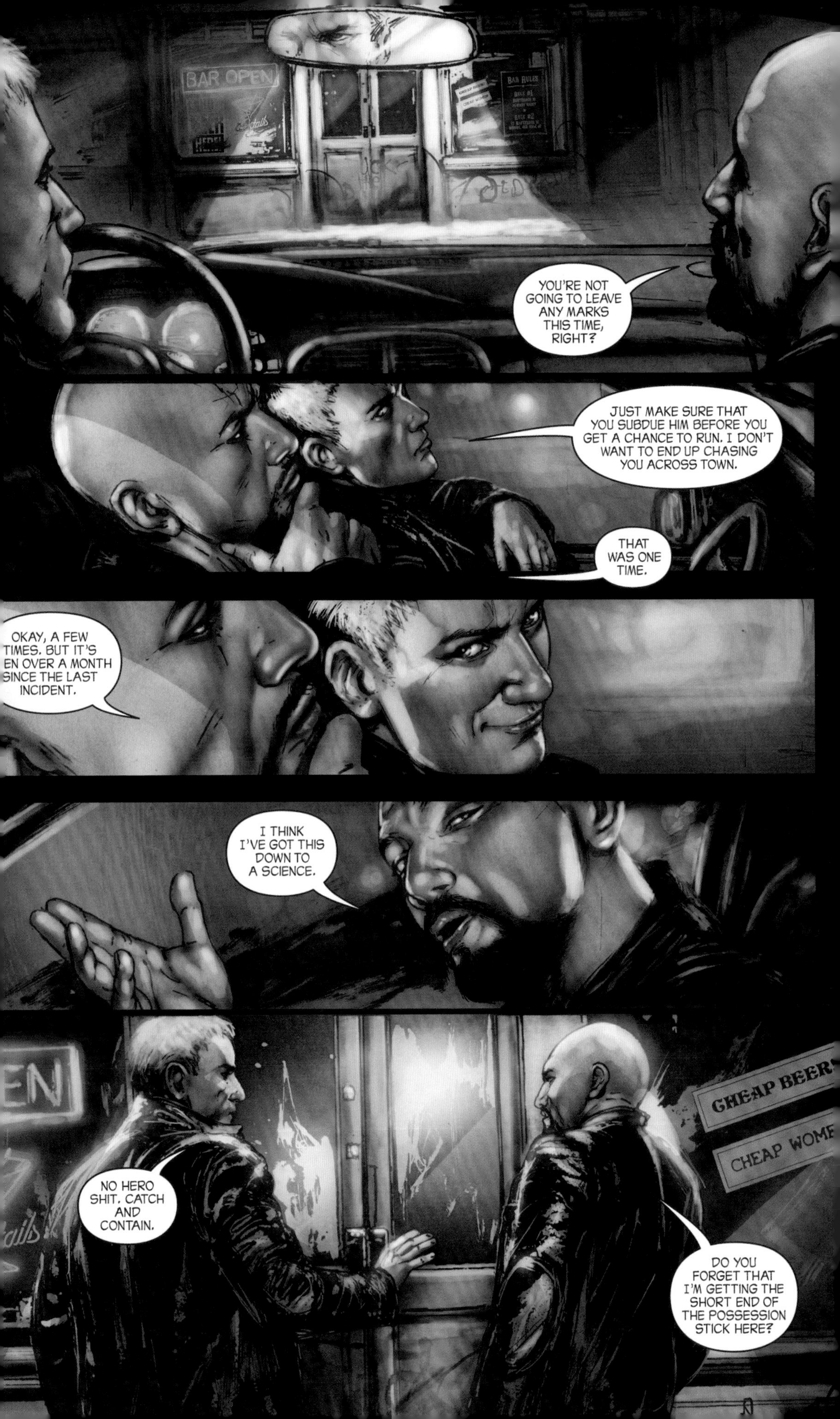
BAR OPEN
BAR RULES
YOU'RE NOT GOING TO LEAVE ANY MARKS THIS TIME, RIGHT?
JUST MAKE SURE THAT YOU SUBDUE HIM BEFORE YOU GET A CHANCE TO RUN. I DON'T WANT TO END UP CHASING YOU ACROSS TOWN.
THAT WAS ONE TIME.
OKAY, A FEW TIMES. BUT IT'S EN OVER A MONTH SINCE THE LAST INCIDENT.
I THINK I'VE GOT THIS DOWN TO A SCIENCE.
EN
CHEAP BEER
CHEAP WOME
NO HERO SHIT. CATCH AND CONTAIN.
DO YOU FORGET THAT I'M GETTING THE SHORT END OF THE POSSESSION STICK HERE?

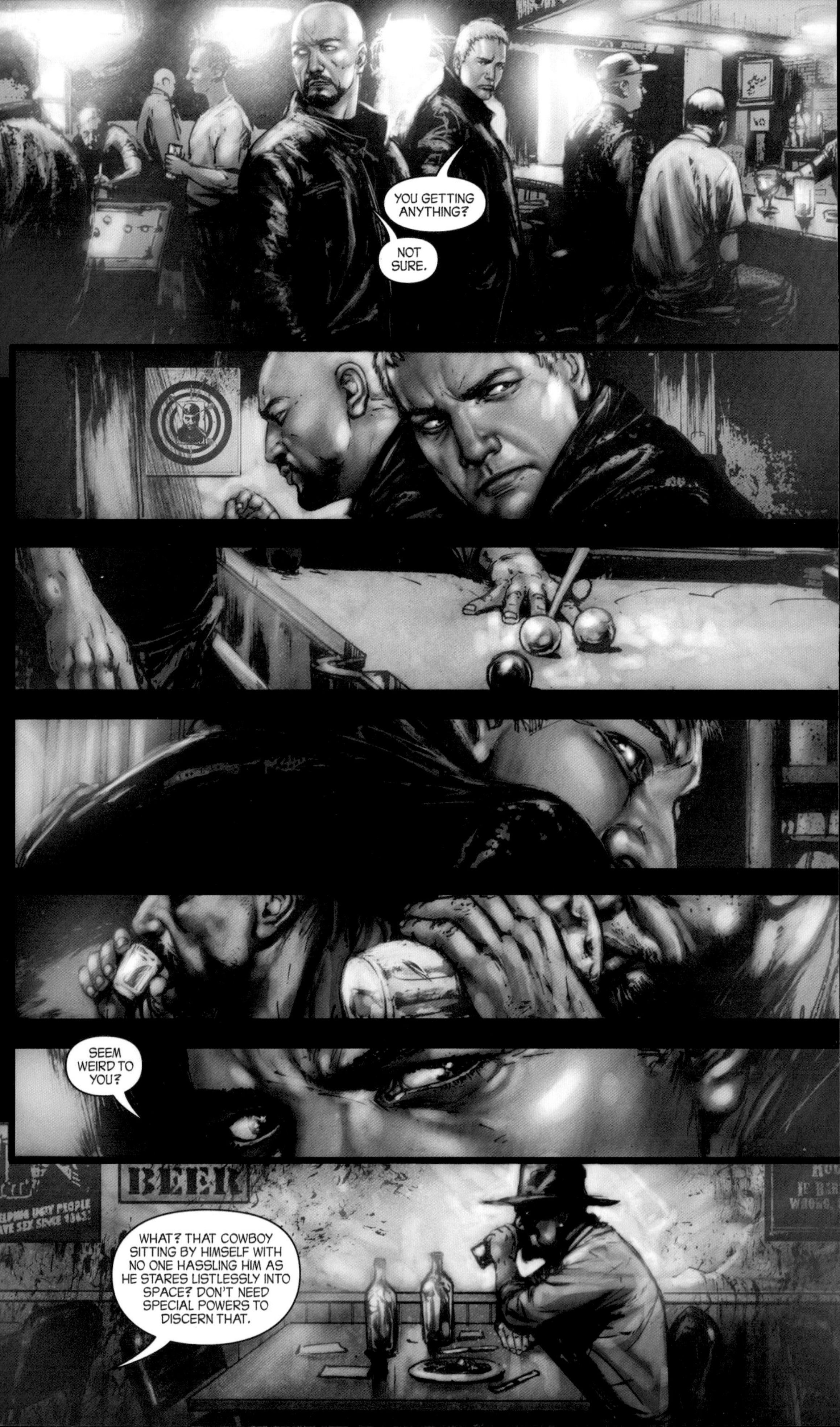
YOU GETTING ANYTHING?
NOT SURE.
SEEM WEIRD TO YOU?
BEER
WHAT? THAT COWBOY SITTING BY HIMSELF WITH NO ONE HASSLING HIM AS HE STARES LISTLESSLY INTO SPACE? DON'T NEED SPECIAL POWERS TO DISCERN THAT.

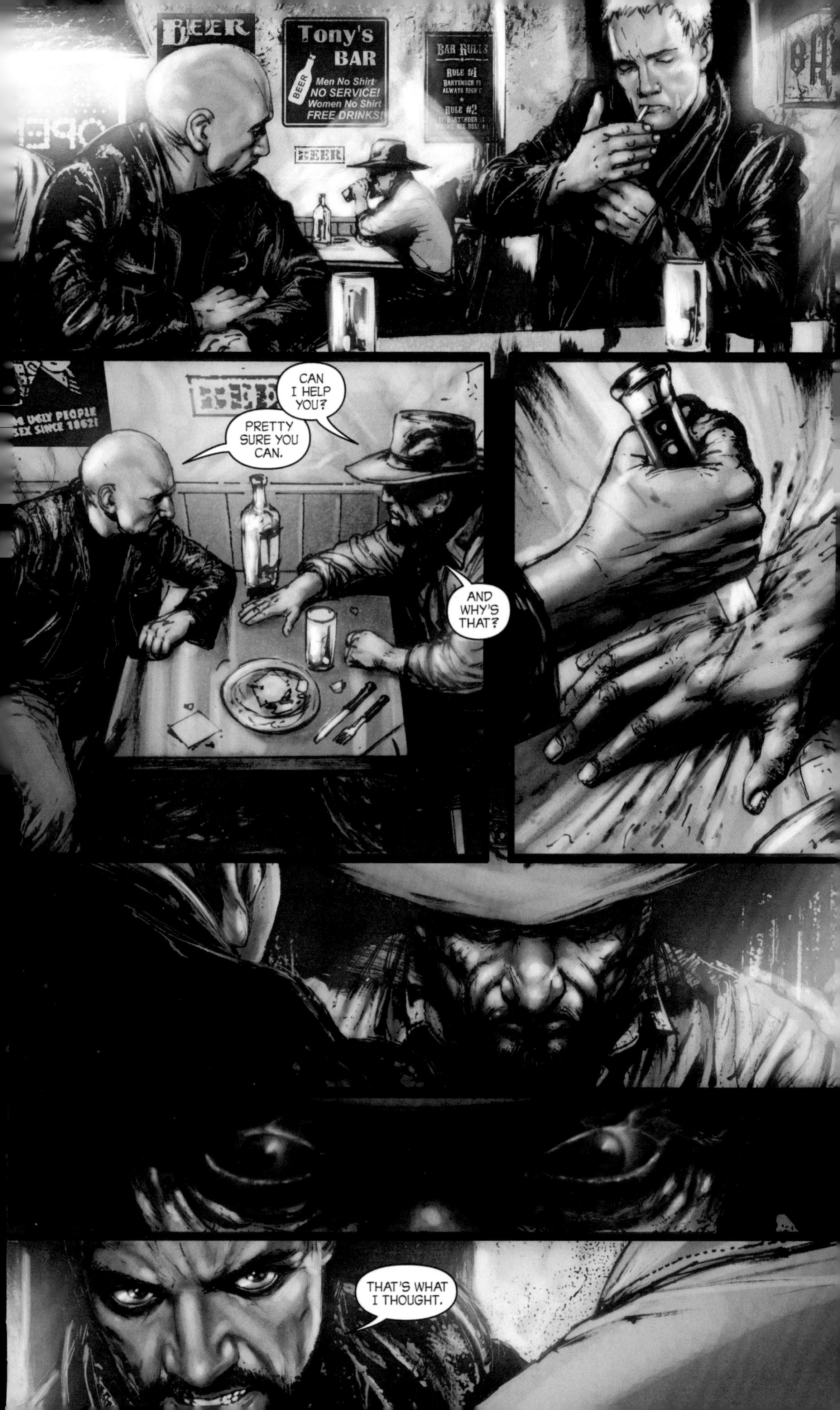
BEER
Tony's BAR
BEER
Men No Shirt NO SERVICE!
Women No Shirt FREE DRINKS!
BAR RULES
RULE #1
BARTENDER IS ALWAYS RIGHT
RULE #2
BEER
CAN I HELP YOU?
PRETTY SURE YOU CAN.
AND WHY'S THAT?
THAT'S WHAT I THOUGHT.

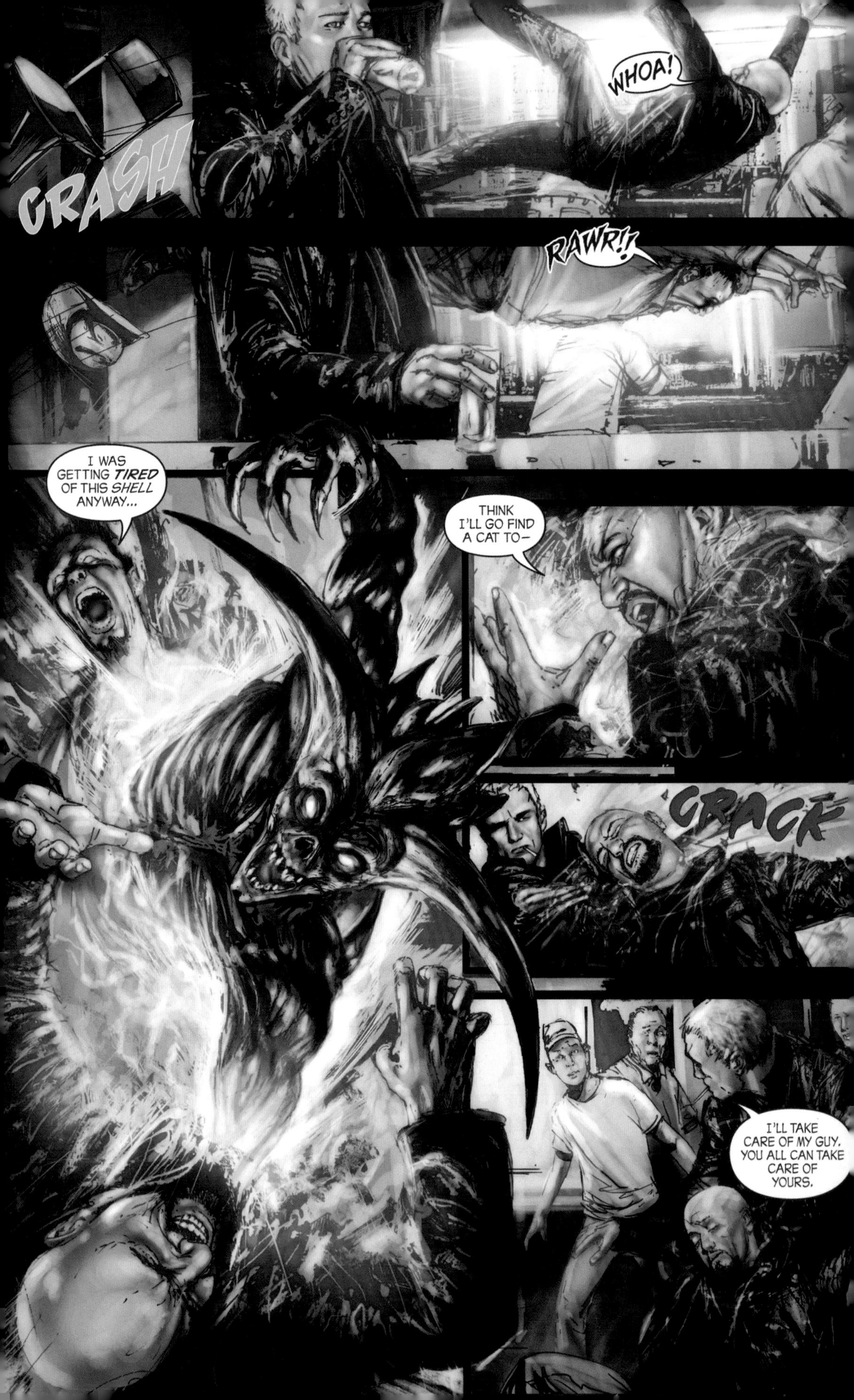

CRASH
WHOA!
RAWR!!
I WAS GETTING *TIRED* OF THIS *SHELL* ANYWAY...
THINK I'LL GO FIND A CAT TO—
CRACK
I'LL TAKE CARE OF MY GUY. YOU ALL CAN TAKE CARE OF YOURS.

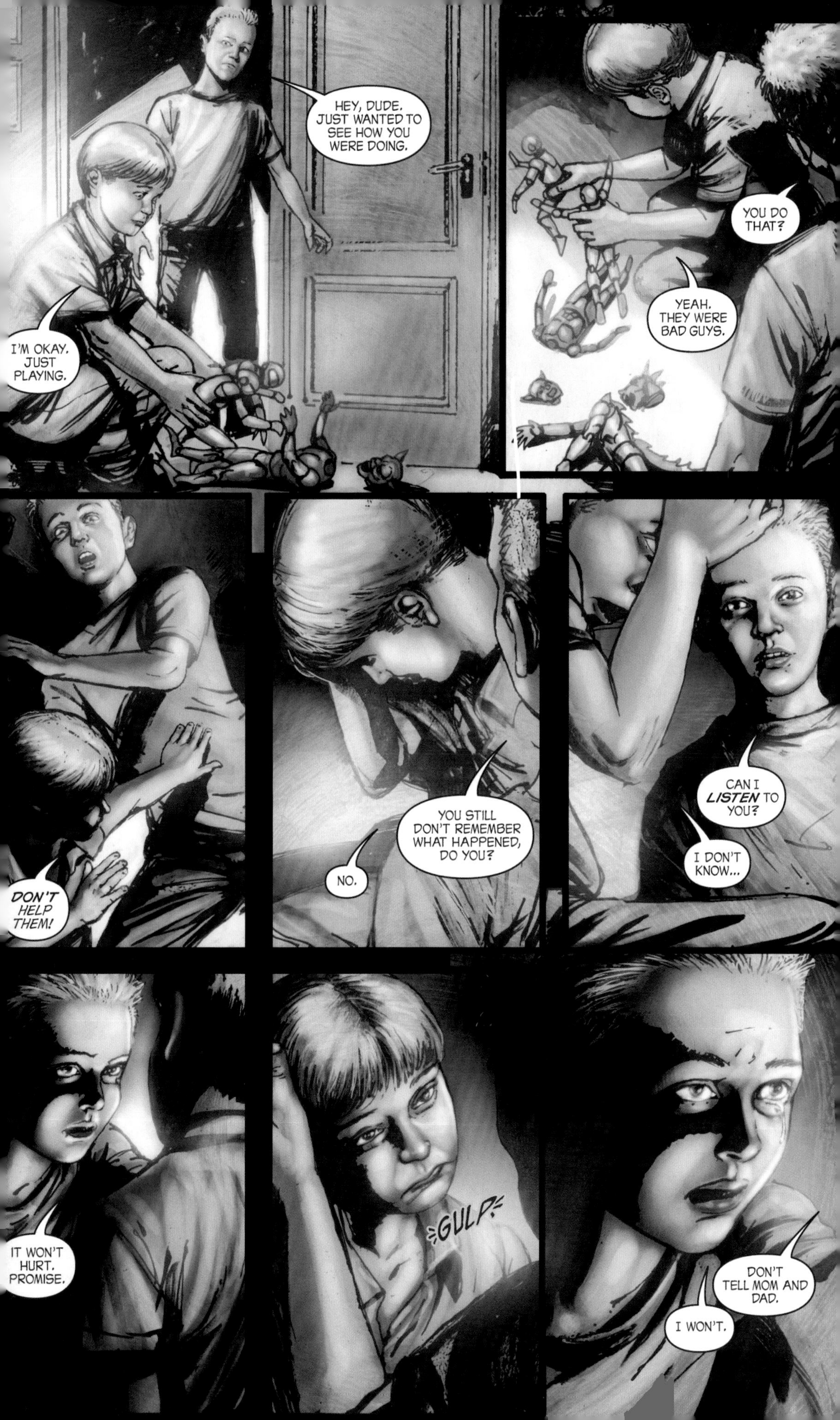
HEY, DUDE. JUST WANTED TO SEE HOW YOU WERE DOING.
I'M OKAY. JUST PLAYING.
YOU DO THAT?
YEAH. THEY WERE BAD GUYS.
DON'T HELP THEM!
YOU STILL DON'T REMEMBER WHAT HAPPENED, DO YOU?
NO.
CAN I LISTEN TO YOU?
I DON'T KNOW...
IT WON'T HURT. PROMISE.
GULP!
DON'T TELL MOM AND DAD.
I WON'T.

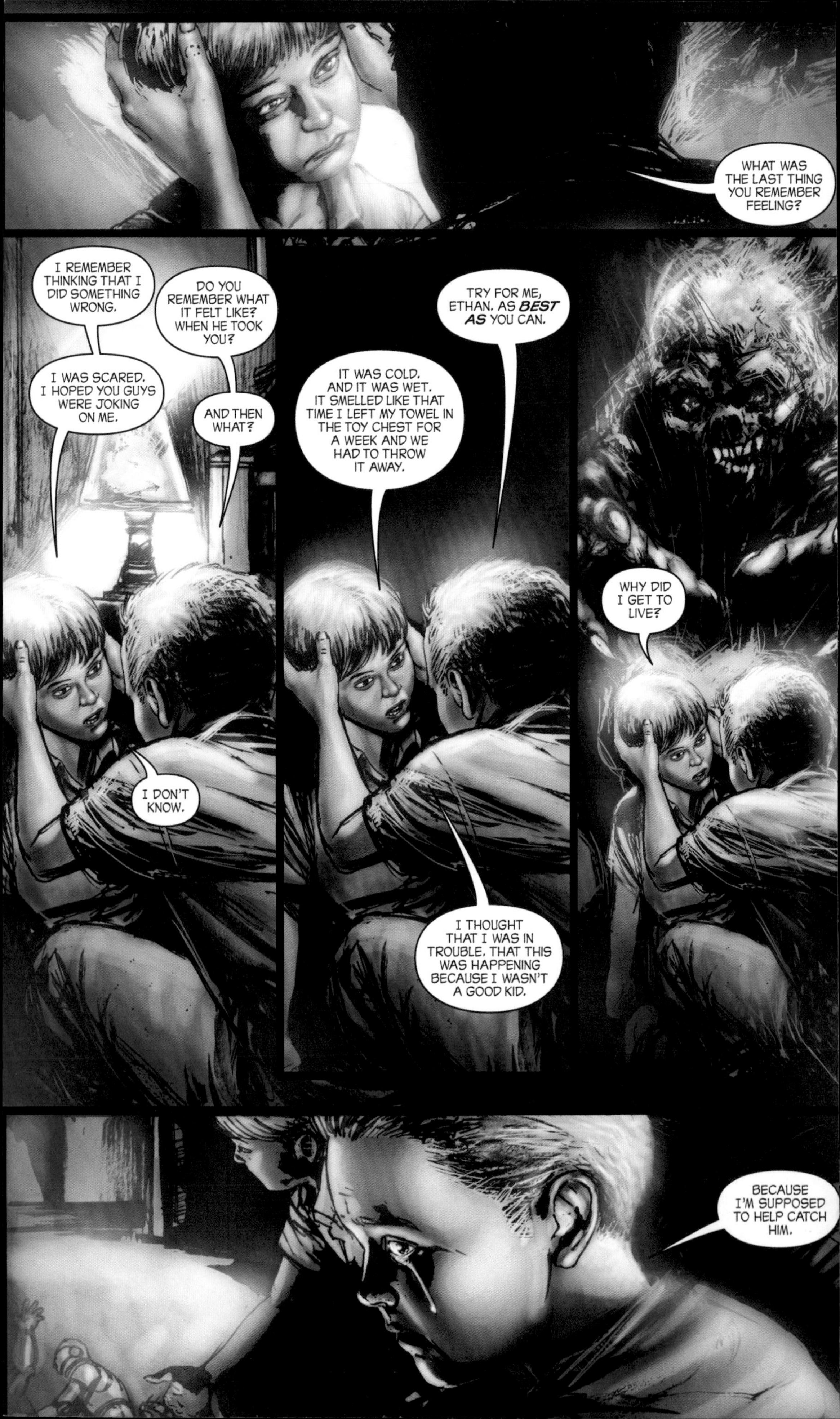
WHAT WAS THE LAST THING YOU REMEMBER FEELING?
I REMEMBER THINKING THAT I DID SOMETHING WRONG.
I WAS SCARED. I HOPED YOU GUYS WERE JOKING ON ME.
DO YOU REMEMBER WHAT IT FELT LIKE? WHEN HE TOOK YOU?
AND THEN WHAT?
I DON'T KNOW.
TRY FOR ME, ETHAN. AS BEST AS YOU CAN.
IT WAS COLD. AND IT WAS WET. IT SMELLED LIKE THAT TIME I LEFT MY TOWEL IN THE TOY CHEST FOR A WEEK AND WE HAD TO THROW IT AWAY.
I THOUGHT THAT I WAS IN TROUBLE. THAT THIS WAS HAPPENING BECAUSE I WASN'T A GOOD KID.
WHY DID I GET TO LIVE?
BECAUSE I'M SUPPOSED TO HELP CATCH HIM.

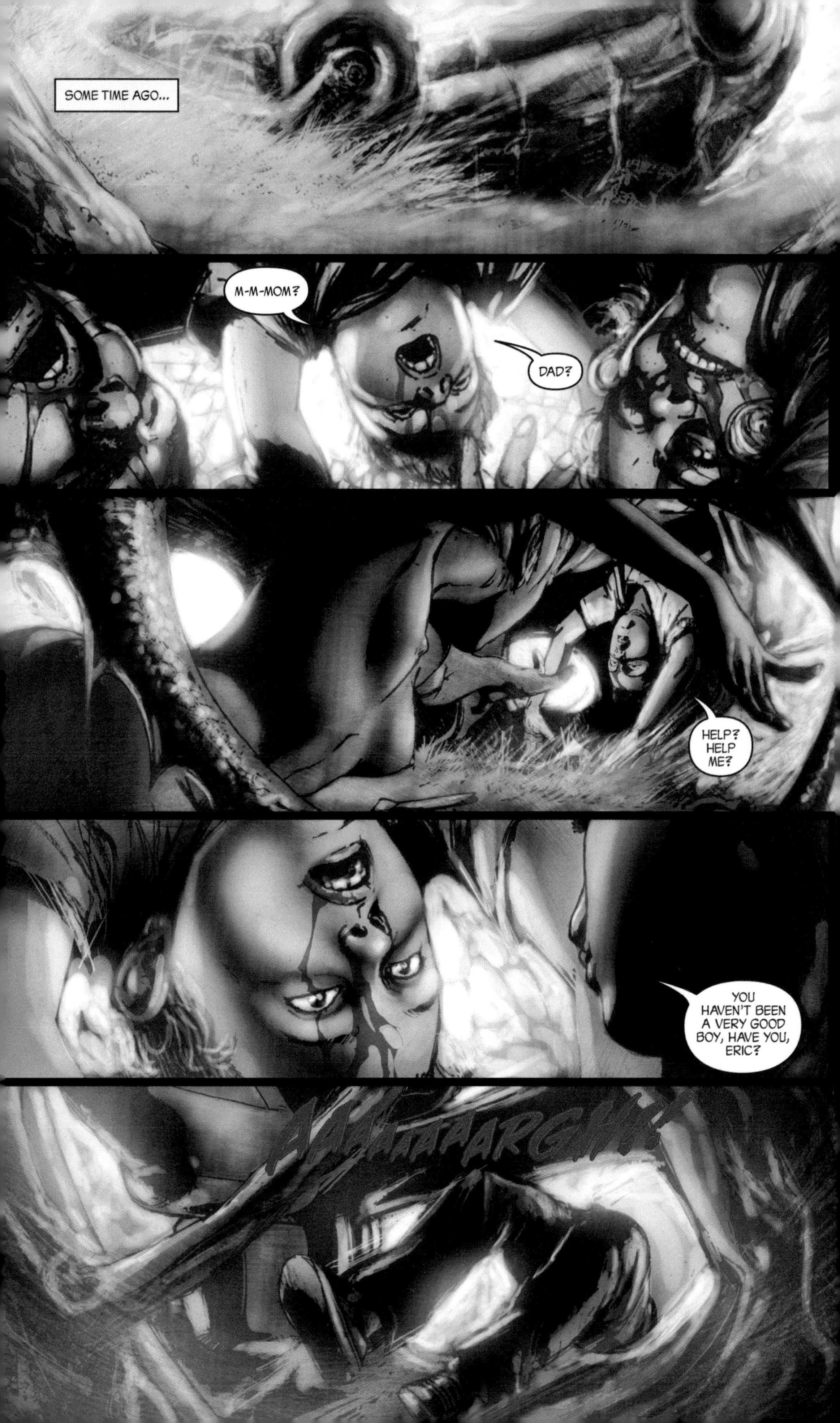
SOME TIME AGO...
M-M-MOM?
DAD?
HELP? HELP ME?
YOU HAVEN'T BEEN A VERY GOOD BOY, HAVE YOU, ERIC?
AAAAAAARGH!!

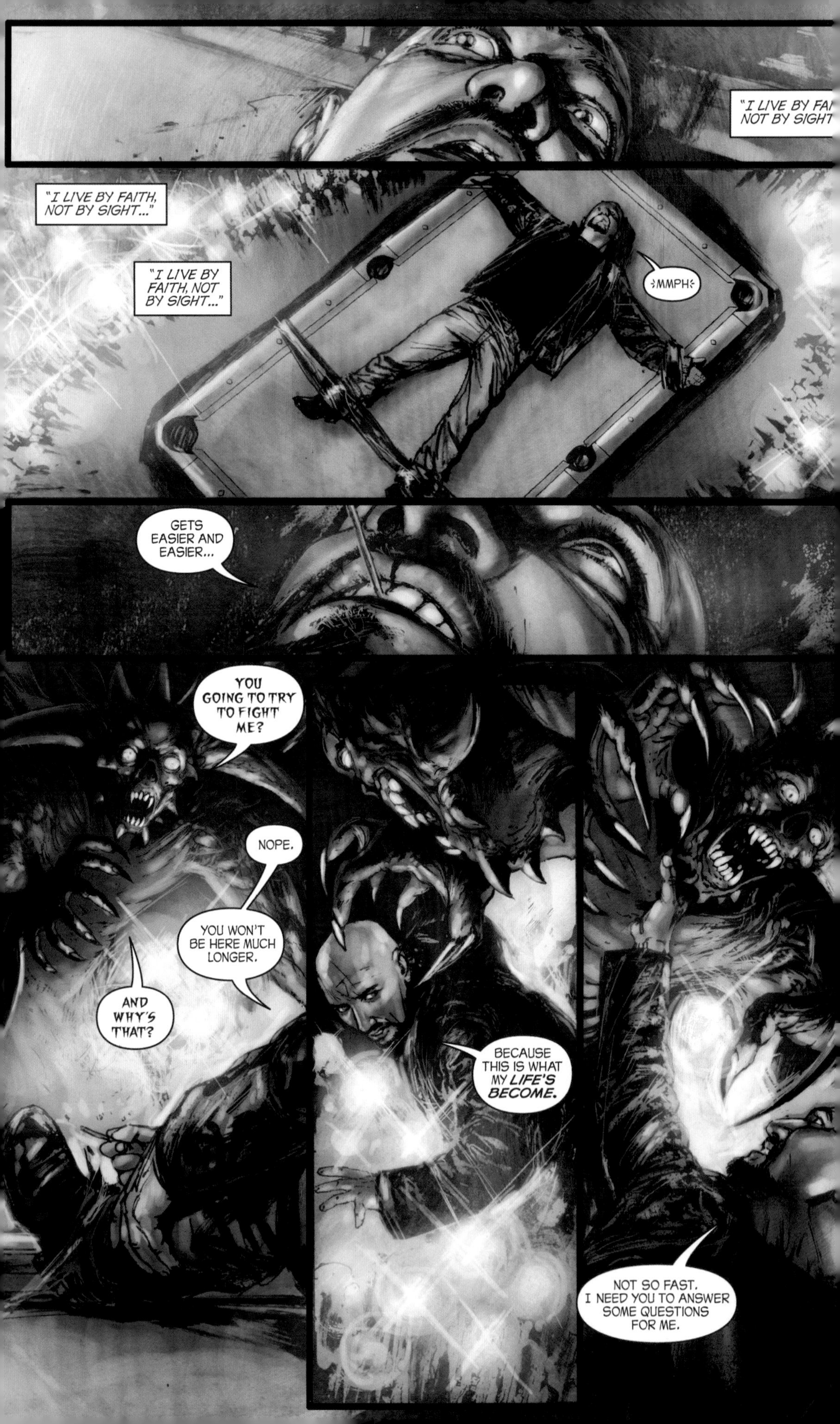
"I LIVE BY FAI
NOT BY SIGHT
"I LIVE BY FAITH, NOT BY SIGHT..."
"I LIVE BY FAITH, NOT BY SIGHT..."
MMPH
GETS EASIER AND EASIER...
YOU GOING TO TRY TO FIGHT ME?
NOPE.
YOU WON'T BE HERE MUCH LONGER.
AND WHY'S THAT?
BECAUSE THIS IS WHAT MY *LIFE'S BECOME*.
NOT SO FAST. I NEED YOU TO ANSWER SOME QUESTIONS FOR ME.

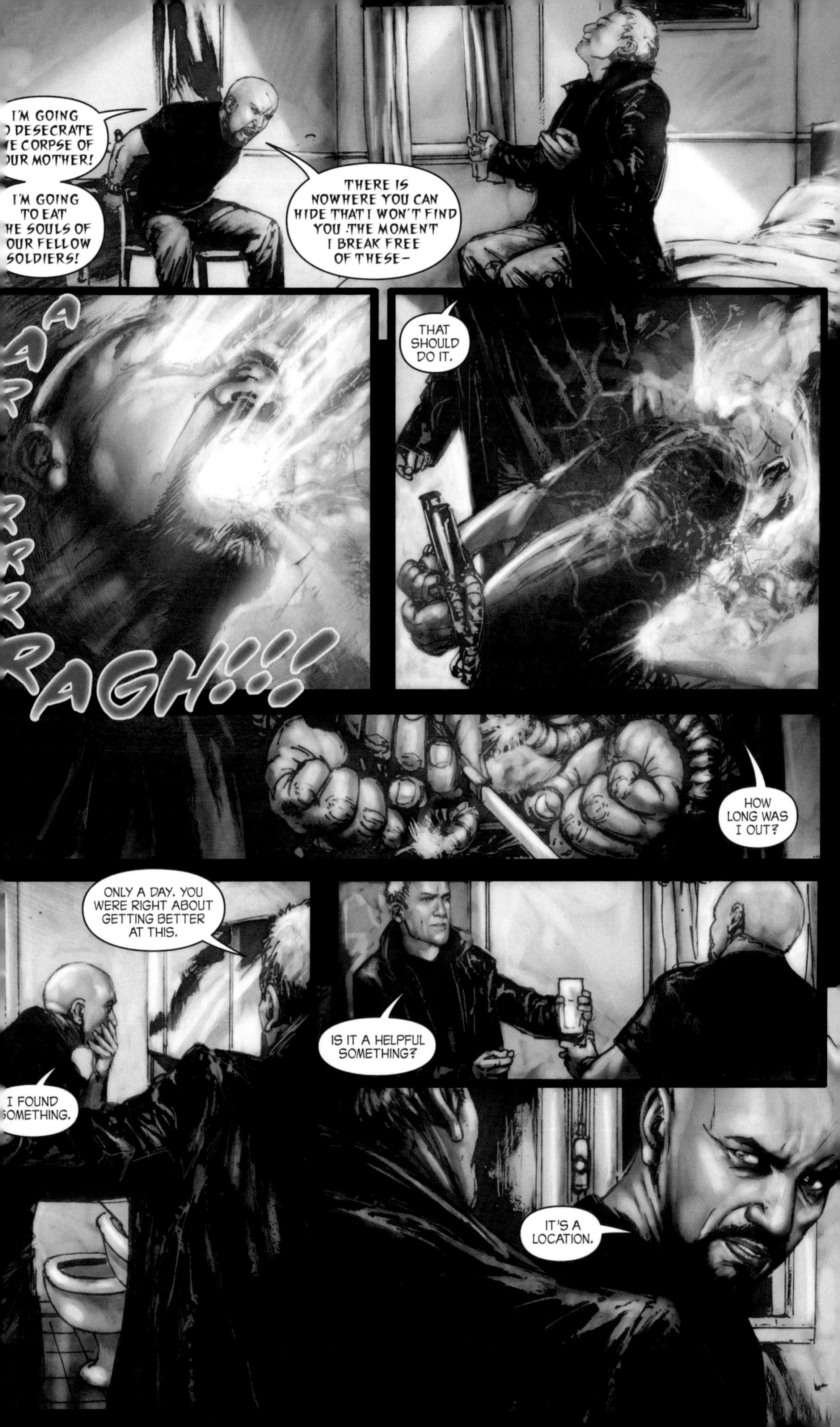
I'M GOING
DESECRATE
E CORPSE OF
OUR MOTHER!
I'M GOING TO EAT
HE SOULS OF
OUR FELLOW SOLDIERS!
THERE IS NOWHERE YOU CAN HIDE THAT I WON'T FIND YOU. THE MOMENT I BREAK FREE OF THESE–
AAARRRRRAGH!!!
THAT SHOULD DO IT.
HOW LONG WAS I OUT?
ONLY A DAY. YOU WERE RIGHT ABOUT GETTING BETTER AT THIS.
I FOUND
OMETHING.
IS IT A HELPFUL SOMETHING?
IT'S A LOCATION.

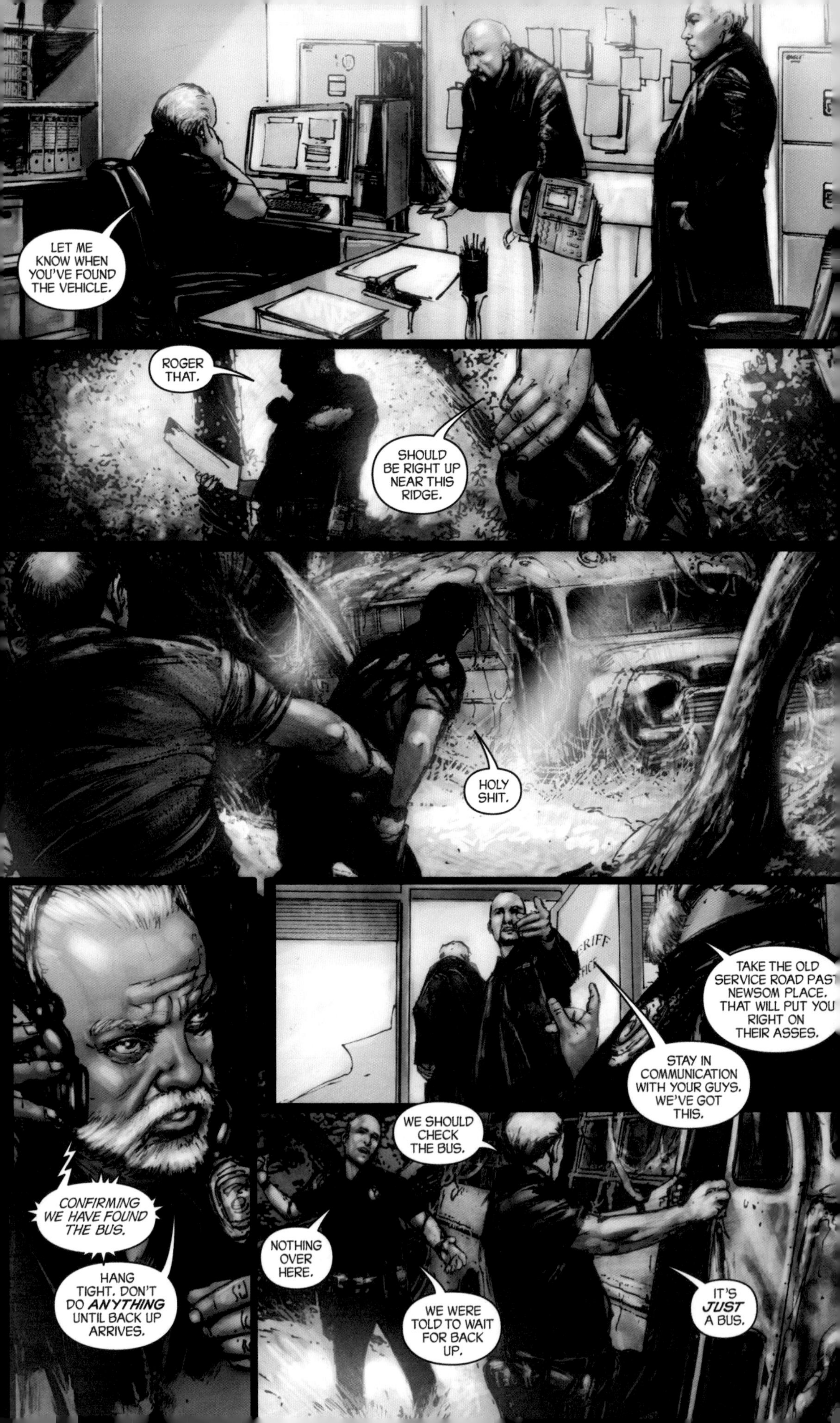
LET ME KNOW WHEN YOU'VE FOUND THE VEHICLE.
ROGER THAT.
SHOULD BE RIGHT UP NEAR THIS RIDGE.
HOLY SHIT.
CONFIRMING WE HAVE FOUND THE BUS.
HANG TIGHT. DON'T DO *ANYTHING* UNTIL BACK UP ARRIVES.
TAKE THE OLD SERVICE ROAD PAST NEWSOM PLACE. THAT WILL PUT YOU RIGHT ON THEIR ASSES.
STAY IN COMMUNICATION WITH YOUR GUYS. WE'VE GOT THIS.
WE SHOULD CHECK THE BUS.
NOTHING OVER HERE.
WE WERE TOLD TO WAIT FOR BACK UP.
IT'S *JUST* A BUS.

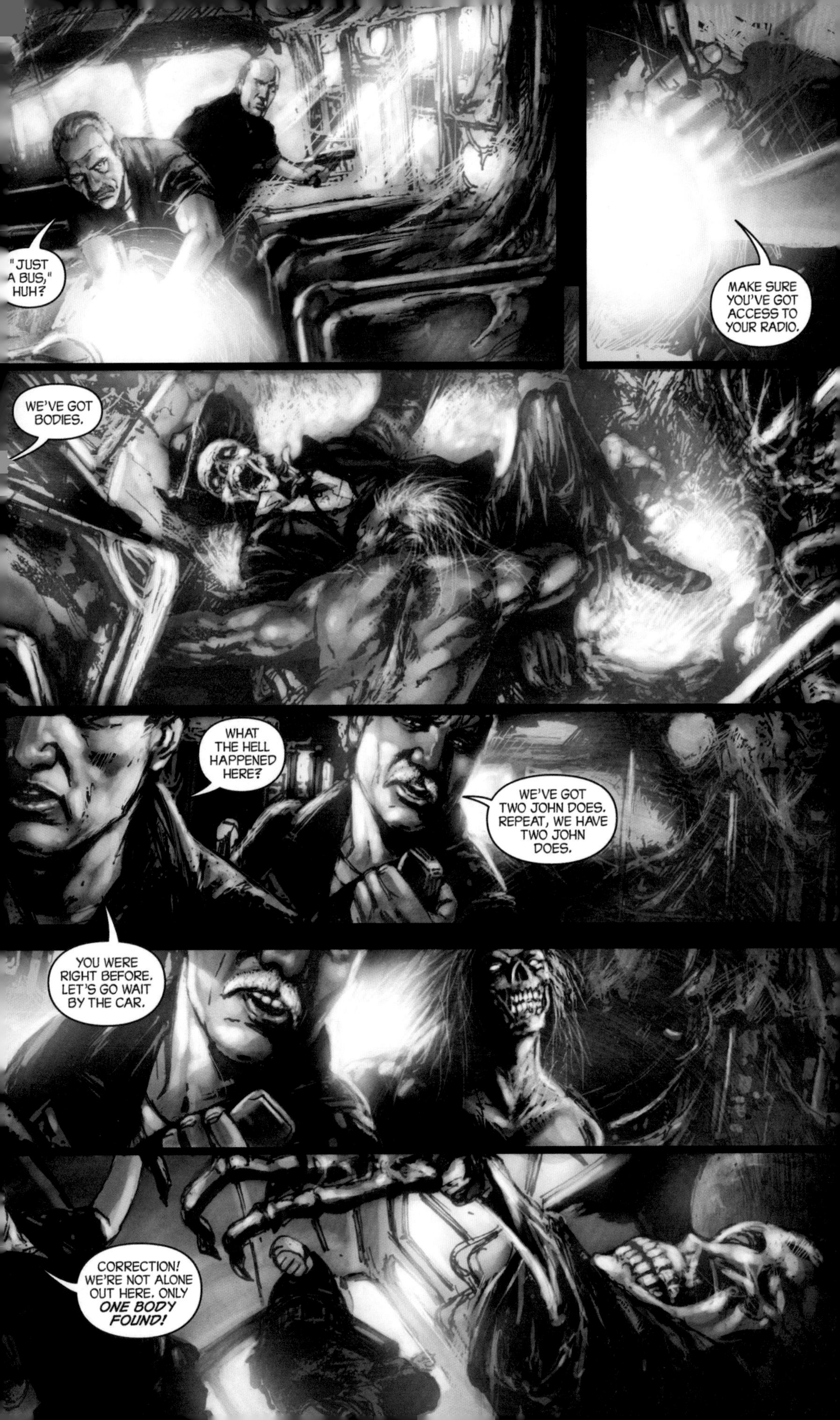
"JUST A BUS," HUH?
MAKE SURE YOU'VE GOT ACCESS TO YOUR RADIO.
WE'VE GOT BODIES.
WHAT THE HELL HAPPENED HERE?
WE'VE GOT TWO JOHN DOES. REPEAT, WE HAVE TWO JOHN DOES.
YOU WERE RIGHT BEFORE. LET'S GO WAIT BY THE CAR.
CORRECTION! WE'RE NOT ALONE OUT HERE. ONLY *ONE BODY FOUND!*

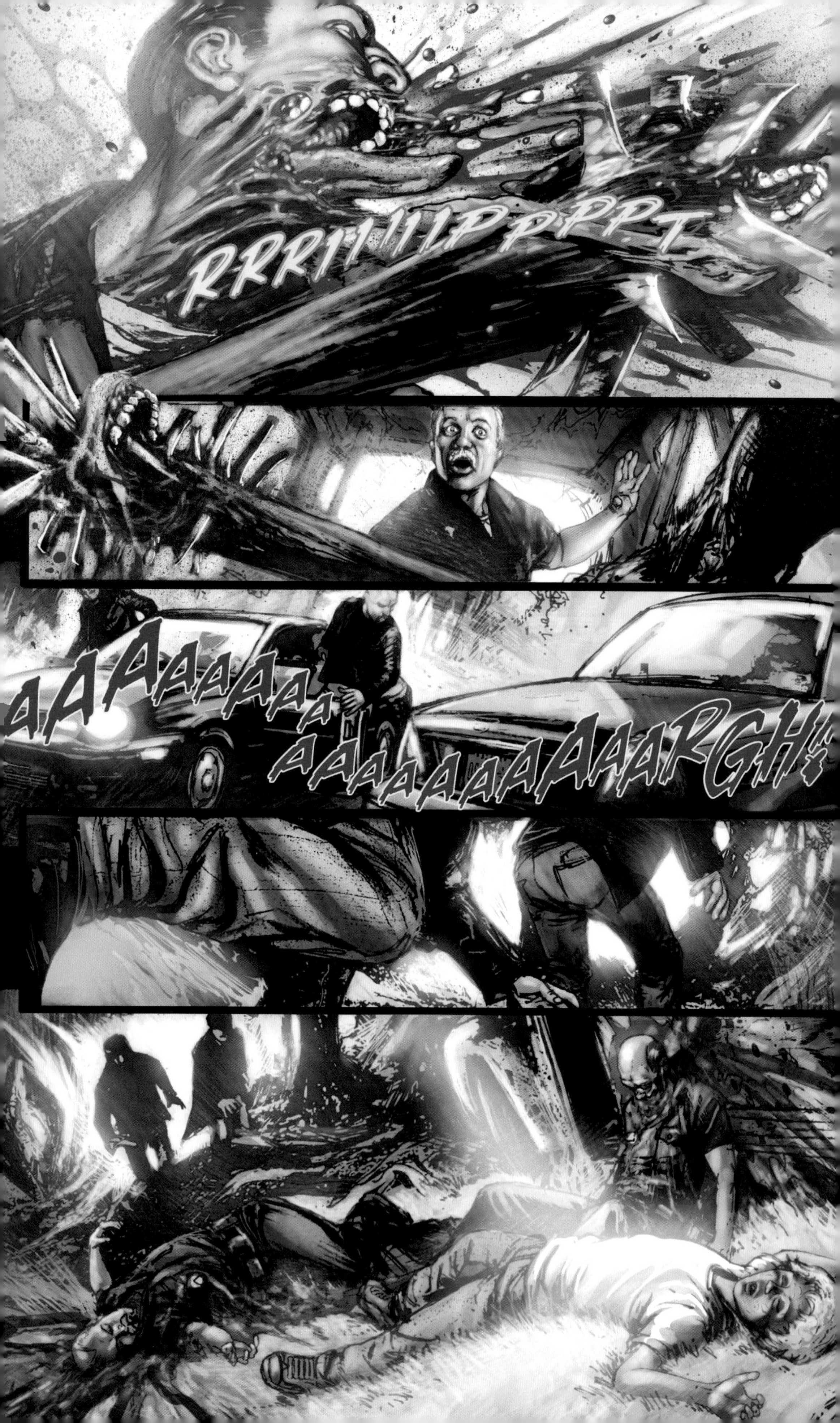
RRRIIIIIPPPPT
AAAAAAAAAAAAAAAAAAAAARGH!!

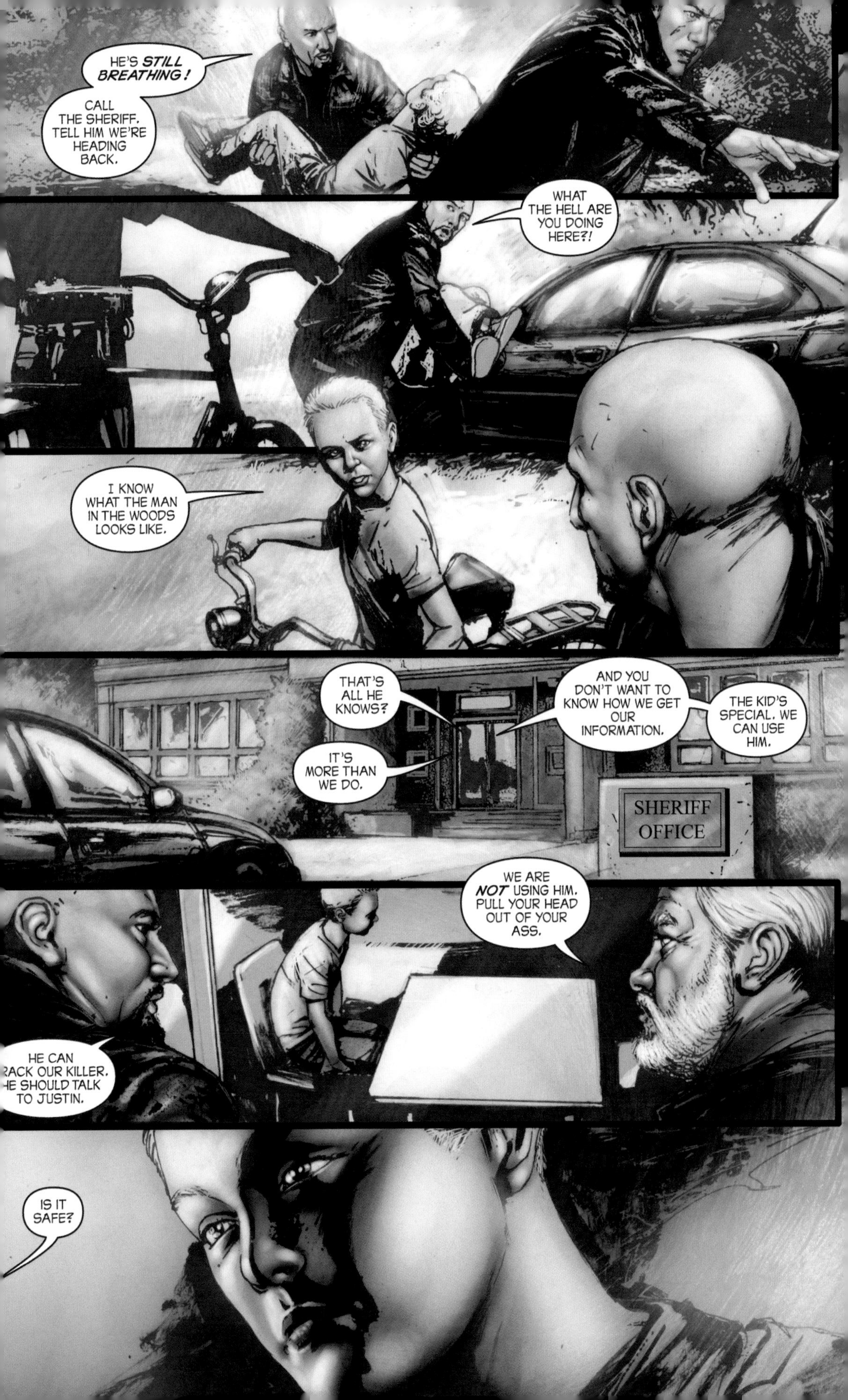
HE'S ***STILL BREATHING!***
CALL THE SHERIFF. TELL HIM WE'RE HEADING BACK.
WHAT THE HELL ARE YOU DOING HERE?!
I KNOW WHAT THE MAN IN THE WOODS LOOKS LIKE.
THAT'S ALL HE KNOWS?
IT'S MORE THAN WE DO.
AND YOU DON'T WANT TO KNOW HOW WE GET OUR INFORMATION.
THE KID'S SPECIAL. WE CAN USE HIM.
SHERIFF OFFICE
HE CAN ACK OUR KILLER. HE SHOULD TALK TO JUSTIN.
WE ARE ***NOT*** USING HIM. PULL YOUR HEAD OUT OF YOUR ASS.
IS IT SAFE?

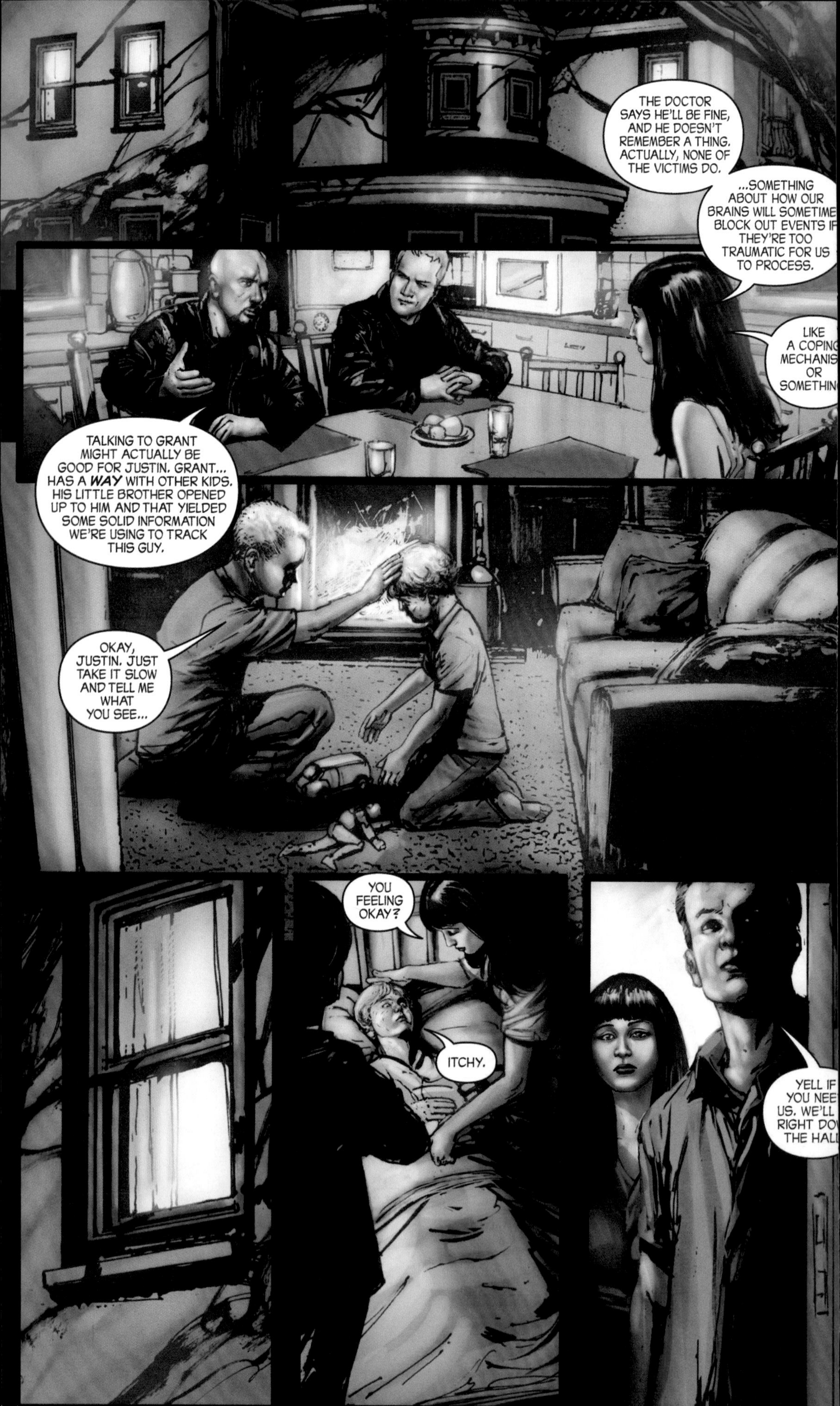
THE DOCTOR SAYS HE'LL BE FINE, AND HE DOESN'T REMEMBER A THING. ACTUALLY, NONE OF THE VICTIMS DO.
...SOMETHING ABOUT HOW OUR BRAINS WILL SOMETIME BLOCK OUT EVENTS IF THEY'RE TOO TRAUMATIC FOR US TO PROCESS.
LIKE A COPING MECHANIS OR SOMETHIN
TALKING TO GRANT MIGHT ACTUALLY BE GOOD FOR JUSTIN. GRANT... HAS A WAY WITH OTHER KIDS. HIS LITTLE BROTHER OPENED UP TO HIM AND THAT YIELDED SOME SOLID INFORMATION WE'RE USING TO TRACK THIS GUY.
OKAY, JUSTIN. JUST TAKE IT SLOW AND TELL ME WHAT YOU SEE...
YOU FEELING OKAY?
ITCHY.
YELL IF YOU NEE US. WE'LL RIGHT DOW THE HAL

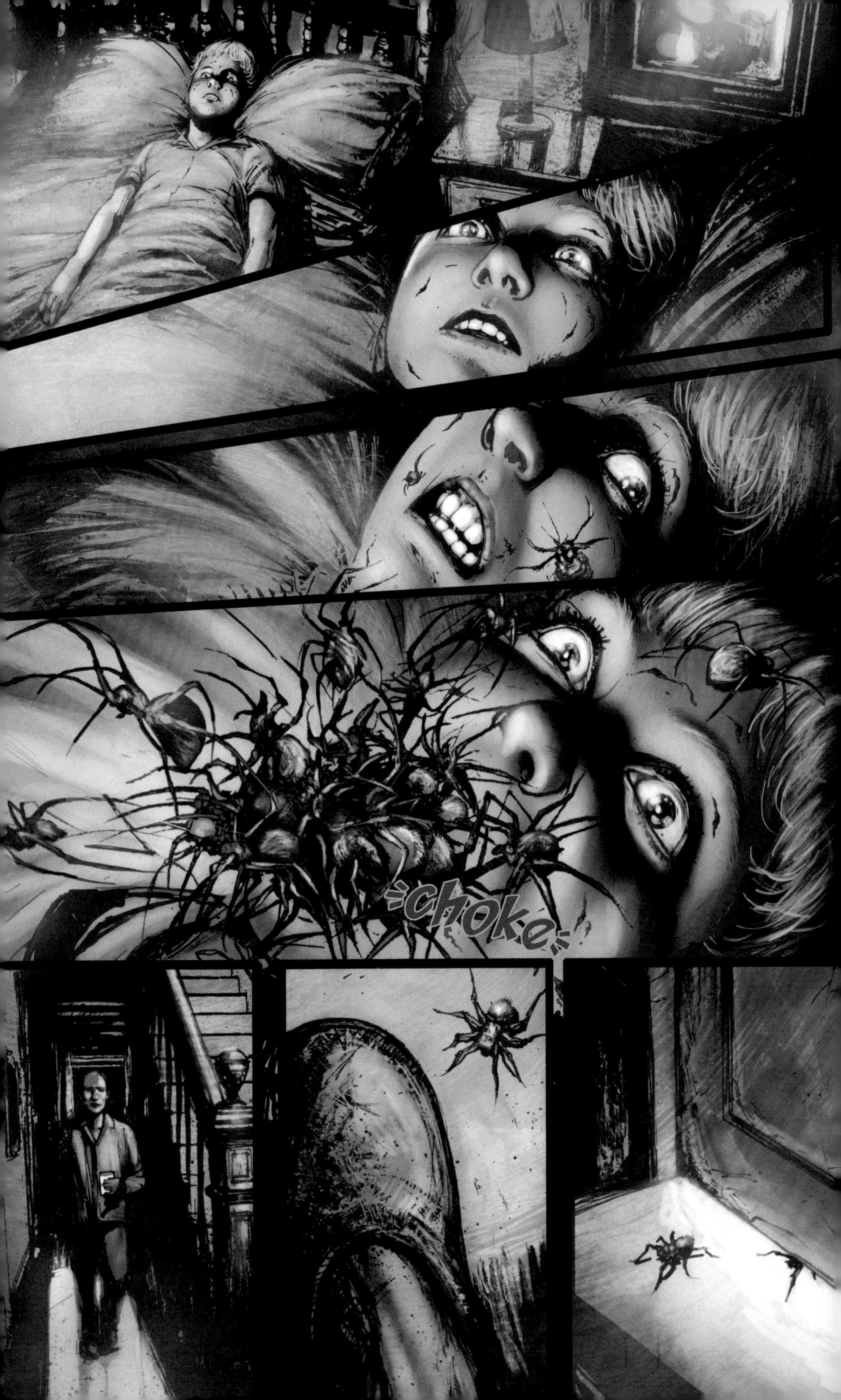
choke

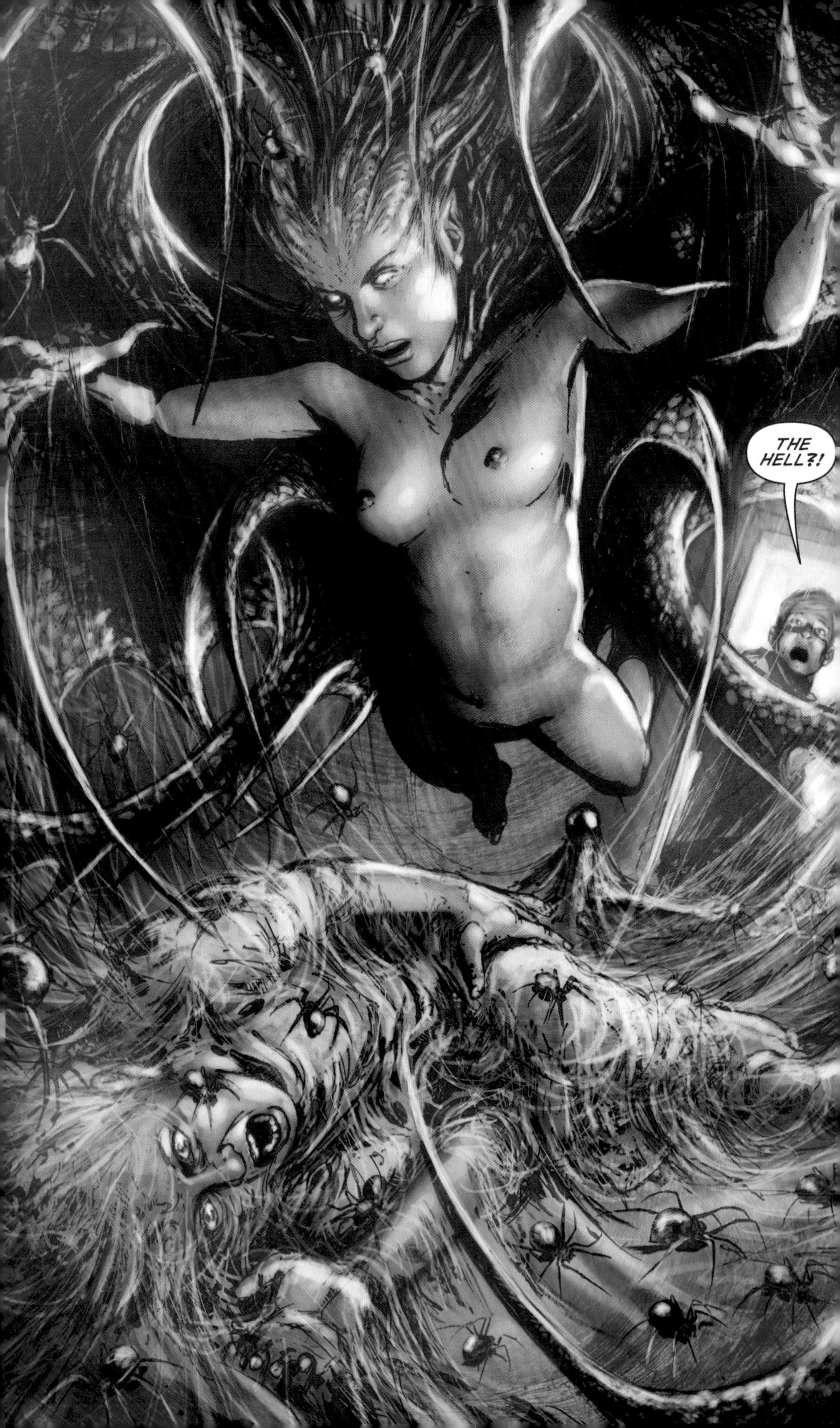
THE HELL?!

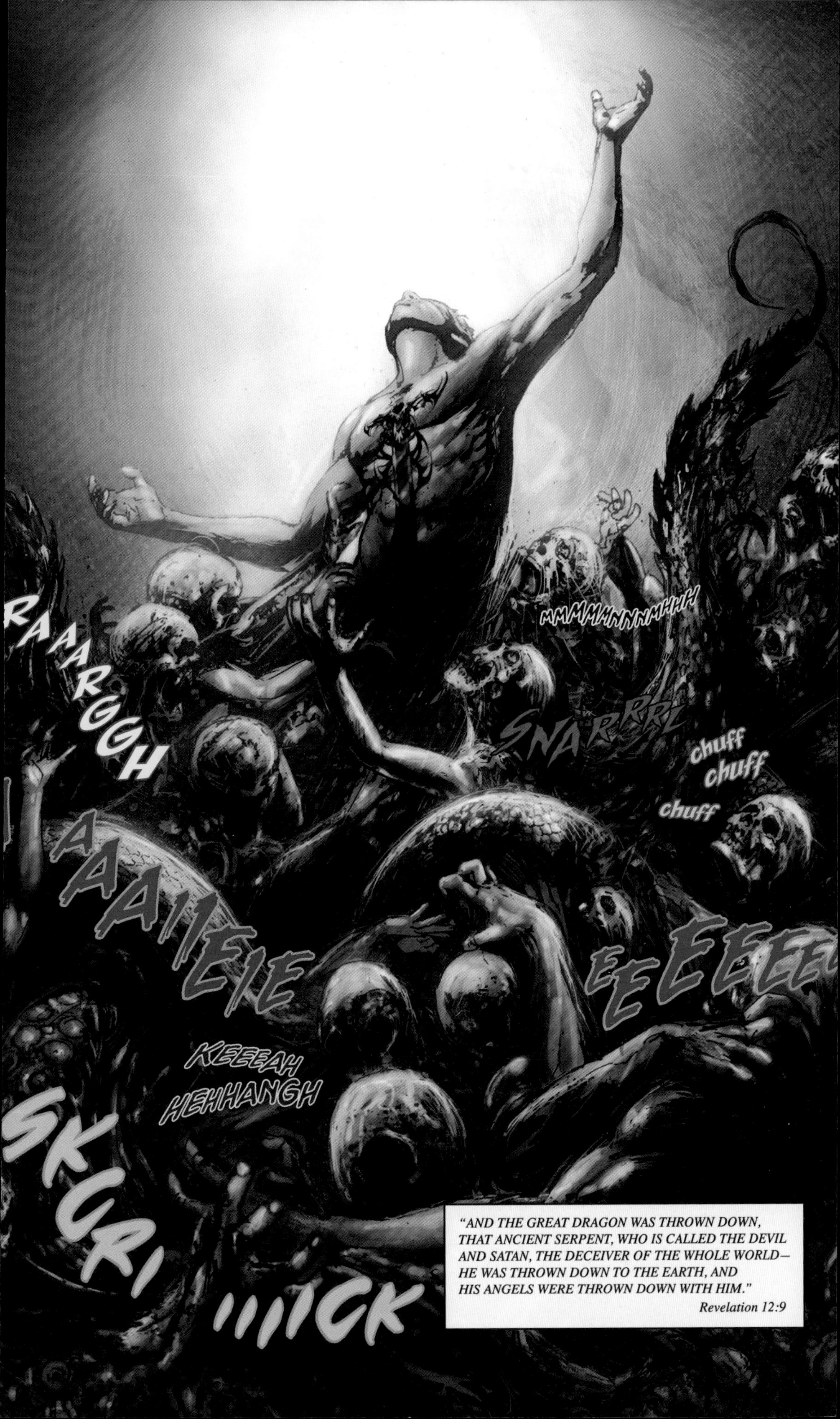
RAAARGGGH
MMMMMNNNMHHH
SNARRRL
chuff chuff chuff
AAAIIEIE
EEEEEE
KEEEEAH HEHHANGH
SKURIIIIICK
"AND THE GREAT DRAGON WAS THROWN DOWN, THAT ANCIENT SERPENT, WHO IS CALLED THE DEVIL AND SATAN, THE DECEIVER OF THE WHOLE WORLD– HE WAS THROWN DOWN TO THE EARTH, AND HIS ANGELS WERE THROWN DOWN WITH HIM."
Revelation 12:9

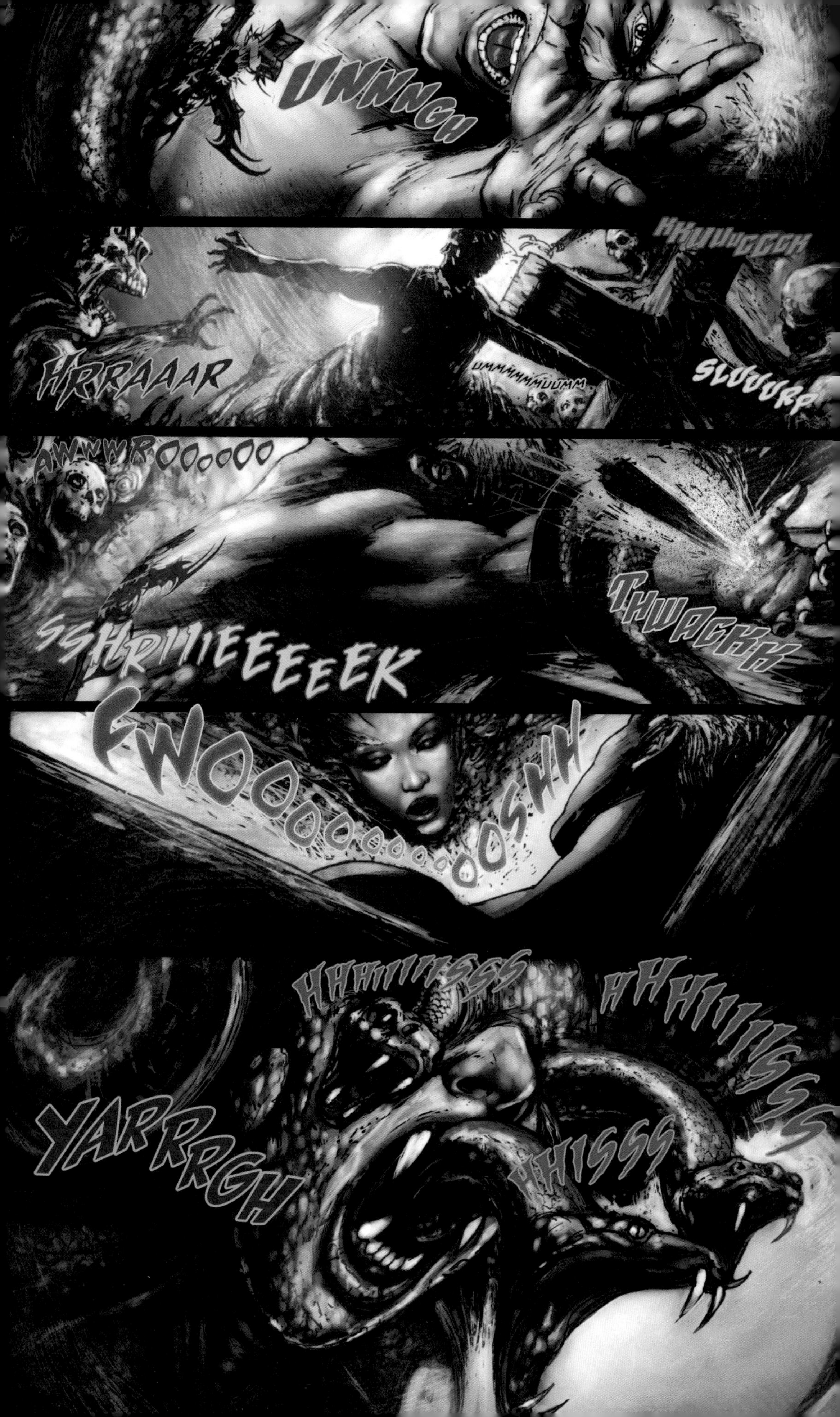
UNNNGH
HRRAAAR
UMMMMMMUUMM
KKUUUGGCH
SLUUURP
AWWWROOoooo
SSHRIIIEEEEEK
THWACKK
FWOOOOooooooOOSHH
HHIIIIISSS
YARRRGH
HHISSS
HHHIIIIISSSS

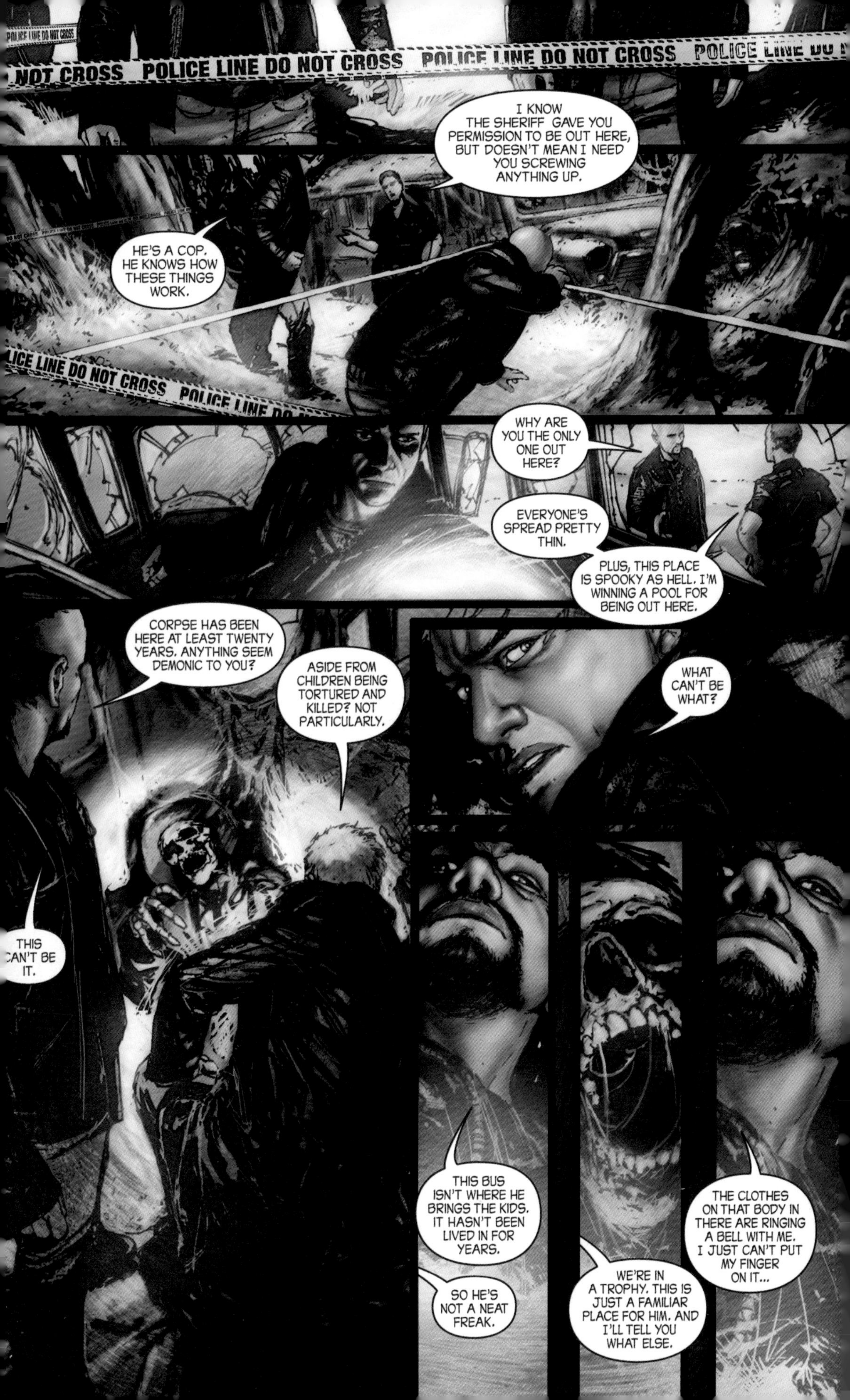

NOT CROSS POLICE LINE DO NOT CROSS POLICE LINE DO NOT CROSS
I KNOW THE SHERIFF GAVE YOU PERMISSION TO BE OUT HERE, BUT DOESN'T MEAN I NEED YOU SCREWING ANYTHING UP.
HE'S A COP. HE KNOWS HOW THESE THINGS WORK.
LICE LINE DO NOT CROSS
WHY ARE YOU THE ONLY ONE OUT HERE?
EVERYONE'S SPREAD PRETTY THIN.
PLUS, THIS PLACE IS SPOOKY AS HELL. I'M WINNING A POOL FOR BEING OUT HERE.
CORPSE HAS BEEN HERE AT LEAST TWENTY YEARS. ANYTHING SEEM DEMONIC TO YOU?
ASIDE FROM CHILDREN BEING TORTURED AND KILLED? NOT PARTICULARLY.
THIS CAN'T BE IT.
WHAT CAN'T BE WHAT?
THIS BUS ISN'T WHERE HE BRINGS THE KIDS. IT HASN'T BEEN LIVED IN FOR YEARS.
SO HE'S NOT A NEAT FREAK.
WE'RE IN A TROPHY. THIS IS JUST A FAMILIAR PLACE FOR HIM. AND I'LL TELL YOU WHAT ELSE.
THE CLOTHES ON THAT BODY IN THERE ARE RINGING A BELL WITH ME. I JUST CAN'T PUT MY FINGER ON IT...

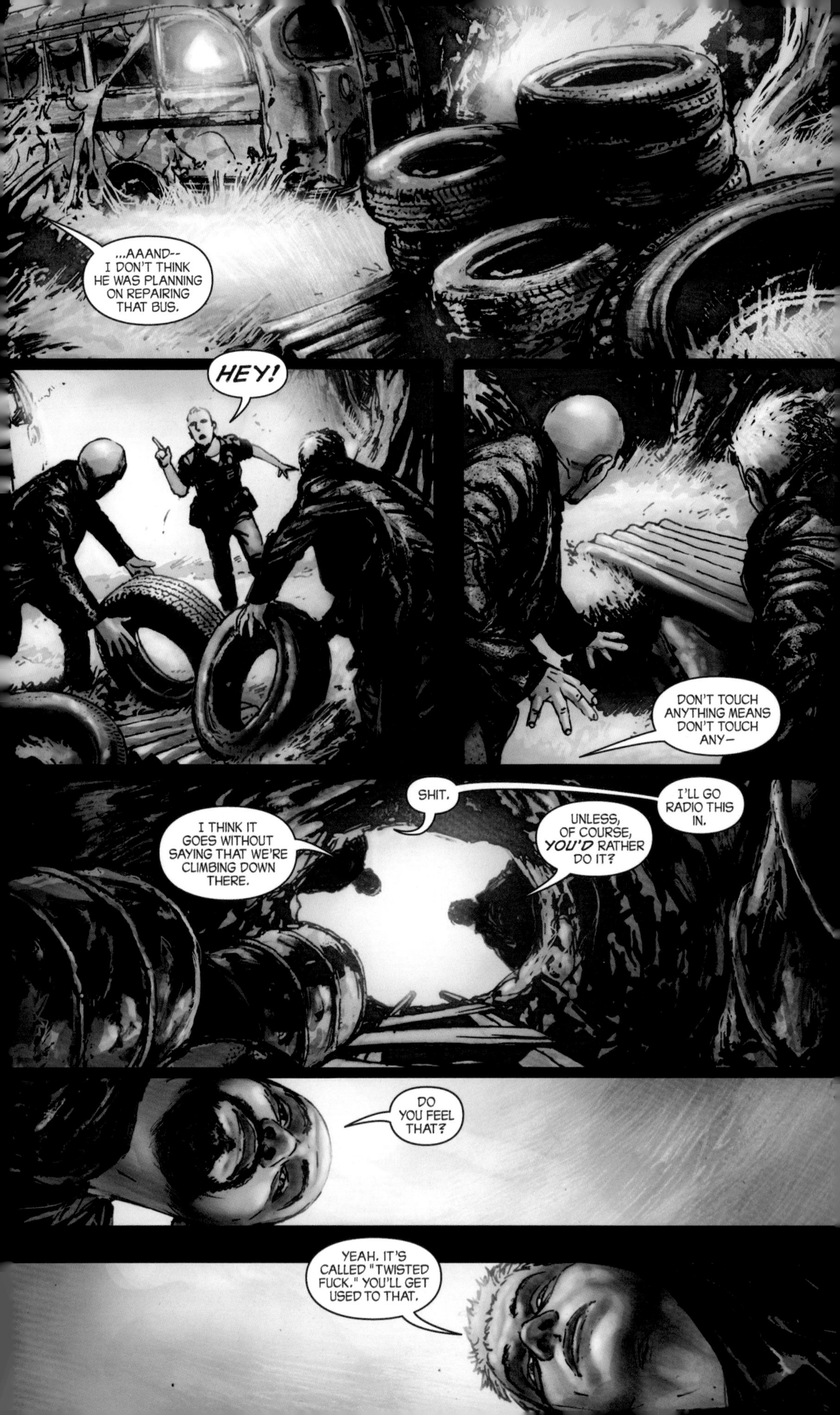
...AAAND-- I DON'T THINK HE WAS PLANNING ON REPAIRING THAT BUS.
HEY!
DON'T TOUCH ANYTHING MEANS DON'T TOUCH ANY--
I THINK IT GOES WITHOUT SAYING THAT WE'RE CLIMBING DOWN THERE.
SHIT.
UNLESS, OF COURSE, *YOU'D* RATHER DO IT?
I'LL GO RADIO THIS IN.
DO YOU FEEL THAT?
YEAH. IT'S CALLED "TWISTED FUCK." YOU'LL GET USED TO THAT.

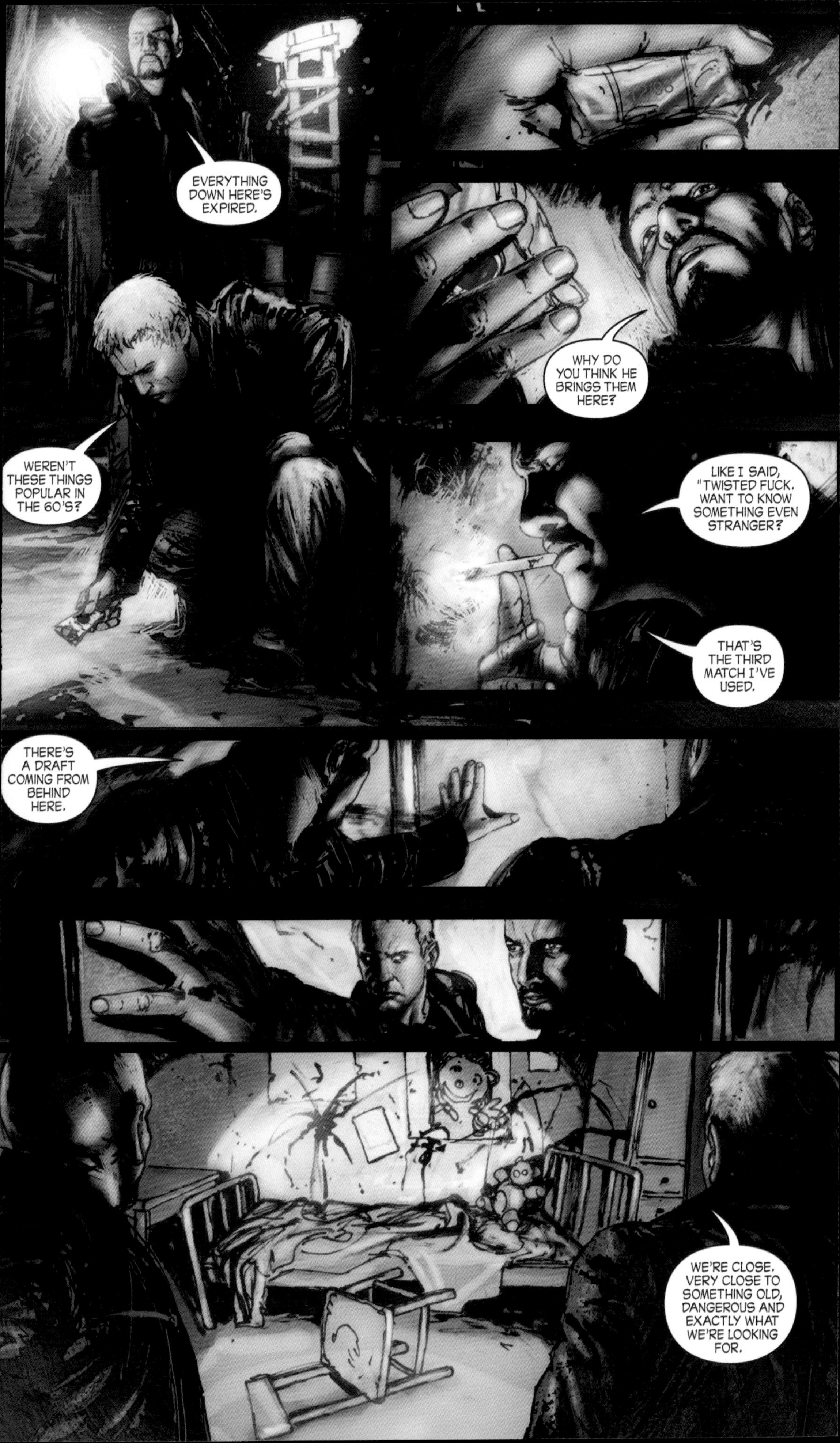
EVERYTHING DOWN HERE'S EXPIRED.
WEREN'T THESE THINGS POPULAR IN THE 60'S?
WHY DO YOU THINK HE BRINGS THEM HERE?
LIKE I SAID, "TWISTED FUCK. WANT TO KNOW SOMETHING EVEN STRANGER?
THAT'S THE THIRD MATCH I'VE USED.
THERE'S A DRAFT COMING FROM BEHIND HERE.
WE'RE CLOSE. VERY CLOSE TO SOMETHING OLD, DANGEROUS AND EXACTLY WHAT WE'RE LOOKING FOR.

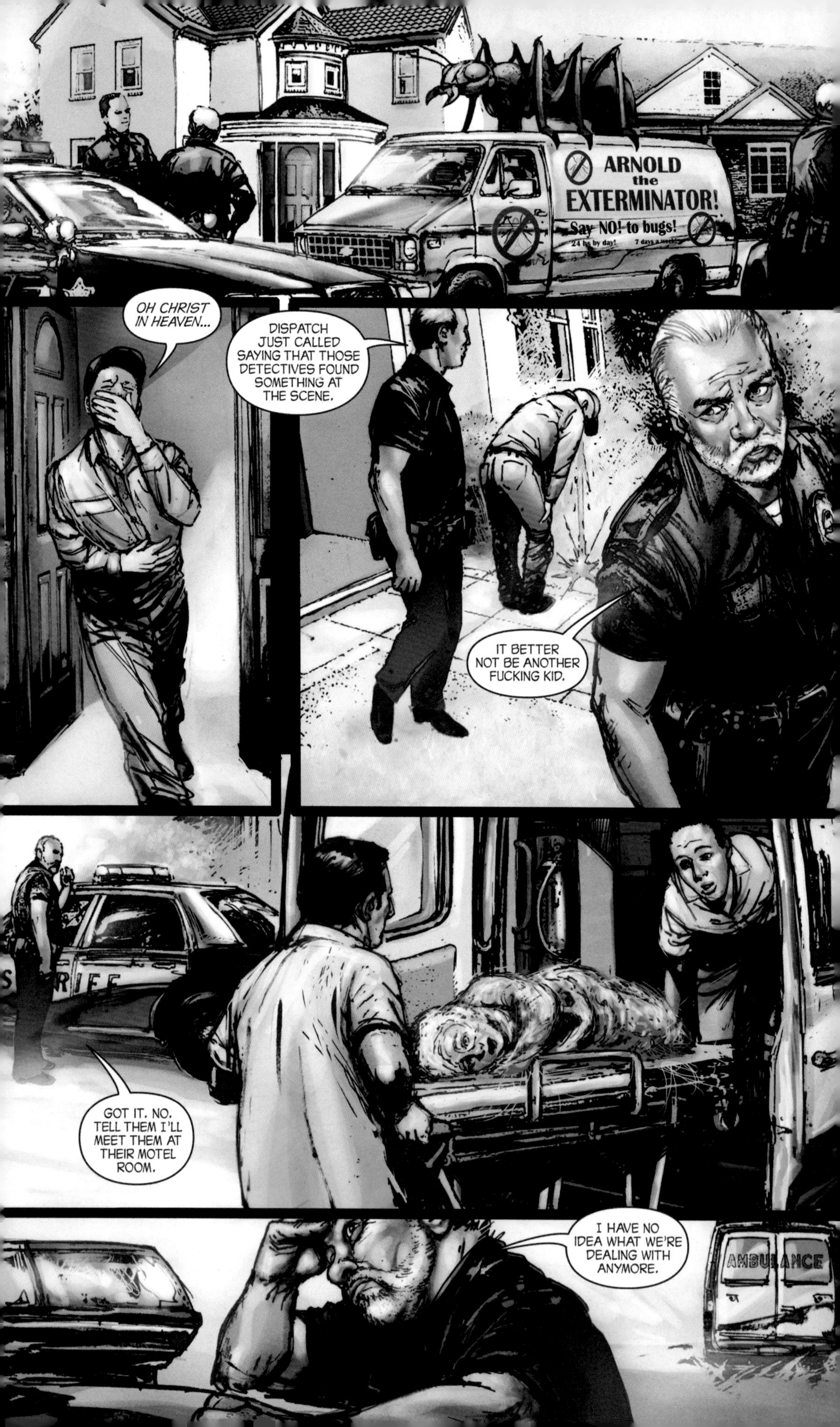
ARNOLD the EXTERMINATOR!
Say NO! to bugs!
24 hs by day! 7 days a week!
OH CHRIST IN HEAVEN...
DISPATCH JUST CALLED SAYING THAT THOSE DETECTIVES FOUND SOMETHING AT THE SCENE.
IT BETTER NOT BE ANOTHER FUCKING KID.
GOT IT. NO. TELL THEM I'LL MEET THEM AT THEIR MOTEL ROOM.
I HAVE NO IDEA WHAT WE'RE DEALING WITH ANYMORE.
AMBULANCE

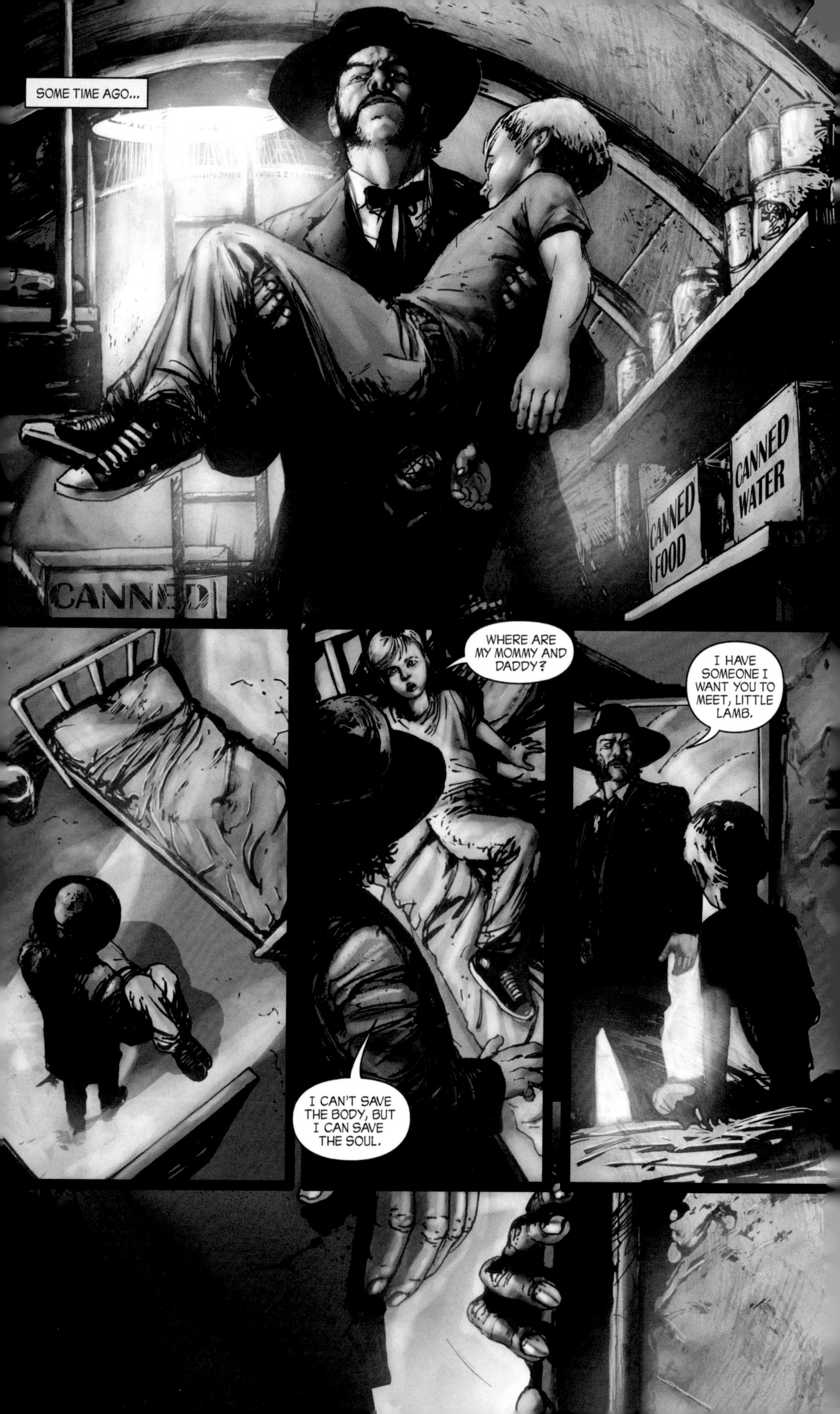
SOME TIME AGO...
CANNED
CANNED FOOD
CANNED WATER
WHERE ARE MY MOMMY AND DADDY?
I CAN'T SAVE THE BODY, BUT I CAN SAVE THE SOUL.
I HAVE SOMEONE I WANT YOU TO MEET, LITTLE LAMB.

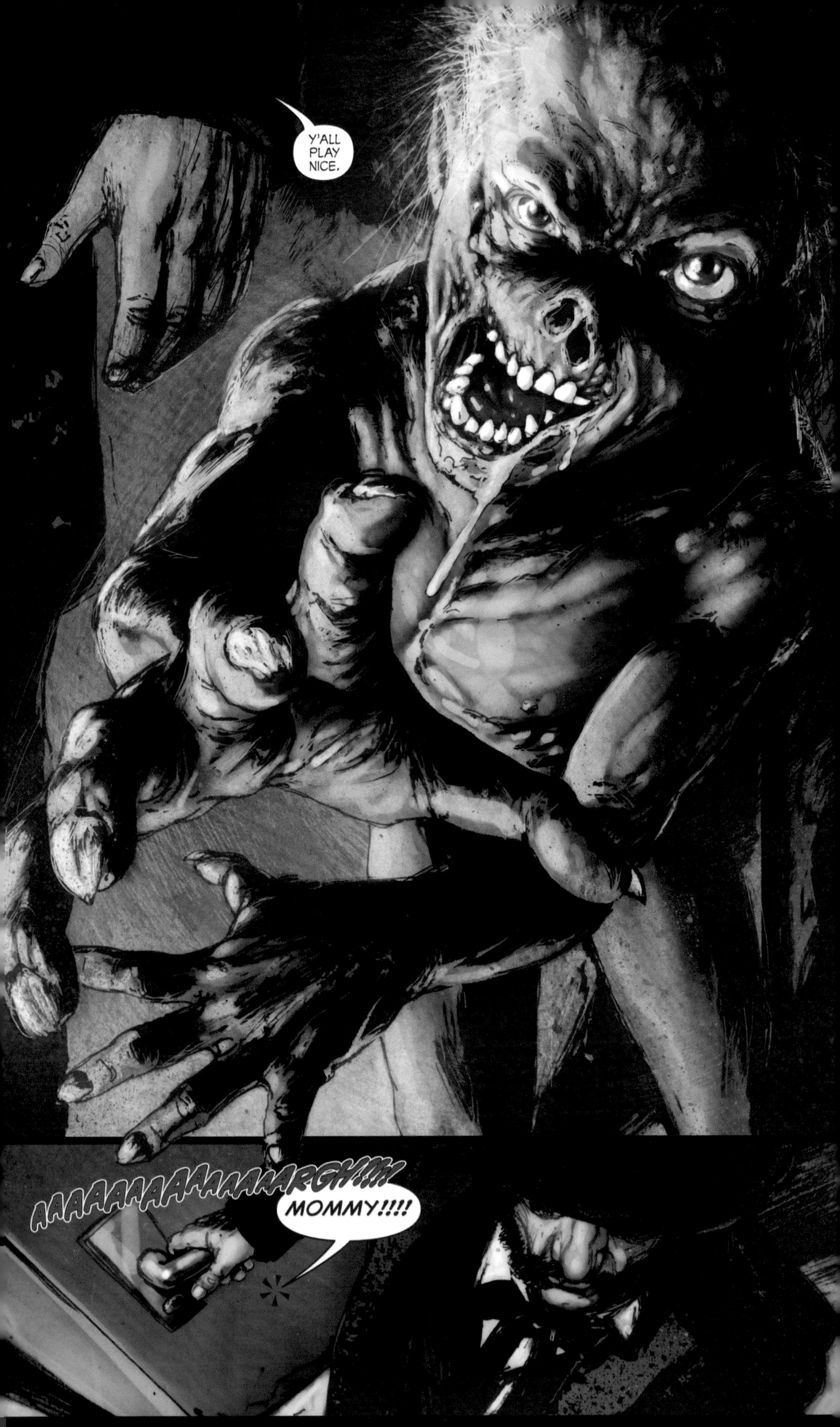
Y'ALL PLAY NICE.
AAAAAAAAAAAAAARGH!!!!
MOMMY!!!!!

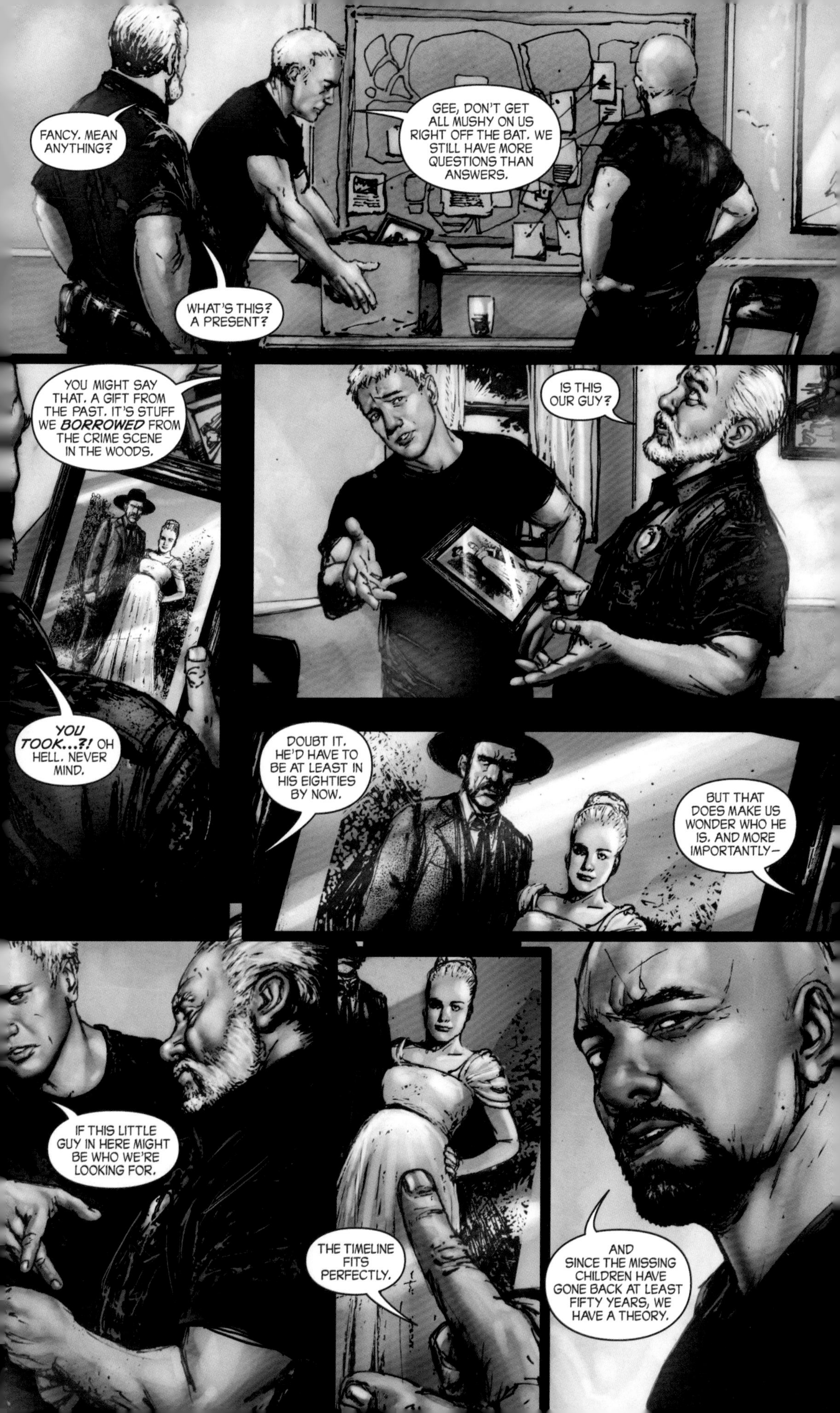
FANCY. MEAN ANYTHING?
GEE, DON'T GET ALL MUSHY ON US RIGHT OFF THE BAT. WE STILL HAVE MORE QUESTIONS THAN ANSWERS.
WHAT'S THIS? A PRESENT?
YOU MIGHT SAY THAT. A GIFT FROM THE PAST. IT'S STUFF WE BORROWED FROM THE CRIME SCENE IN THE WOODS.
YOU TOOK...?! OH HELL. NEVER MIND.
IS THIS OUR GUY?
DOUBT IT. HE'D HAVE TO BE AT LEAST IN HIS EIGHTIES BY NOW.
BUT THAT DOES MAKE US WONDER WHO HE IS. AND MORE IMPORTANTLY—
IF THIS LITTLE GUY IN HERE MIGHT BE WHO WE'RE LOOKING FOR.
THE TIMELINE FITS PERFECTLY.
AND SINCE THE MISSING CHILDREN HAVE GONE BACK AT LEAST FIFTY YEARS, WE HAVE A THEORY.

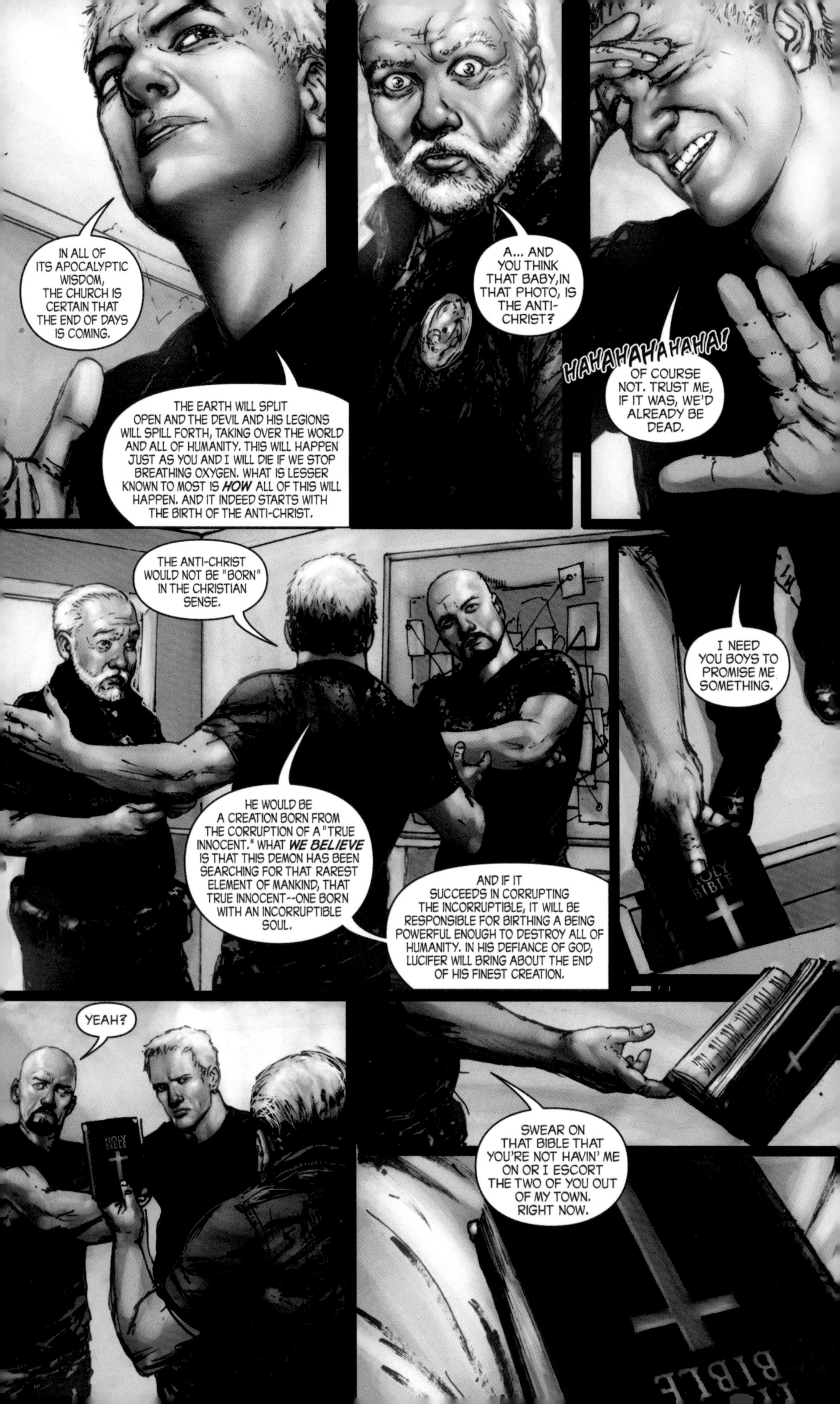
IN ALL OF ITS APOCALYPTIC WISDOM, THE CHURCH IS CERTAIN THAT THE END OF DAYS IS COMING.
THE EARTH WILL SPLIT OPEN AND THE DEVIL AND HIS LEGIONS WILL SPILL FORTH, TAKING OVER THE WORLD AND ALL OF HUMANITY. THIS WILL HAPPEN JUST AS YOU AND I WILL DIE IF WE STOP BREATHING OXYGEN. WHAT IS LESSER KNOWN TO MOST IS *HOW* ALL OF THIS WILL HAPPEN. AND IT INDEED STARTS WITH THE BIRTH OF THE ANTI-CHRIST.
A... AND YOU THINK THAT BABY, IN THAT PHOTO, IS THE ANTI-CHRIST?
HAHAHAHAHAHA!
OF COURSE NOT. TRUST ME, IF IT WAS, WE'D ALREADY BE DEAD.
THE ANTI-CHRIST WOULD NOT BE "BORN" IN THE CHRISTIAN SENSE.
HE WOULD BE A CREATION BORN FROM THE CORRUPTION OF A "TRUE INNOCENT." WHAT *WE BELIEVE* IS THAT THIS DEMON HAS BEEN SEARCHING FOR THAT RAREST ELEMENT OF MANKIND, THAT TRUE INNOCENT--ONE BORN WITH AN INCORRUPTIBLE SOUL.
AND IF IT SUCCEEDS IN CORRUPTING THE INCORRUPTIBLE, IT WILL BE RESPONSIBLE FOR BIRTHING A BEING POWERFUL ENOUGH TO DESTROY ALL OF HUMANITY. IN HIS DEFIANCE OF GOD, LUCIFER WILL BRING ABOUT THE END OF HIS FINEST CREATION.
I NEED YOU BOYS TO PROMISE ME SOMETHING.
HOLY BIBLE
YEAH?
HOLY BIBLE
SWEAR ON THAT BIBLE THAT YOU'RE NOT HAVIN' ME ON OR I ESCORT THE TWO OF YOU OUT OF MY TOWN. RIGHT NOW.
BIBLE

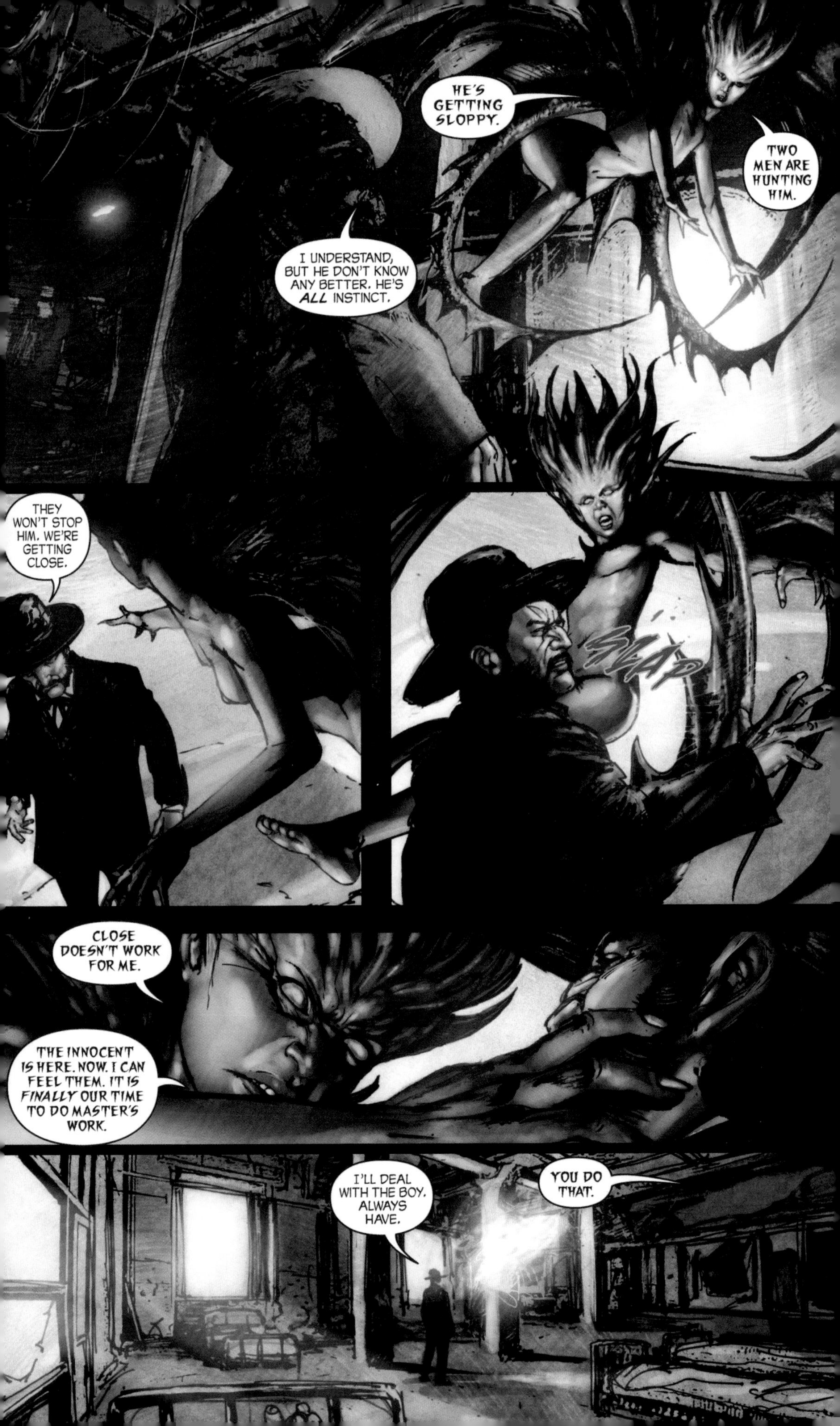
HE'S GETTING SLOPPY.
TWO MEN ARE HUNTING HIM.
I UNDERSTAND, BUT HE DON'T KNOW ANY BETTER. HE'S ALL INSTINCT.
THEY WON'T STOP HIM. WE'RE GETTING CLOSE.
SLAP
CLOSE DOESN'T WORK FOR ME.
THE INNOCENT IS HERE. NOW. I CAN FEEL THEM. IT IS FINALLY OUR TIME TO DO MASTER'S WORK.
I'LL DEAL WITH THE BOY. ALWAYS HAVE.
YOU DO THAT.

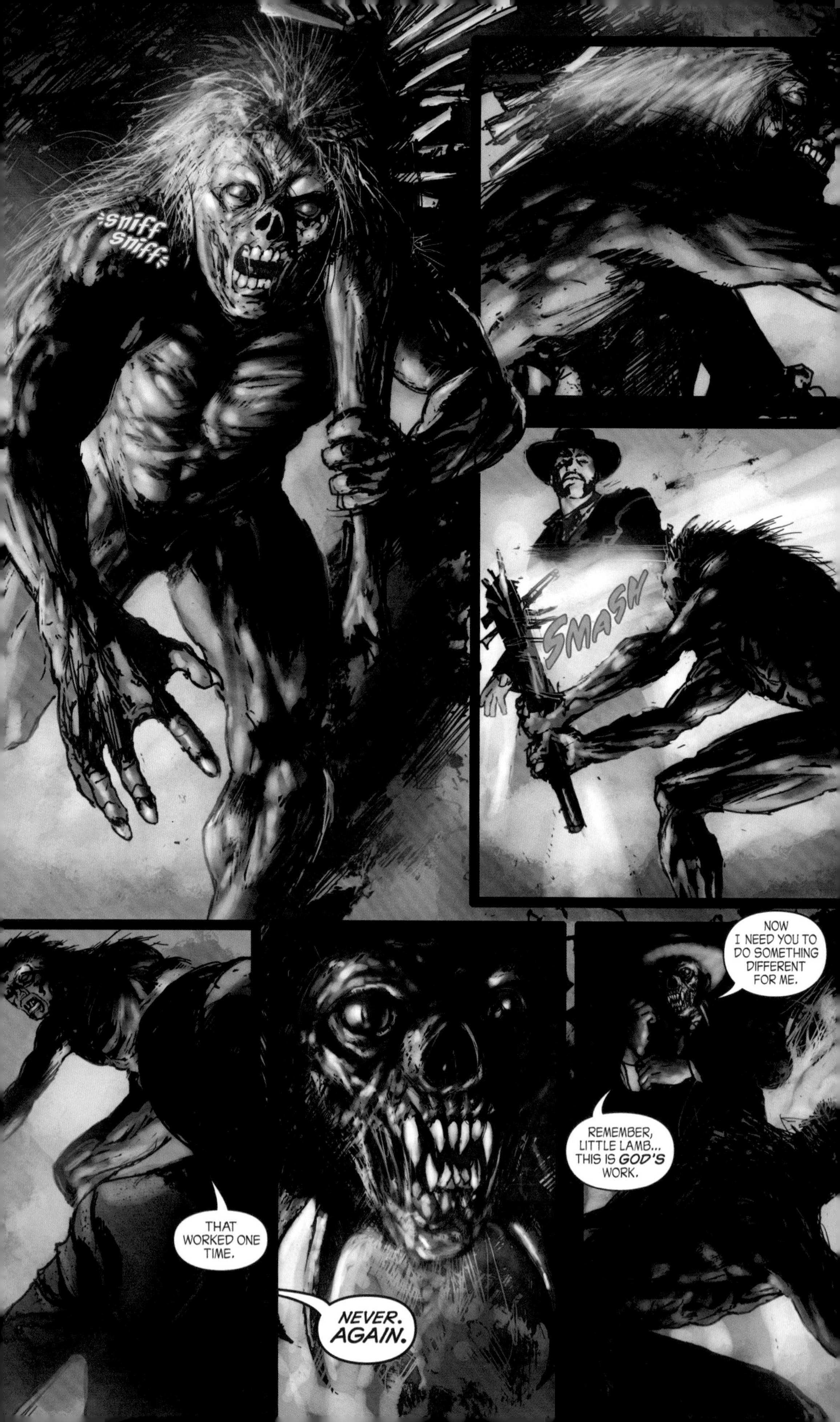
SNIFF SNIFF
SMASH
THAT WORKED ONE TIME.
NEVER. AGAIN.
NOW I NEED YOU TO DO SOMETHING DIFFERENT FOR ME.
REMEMBER, LITTLE LAMB... THIS IS GOD'S WORK.

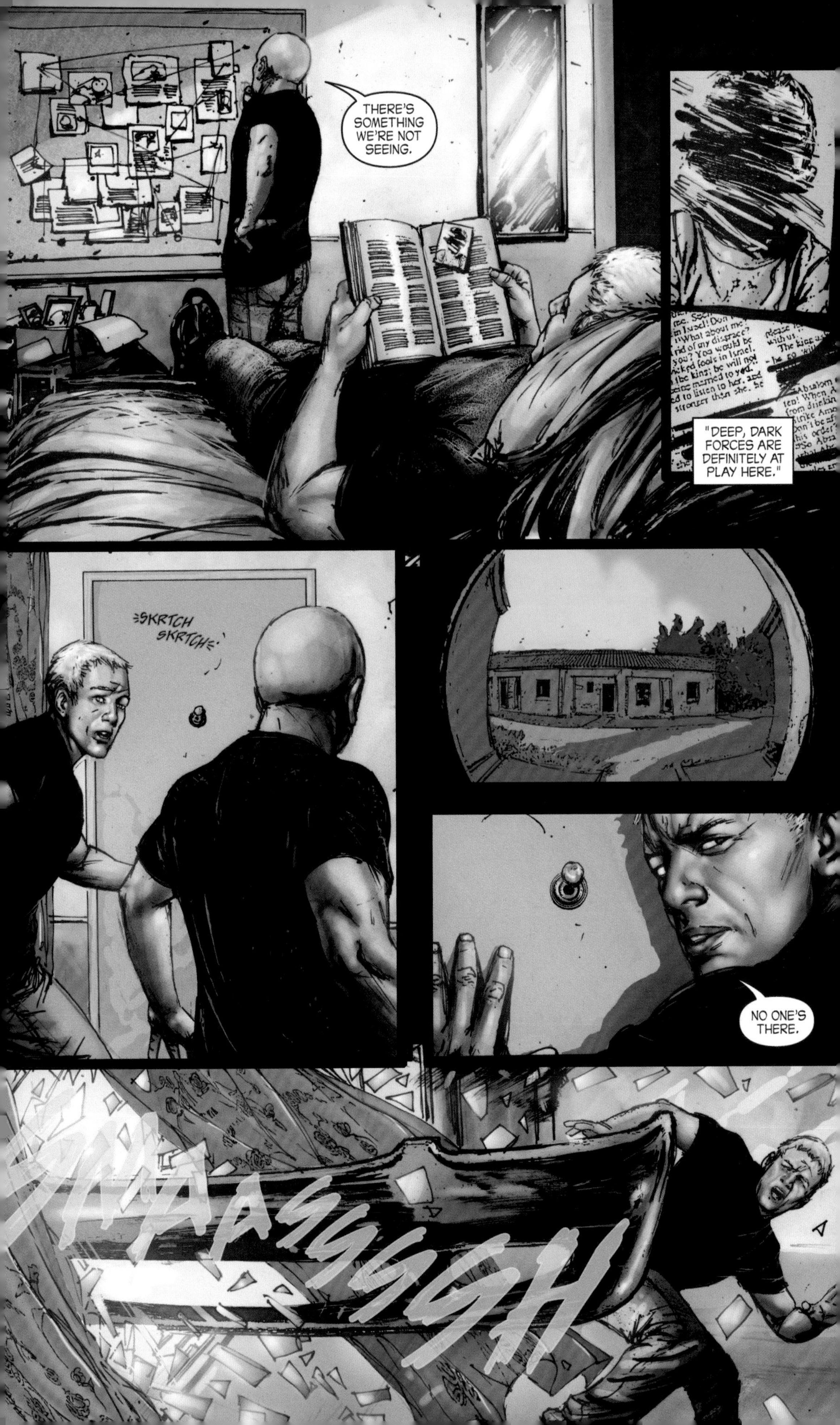
THERE'S SOMETHING WE'RE NOT SEEING.
"DEEP, DARK FORCES ARE DEFINITELY AT PLAY HERE."
SKRTCH SKRTCH
NO ONE'S THERE.

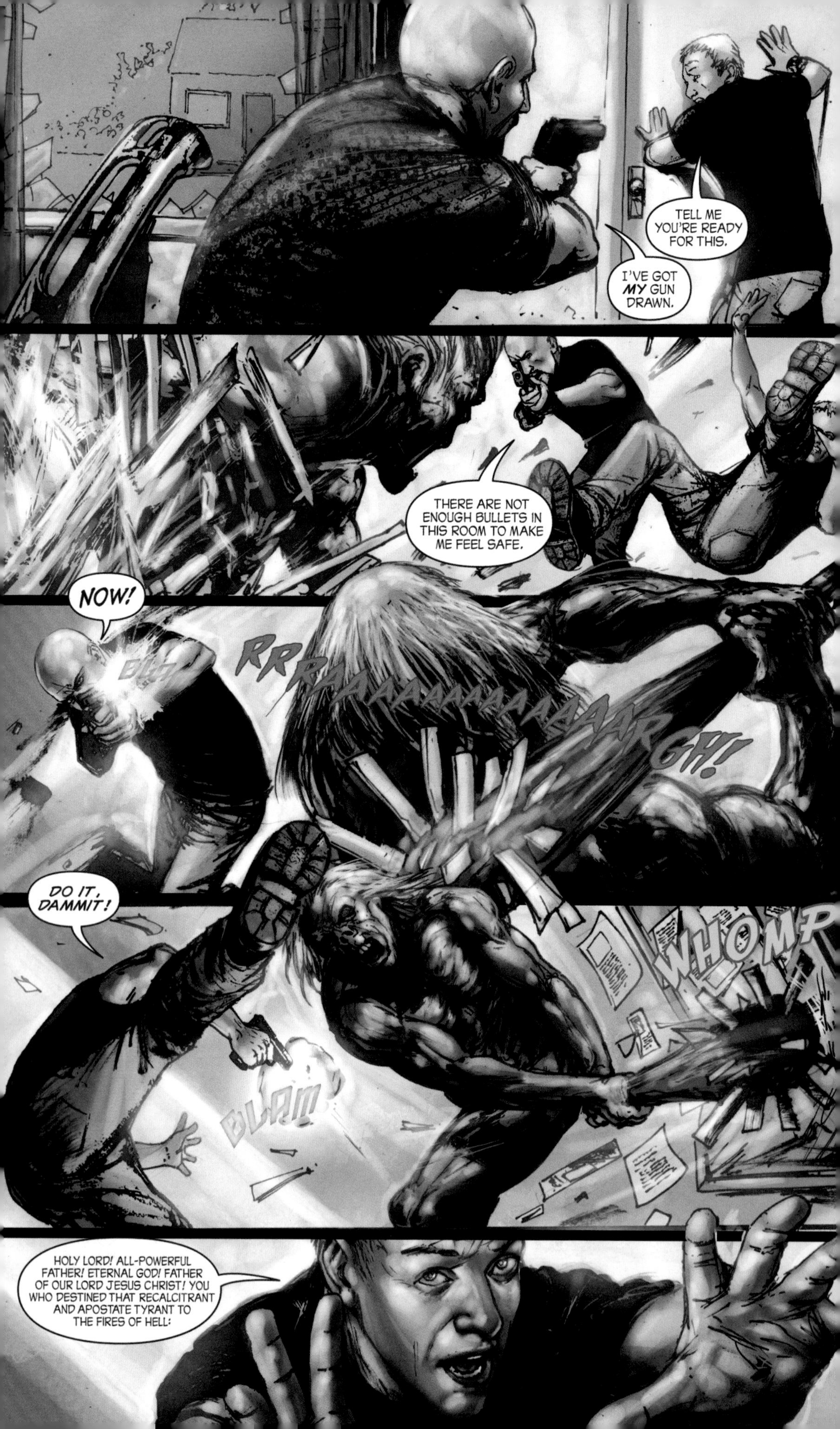
TELL ME YOU'RE READY FOR THIS.
I'VE GOT *MY* GUN DRAWN.
THERE ARE NOT ENOUGH BULLETS IN THIS ROOM TO MAKE ME FEEL SAFE.
NOW!
RRRAAAAAAAAAAAARGH!
DO IT, DAMMIT!
WHOMP
BLAM
HOLY LORD! ALL-POWERFUL FATHER! ETERNAL GOD! FATHER OF OUR LORD JESUS CHRIST! YOU WHO DESTINED THAT RECALCITRANT AND APOSTATE TYRANT TO THE FIRES OF HELL:

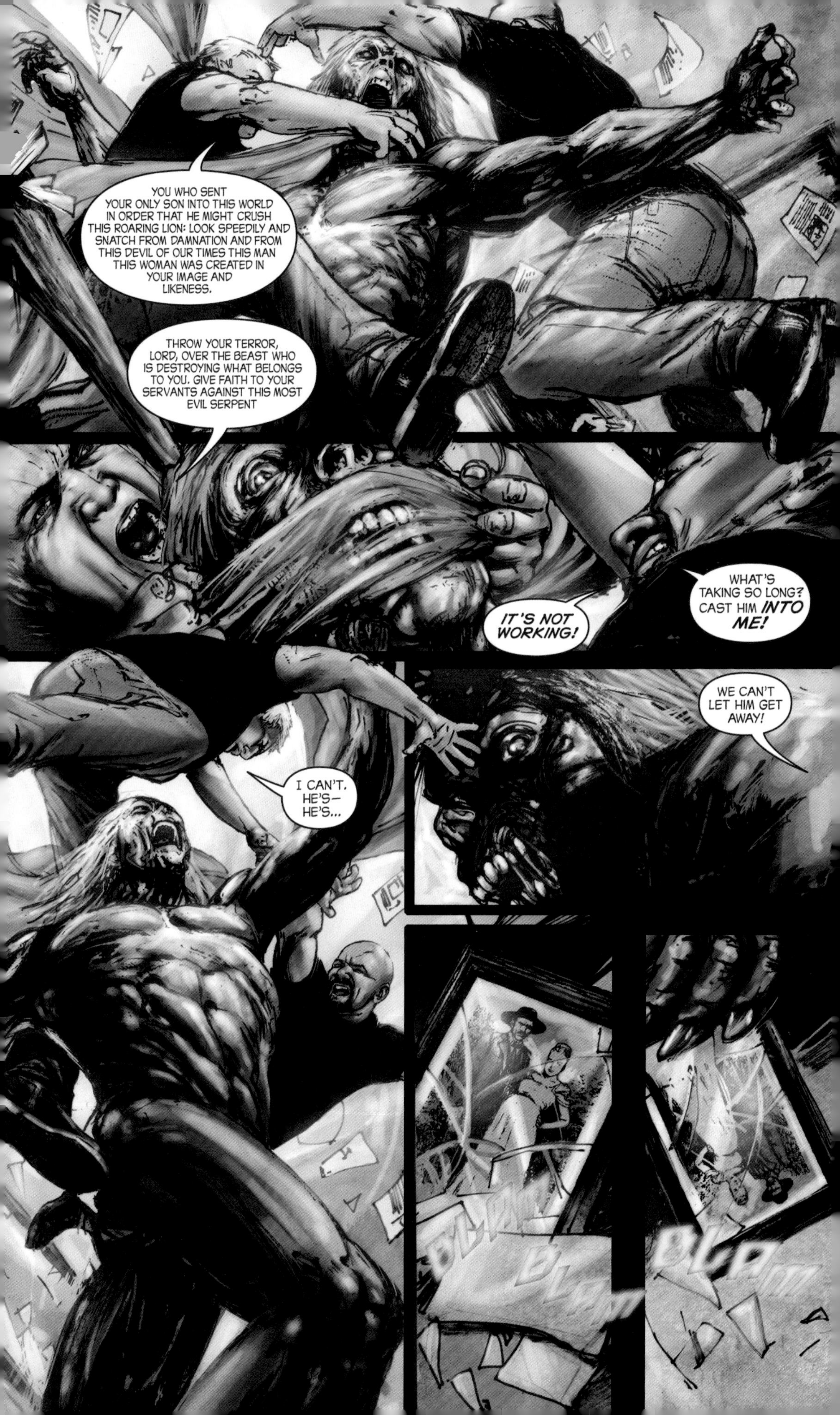
YOU WHO SENT YOUR ONLY SON INTO THIS WORLD IN ORDER THAT HE MIGHT CRUSH THIS ROARING LION: LOOK SPEEDILY AND SNATCH FROM DAMNATION AND FROM THIS DEVIL OF OUR TIMES THIS MAN THIS WOMAN WAS CREATED IN YOUR IMAGE AND LIKENESS.
THROW YOUR TERROR, LORD, OVER THE BEAST WHO IS DESTROYING WHAT BELONGS TO YOU. GIVE FAITH TO YOUR SERVANTS AGAINST THIS MOST EVIL SERPENT
IT'S NOT WORKING!
WHAT'S TAKING SO LONG? CAST HIM INTO ME!
I CAN'T. HE'S— HE'S...
WE CAN'T LET HIM GET AWAY!

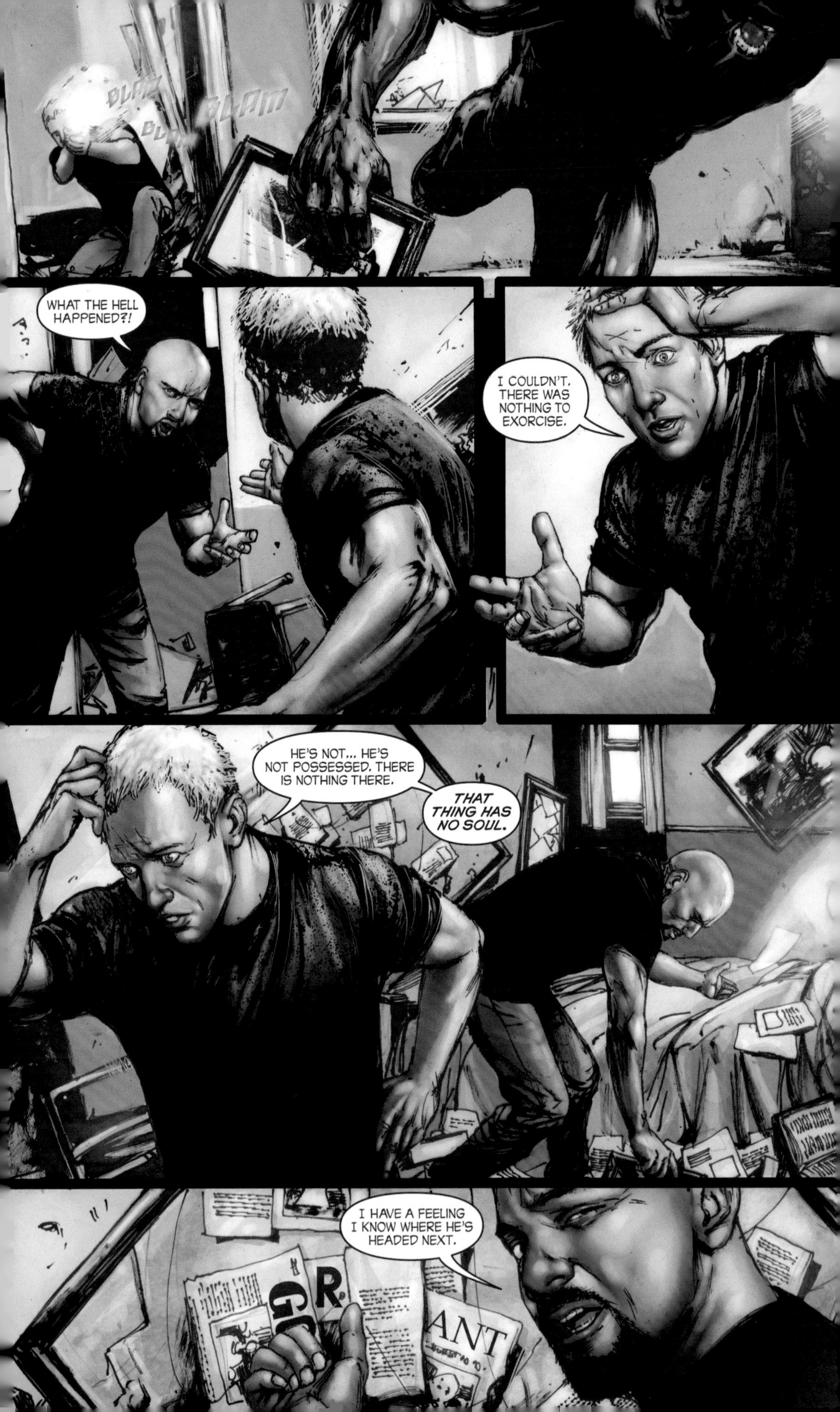
BLAM
BLAM
BLAM
WHAT THE HELL HAPPENED?!
I COULDN'T. THERE WAS NOTHING TO EXORCISE.
HE'S NOT... HE'S NOT POSSESSED. THERE IS NOTHING THERE.
THAT THING HAS NO SOUL.
I HAVE A FEELING I KNOW WHERE HE'S HEADED NEXT.

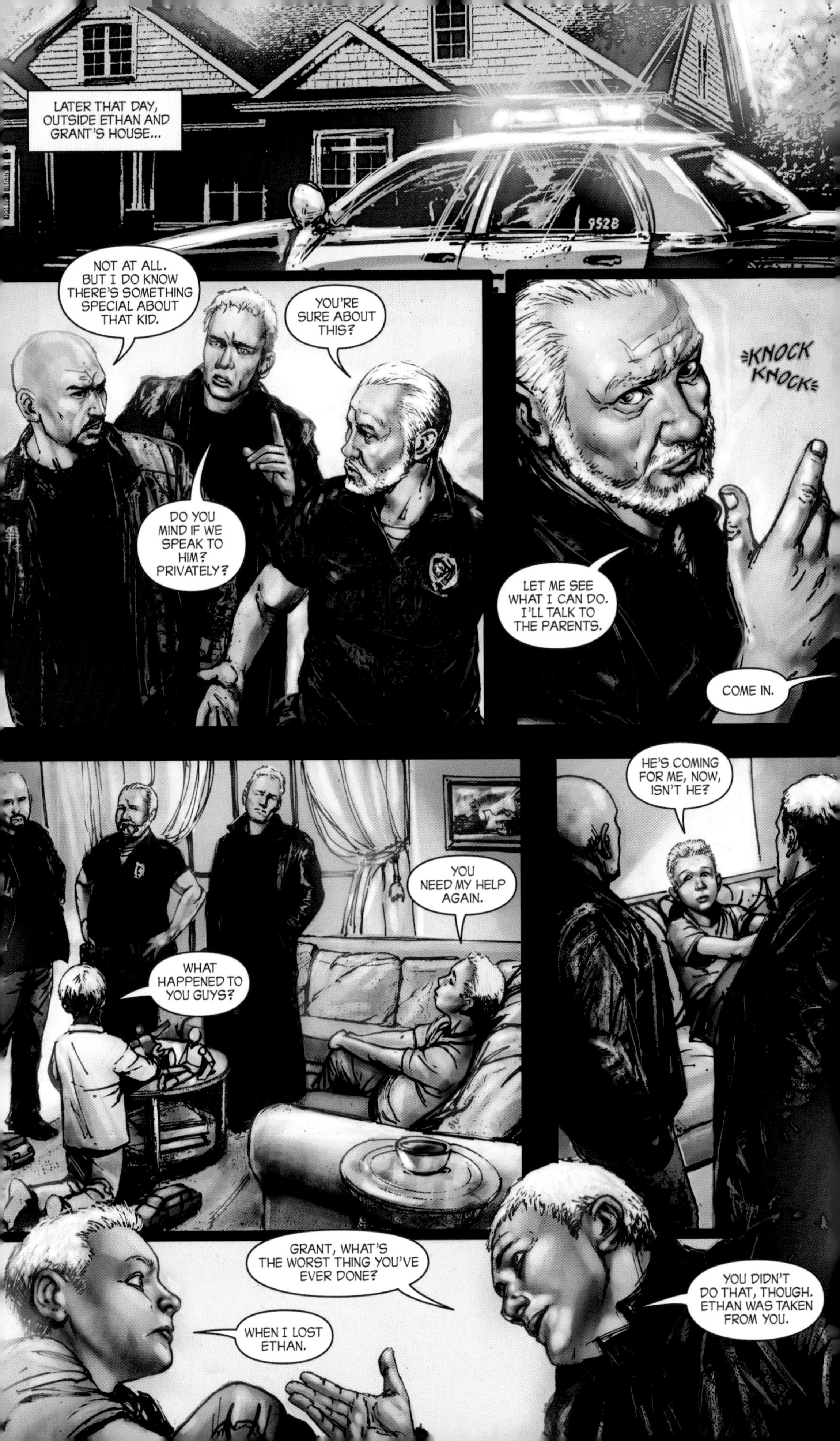
LATER THAT DAY, OUTSIDE ETHAN AND GRANT'S HOUSE...
9528
NOT AT ALL. BUT I DO KNOW THERE'S SOMETHING SPECIAL ABOUT THAT KID.
YOU'RE SURE ABOUT THIS?
DO YOU MIND IF WE SPEAK TO HIM? PRIVATELY?
KNOCK KNOCK
LET ME SEE WHAT I CAN DO. I'LL TALK TO THE PARENTS.
COME IN.
YOU NEED MY HELP AGAIN.
WHAT HAPPENED TO YOU GUYS?
HE'S COMING FOR ME, NOW, ISN'T HE?
GRANT, WHAT'S THE WORST THING YOU'VE EVER DONE?
WHEN I LOST ETHAN.
YOU DIDN'T DO THAT, THOUGH. ETHAN WAS TAKEN FROM YOU.

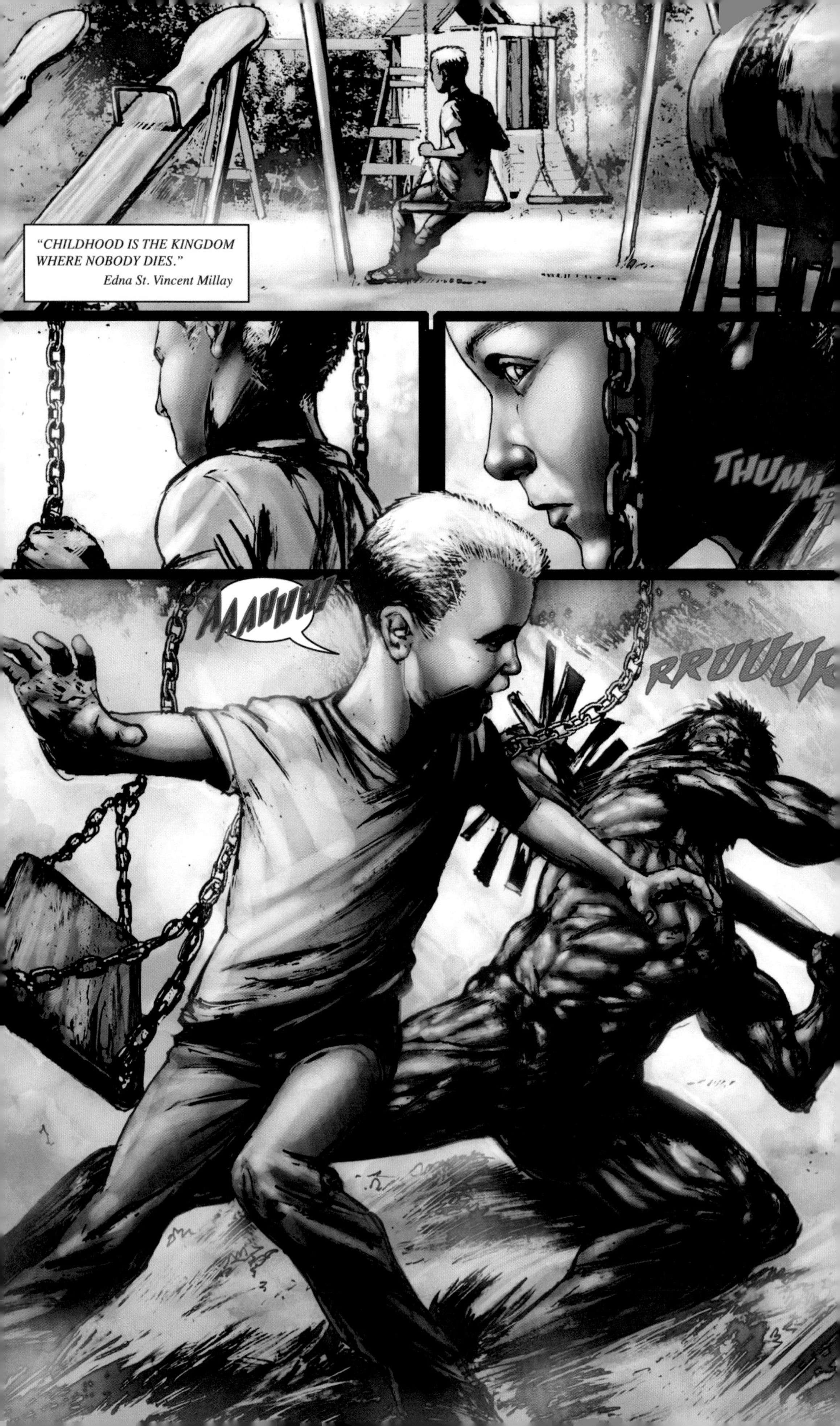
"CHILDHOOD IS THE KINGDOM WHERE NOBODY DIES."
Edna St. Vincent Millay
THUMM
AAAHHH!
RRUUUR

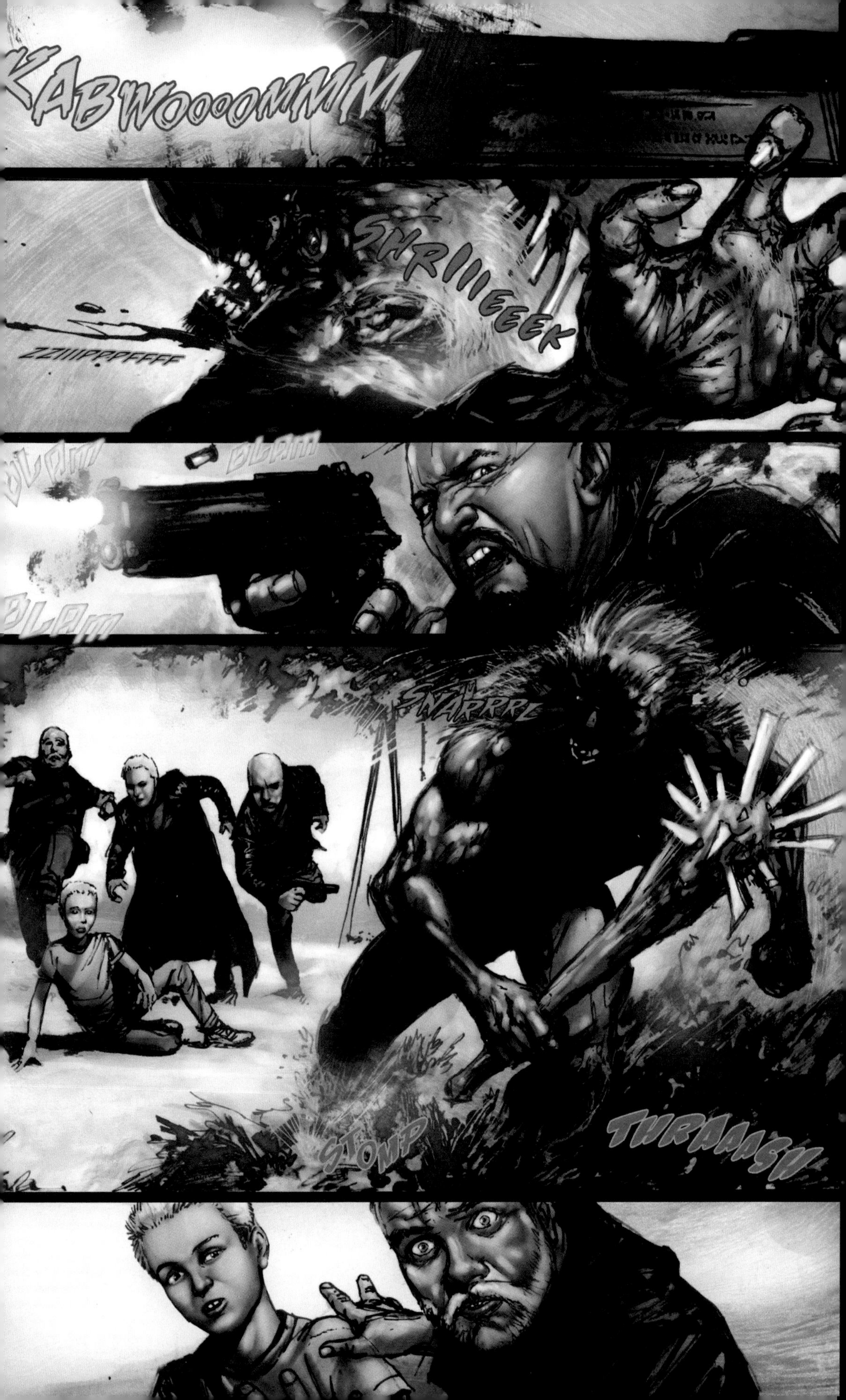
KABWOOOOMMM
SHRIIIIEEEK
ZZIIIPPPFFFF
BLAM
BLAM
BLAM
SNARRRL
STOMP
THRAAASH

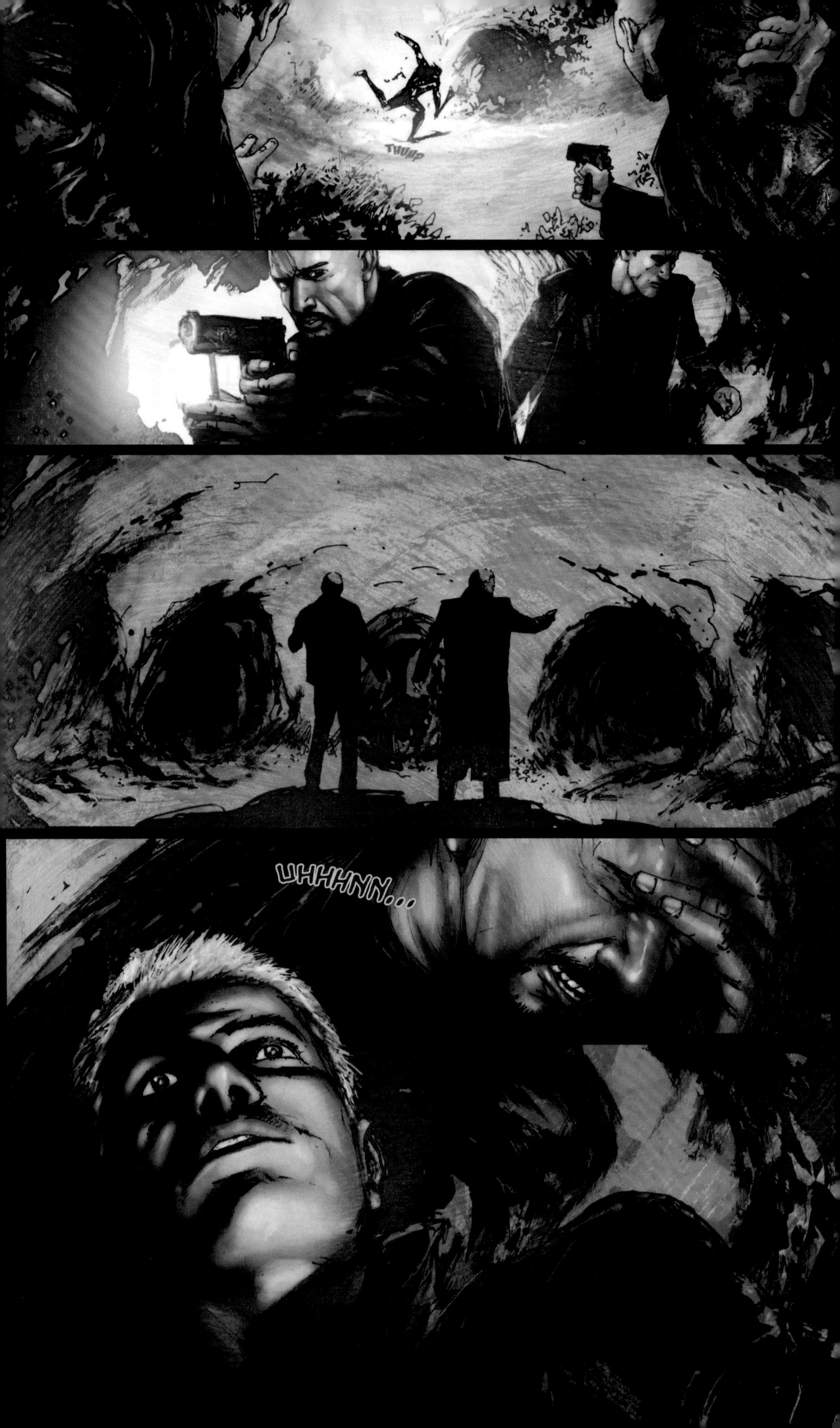
THUMP
UHHHNN...

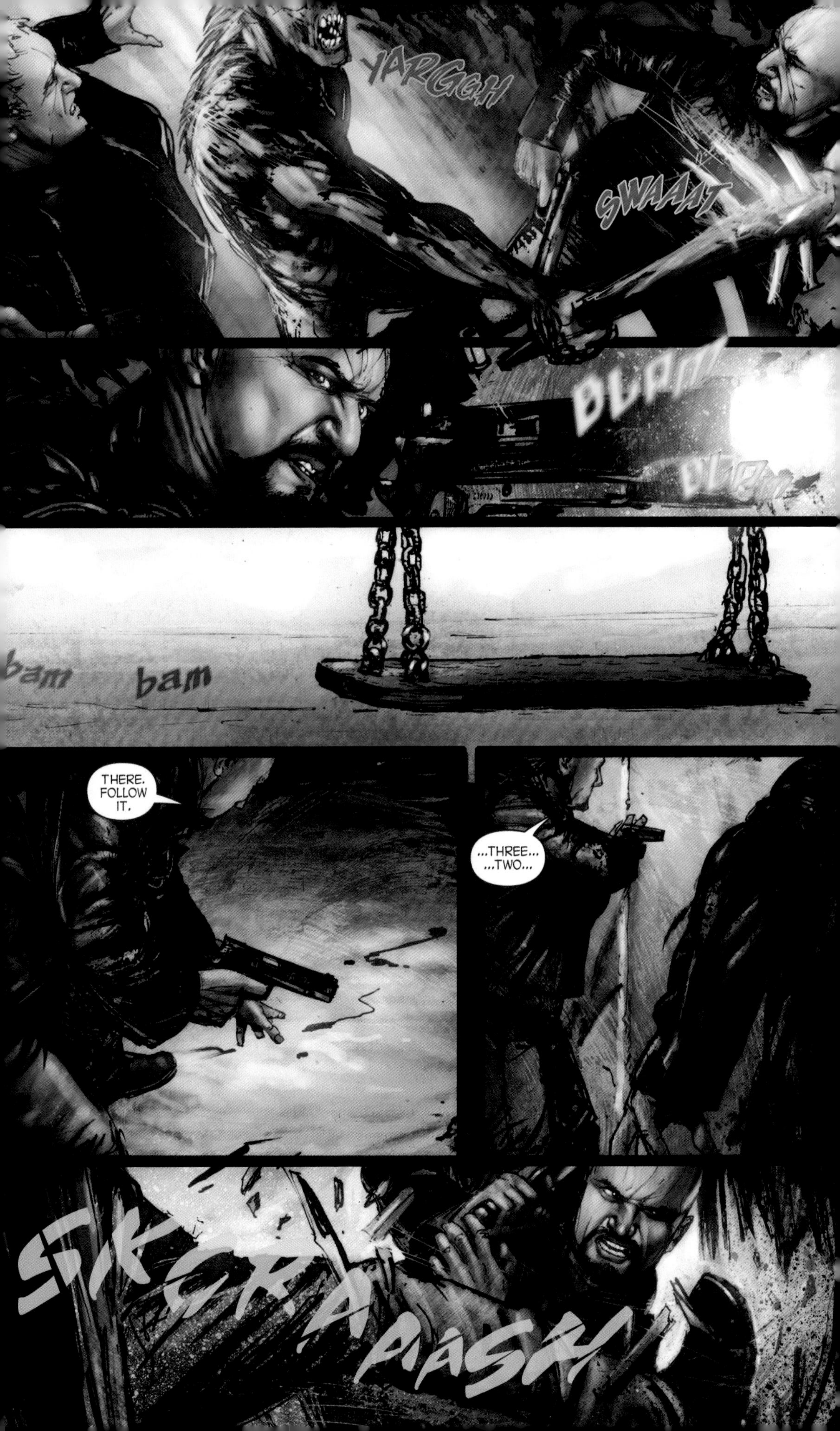
YARGGH
SWAAAT
BLAM
BLAM
bam
bam
THERE. FOLLOW IT.
...THREE... ...TWO...

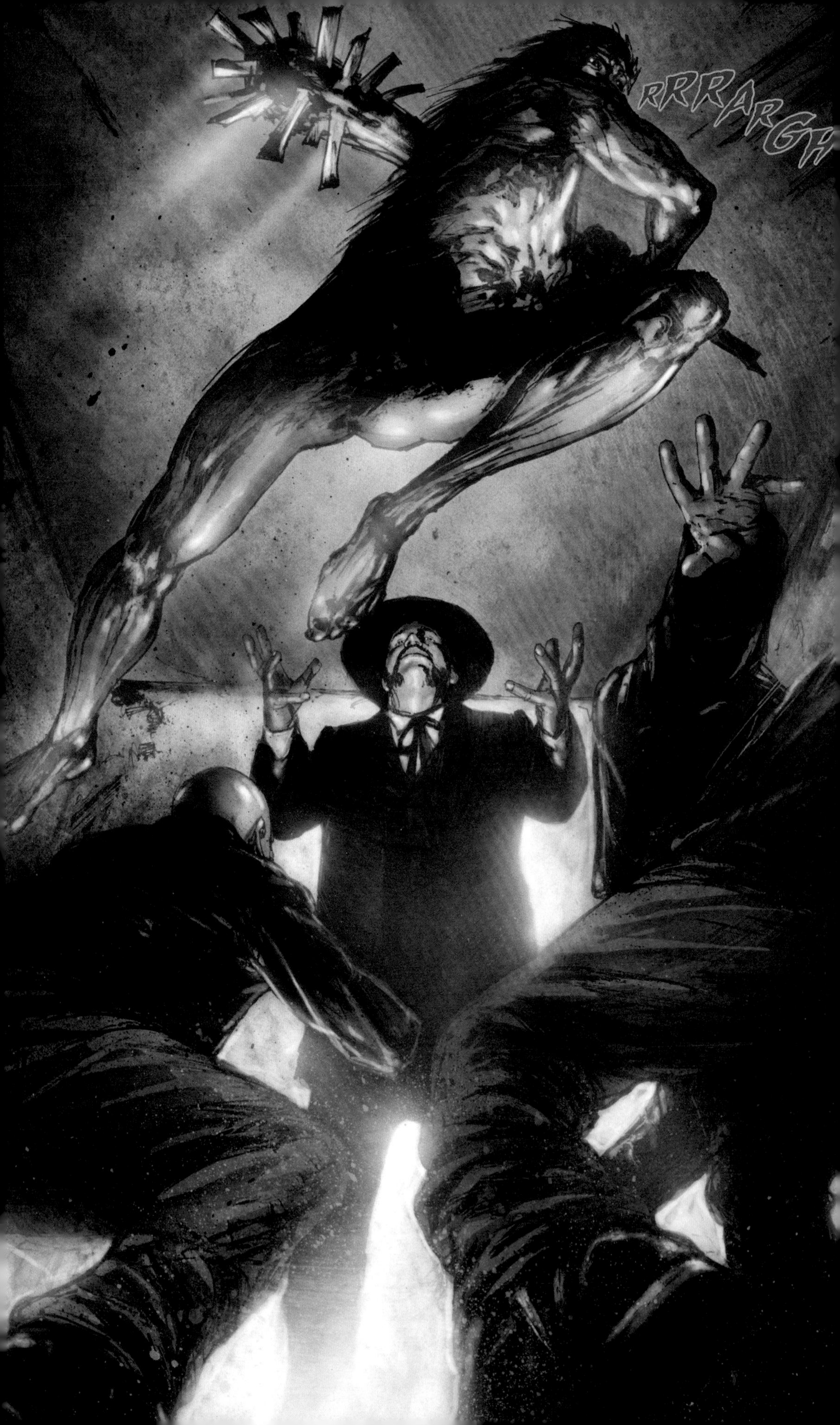
RRRARGH

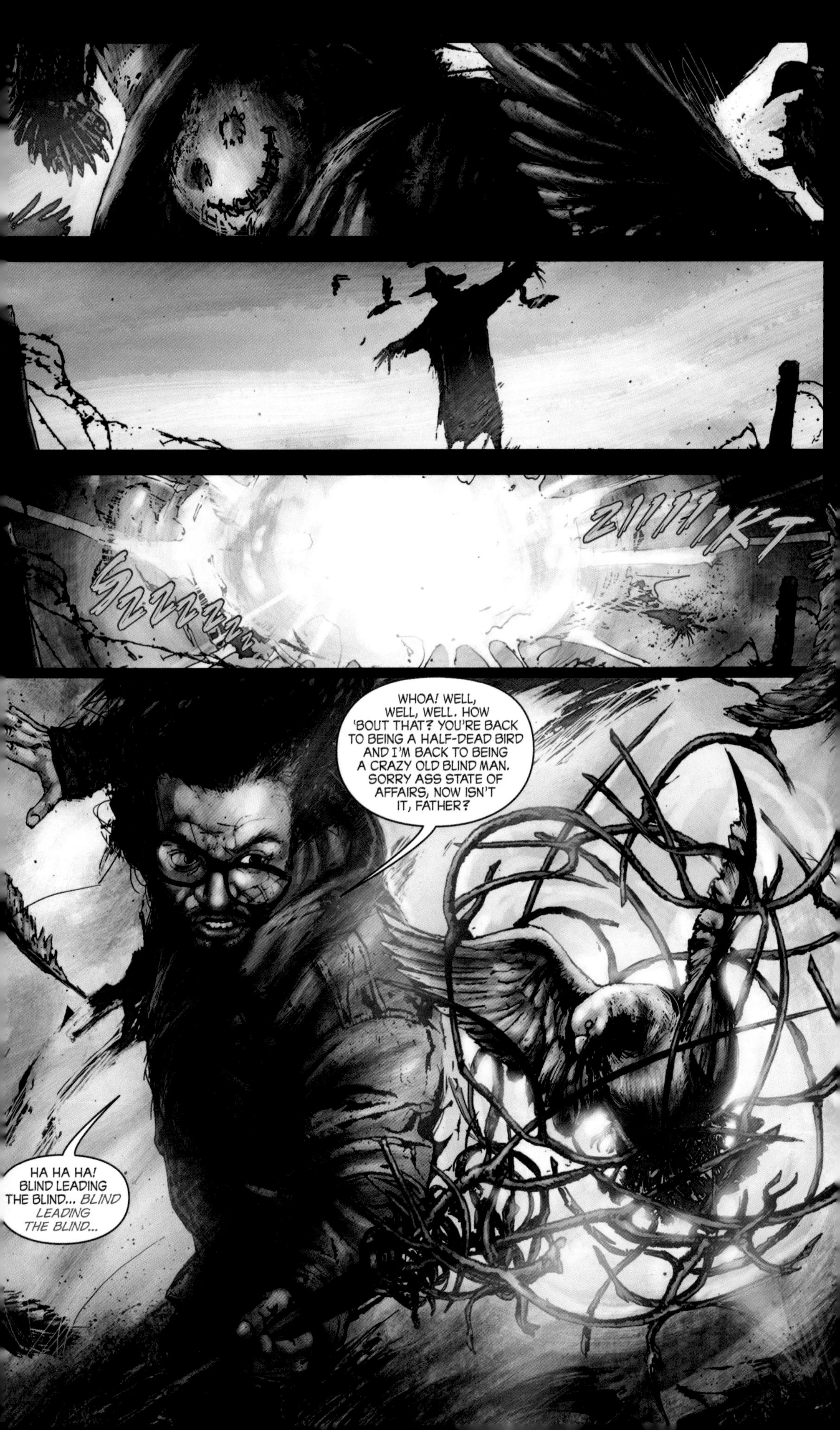
ZIIIIIKT
SZZZZZZZZ
WHOA! WELL, WELL, WELL. HOW 'BOUT THAT? YOU'RE BACK TO BEING A HALF-DEAD BIRD AND I'M BACK TO BEING A CRAZY OLD BLIND MAN. SORRY ASS STATE OF AFFAIRS, NOW ISN'T IT, FATHER?
HA HA HA! BLIND LEADING THE BLIND... *BLIND LEADING THE BLIND...*

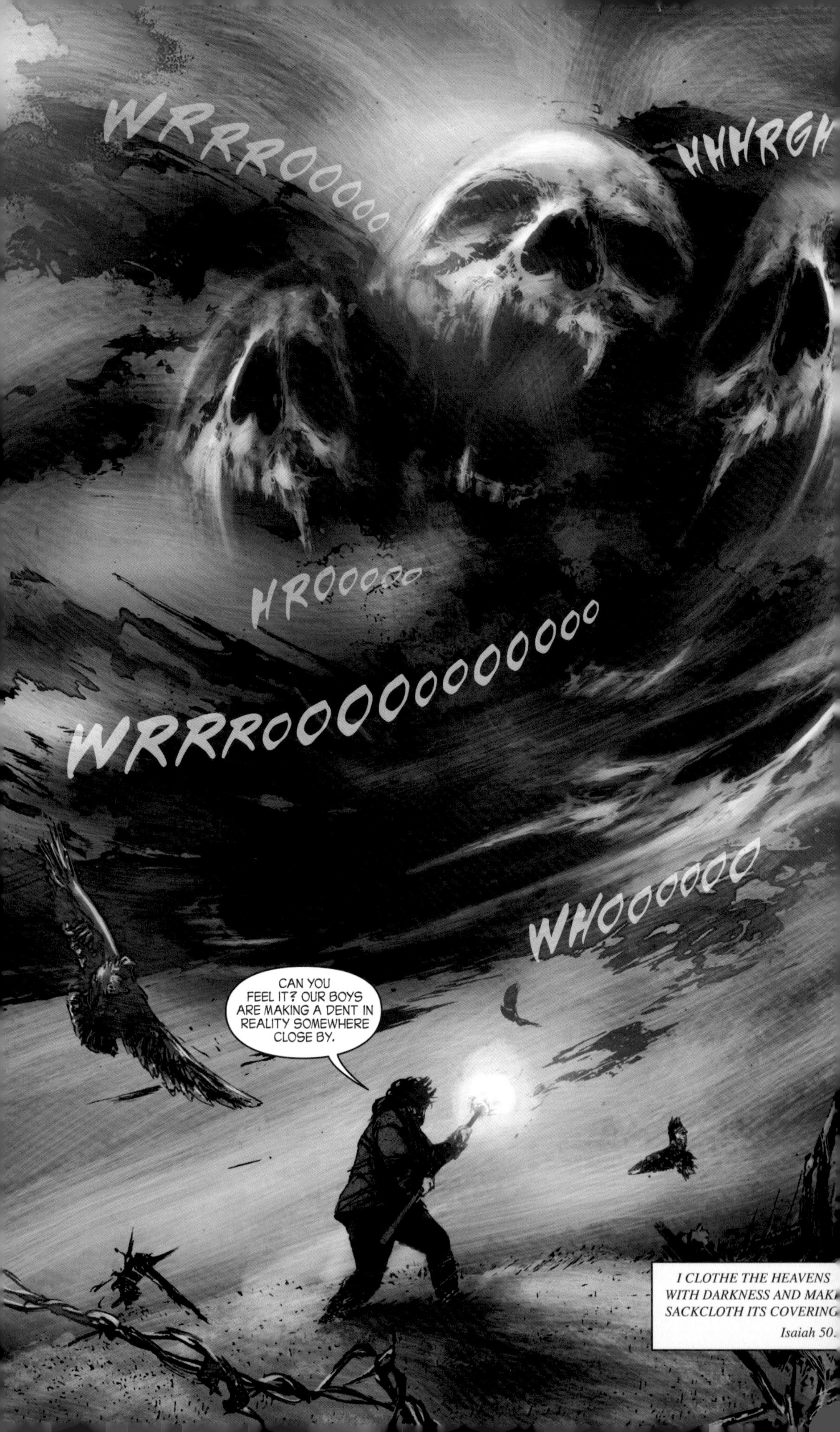
WRRROOOOOO
HHHRGH
HROOOOO
WRRROOOOOOOOOOOO
WHOOOOOO
CAN YOU FEEL IT? OUR BOYS ARE MAKING A DENT IN REALITY SOMEWHERE CLOSE BY.
I CLOTHE THE HEAVENS WITH DARKNESS AND MAK SACKCLOTH ITS COVERING
Isaiah 50.

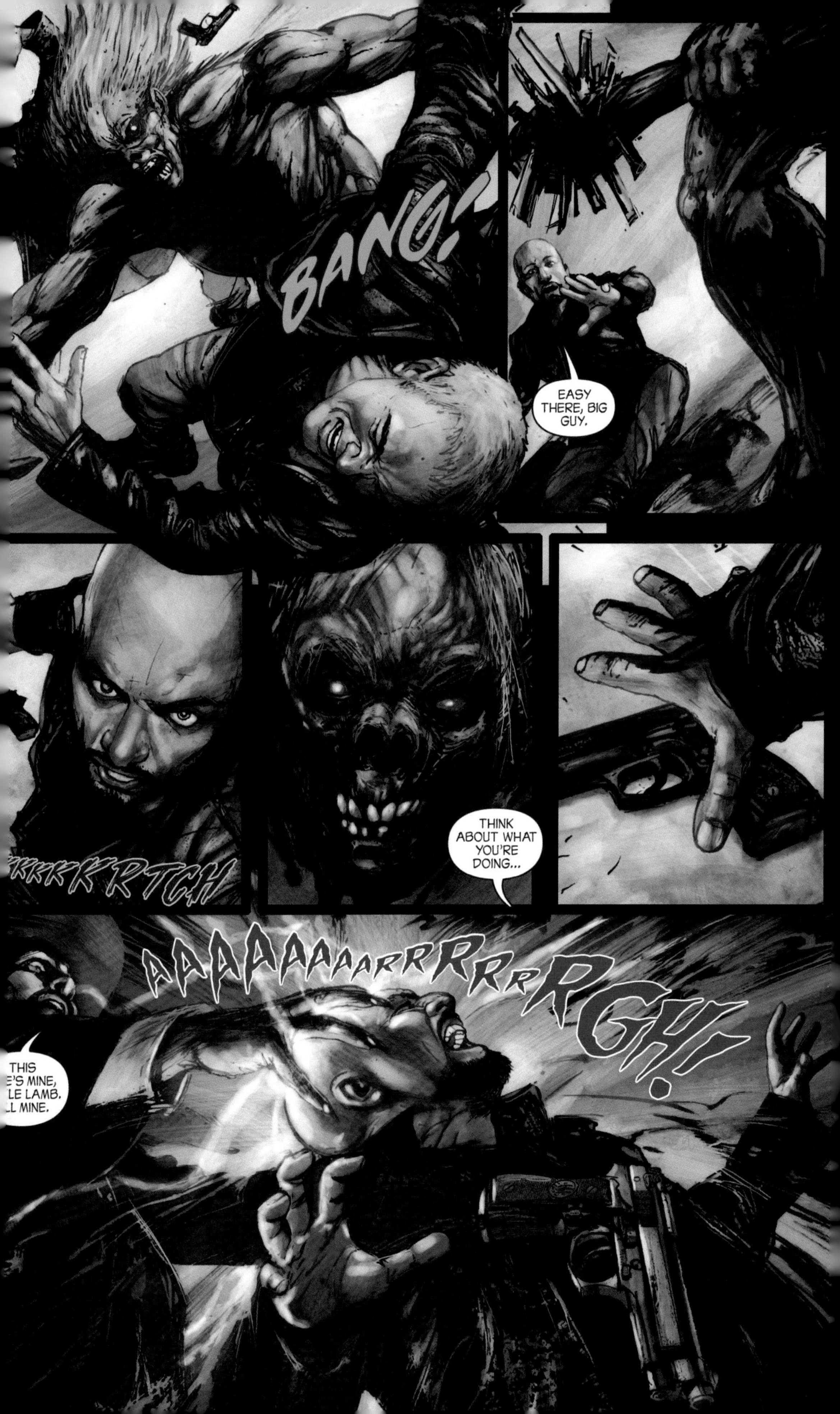
BANG!
EASY THERE, BIG GUY.
KKKKKRTCH
THINK ABOUT WHAT YOU'RE DOING...
AAAAAAAARRRRRRRGH!
THIS
E'S MINE,
LE LAMB.
L MINE.

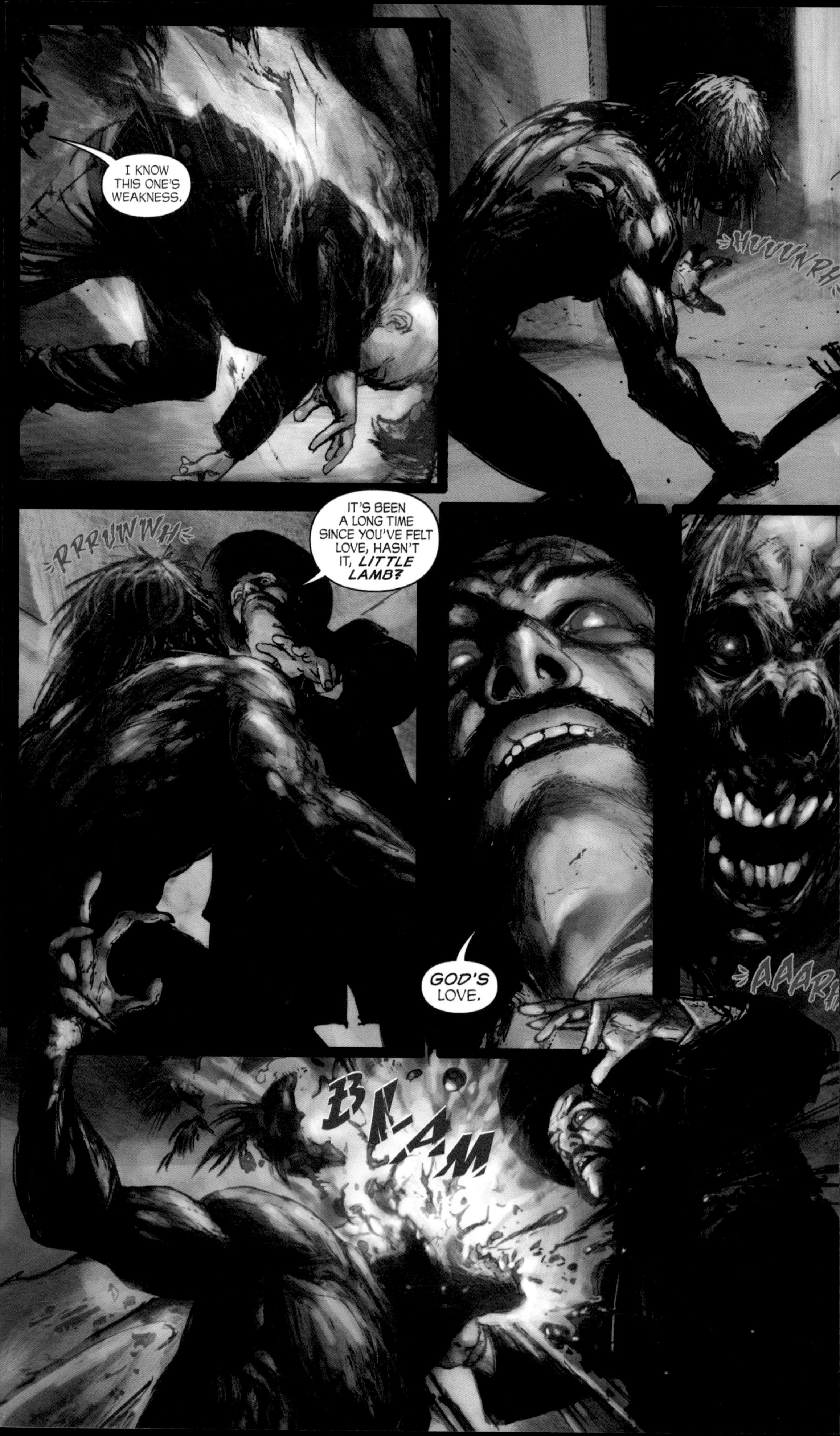
I KNOW THIS ONE'S WEAKNESS.
HUUUNRH
RRRUNWH
IT'S BEEN A LONG TIME SINCE YOU'VE FELT LOVE, HASN'T IT, *LITTLE LAMB?*
GOD'S LOVE.
AAARH
BLAM

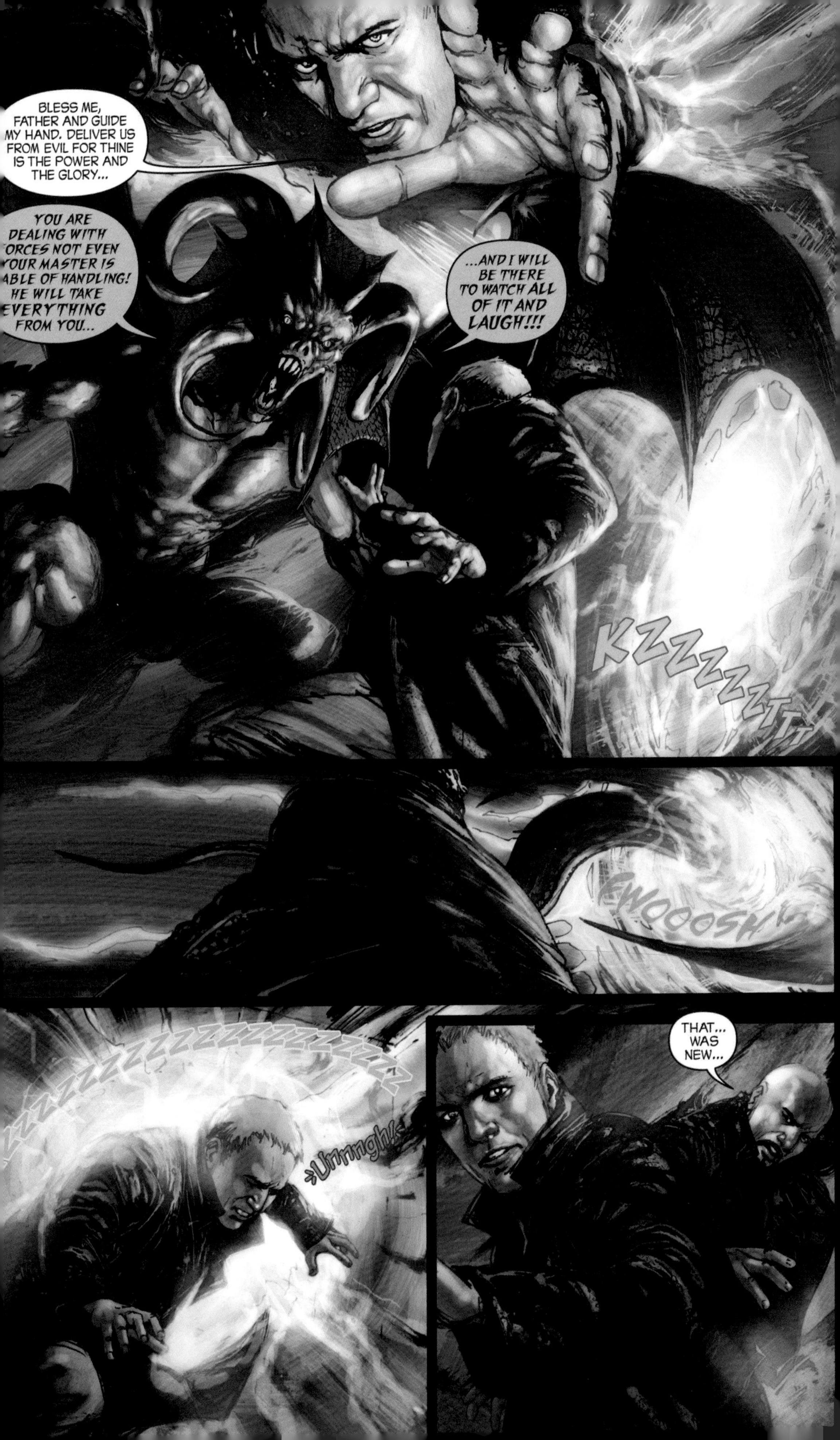
BLESS ME, FATHER AND GUIDE MY HAND. DELIVER US FROM EVIL FOR THINE IS THE POWER AND THE GLORY...
YOU ARE DEALING WITH FORCES NOT EVEN YOUR MASTER IS ABLE OF HANDLING! HE WILL TAKE EVERYTHING FROM YOU...
...AND I WILL BE THERE TO WATCH ALL OF IT AND LAUGH!!!
KZZZZZZTTT
KWOOOSH
ZZZZZZZZZZZZZZZZZZZZZZZ
Unnngh!!
THAT... WAS NEW...

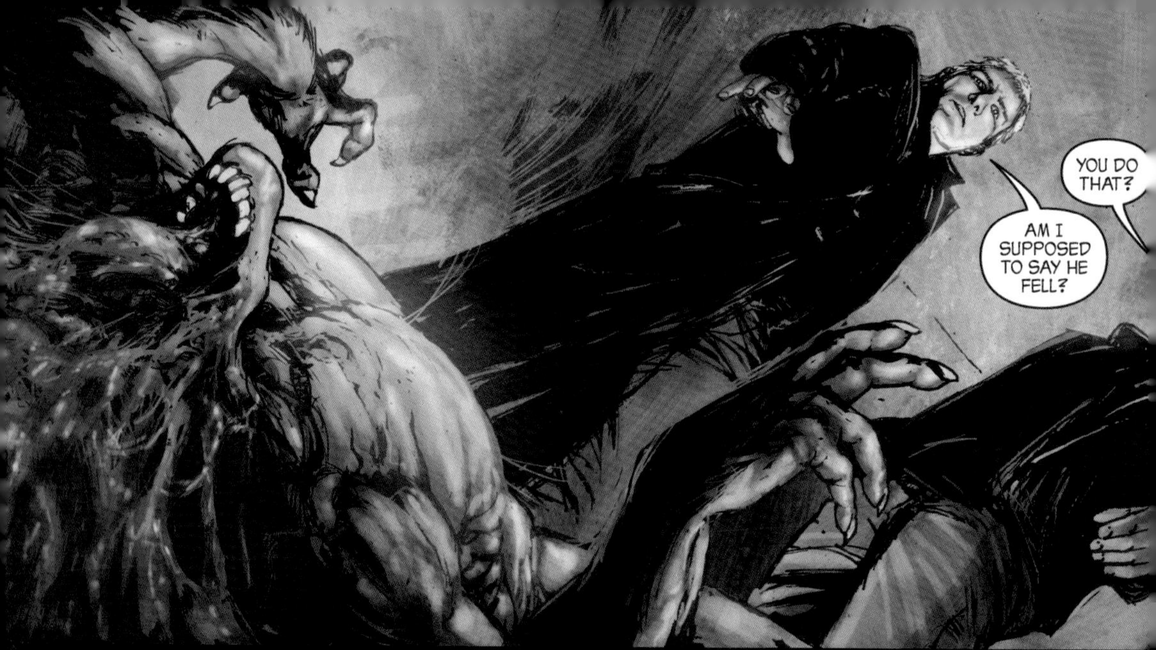
YOU DO THAT?
AM I SUPPOSED TO SAY HE FELL?
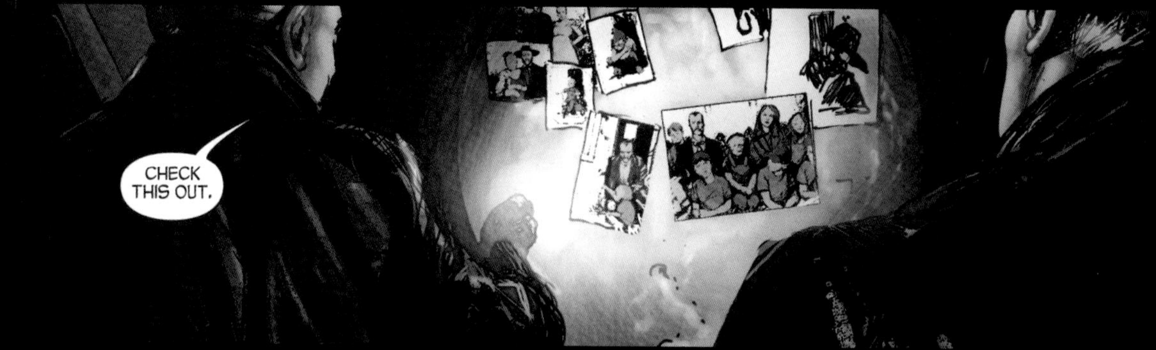
CHECK THIS OUT.
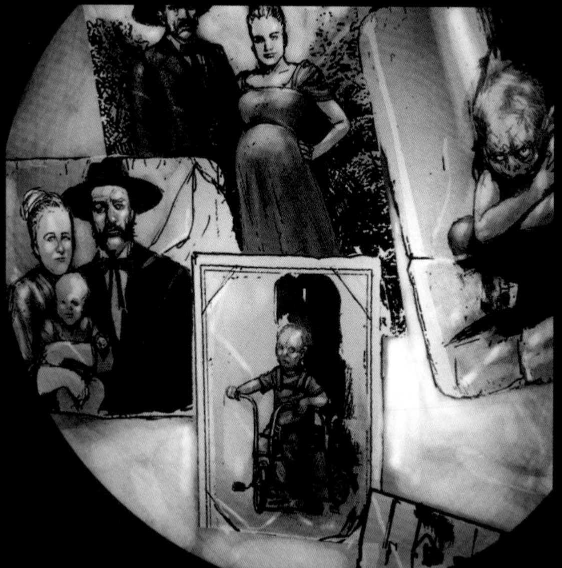
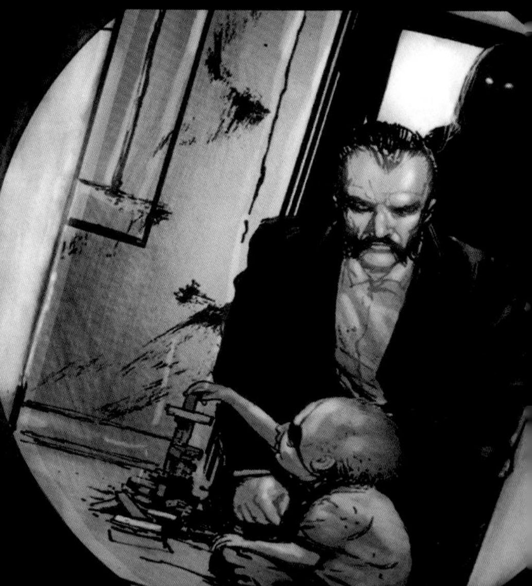
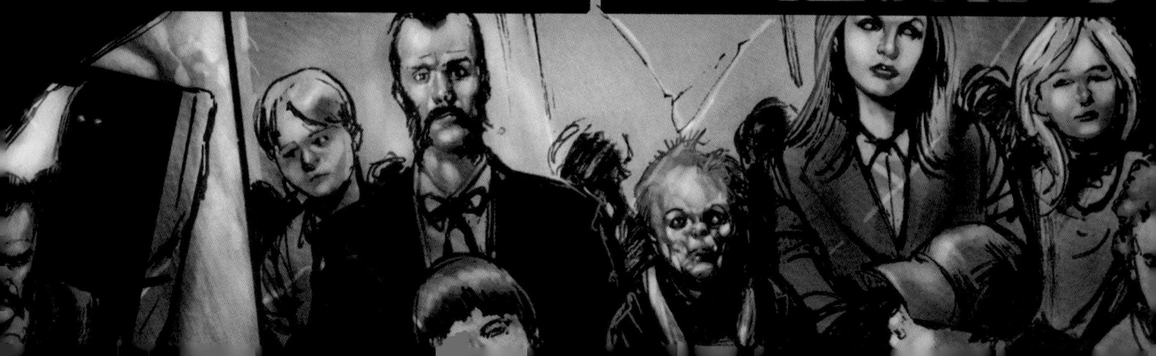

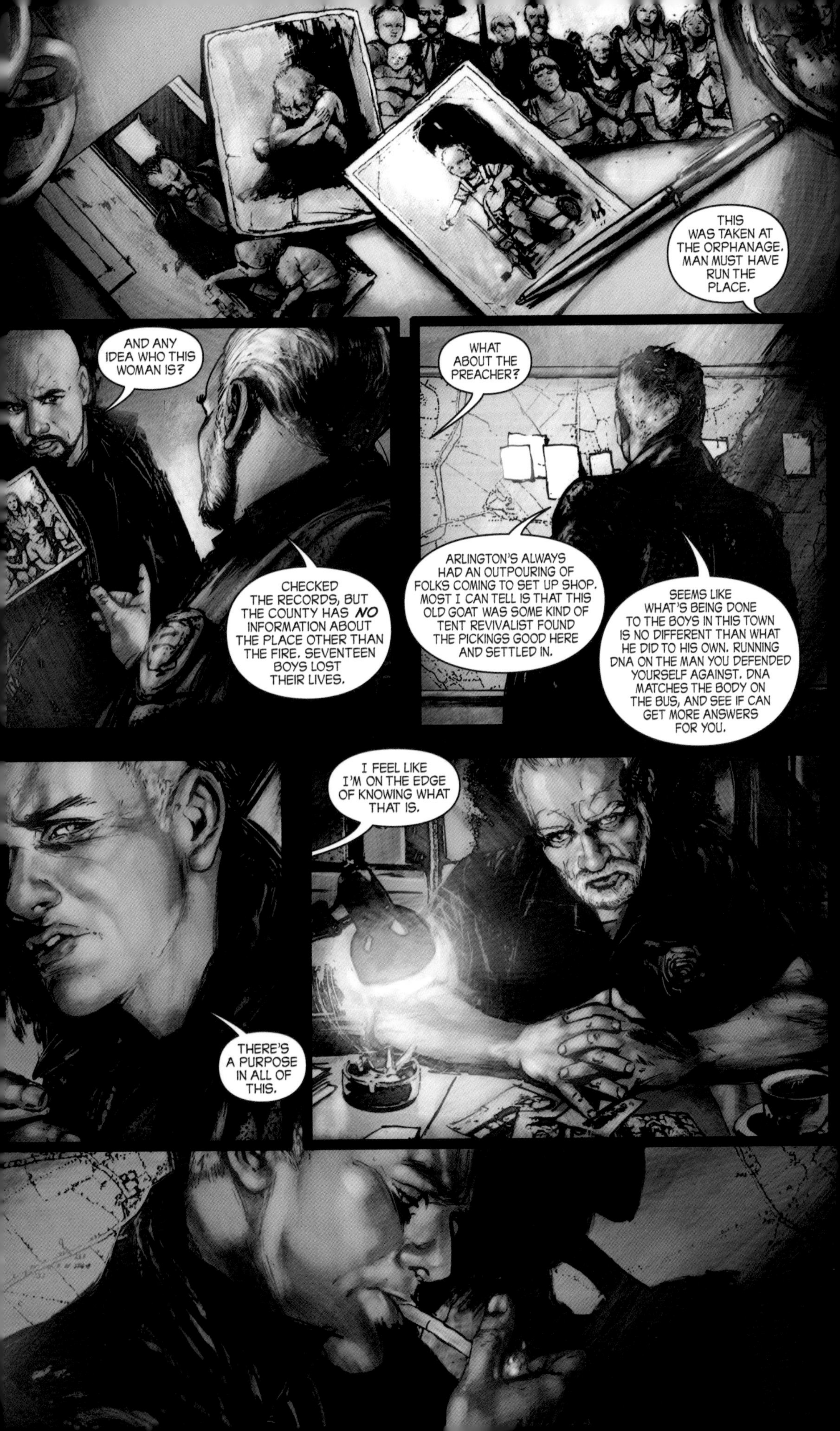

THIS WAS TAKEN AT THE ORPHANAGE. MAN MUST HAVE RUN THE PLACE.
AND ANY IDEA WHO THIS WOMAN IS?
CHECKED THE RECORDS, BUT THE COUNTY HAS NO INFORMATION ABOUT THE PLACE OTHER THAN THE FIRE. SEVENTEEN BOYS LOST THEIR LIVES.
WHAT ABOUT THE PREACHER?
ARLINGTON'S ALWAYS HAD AN OUTPOURING OF FOLKS COMING TO SET UP SHOP. MOST I CAN TELL IS THAT THIS OLD GOAT WAS SOME KIND OF TENT REVIVALIST FOUND THE PICKINGS GOOD HERE AND SETTLED IN.
SEEMS LIKE WHAT'S BEING DONE TO THE BOYS IN THIS TOWN IS NO DIFFERENT THAN WHAT HE DID TO HIS OWN. RUNNING DNA ON THE MAN YOU DEFENDED YOURSELF AGAINST. DNA MATCHES THE BODY ON THE BUS, AND SEE IF CAN GET MORE ANSWERS FOR YOU.
THERE'S A PURPOSE IN ALL OF THIS.
I FEEL LIKE I'M ON THE EDGE OF KNOWING WHAT THAT IS.

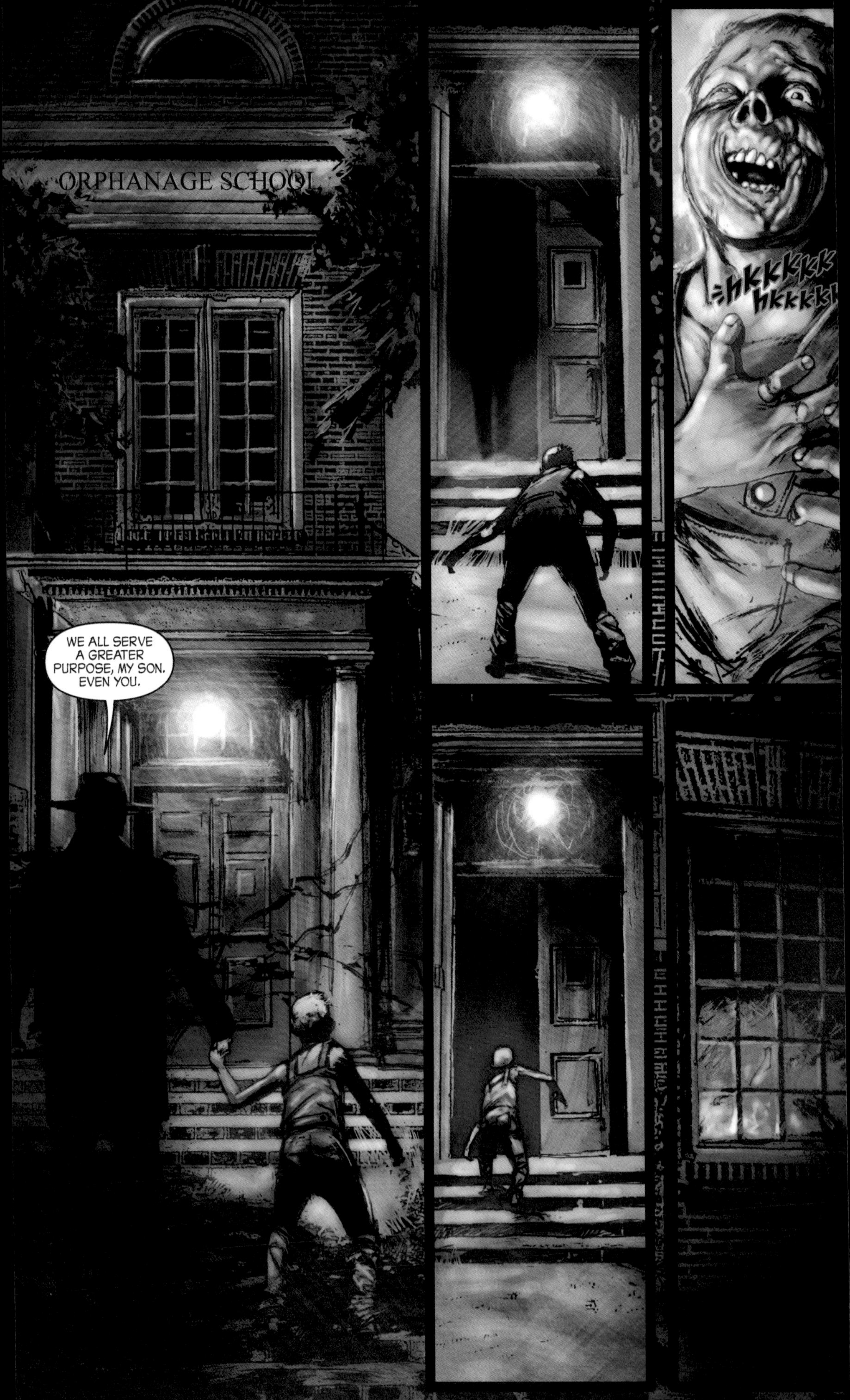
ORPHANAGE SCHOOL
WE ALL SERVE A GREATER PURPOSE, MY SON. EVEN YOU.
HKKKKK HKKKKK

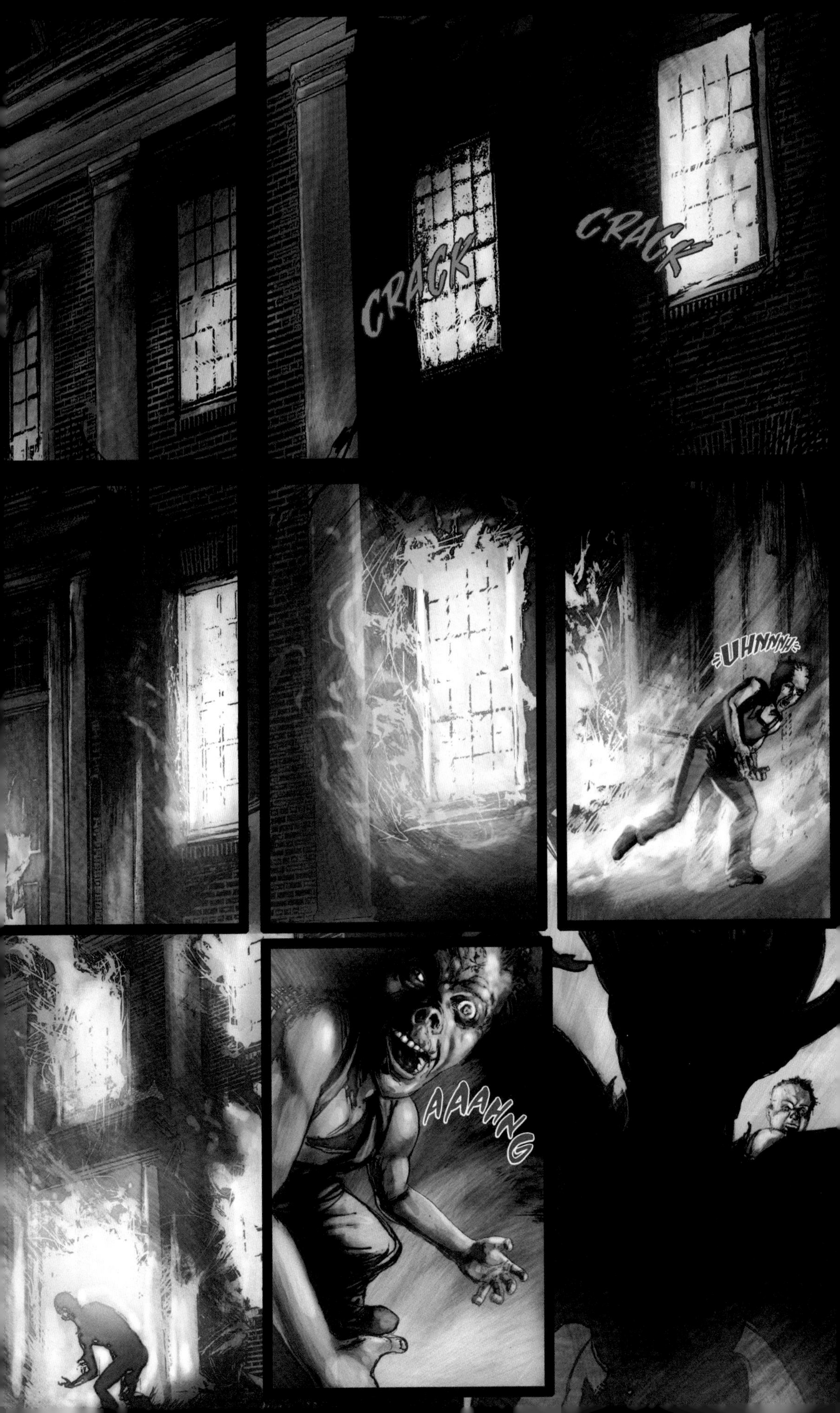
CRACK
CRACK
UHNNNN
AAAHNG

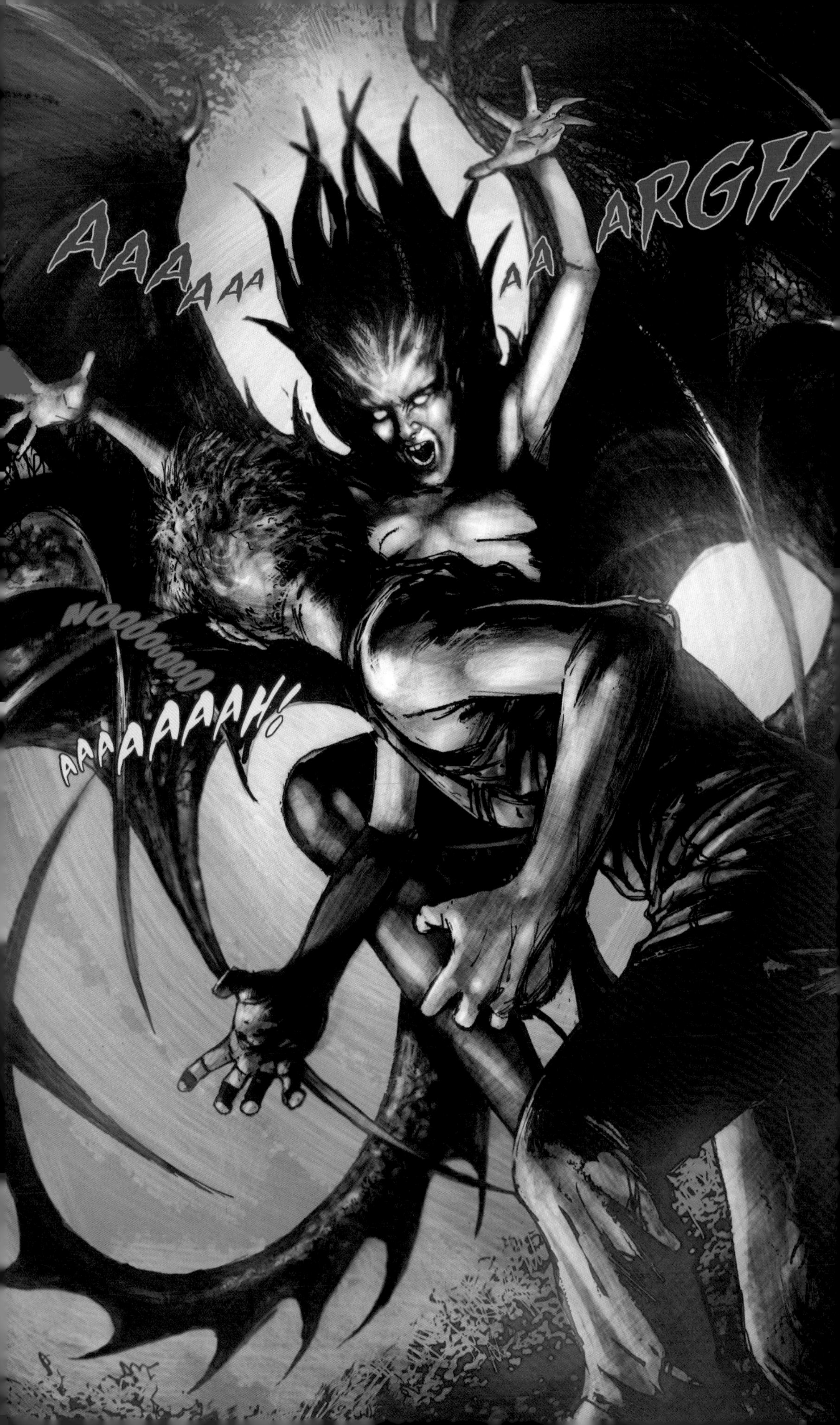
AAAAAA
AAARGH
NOOOOOOOOO
AAAAAAAH!

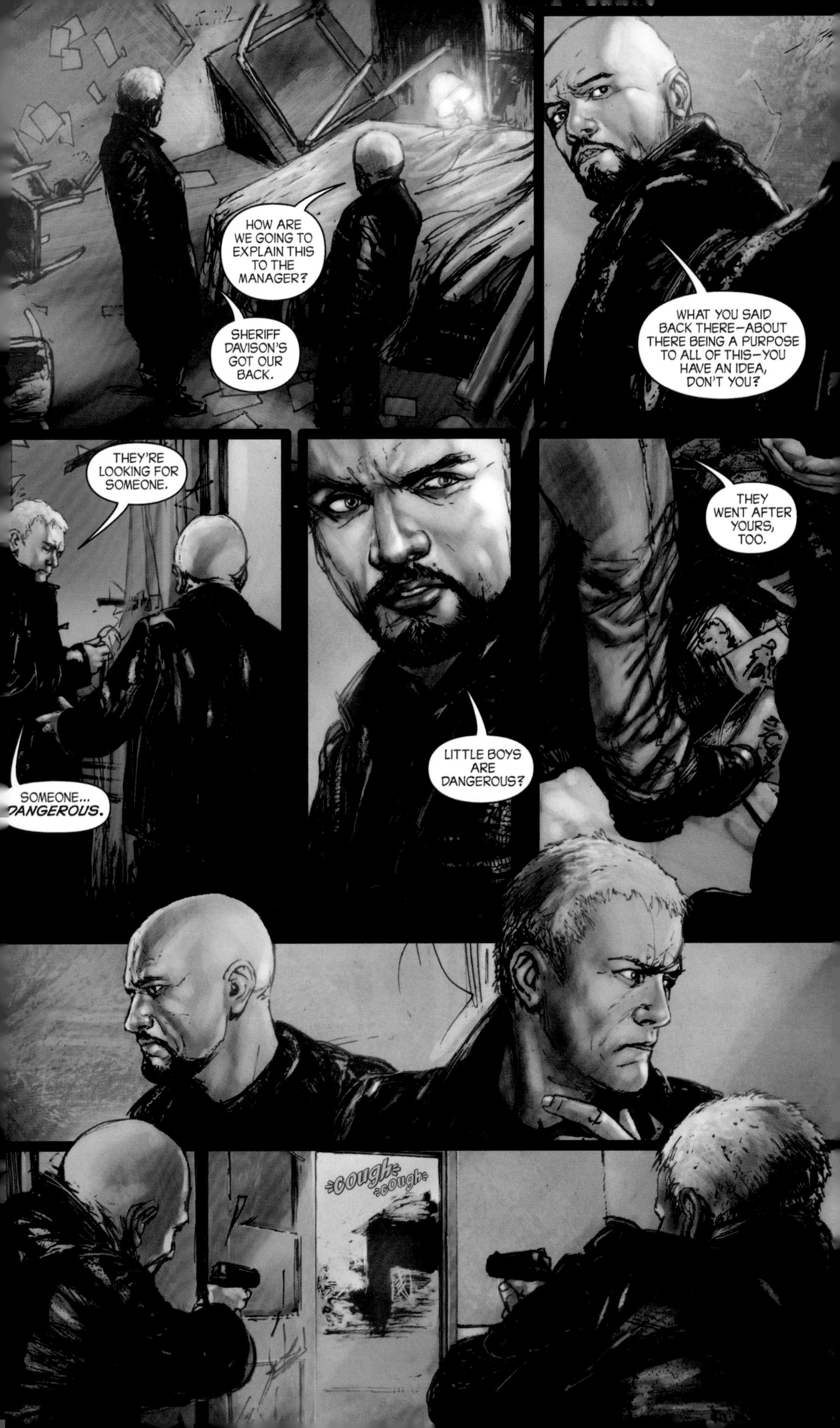
HOW ARE WE GOING TO EXPLAIN THIS TO THE MANAGER?
SHERIFF DAVISON'S GOT OUR BACK.
WHAT YOU SAID BACK THERE—ABOUT THERE BEING A PURPOSE TO ALL OF THIS—YOU HAVE AN IDEA, DON'T YOU?
THEY'RE LOOKING FOR SOMEONE.
SOMEONE... *DANGEROUS.*
LITTLE BOYS ARE DANGEROUS?
THEY WENT AFTER YOURS, TOO.
COUGH COUGH

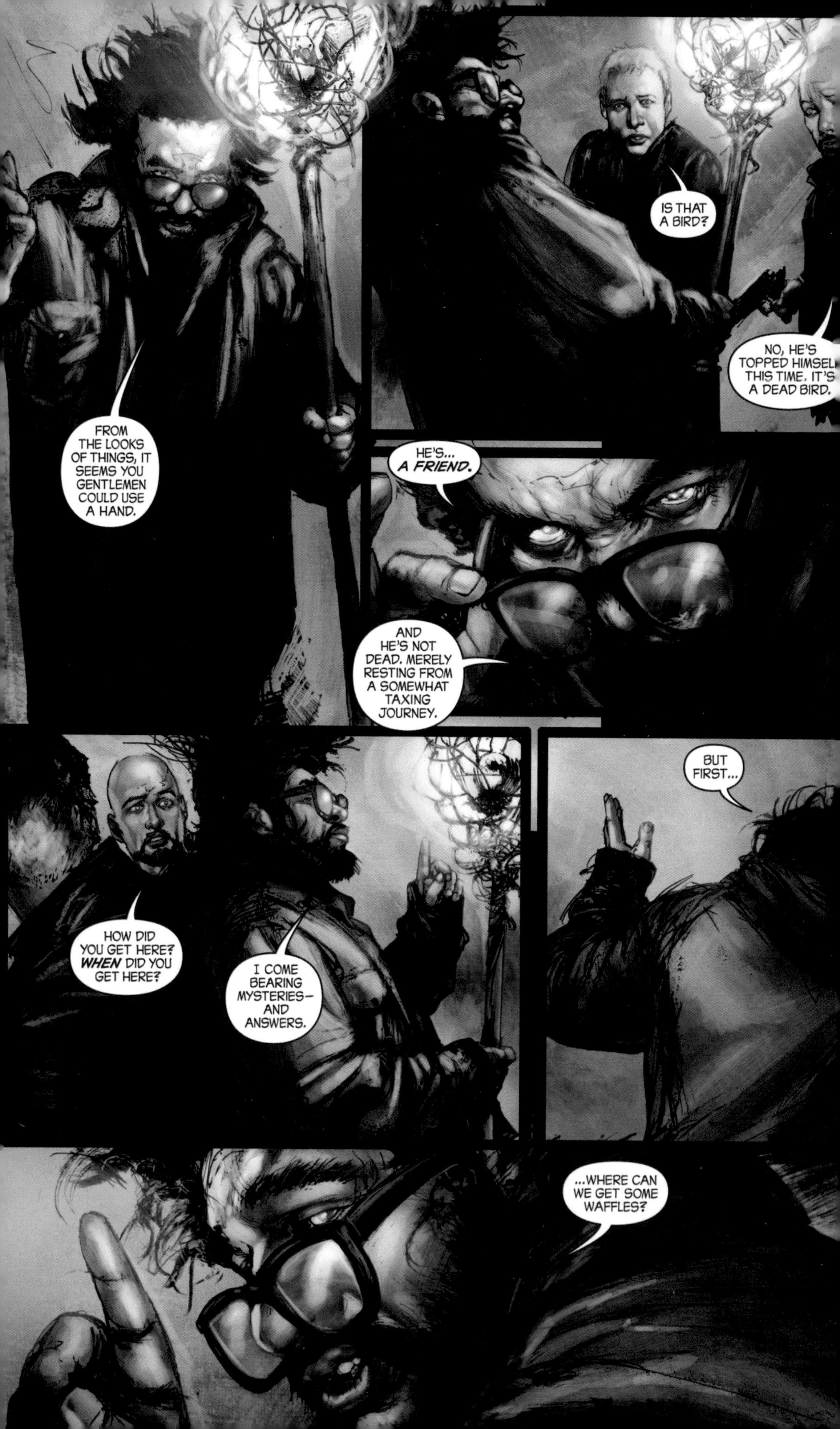
FROM THE LOOKS OF THINGS, IT SEEMS YOU GENTLEMEN COULD USE A HAND.
IS THAT A BIRD?
NO, HE'S TOPPED HIMSEL THIS TIME. IT'S A DEAD BIRD.
HE'S... *A FRIEND.*
AND HE'S NOT DEAD. MERELY RESTING FROM A SOMEWHAT TAXING JOURNEY.
HOW DID YOU GET HERE? *WHEN* DID YOU GET HERE?
I COME BEARING MYSTERIES— AND ANSWERS.
BUT FIRST...
...WHERE CAN WE GET SOME WAFFLES?

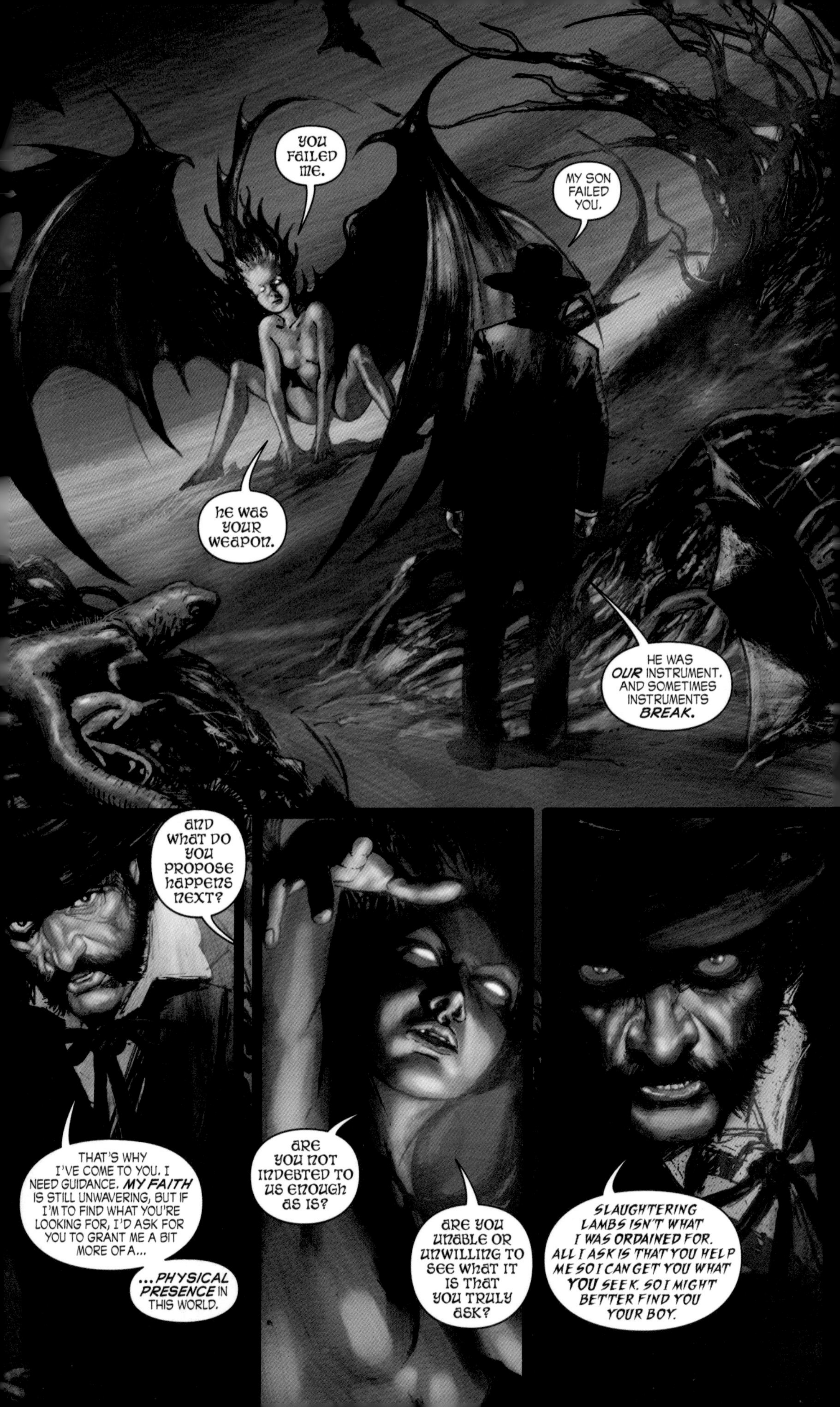
YOU FAILED ME.
MY SON FAILED YOU.
HE WAS YOUR WEAPON.
HE WAS OUR INSTRUMENT. AND SOMETIMES INSTRUMENTS BREAK.
AND WHAT DO YOU PROPOSE HAPPENS NEXT?
THAT'S WHY I'VE COME TO YOU. I NEED GUIDANCE. MY FAITH IS STILL UNWAVERING, BUT IF I'M TO FIND WHAT YOU'RE LOOKING FOR, I'D ASK FOR YOU TO GRANT ME A BIT MORE OF A...
...PHYSICAL PRESENCE IN THIS WORLD.
ARE YOU NOT INDEBTED TO US ENOUGH AS IS?
ARE YOU UNABLE OR UNWILLING TO SEE WHAT IT IS THAT YOU TRULY ASK?
SLAUGHTERING LAMBS ISN'T WHAT I WAS ORDAINED FOR. ALL I ASK IS THAT YOU HELP ME SO I CAN GET YOU WHAT YOU SEEK. SO I MIGHT BETTER FIND YOU YOUR BOY.

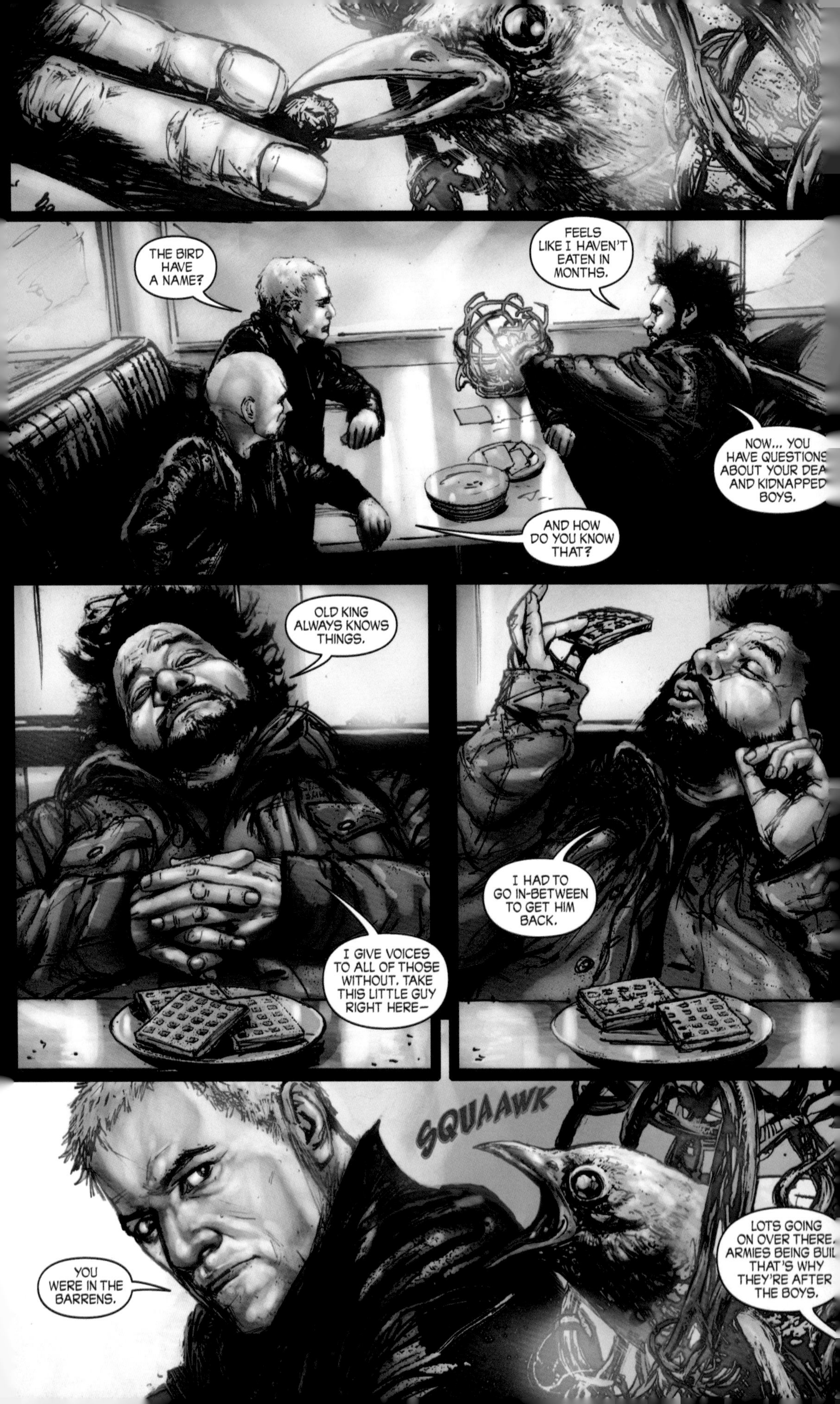
THE BIRD HAVE A NAME?
FEELS LIKE I HAVEN'T EATEN IN MONTHS.
NOW... YOU HAVE QUESTIONS ABOUT YOUR DEA AND KIDNAPPED BOYS.
AND HOW DO YOU KNOW THAT?
OLD KING ALWAYS KNOWS THINGS.
I GIVE VOICES TO ALL OF THOSE WITHOUT. TAKE THIS LITTLE GUY RIGHT HERE—
I HAD TO GO IN-BETWEEN TO GET HIM BACK.
SQUAAWK
YOU WERE IN THE BARRENS.
LOTS GOING ON OVER THERE. ARMIES BEING BUIL THAT'S WHY THEY'RE AFTER THE BOYS.

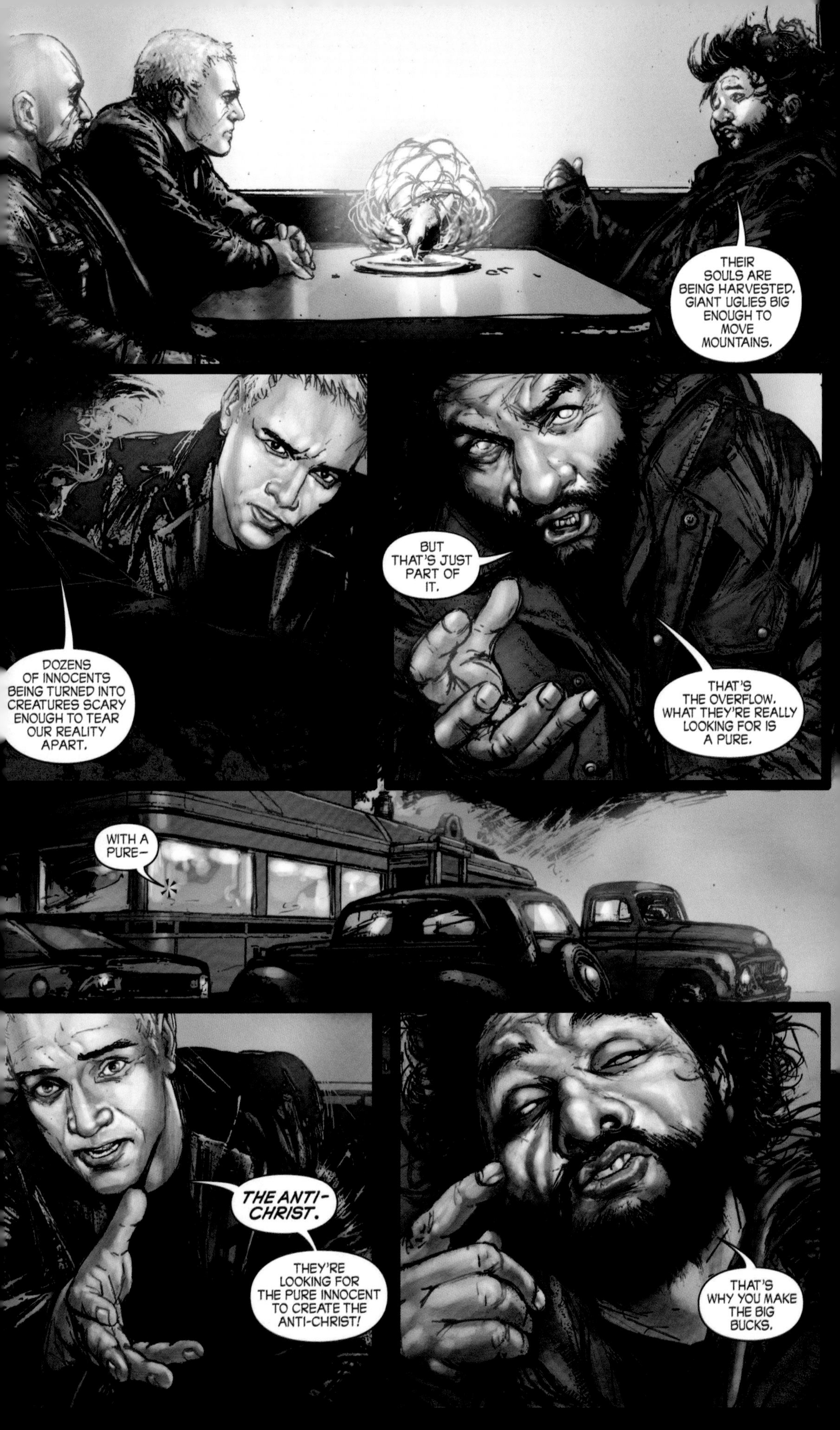
THEIR SOULS ARE BEING HARVESTED. GIANT UGLIES BIG ENOUGH TO MOVE MOUNTAINS.
DOZENS OF INNOCENTS BEING TURNED INTO CREATURES SCARY ENOUGH TO TEAR OUR REALITY APART.
BUT THAT'S JUST PART OF IT.
THAT'S THE OVERFLOW. WHAT THEY'RE REALLY LOOKING FOR IS A PURE.
WITH A PURE—
THE ANTI-CHRIST.
THEY'RE LOOKING FOR THE PURE INNOCENT TO CREATE THE ANTI-CHRIST!
THAT'S WHY YOU MAKE THE BIG BUCKS.

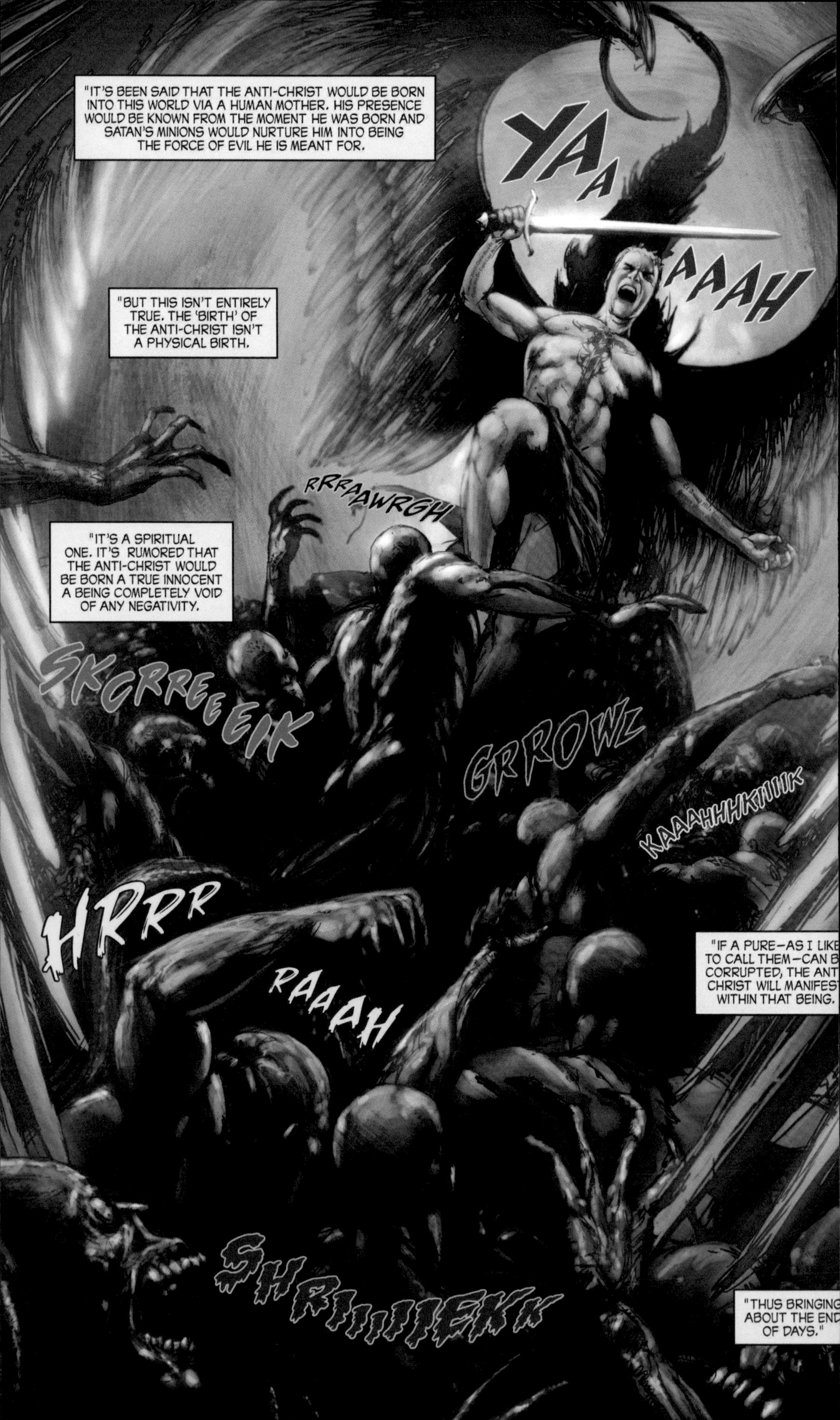
"IT'S BEEN SAID THAT THE ANTI-CHRIST WOULD BE BORN INTO THIS WORLD VIA A HUMAN MOTHER. HIS PRESENCE WOULD BE KNOWN FROM THE MOMENT HE WAS BORN AND SATAN'S MINIONS WOULD NURTURE HIM INTO BEING THE FORCE OF EVIL HE IS MEANT FOR.
YAAAAAAH
"BUT THIS ISN'T ENTIRELY TRUE. THE 'BIRTH' OF THE ANTI-CHRIST ISN'T A PHYSICAL BIRTH.
RRRAAWRGH
"IT'S A SPIRITUAL ONE. IT'S RUMORED THAT THE ANTI-CHRIST WOULD BE BORN A TRUE INNOCENT A BEING COMPLETELY VOID OF ANY NEGATIVITY.
SKCRREEEIK
GRROWL
KAAAHHHKIIIIK
HRRR
RAAAH
"IF A PURE—AS I LIKE TO CALL THEM—CAN B CORRUPTED, THE ANT CHRIST WILL MANIFEST WITHIN THAT BEING.
SHRIIIIIEKK
"THUS BRINGING ABOUT THE END OF DAYS."

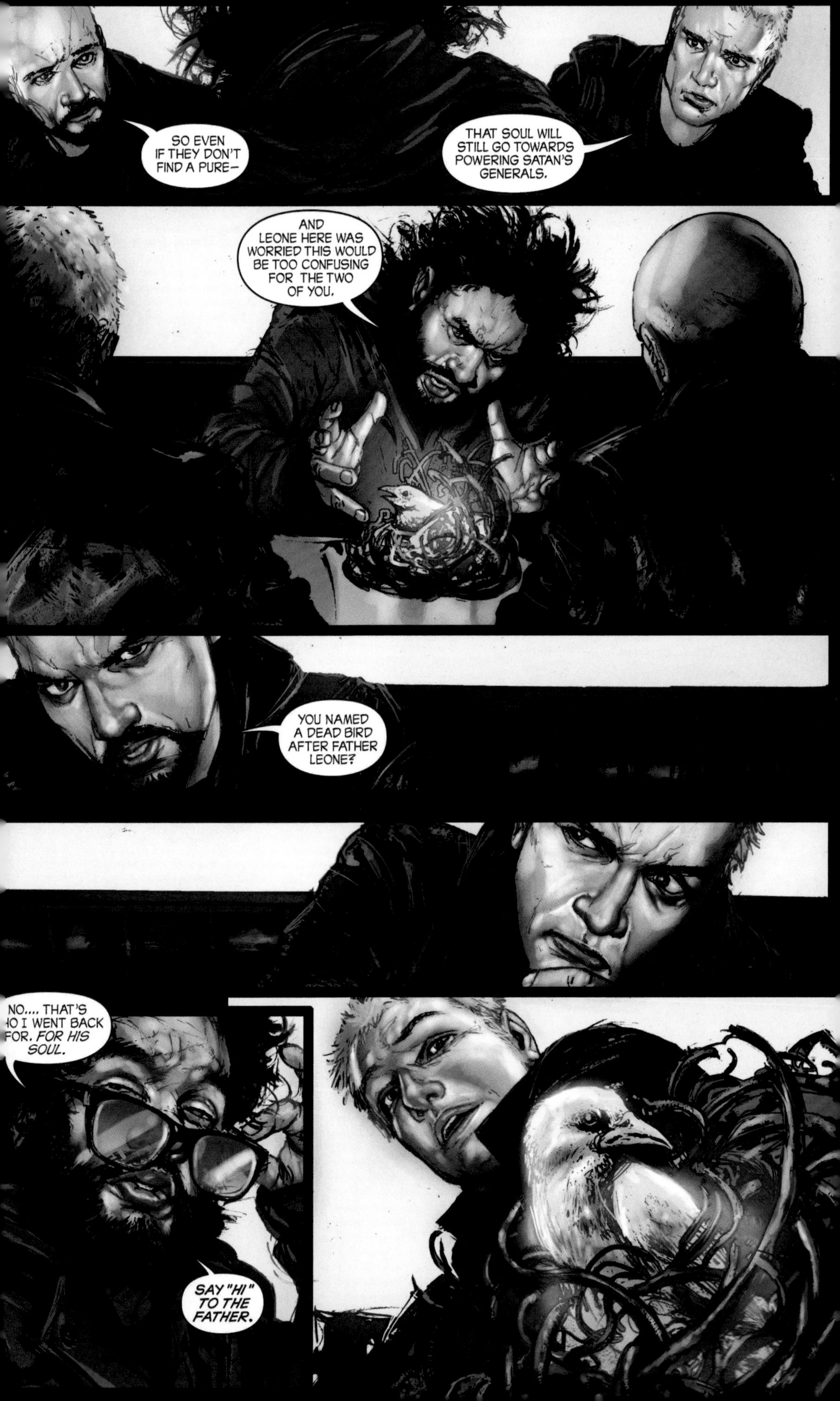
SO EVEN IF THEY DON'T FIND A PURE—
THAT SOUL WILL STILL GO TOWARDS POWERING SATAN'S GENERALS.
AND LEONE HERE WAS WORRIED THIS WOULD BE TOO CONFUSING FOR THE TWO OF YOU.
YOU NAMED A DEAD BIRD AFTER FATHER LEONE?
NO.... THAT'S IO I WENT BACK FOR. *FOR HIS SOUL.*
SAY "*HI*" *TO THE FATHER.*

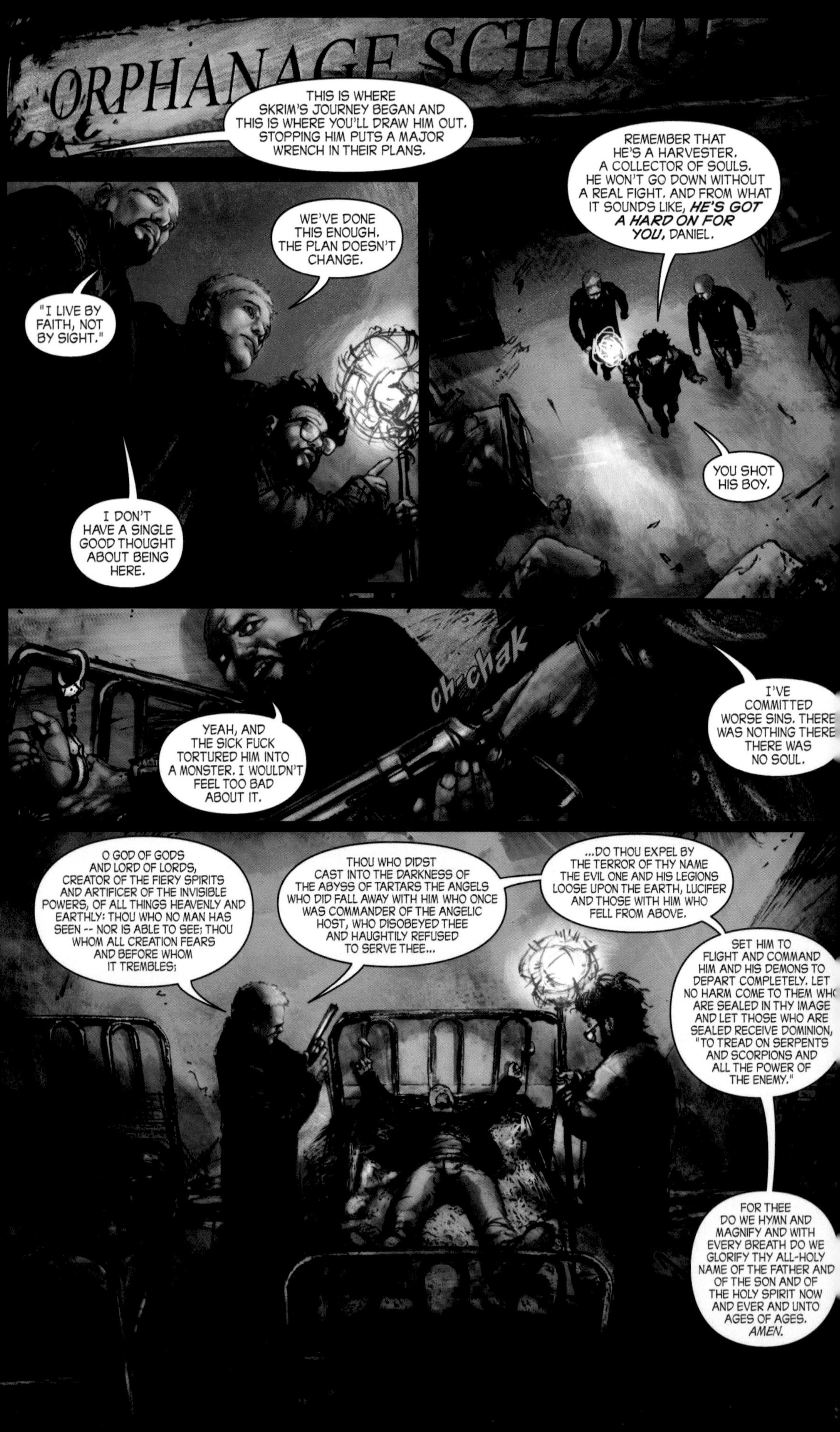
ORPHANAGE SCHO
THIS IS WHERE SKRIM'S JOURNEY BEGAN AND THIS IS WHERE YOU'LL DRAW HIM OUT. STOPPING HIM PUTS A MAJOR WRENCH IN THEIR PLANS.
"I LIVE BY FAITH, NOT BY SIGHT."
WE'VE DONE THIS ENOUGH. THE PLAN DOESN'T CHANGE.
I DON'T HAVE A SINGLE GOOD THOUGHT ABOUT BEING HERE.
REMEMBER THAT HE'S A HARVESTER. A COLLECTOR OF SOULS. HE WON'T GO DOWN WITHOUT A REAL FIGHT. AND FROM WHAT IT SOUNDS LIKE, HE'S GOT A HARD ON FOR YOU, DANIEL.
YOU SHOT HIS BOY.
YEAH, AND THE SICK FUCK TORTURED HIM INTO A MONSTER. I WOULDN'T FEEL TOO BAD ABOUT IT.
ch-chak
I'VE COMMITTED WORSE SINS. THERE WAS NOTHING THERE THERE WAS NO SOUL.
O GOD OF GODS AND LORD OF LORDS, CREATOR OF THE FIERY SPIRITS AND ARTIFICER OF THE INVISIBLE POWERS, OF ALL THINGS HEAVENLY AND EARTHLY: THOU WHO NO MAN HAS SEEN -- NOR IS ABLE TO SEE; THOU WHOM ALL CREATION FEARS AND BEFORE WHOM IT TREMBLES;
THOU WHO DIDST CAST INTO THE DARKNESS OF THE ABYSS OF TARTARS THE ANGELS WHO DID FALL AWAY WITH HIM WHO ONCE WAS COMMANDER OF THE ANGELIC HOST, WHO DISOBEYED THEE AND HAUGHTILY REFUSED TO SERVE THEE...
...DO THOU EXPEL BY THE TERROR OF THY NAME THE EVIL ONE AND HIS LEGIONS LOOSE UPON THE EARTH, LUCIFER AND THOSE WITH HIM WHO FELL FROM ABOVE.
SET HIM TO FLIGHT AND COMMAND HIM AND HIS DEMONS TO DEPART COMPLETELY. LET NO HARM COME TO THEM WHO ARE SEALED IN THY IMAGE AND LET THOSE WHO ARE SEALED RECEIVE DOMINION, "TO TREAD ON SERPENTS AND SCORPIONS AND ALL THE POWER OF THE ENEMY."
FOR THEE DO WE HYMN AND MAGNIFY AND WITH EVERY BREATH DO WE GLORIFY THY ALL-HOLY NAME OF THE FATHER AND OF THE SON AND OF THE HOLY SPIRIT NOW AND EVER AND UNTO AGES OF AGES. AMEN.

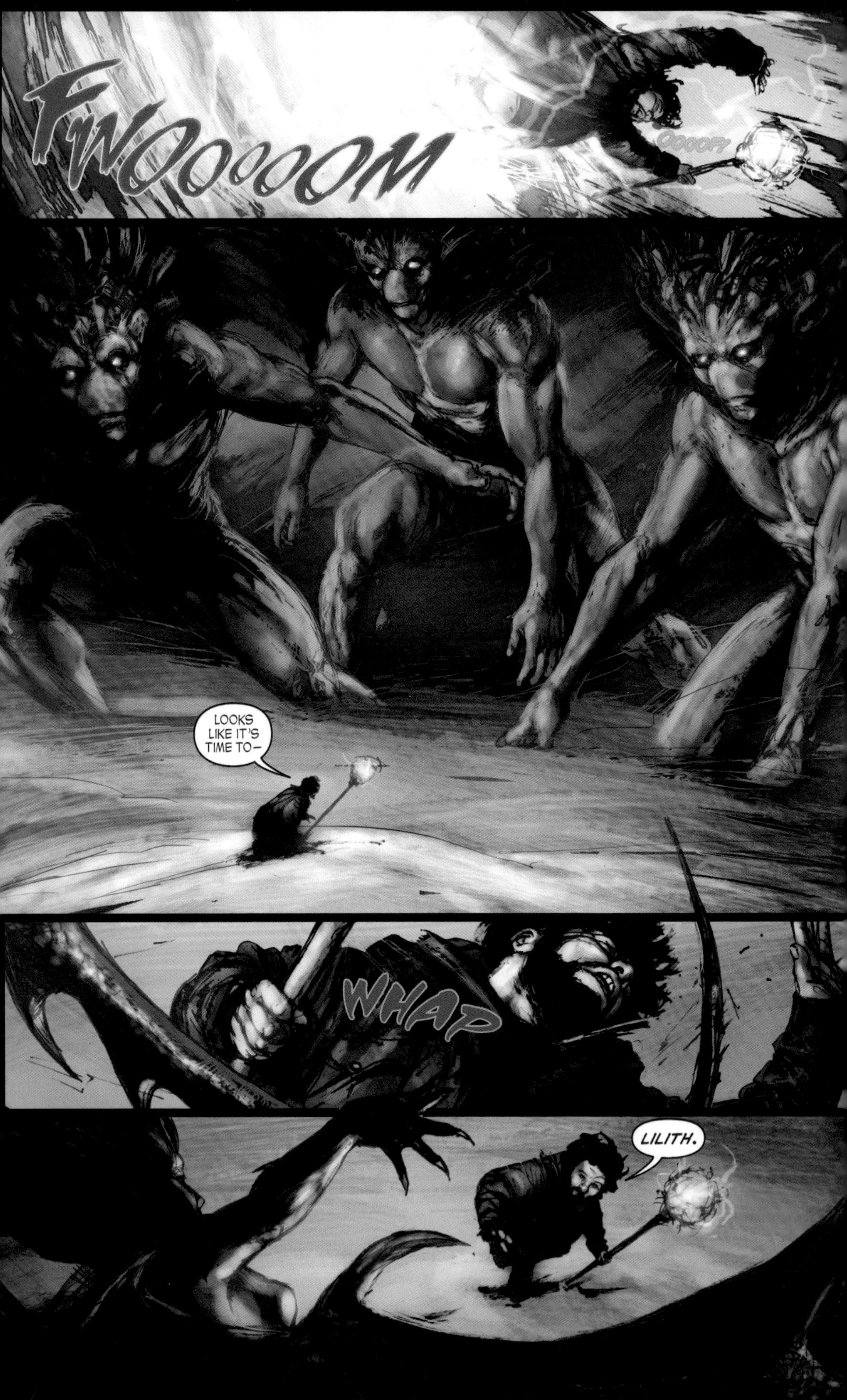
FWOOOOOM
OOOOF
LOOKS LIKE IT'S TIME TO—
WHAP
LILITH.

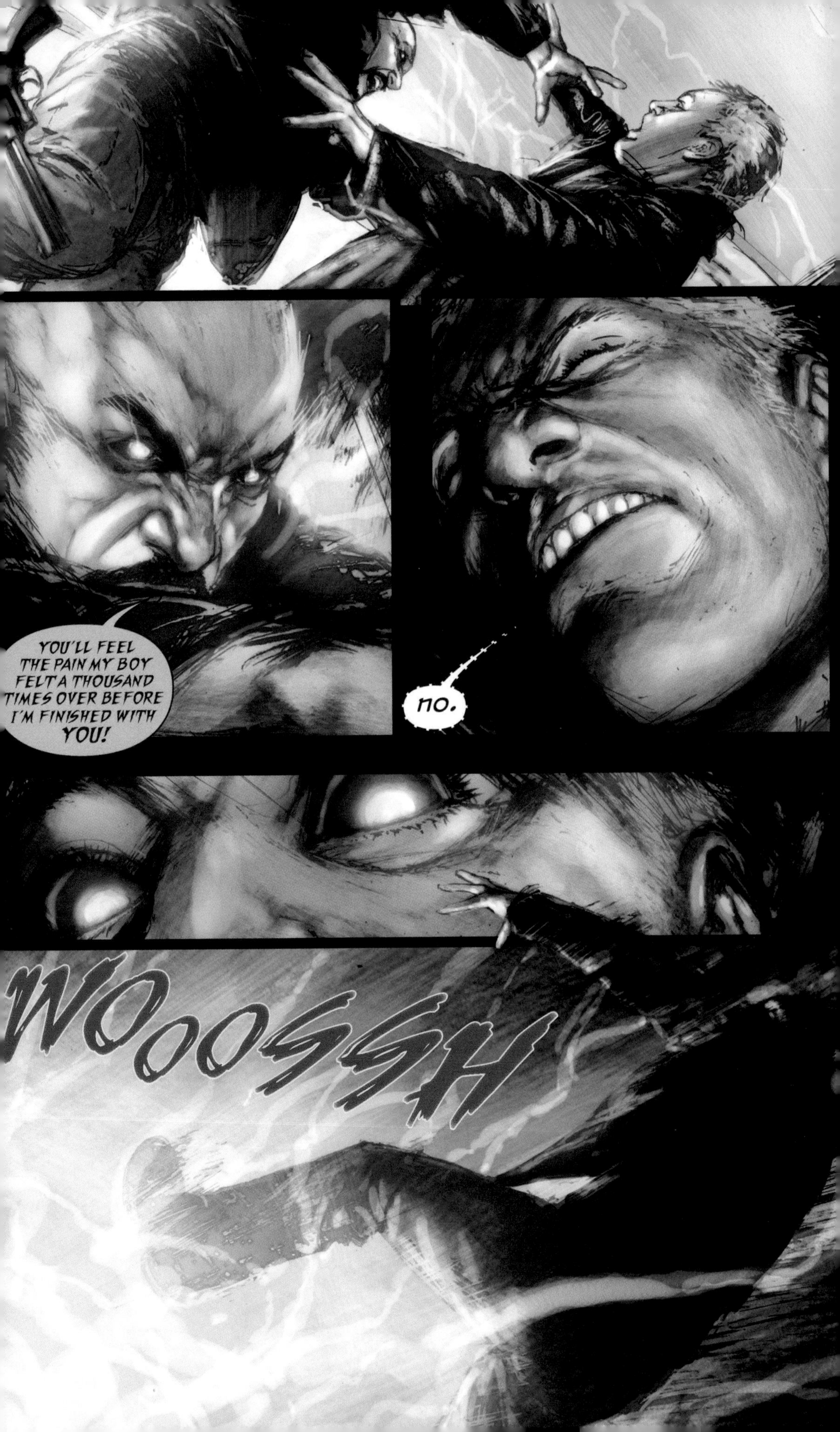
YOU'LL FEEL THE PAIN MY BOY FELT A THOUSAND TIMES OVER BEFORE I'M FINISHED WITH YOU!
NO.
WOOOSH

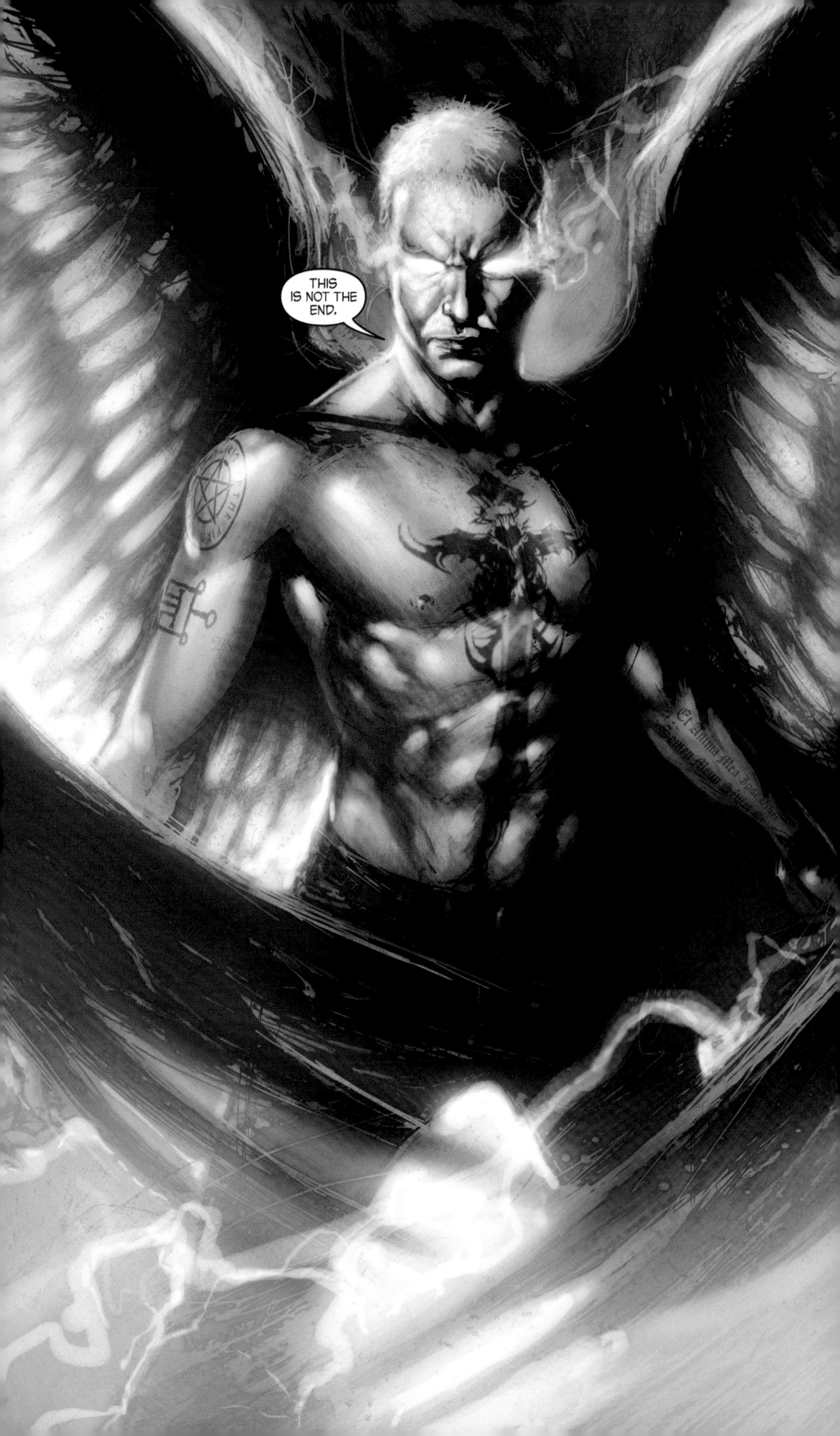
THIS IS NOT THE END.

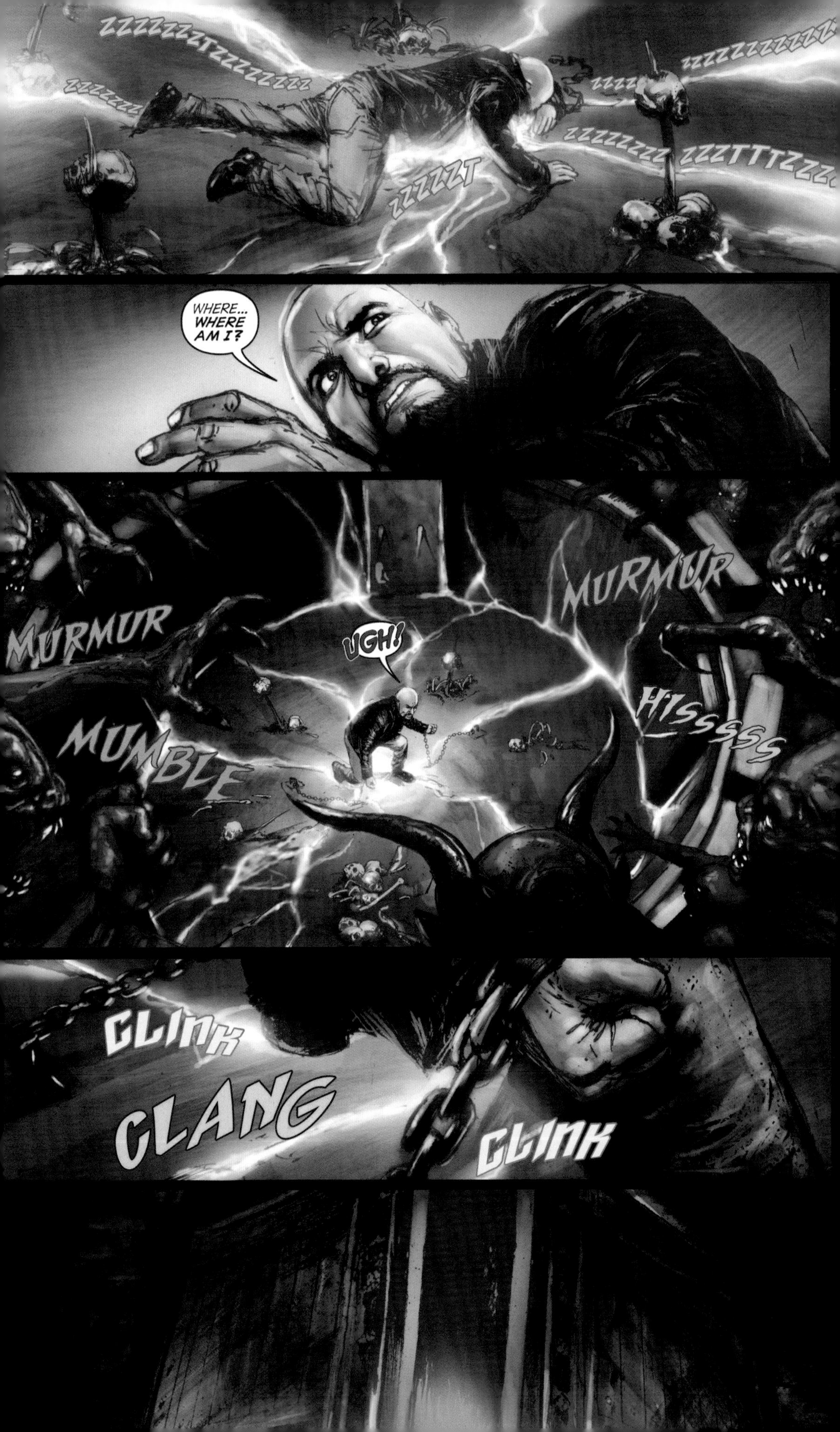
ZZZZZZZZTZZZZZZZZZZ
ZZZZZZZZ
ZZZZ
ZZZZZZZZZZZZZ
ZZZZZZZZZ
ZZZZZT
ZZZTTTTZZZ
WHERE... WHERE AM I?
MURMUR
MUMBLE
UGH!
MURMUR
HISSSSS
CLINK
CLANG
CLINK

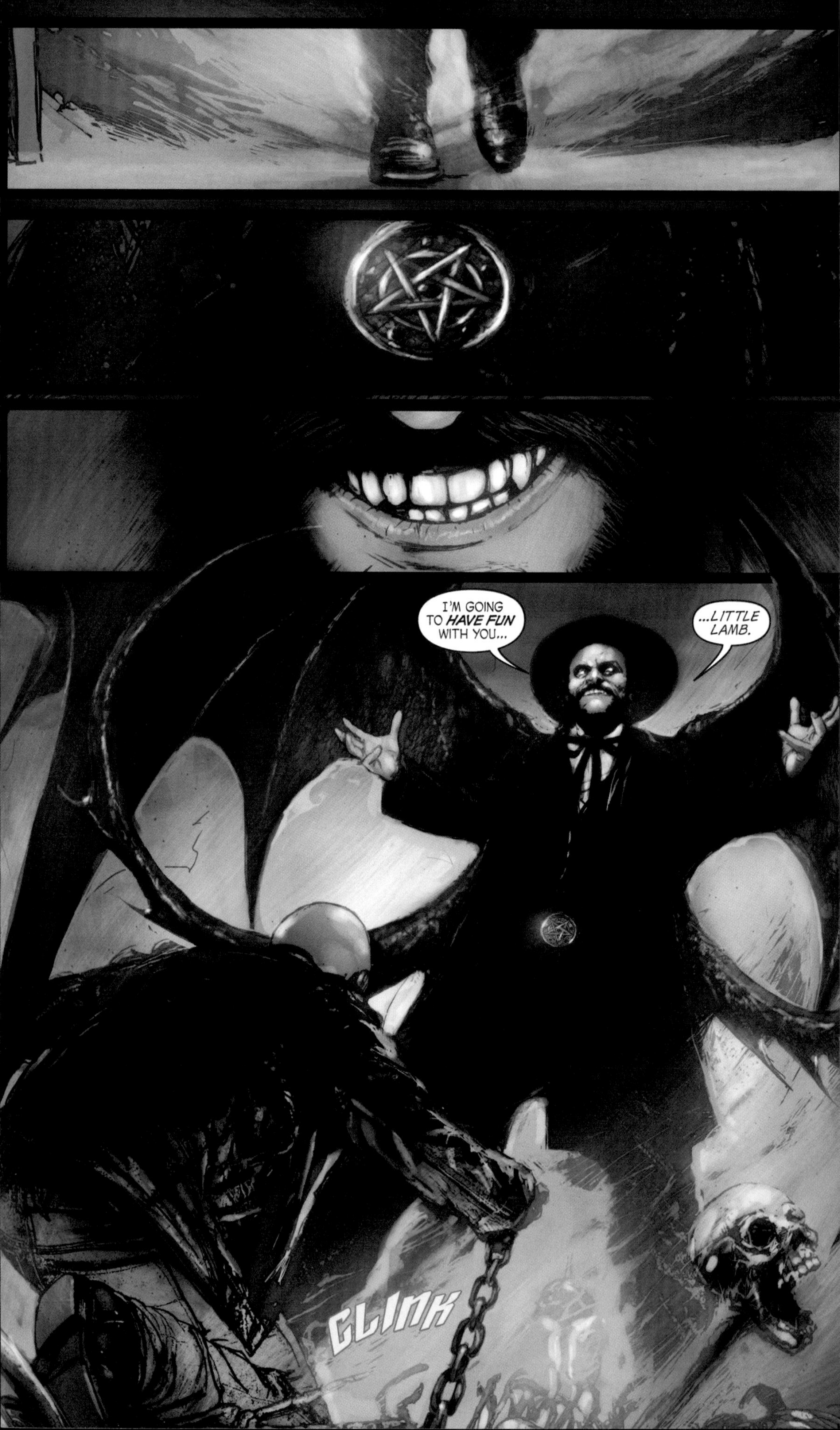
I'M GOING TO HAVE FUN WITH YOU...
...LITTLE LAMB.
CLINK

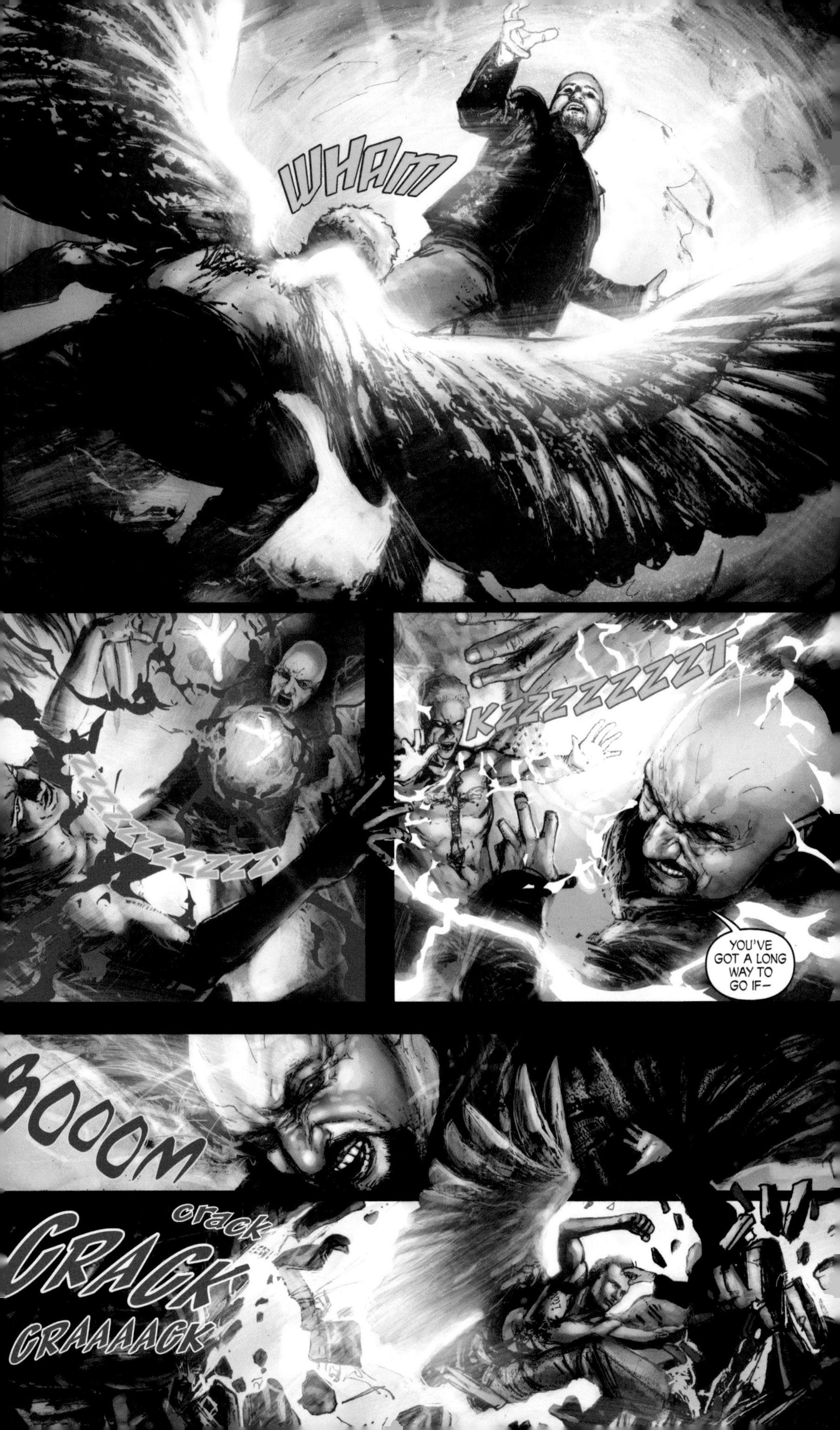
WHAM
ZZZZZZZZZZZ
KZZZZZZZT
YOU'VE GOT A LONG WAY TO GO IF—
BOOOM
crack
CRACK
CRAAAACK

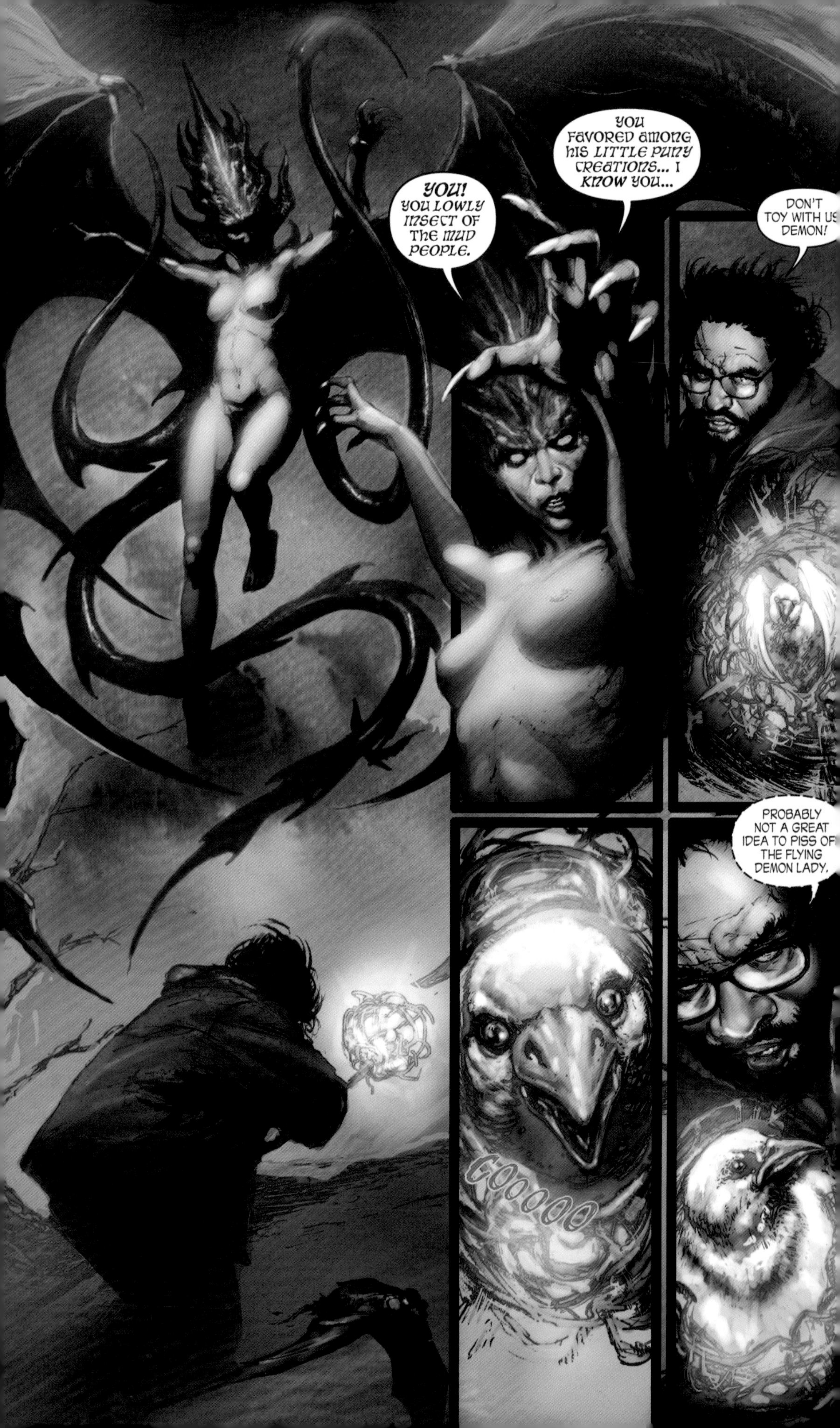
YOU! YOU LOWLY INSECT OF THE MUD PEOPLE.
YOU FAVORED AMONG HIS LITTLE PUNY CREATIONS... I KNOW YOU...
DON'T TOY WITH US DEMON!
GOOOOO
PROBABLY NOT A GREAT IDEA TO PISS OFF THE FLYING DEMON LADY.

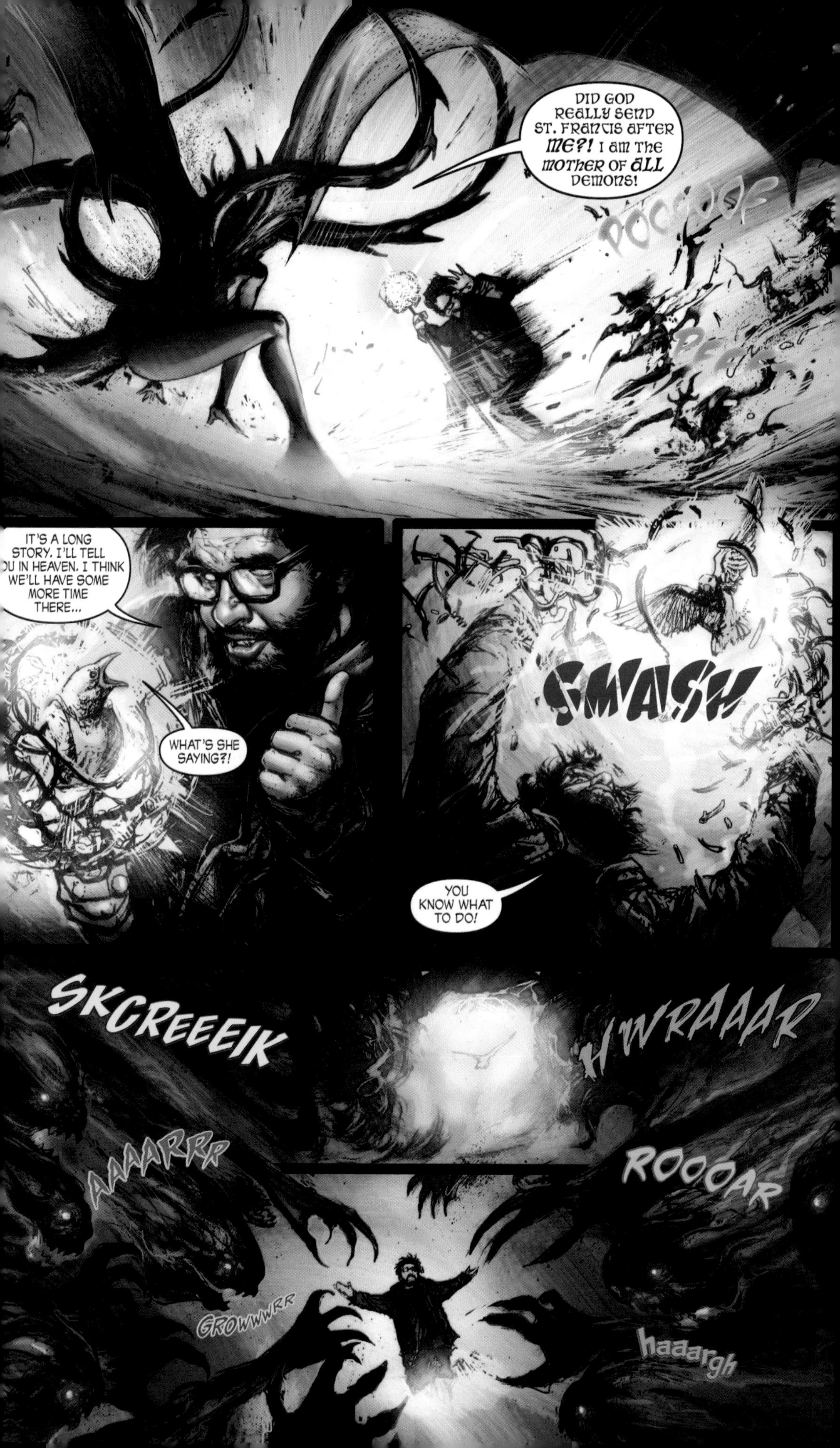
DID GOD REALLY SEND ST. FRANCIS AFTER *ME?!* I AM THE *MOTHER* OF *ALL* DEMONS!
POOOOF
IT'S A LONG STORY. I'LL TELL OU IN HEAVEN. I THINK WE'LL HAVE SOME MORE TIME THERE...
WHAT'S SHE SAYING?!
SMASH
YOU KNOW WHAT TO DO!
SKCREEEIK
HWRAAAR
AAAARRR
ROOOAR
GROWWWRR
haaargh

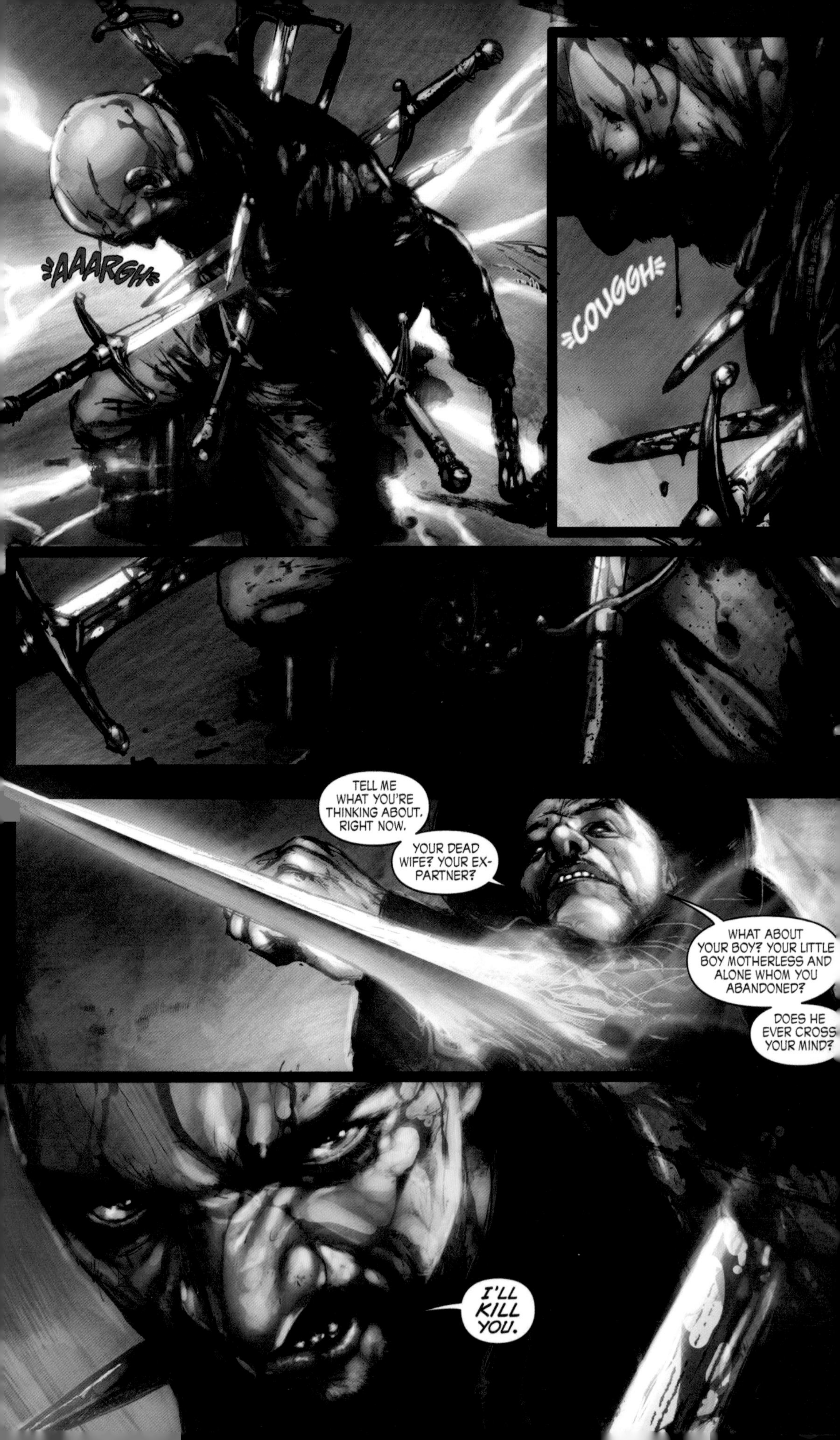
AAARGH
COUGGH
TELL ME WHAT YOU'RE THINKING ABOUT. RIGHT NOW.
YOUR DEAD WIFE? YOUR EX-PARTNER?
WHAT ABOUT YOUR BOY? YOUR LITTLE BOY MOTHERLESS AND ALONE WHOM YOU ABANDONED?
DOES HE EVER CROSS YOUR MIND?
I'LL KILL YOU.

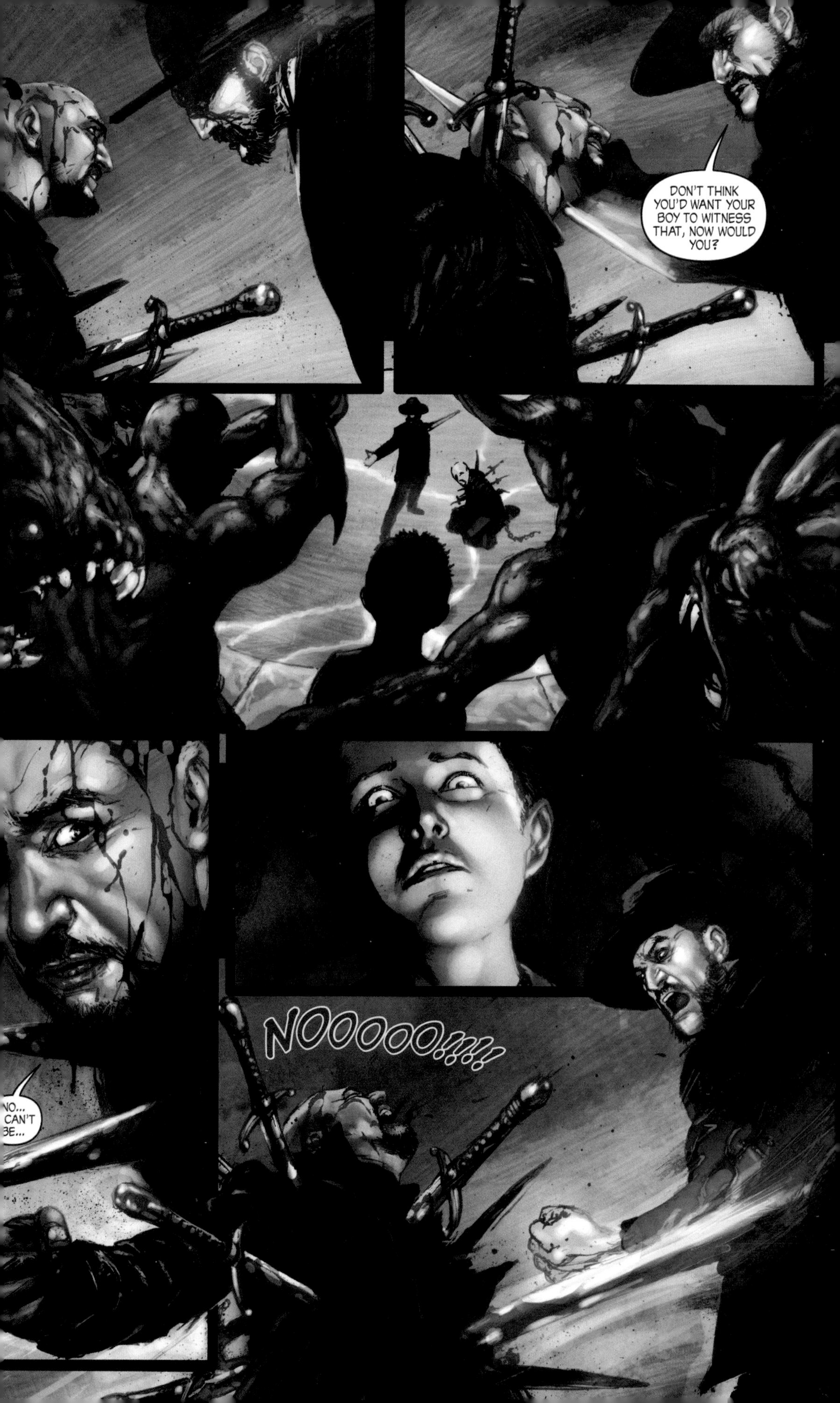
DON'T THINK YOU'D WANT YOUR BOY TO WITNESS THAT, NOW WOULD YOU?
NO... CAN'T BE...
NOOOOO!!!!

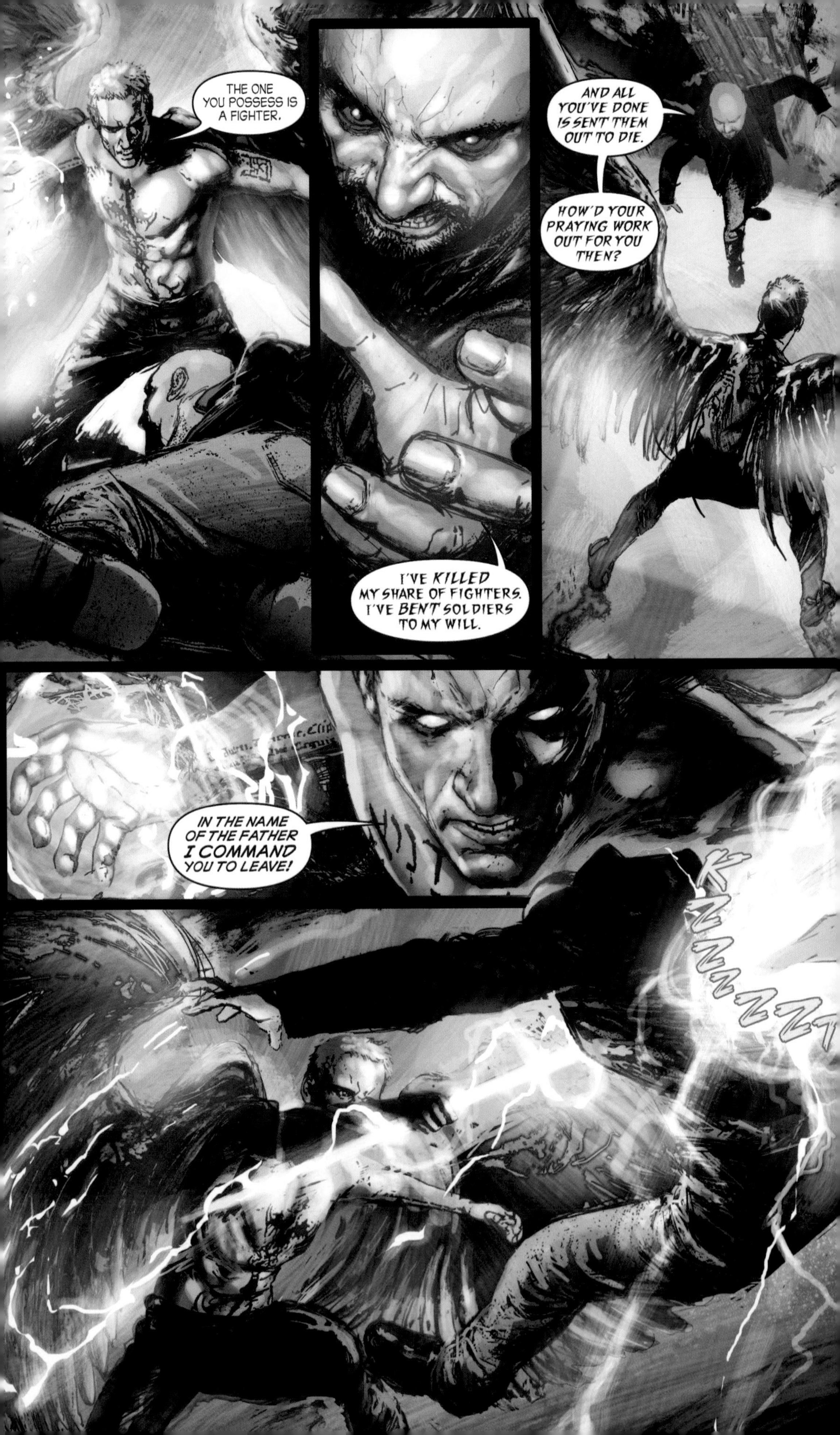
THE ONE YOU POSSESS IS A FIGHTER.
I'VE KILLED MY SHARE OF FIGHTERS. I'VE BENT SOLDIERS TO MY WILL.
AND ALL YOU'VE DONE IS SENT THEM OUT TO DIE.
HOW'D YOUR PRAYING WORK OUT FOR YOU THEN?
IN THE NAME OF THE FATHER I COMMAND YOU TO LEAVE!
KZZZZZT

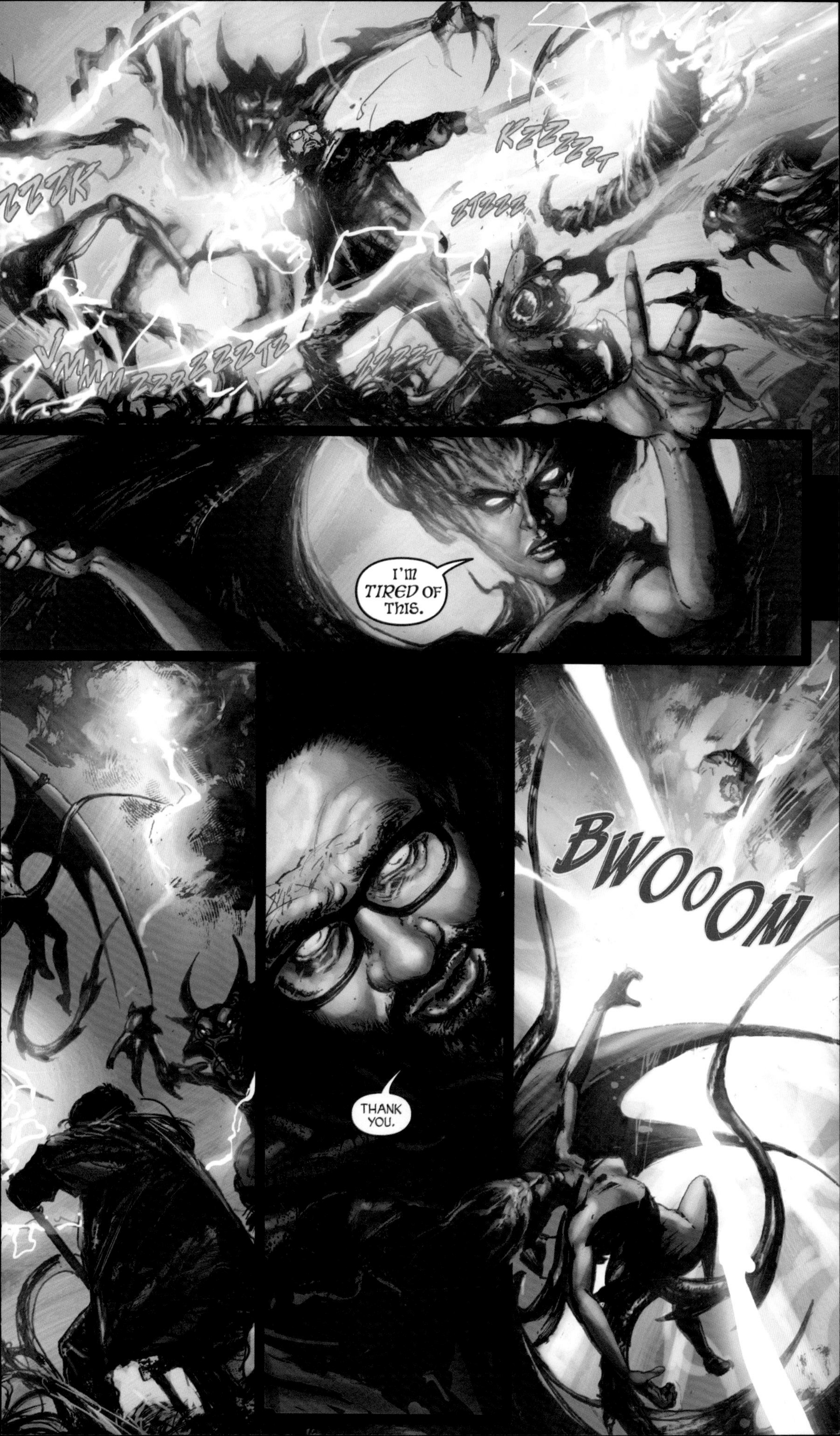
ZZZZK
KZZZZZZT
ZZZZZ
VMMMZZZZZZTZ
ZZZZZT
I'M *TIRED* OF THIS.
THANK YOU.
BWOOOM

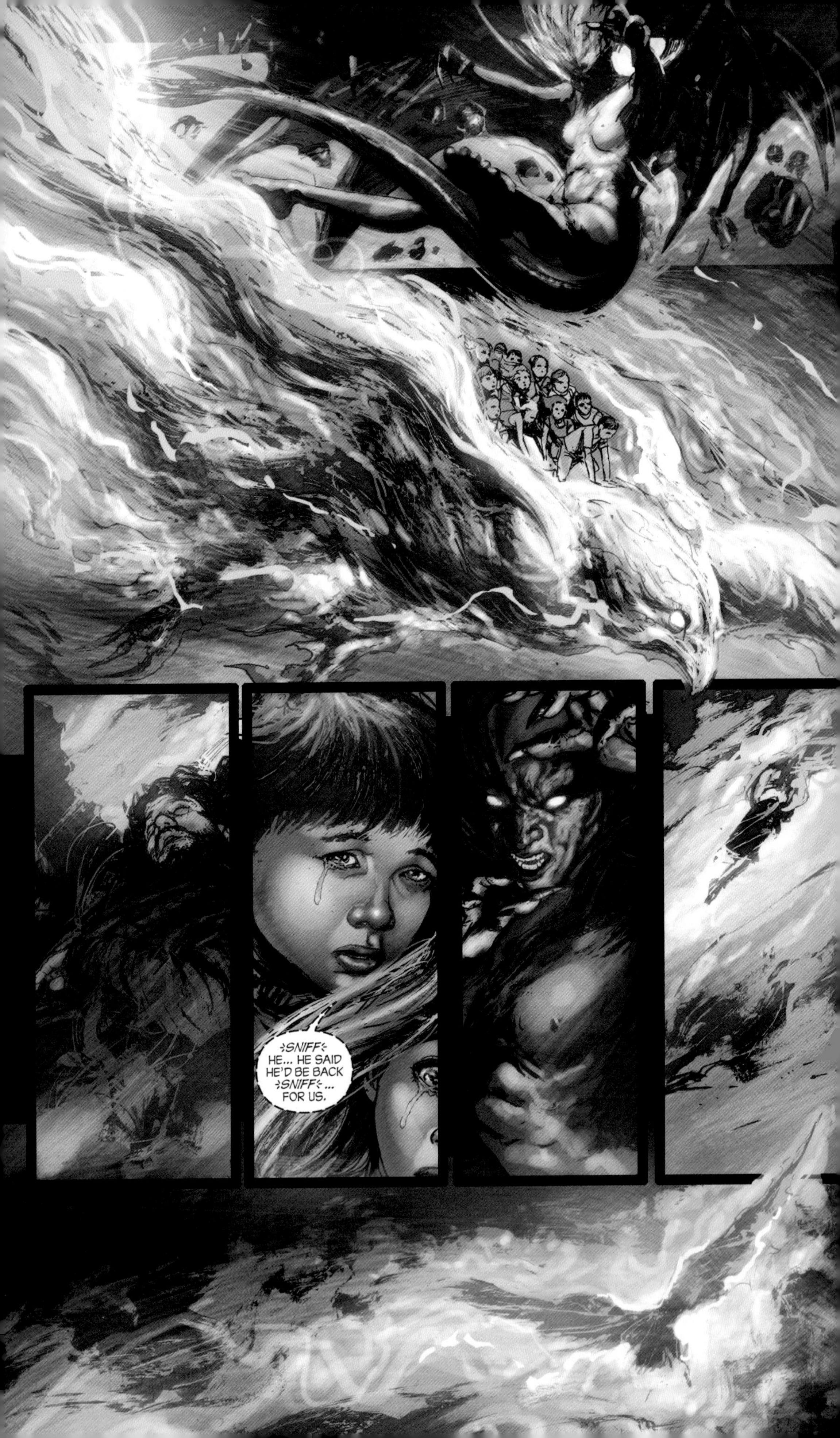
SNIFF HE... HE SAID HE'D BE BACK *SNIFF*... FOR US.

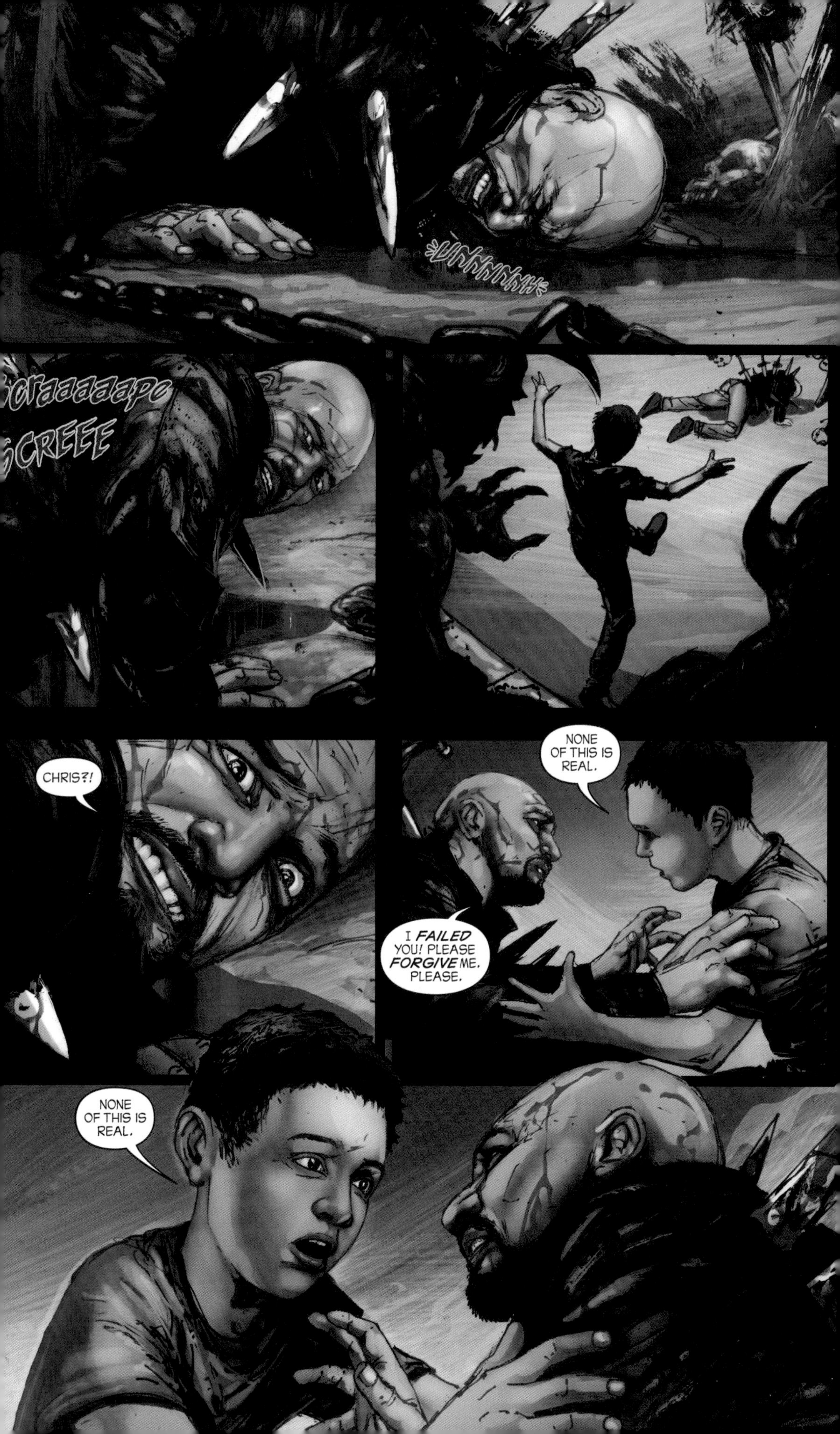

UHHHHHH
scraaaaape
SCREEE
CHRIS?!
NONE OF THIS IS REAL.
I *FAILED* YOU! PLEASE *FORGIVE* ME. PLEASE.
NONE OF THIS IS REAL.

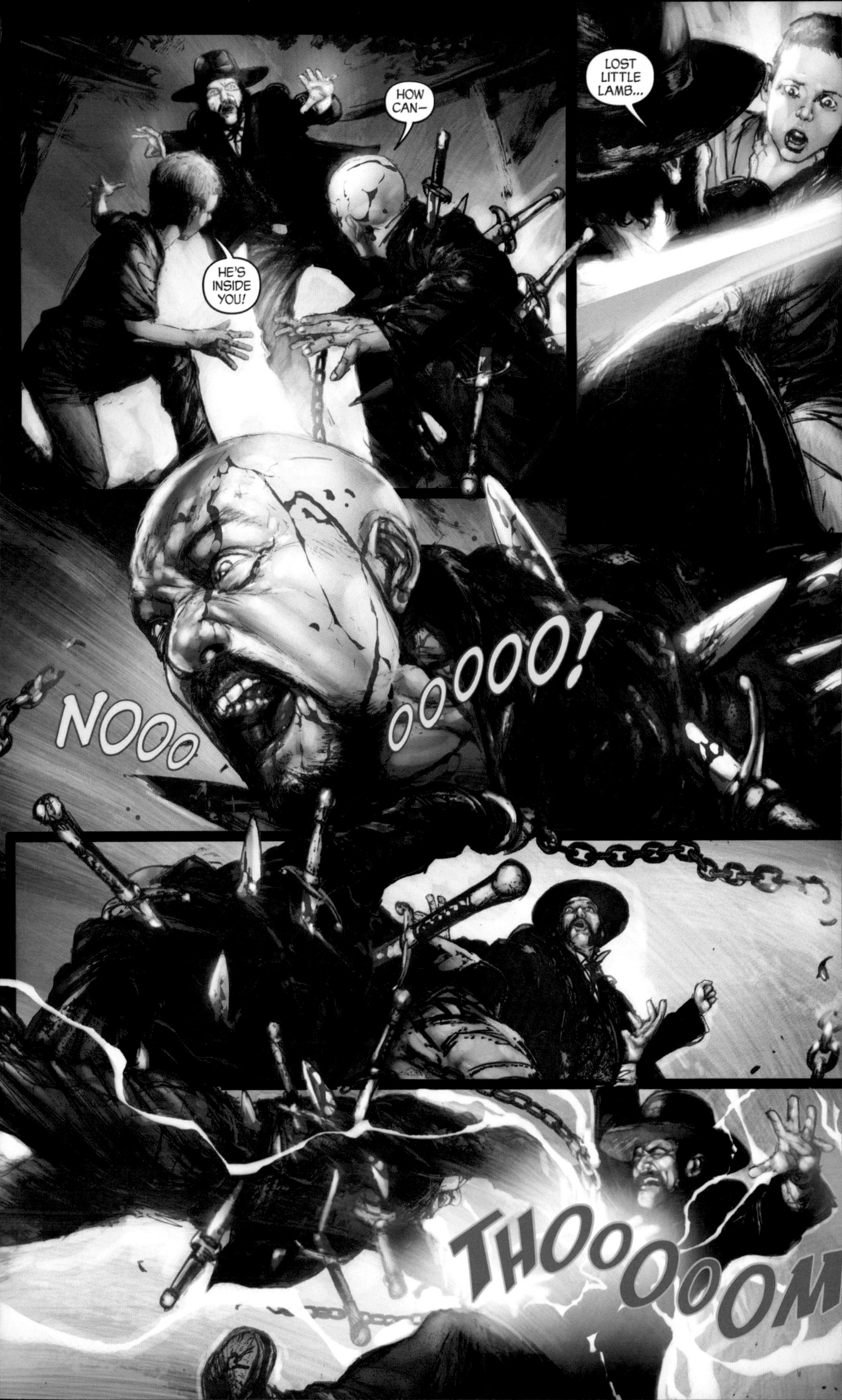
HOW CAN–
HE'S INSIDE YOU!
LOST LITTLE LAMB...
NOOOOOOOO!
THOOOOOM

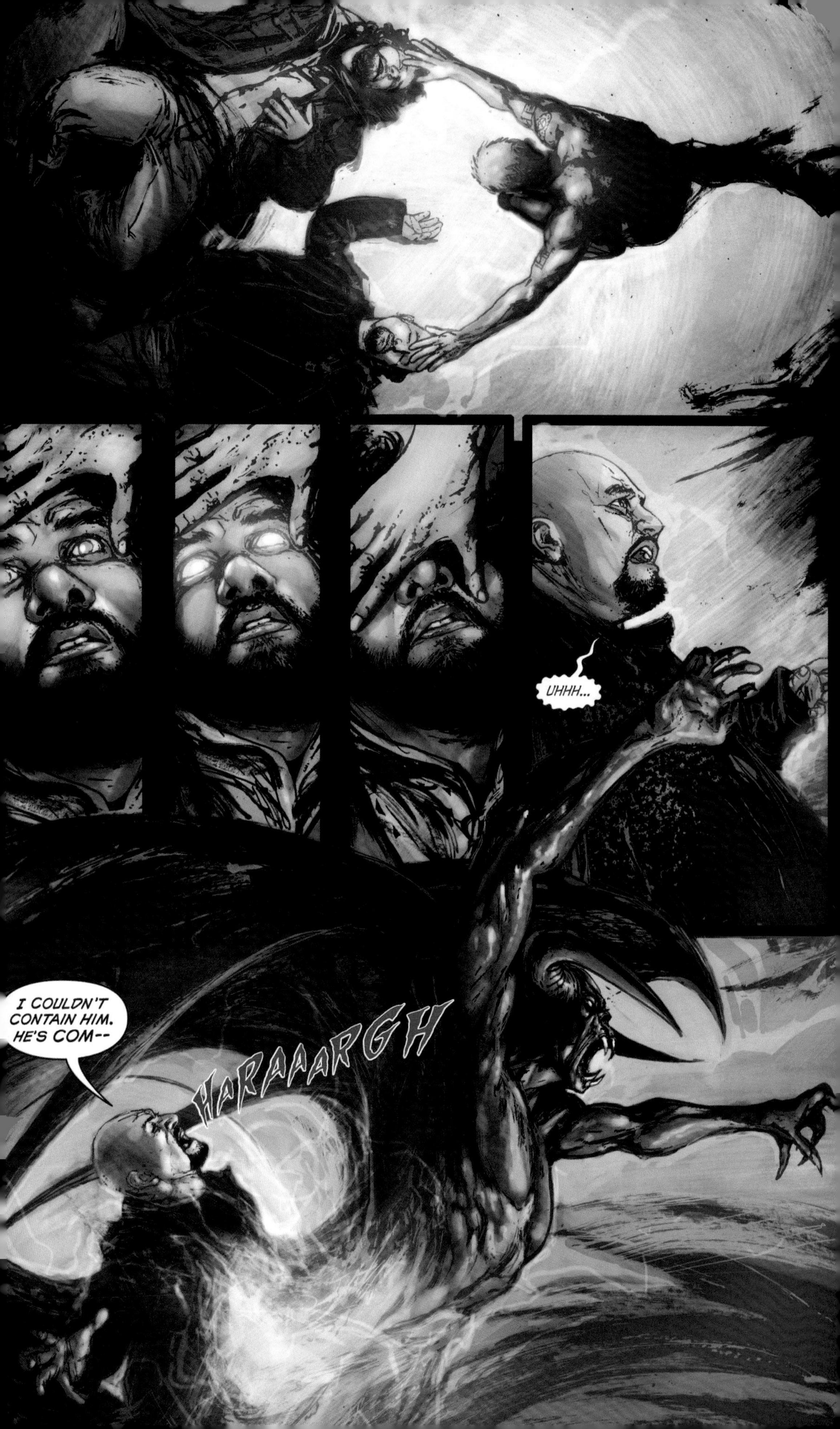
UHHH...
I COULDN'T CONTAIN HIM. HE'S COM--
HARAAARGH

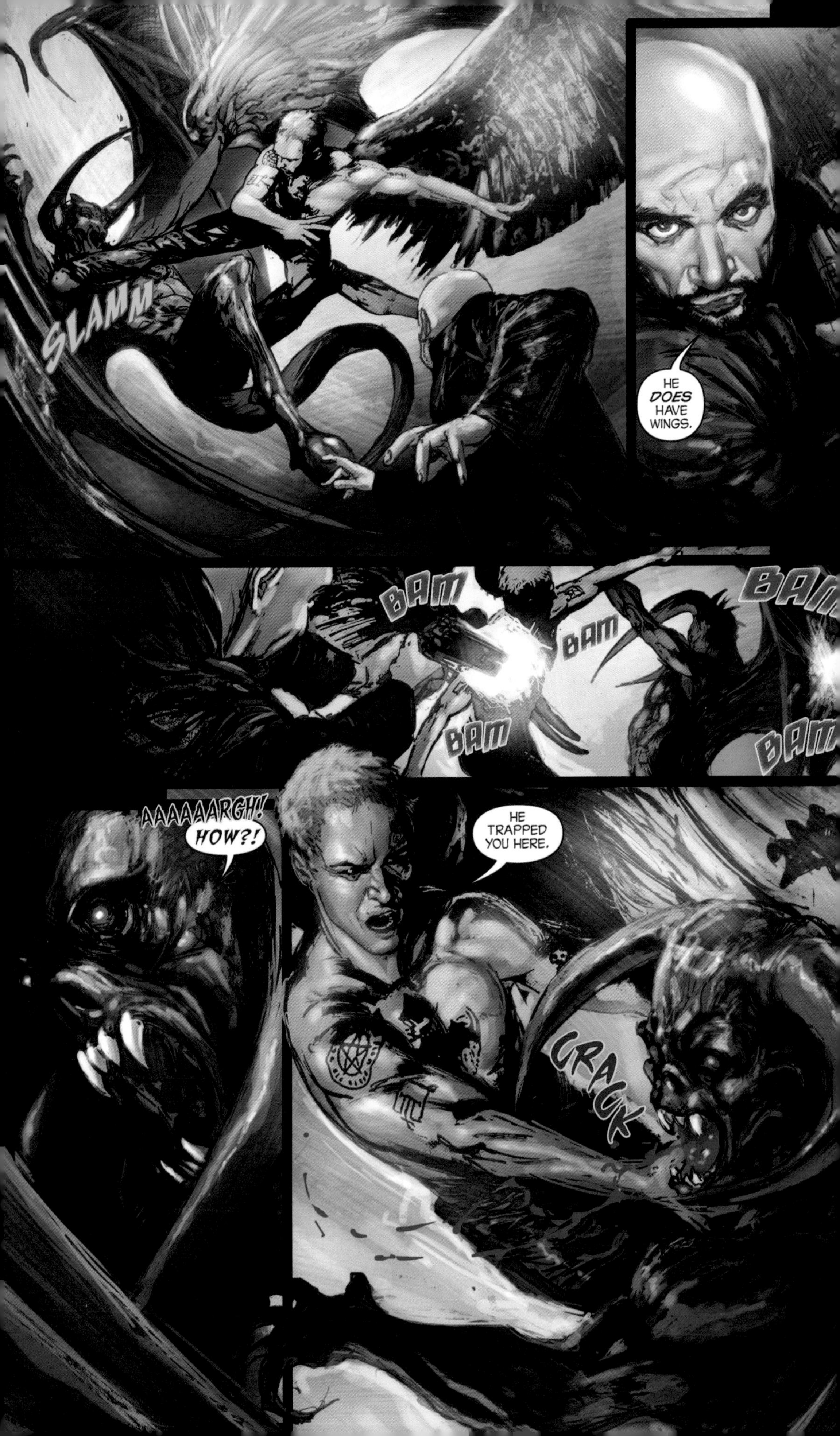
SLAMM
HE DOES HAVE WINGS.
BAM
BAM
BAM
BAM
BAM
AAAAAARGH!
HOW?!
HE TRAPPED YOU HERE.
CRACK

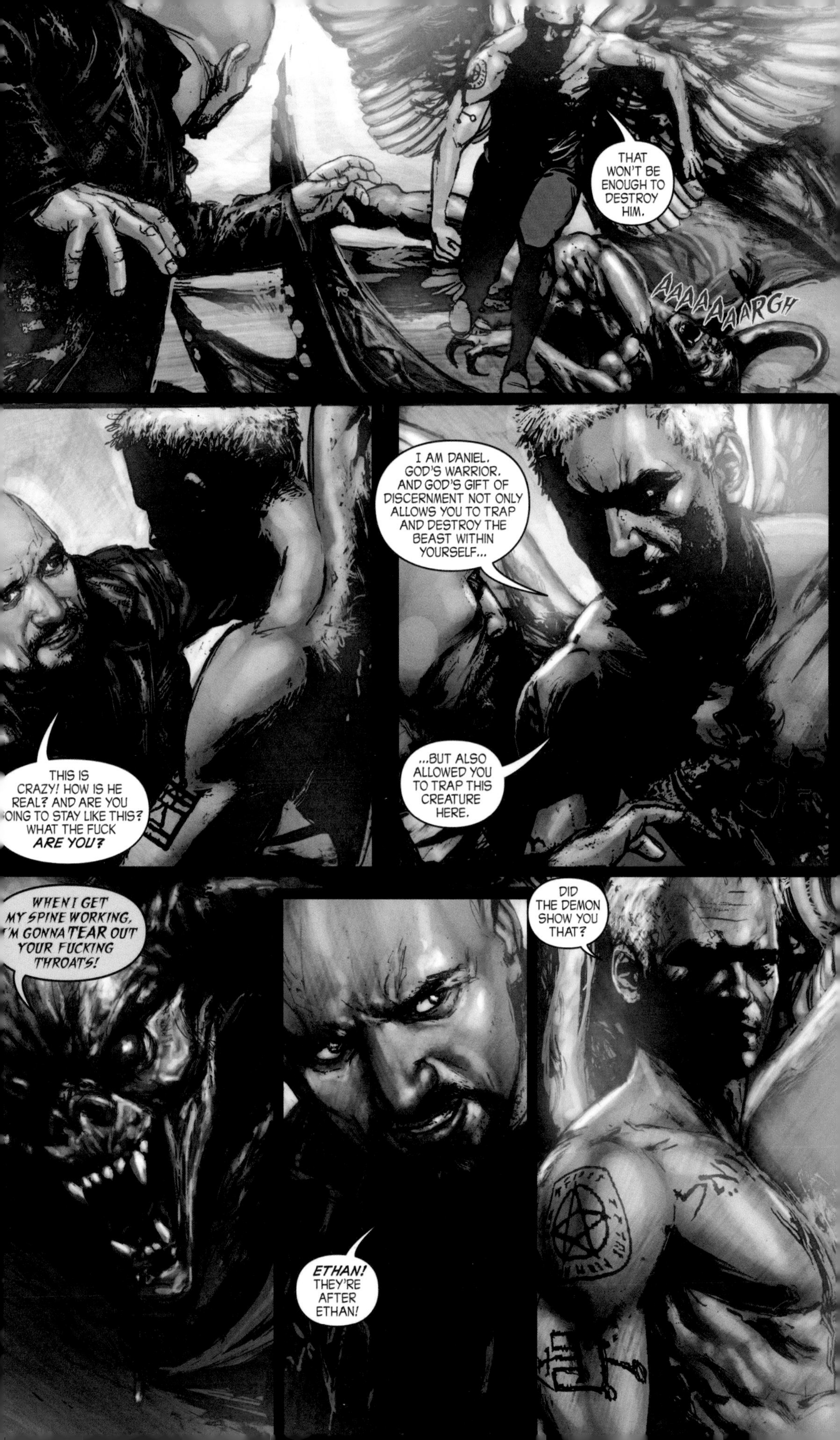
THAT WON'T BE ENOUGH TO DESTROY HIM.
AAAAAAARGH
THIS IS CRAZY! HOW IS HE REAL? AND ARE YOU OING TO STAY LIKE THIS? WHAT THE FUCK ARE YOU?
I AM DANIEL, GOD'S WARRIOR, AND GOD'S GIFT OF DISCERNMENT NOT ONLY ALLOWS YOU TO TRAP AND DESTROY THE BEAST WITHIN YOURSELF...
...BUT ALSO ALLOWED YOU TO TRAP THIS CREATURE HERE.
WHEN I GET MY SPINE WORKING, 'M GONNA TEAR OUT YOUR FUCKING THROATS!
ETHAN! THEY'RE AFTER ETHAN!
DID THE DEMON SHOW YOU THAT?

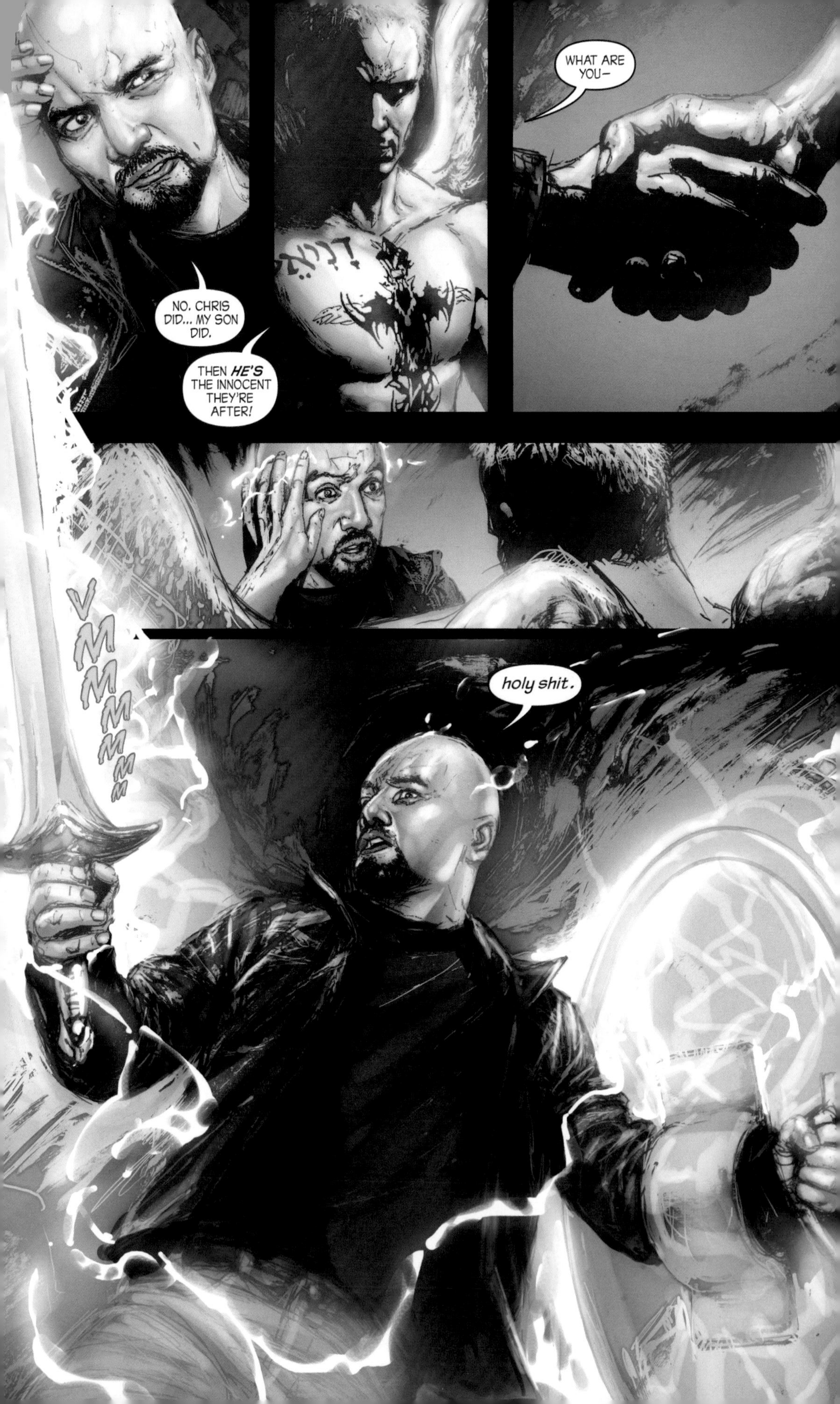
NO. CHRIS DID... MY SON DID.
THEN HE'S THE INNOCENT THEY'RE AFTER!
WHAT ARE YOU–
VMMMMMMM
holy shit.

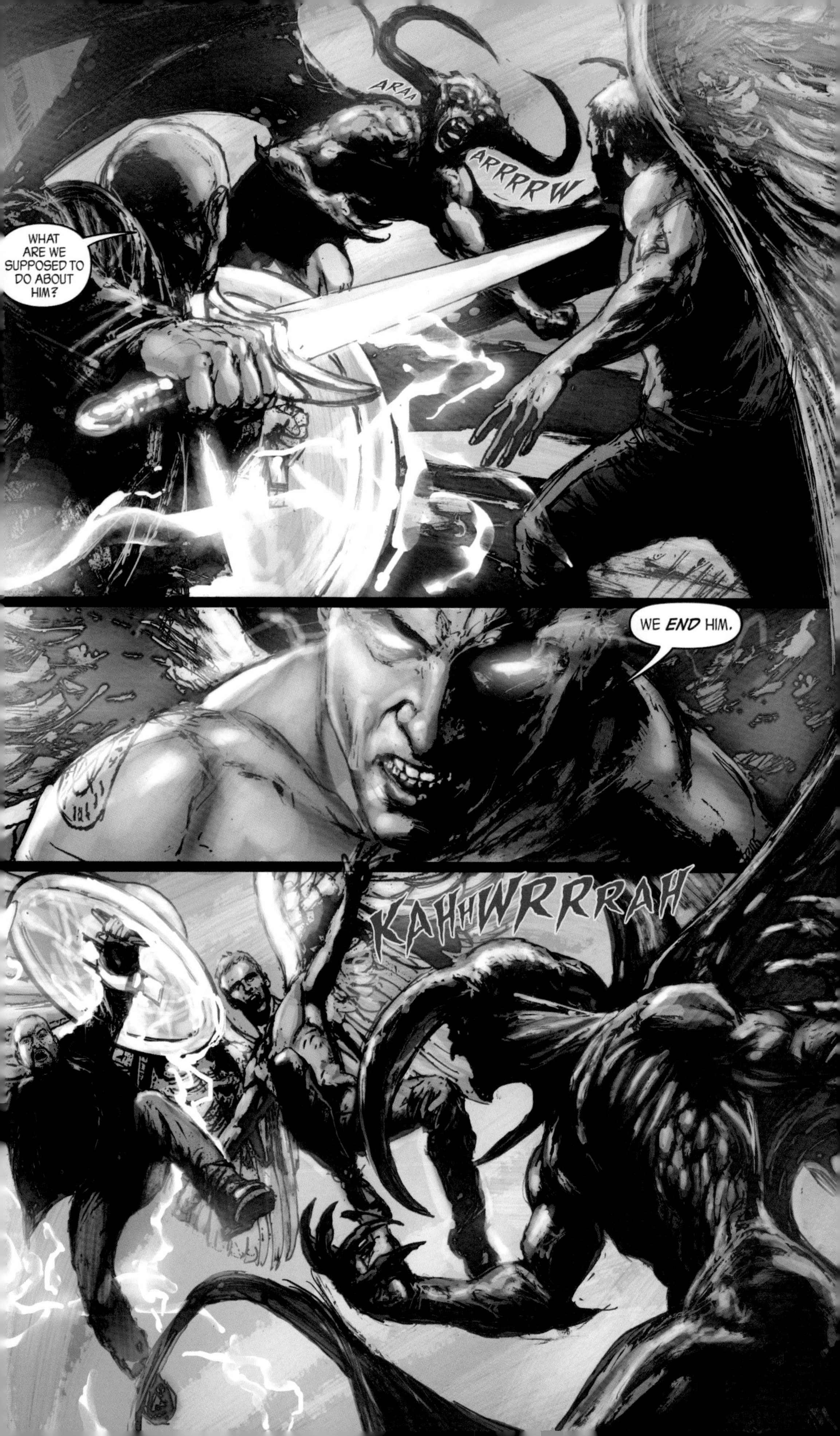
ARAA
ARRRRW
WHAT ARE WE SUPPOSED TO DO ABOUT HIM?
WE END HIM.
KAHHWRRRAH

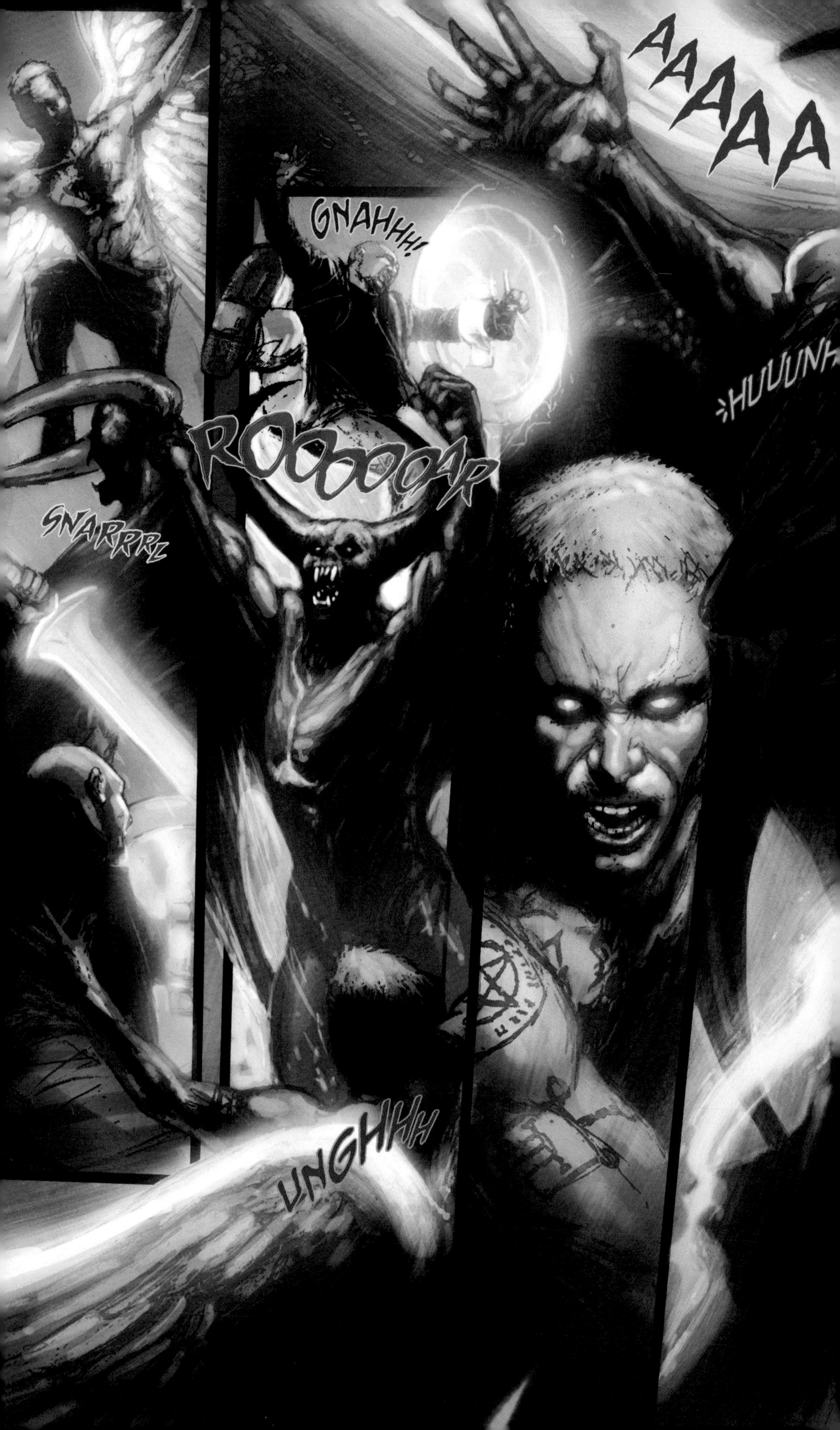

GNAHHH!
AAAAA
HUUUNH
ROOOOOOAR
SNARRRL
UNGHHH

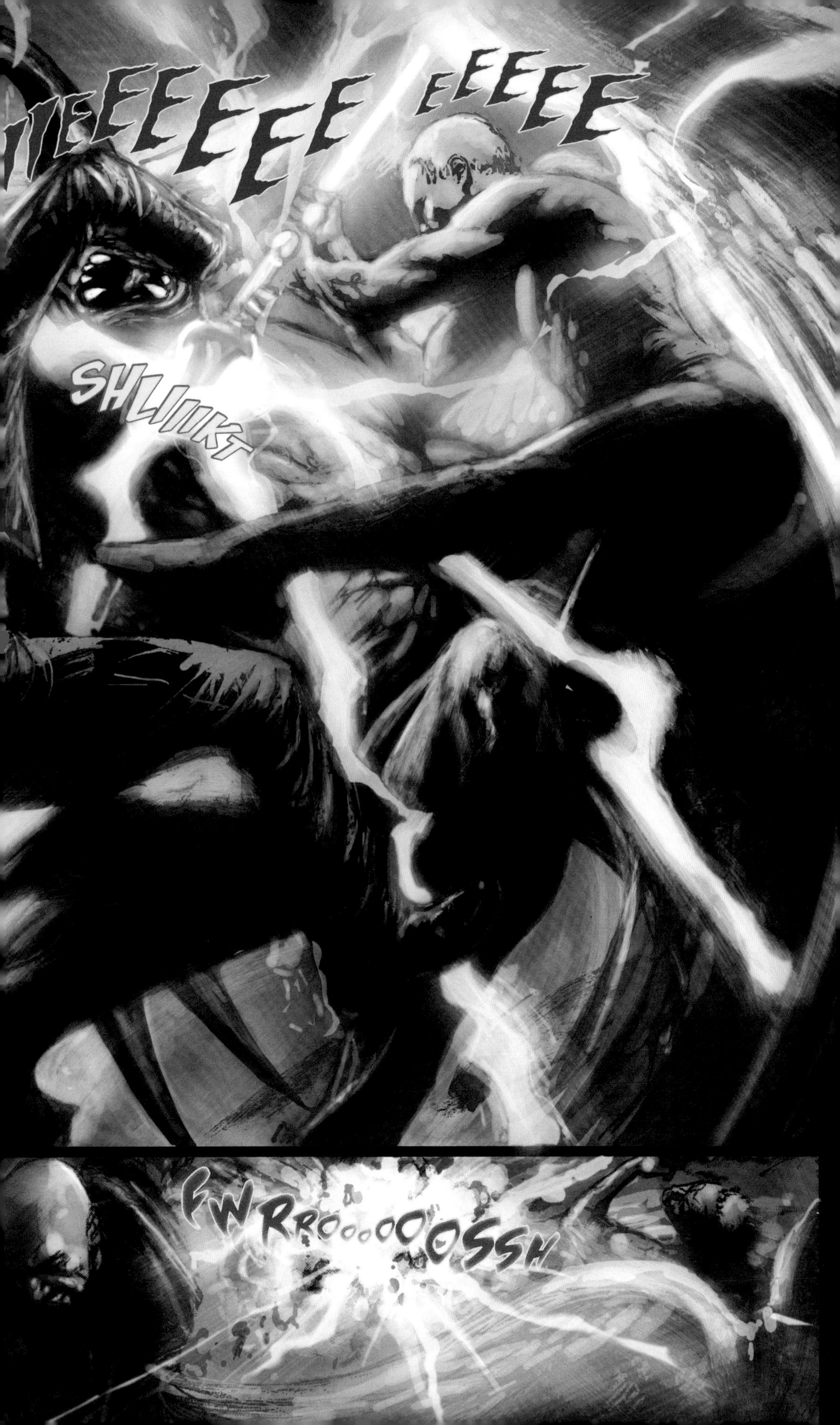
IIEEEEEEE EEEEE
SHLIIIKT
FWRROOOOOOSSH

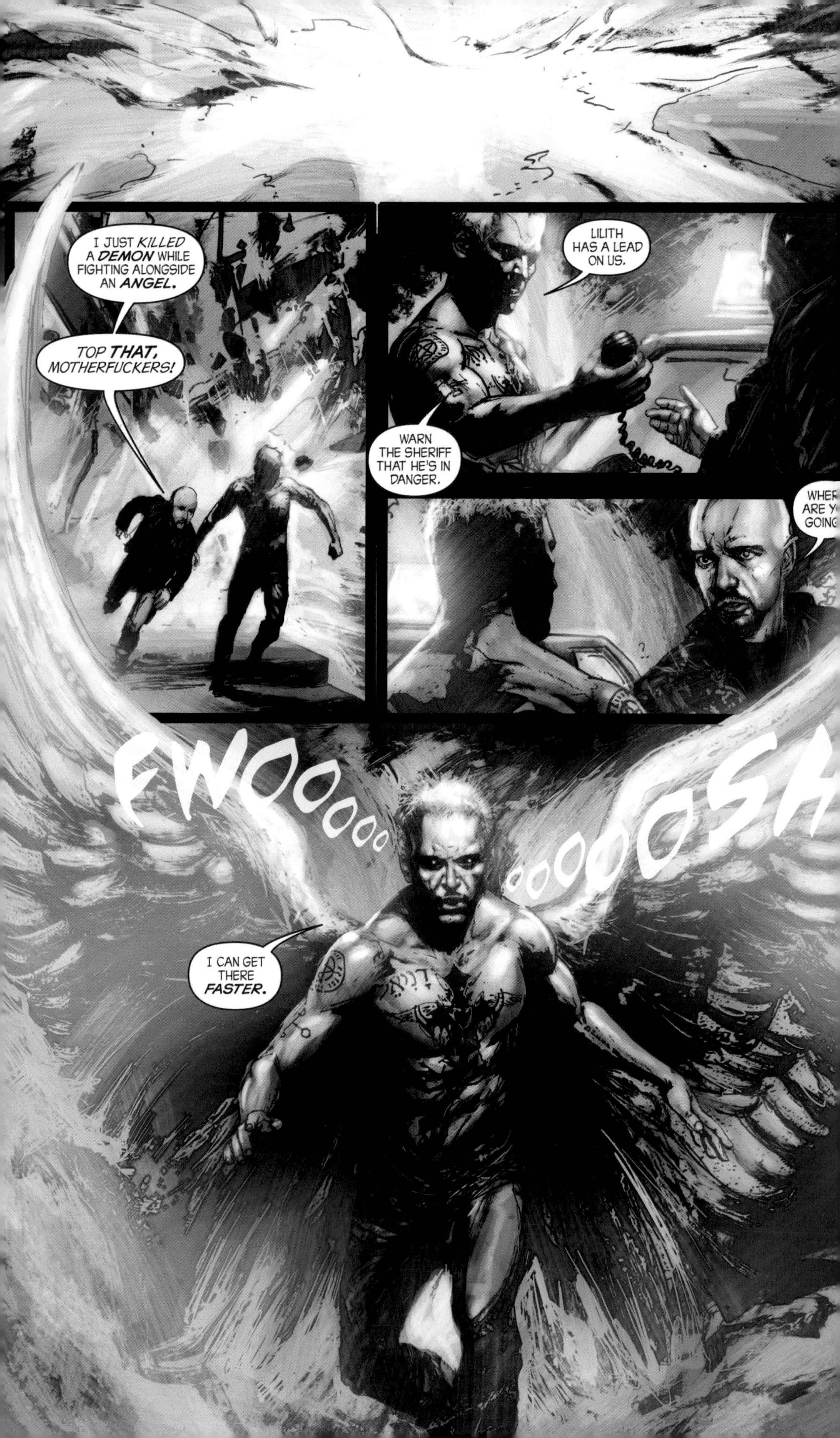
I JUST *KILLED* A ***DEMON*** WHILE FIGHTING ALONGSIDE AN ***ANGEL.***
TOP ***THAT,*** *MOTHERFUCKERS!*
LILITH HAS A LEAD ON US.
WARN THE SHERIFF THAT HE'S IN DANGER.
FWOOOOOOOOOOOSH
I CAN GET THERE ***FASTER.***

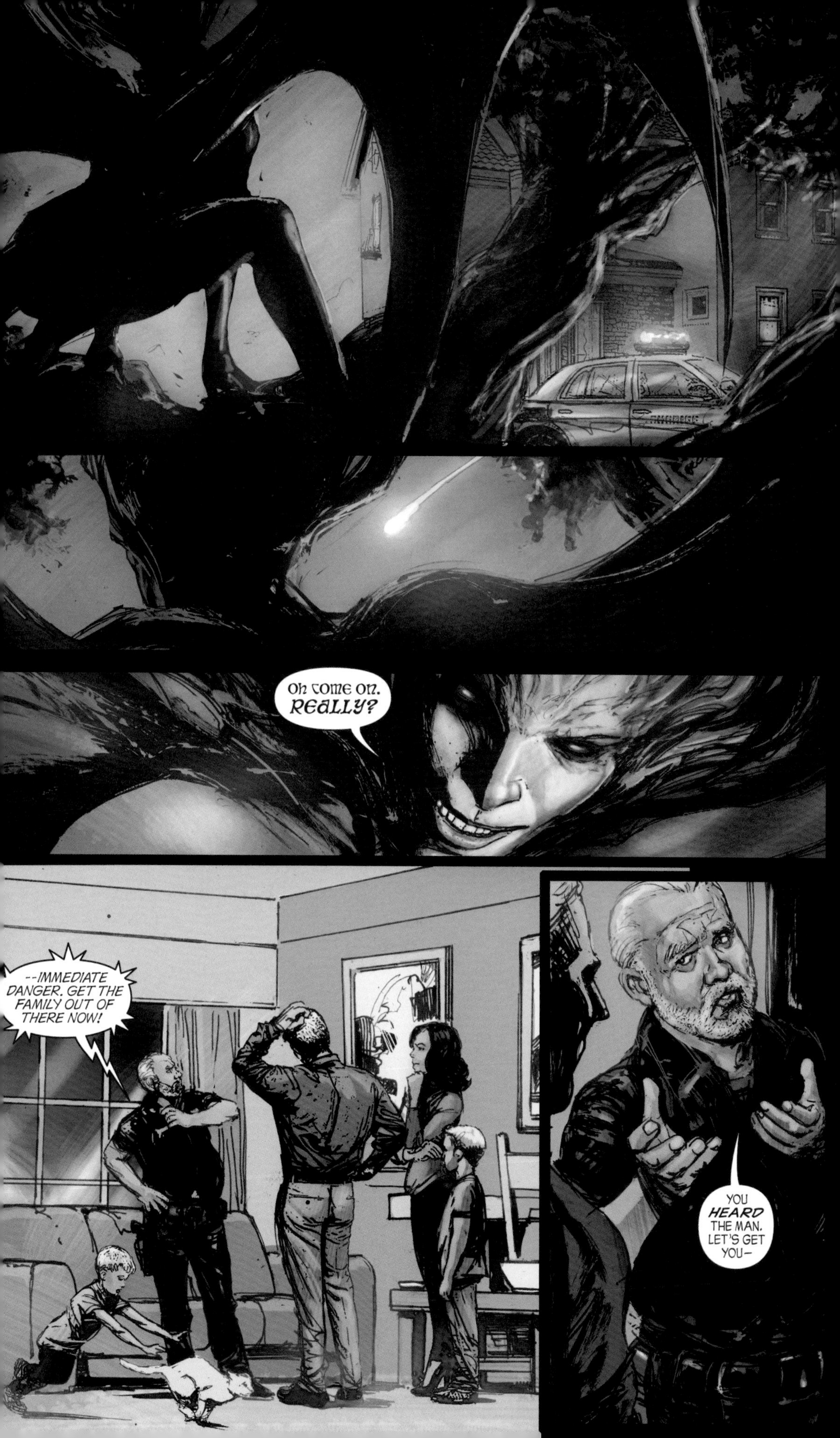
Oh come on. REALLY?
--IMMEDIATE DANGER. GET THE FAMILY OUT OF THERE NOW!
YOU HEARD THE MAN. LET'S GET YOU—

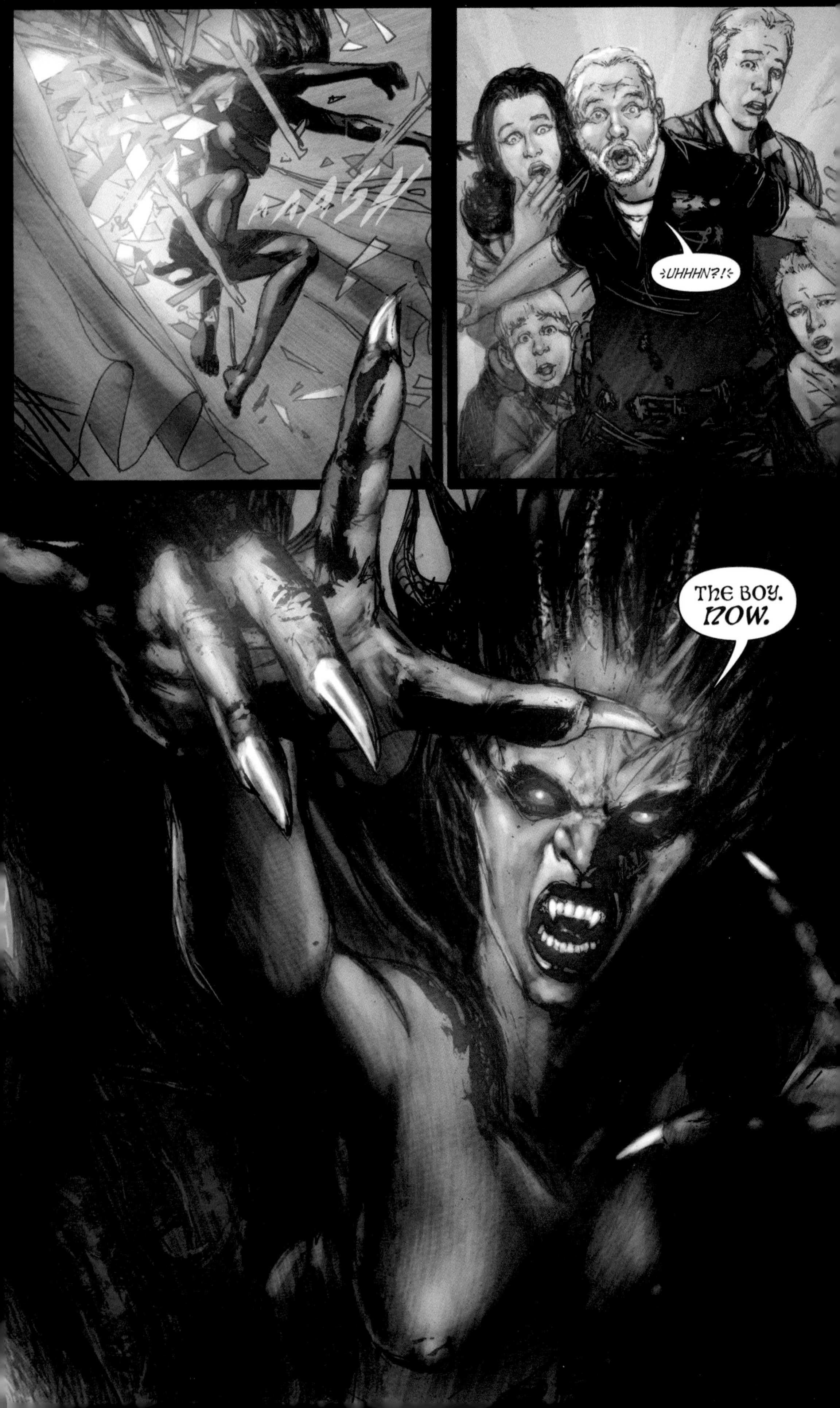
RAASH
UHHHN?!
THE BOY. NOW.

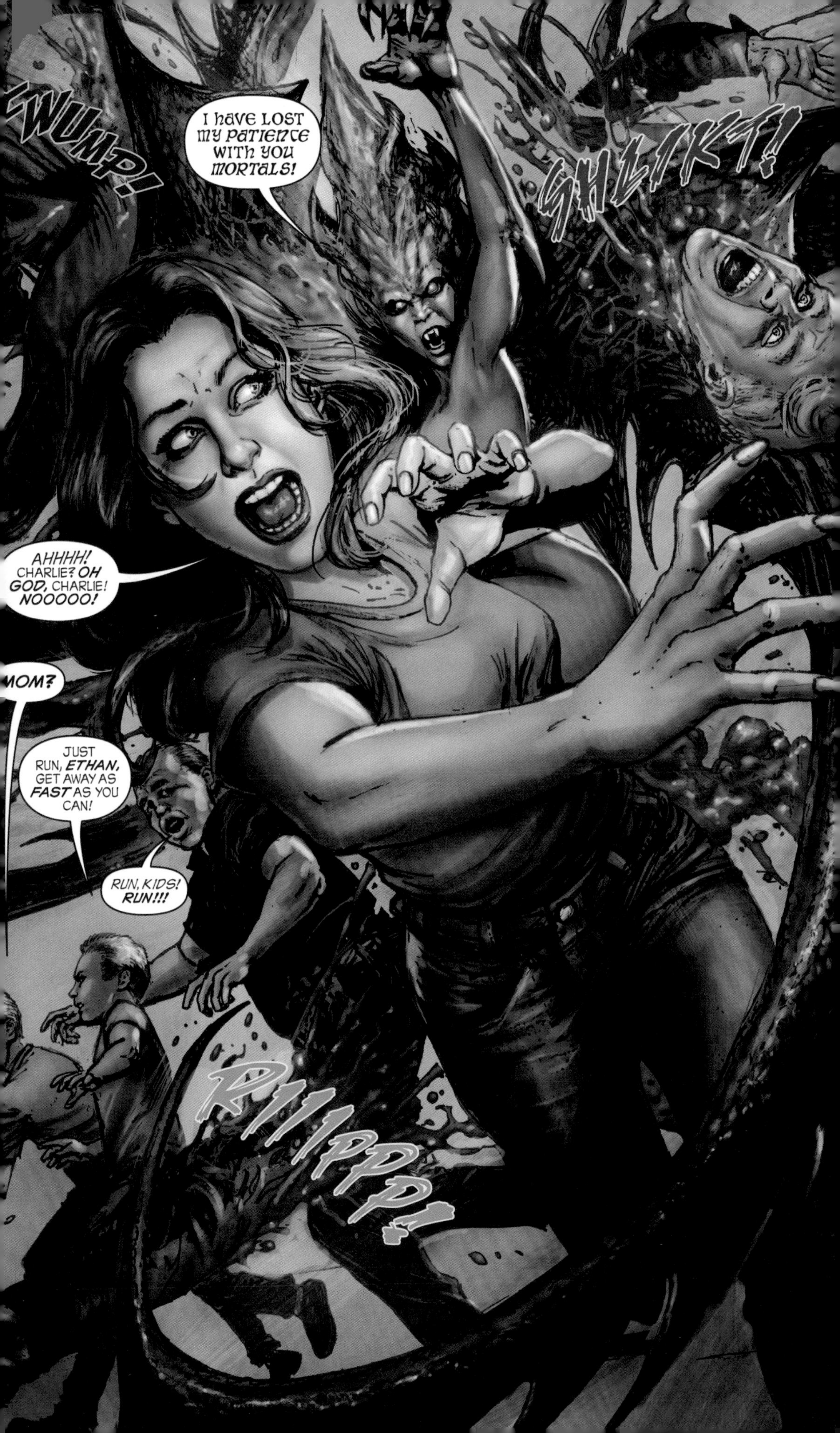
WUMP!
I HAVE LOST MY PATIENCE WITH YOU MORTALS!
SHLIKT!
AHHHH! CHARLIE? OH GOD, CHARLIE! NOOOOO!
MOM?
JUST RUN, ETHAN, GET AWAY AS FAST AS YOU CAN!
RUN, KIDS! RUN!!!
RIIIPPP!

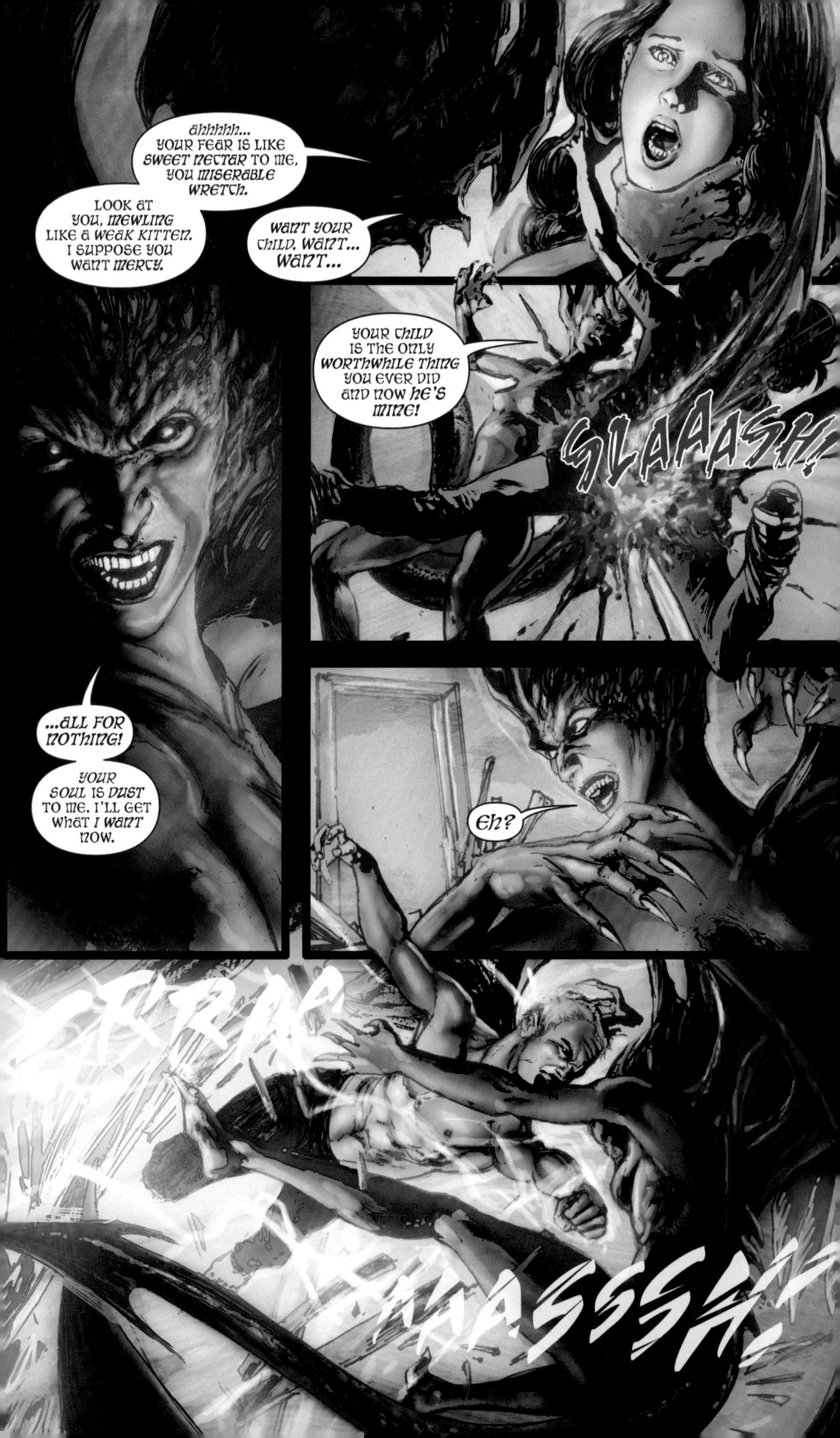
Ahhhhh... YOUR FEAR IS LIKE SWEET NECTAR TO ME, YOU MISERABLE WRETCH.
LOOK AT YOU, MEWLING LIKE A WEAK KITTEN. I SUPPOSE YOU WANT MERCY.
WANT YOUR CHILD. WANT... WANT...
...ALL FOR NOTHING!
YOUR SOUL IS DUST TO ME. I'LL GET WHAT I WANT NOW.
YOUR CHILD IS THE ONLY WORTHWHILE THING YOU EVER DID AND NOW HE'S MINE!
SLAAASH!
Eh?

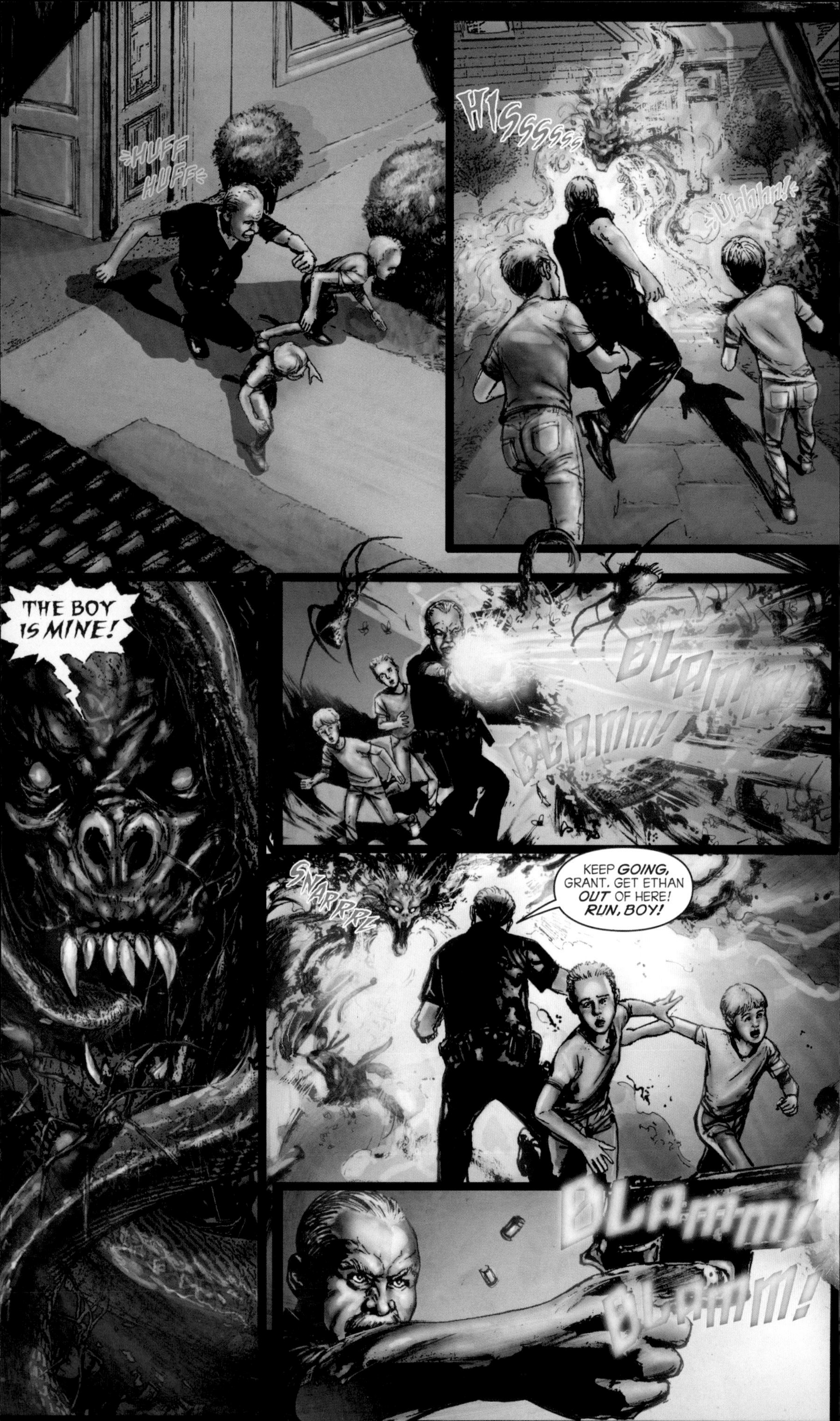
HUFF HUFF
HISSsss
Uhhhn!
THE BOY IS MINE!
BLAMMM!
BLAMMM!
SNARRRRZ
KEEP GOING, GRANT. GET ETHAN OUT OF HERE! RUN, BOY!
BLAMMM!
BLAMMM!

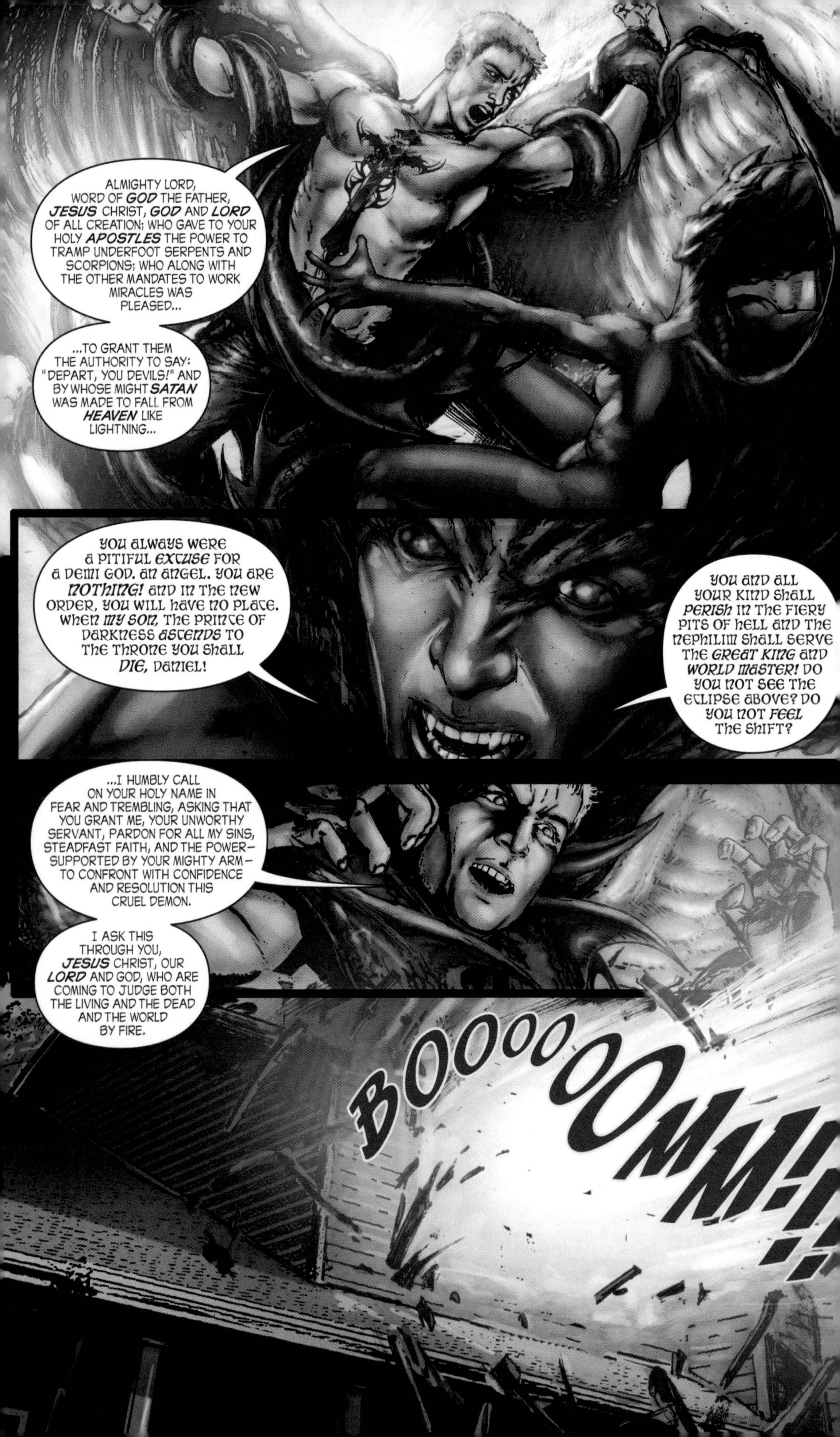
ALMIGHTY LORD, WORD OF GOD THE FATHER, JESUS CHRIST, GOD AND LORD OF ALL CREATION; WHO GAVE TO YOUR HOLY APOSTLES THE POWER TO TRAMP UNDERFOOT SERPENTS AND SCORPIONS; WHO ALONG WITH THE OTHER MANDATES TO WORK MIRACLES WAS PLEASED...
...TO GRANT THEM THE AUTHORITY TO SAY: "DEPART, YOU DEVILS!" AND BY WHOSE MIGHT SATAN WAS MADE TO FALL FROM HEAVEN LIKE LIGHTNING...
YOU ALWAYS WERE A PITIFUL EXCUSE FOR A DEMI GOD. AN ANGEL. YOU ARE NOTHING! AND IN THE NEW ORDER, YOU WILL HAVE NO PLACE. WHEN MY SON, THE PRINCE OF DARKNESS ASCENDS TO THE THRONE YOU SHALL DIE, DANIEL!
YOU AND ALL YOUR KIND SHALL PERISH IN THE FIERY PITS OF HELL AND THE NEPHILIM SHALL SERVE THE GREAT KING AND WORLD MASTER! DO YOU NOT SEE THE ECLIPSE ABOVE? DO YOU NOT FEEL THE SHIFT?
...I HUMBLY CALL ON YOUR HOLY NAME IN FEAR AND TREMBLING, ASKING THAT YOU GRANT ME, YOUR UNWORTHY SERVANT, PARDON FOR ALL MY SINS, STEADFAST FAITH, AND THE POWER—SUPPORTED BY YOUR MIGHTY ARM—TO CONFRONT WITH CONFIDENCE AND RESOLUTION THIS CRUEL DEMON.
I ASK THIS THROUGH YOU, JESUS CHRIST, OUR LORD AND GOD, WHO ARE COMING TO JUDGE BOTH THE LIVING AND THE DEAD AND THE WORLD BY FIRE.
BOOOOOOMM!!

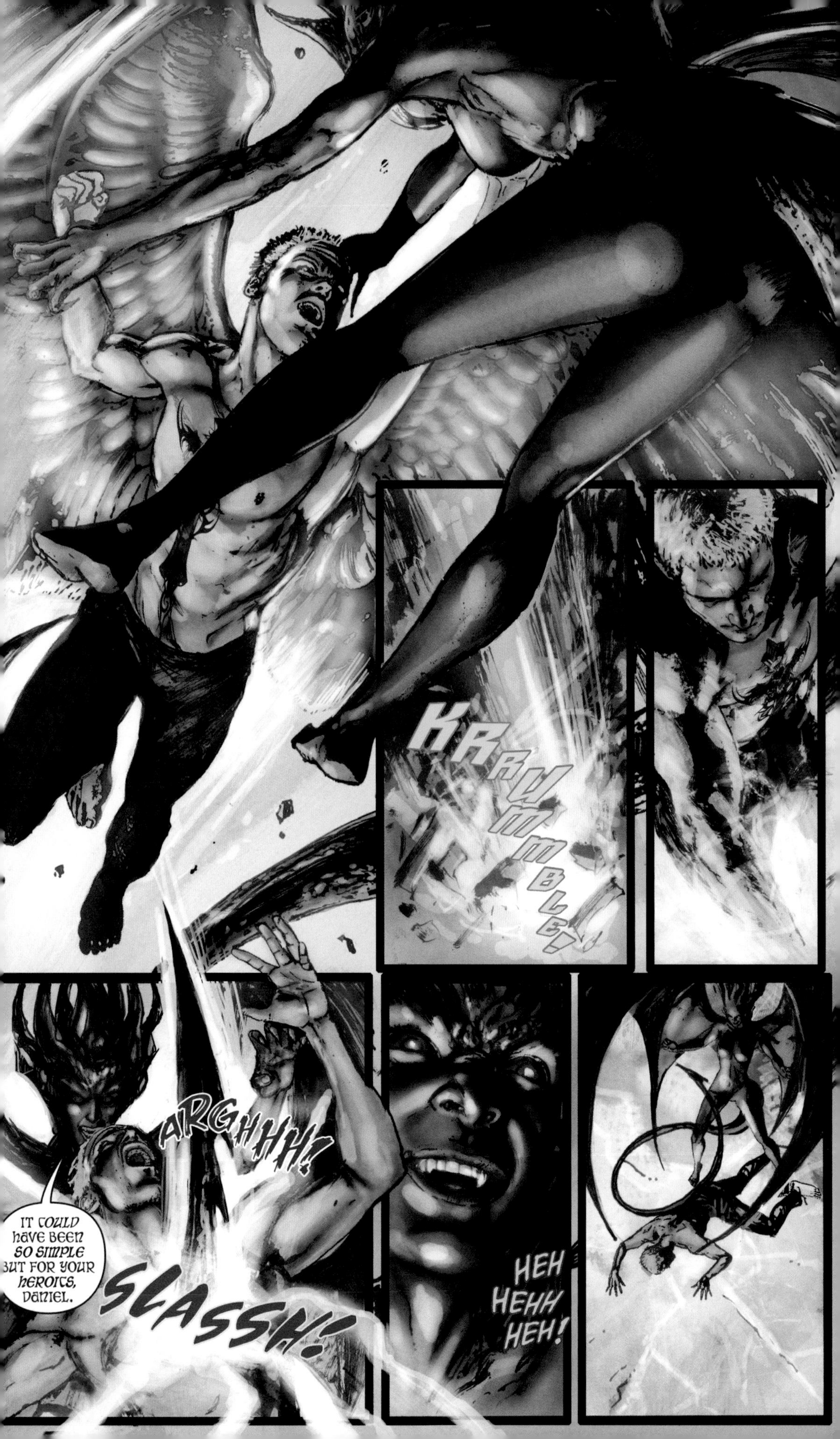
KRRUMMBLE!
ARGHHH!
IT COULD HAVE BEEN SO SIMPLE BUT FOR YOUR HEROICS, DANIEL.
SLASSH!
HEH HEHH HEH!

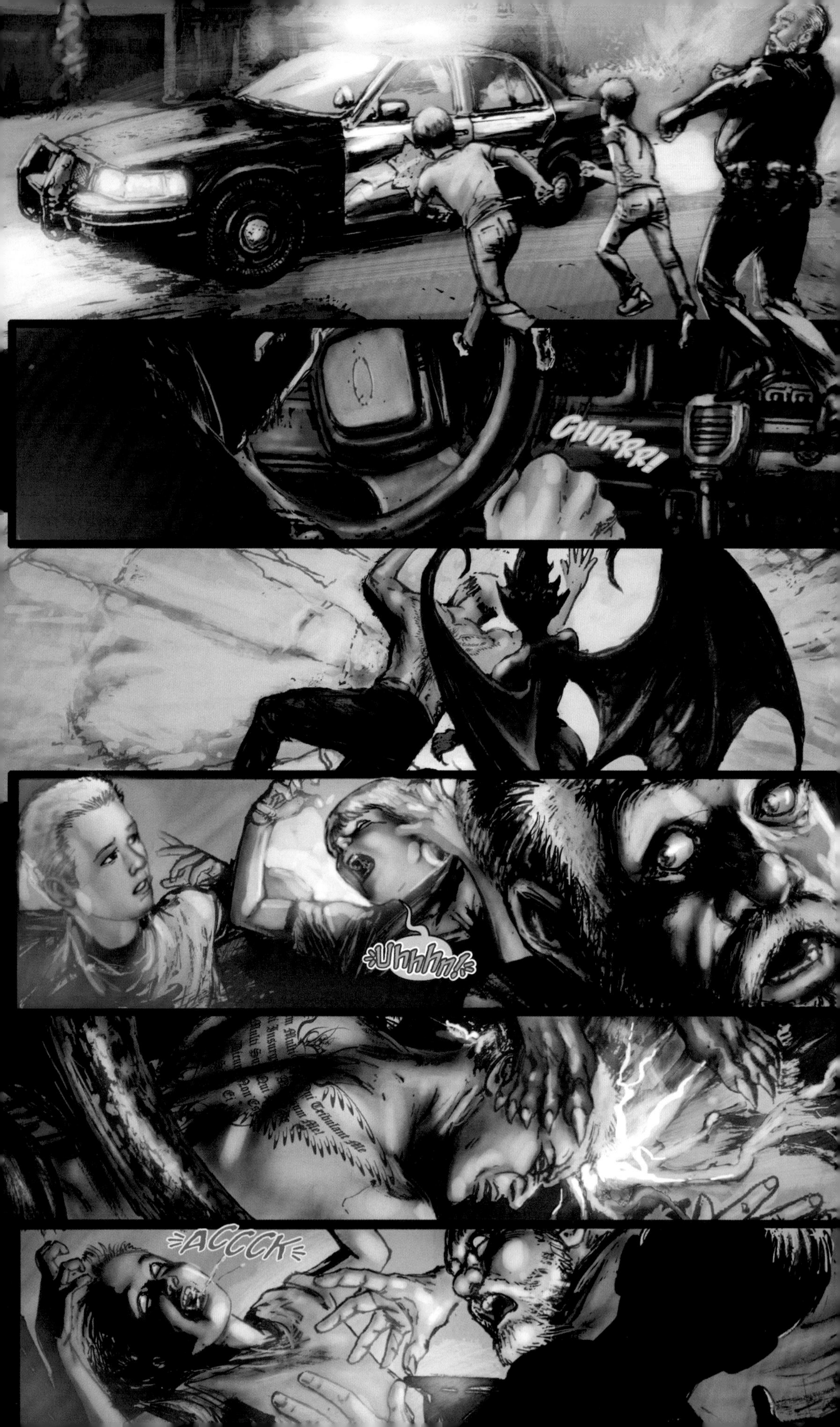
CHURRR!
Uhhhn!
ACCCK

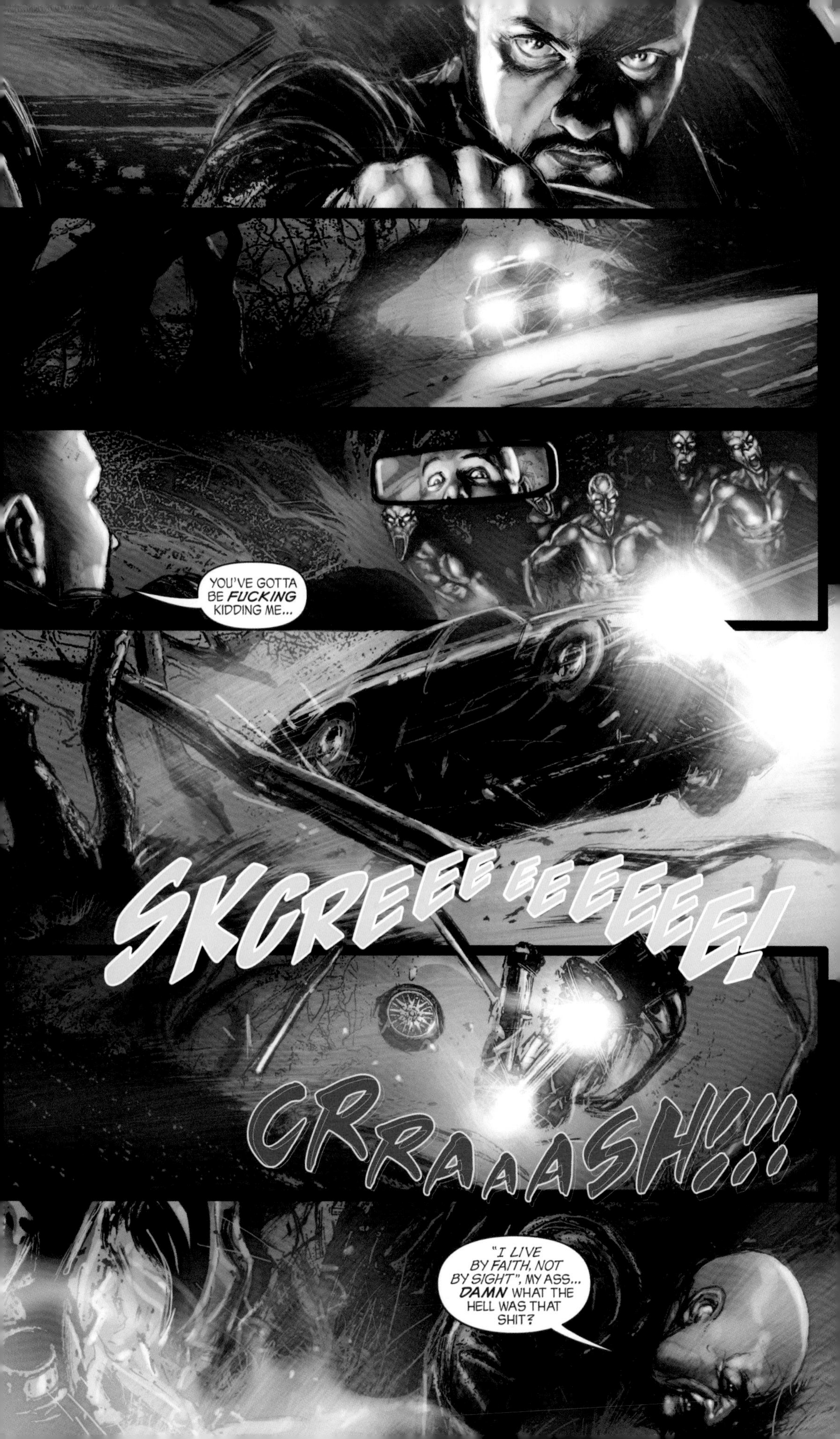
YOU'VE GOTTA BE FUCKING KIDDING ME...
SKCREEEEEEEEE!
CRRAAASH!!!
"I LIVE BY FAITH, NOT BY SIGHT", MY ASS... DAMN WHAT THE HELL WAS THAT SHIT?

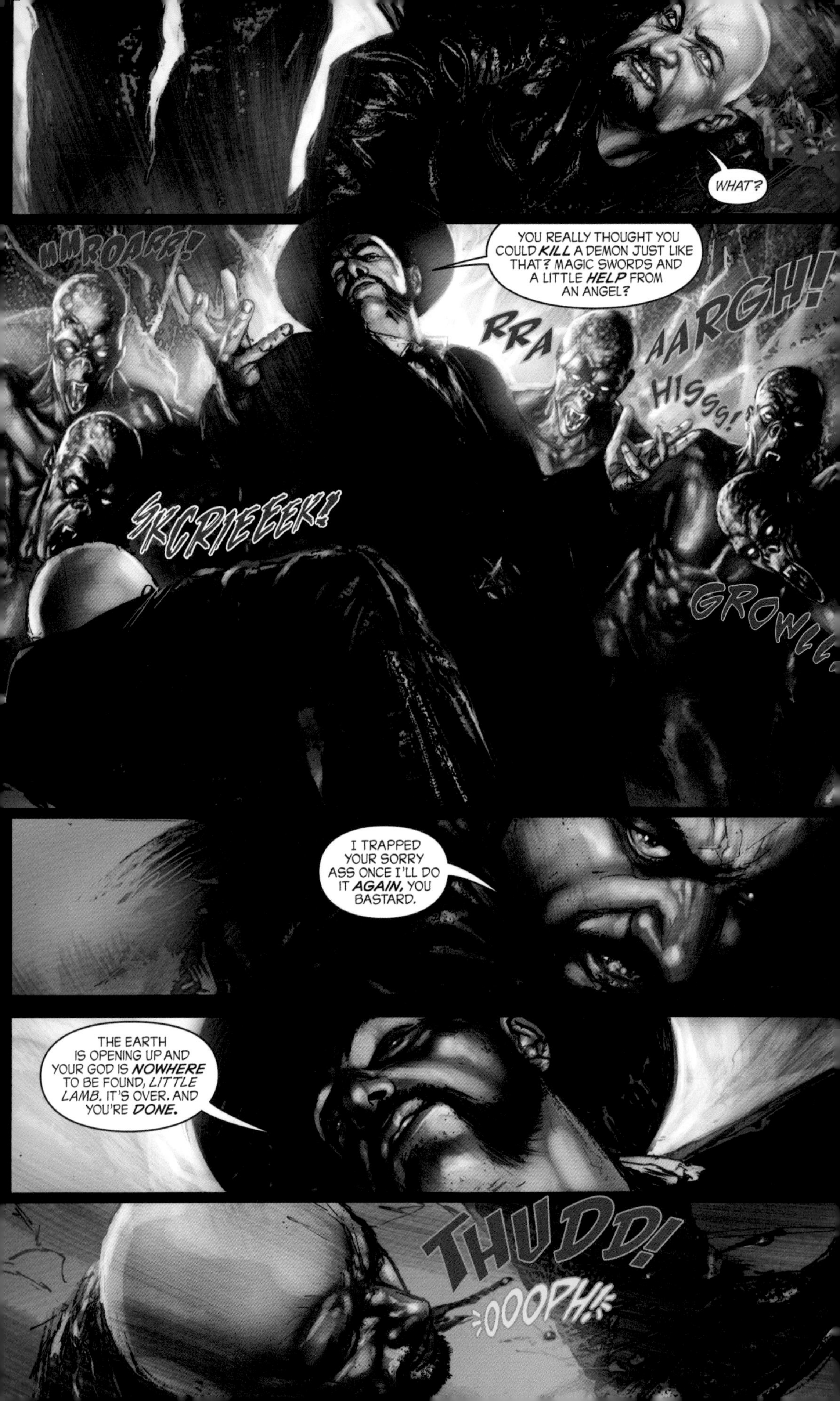
WHAT?
MMROARR!
YOU REALLY THOUGHT YOU COULD ***KILL*** A DEMON JUST LIKE THAT? MAGIC SWORDS AND A LITTLE ***HELP*** FROM AN ANGEL?
RRA
AARGH!
HISSS!
SKCRIEEEK!
GROWLL
I TRAPPED YOUR SORRY ASS ONCE I'LL DO IT ***AGAIN,*** YOU BASTARD.
THE EARTH IS OPENING UP AND YOUR GOD IS ***NOWHERE*** TO BE FOUND, *LITTLE LAMB.* IT'S OVER. AND YOU'RE ***DONE.***
THUDD!
OOOPH!

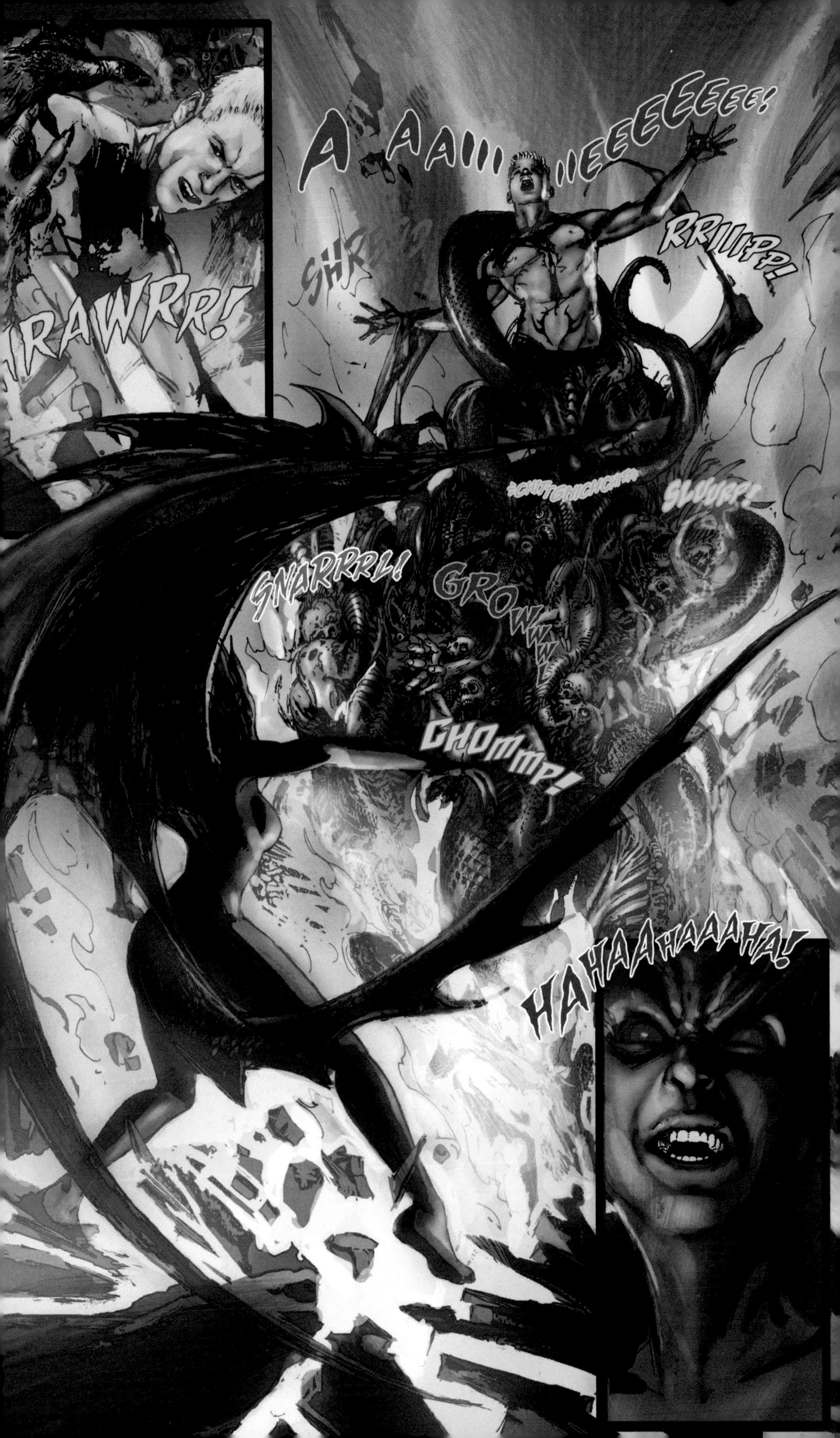
RAWRR!
AAAIII...EEEEEeee!
RRIIIPP!
SLUURP!
SNARRRL!
GROWWWL
CHOMMP!
HAHAAHAAAHA!

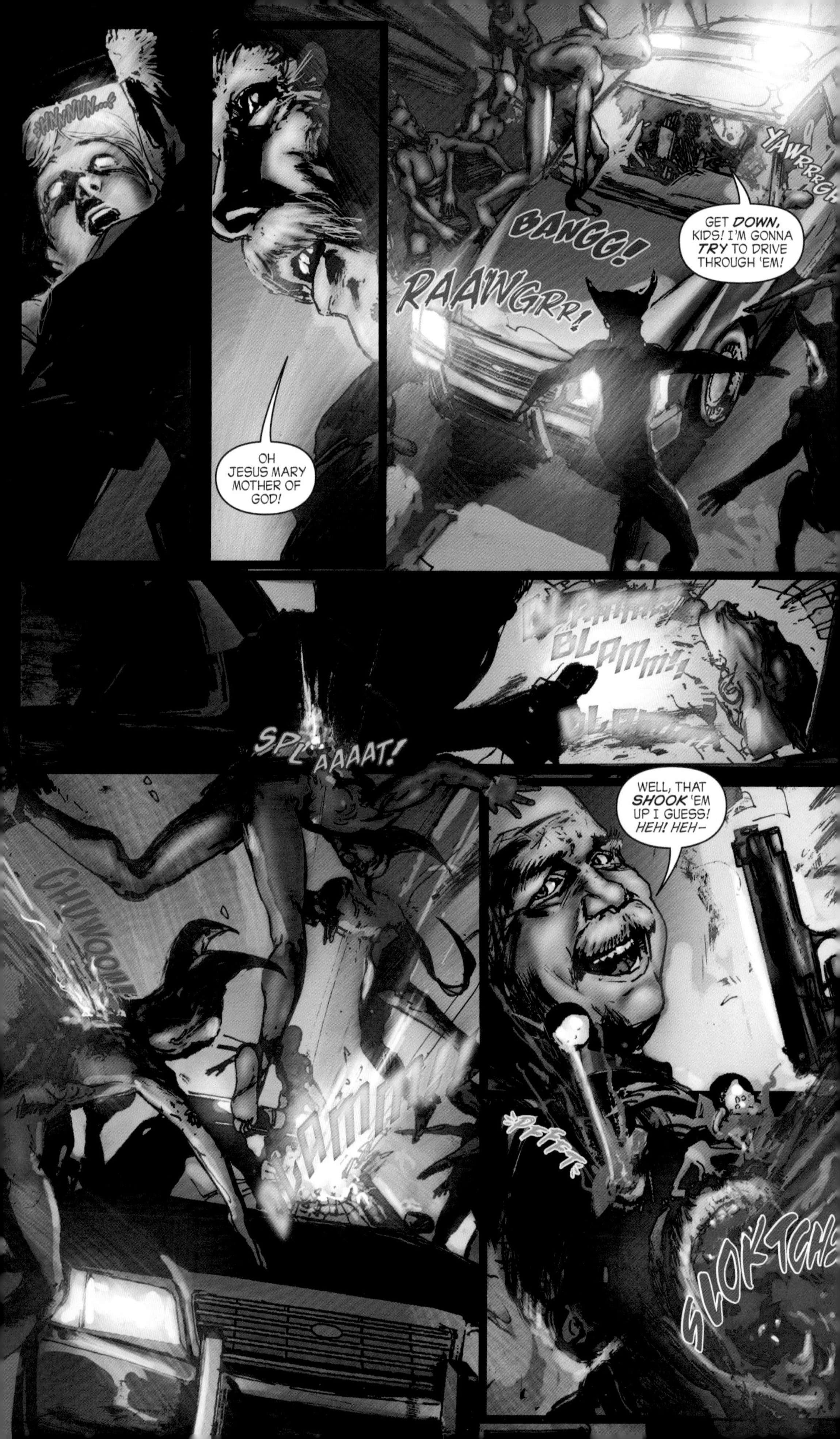
HNNNNN...!
OH JESUS MARY MOTHER OF GOD!
BANGG!
RAAWGRR!
YAWRRRGH!
GET DOWN, KIDS! I'M GONNA TRY TO DRIVE THROUGH 'EM!
BLAMM!
SPLAAAAT!
CHUWOOM!
WELL, THAT SHOOK 'EM UP I GUESS! HEH! HEH–
PFFFT
SLOK'TCHE

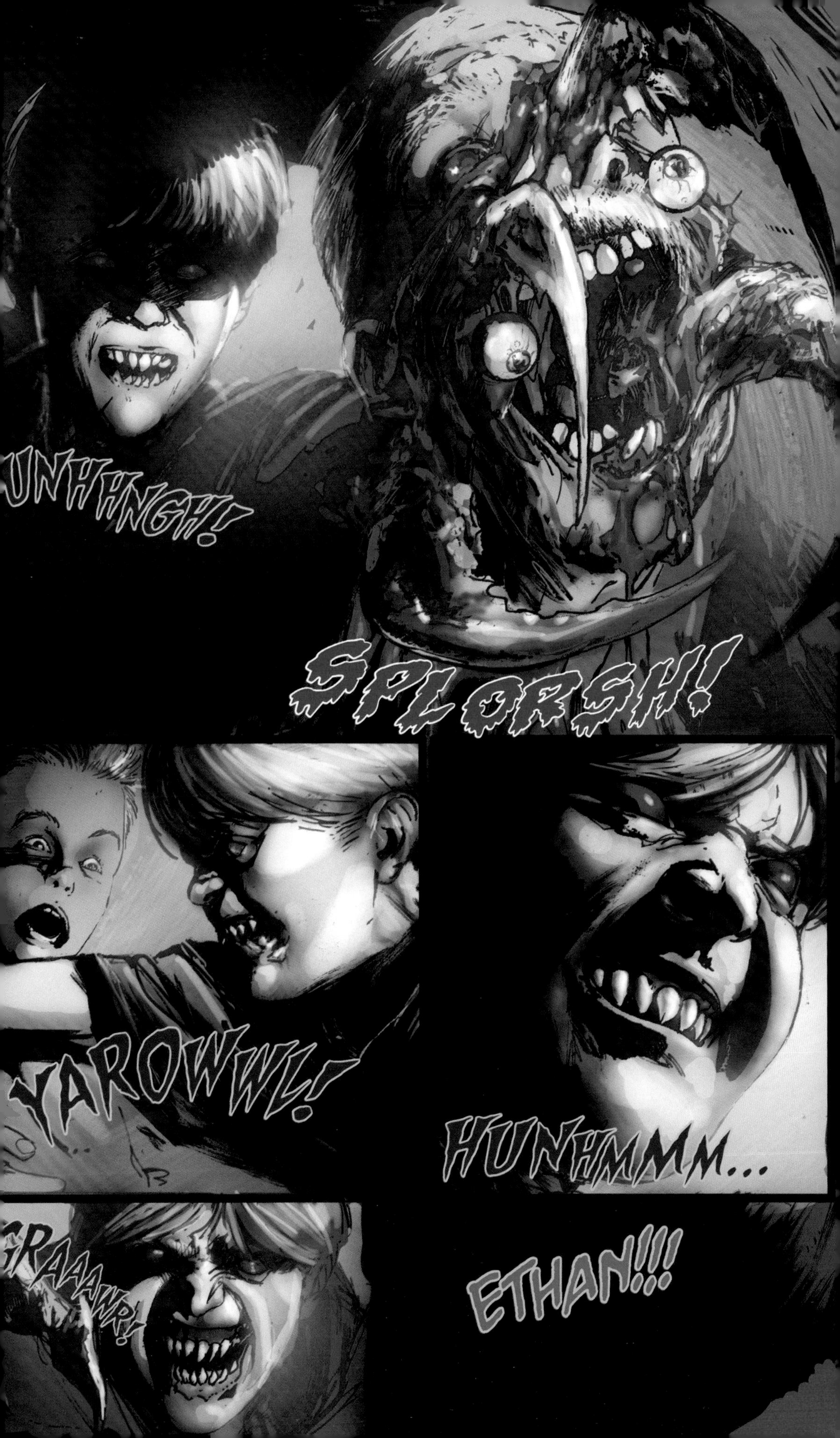
UNHHNGH!
SPLORSH!
YAROWWL!
HUNHMMM...
GRAAAWR!
ETHAN!!!

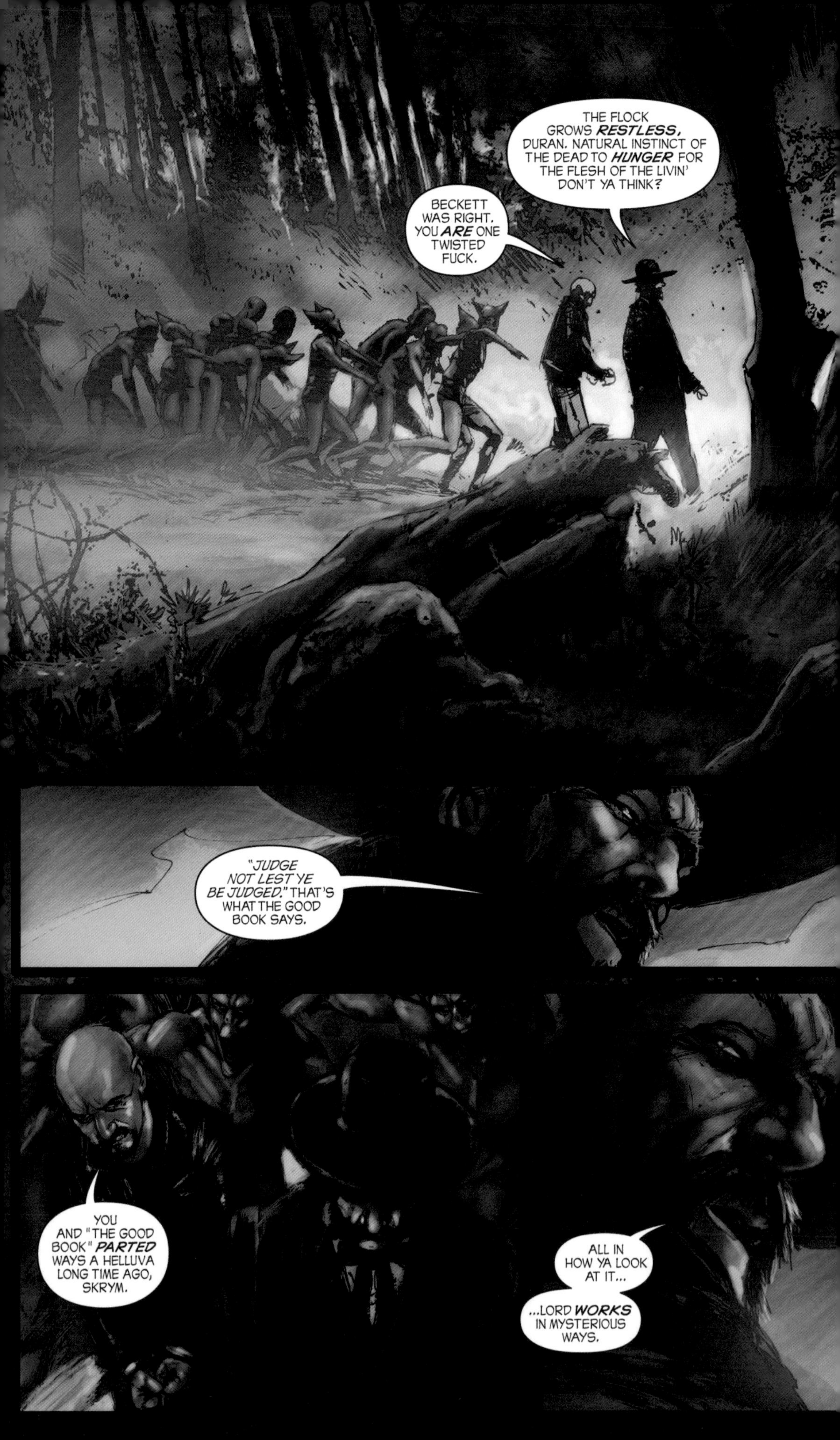

BECKETT WAS RIGHT. YOU ARE ONE TWISTED FUCK.
THE FLOCK GROWS RESTLESS, DURAN. NATURAL INSTINCT OF THE DEAD TO HUNGER FOR THE FLESH OF THE LIVIN' DON'T YA THINK?
"JUDGE NOT LEST YE BE JUDGED." THAT'S WHAT THE GOOD BOOK SAYS.
YOU AND "THE GOOD BOOK" PARTED WAYS A HELLUVA LONG TIME AGO, SKRYM.
ALL IN HOW YA LOOK AT IT...
...LORD WORKS IN MYSTERIOUS WAYS.

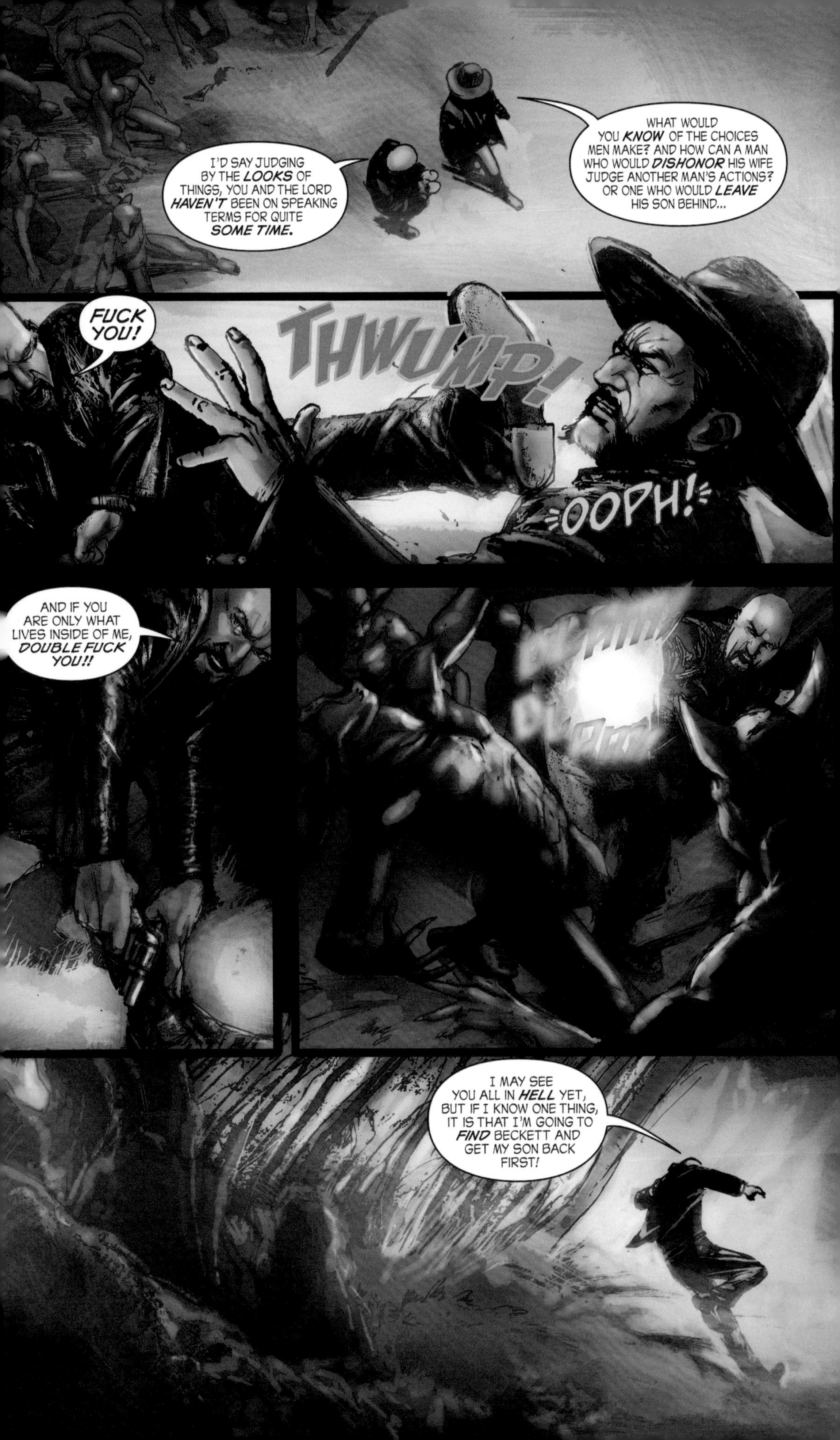

I'D SAY JUDGING BY THE ***LOOKS*** OF THINGS, YOU AND THE LORD ***HAVEN'T*** BEEN ON SPEAKING TERMS FOR QUITE ***SOME TIME.***
WHAT WOULD YOU ***KNOW*** OF THE CHOICES MEN MAKE? AND HOW CAN A MAN WHO WOULD ***DISHONOR*** HIS WIFE JUDGE ANOTHER MAN'S ACTIONS? OR ONE WHO WOULD ***LEAVE*** HIS SON BEHIND...
FUCK YOU!
THWUMP!
OOPH!
AND IF YOU ARE ONLY WHAT LIVES INSIDE OF ME, ***DOUBLE FUCK YOU!!***
I MAY SEE YOU ALL IN ***HELL*** YET, BUT IF I KNOW ONE THING, IT IS THAT I'M GOING TO ***FIND*** BECKETT AND GET MY SON BACK FIRST!

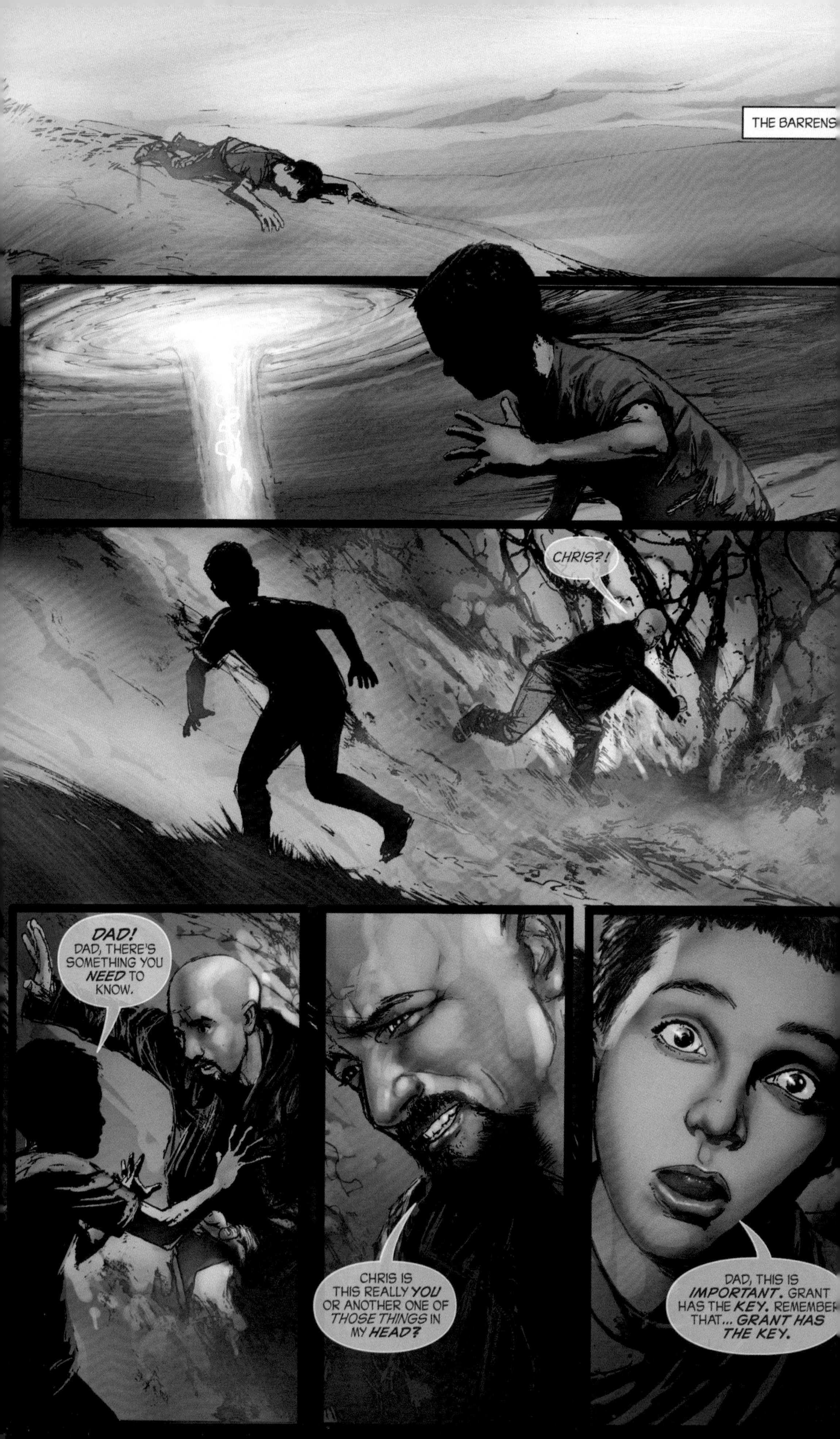
THE BARRENS
CHRIS?!
DAD! DAD, THERE'S SOMETHING YOU NEED TO KNOW.
CHRIS IS THIS REALLY YOU OR ANOTHER ONE OF THOSE THINGS IN MY HEAD?
DAD, THIS IS IMPORTANT. GRANT HAS THE KEY. REMEMBER THAT... GRANT HAS THE KEY.

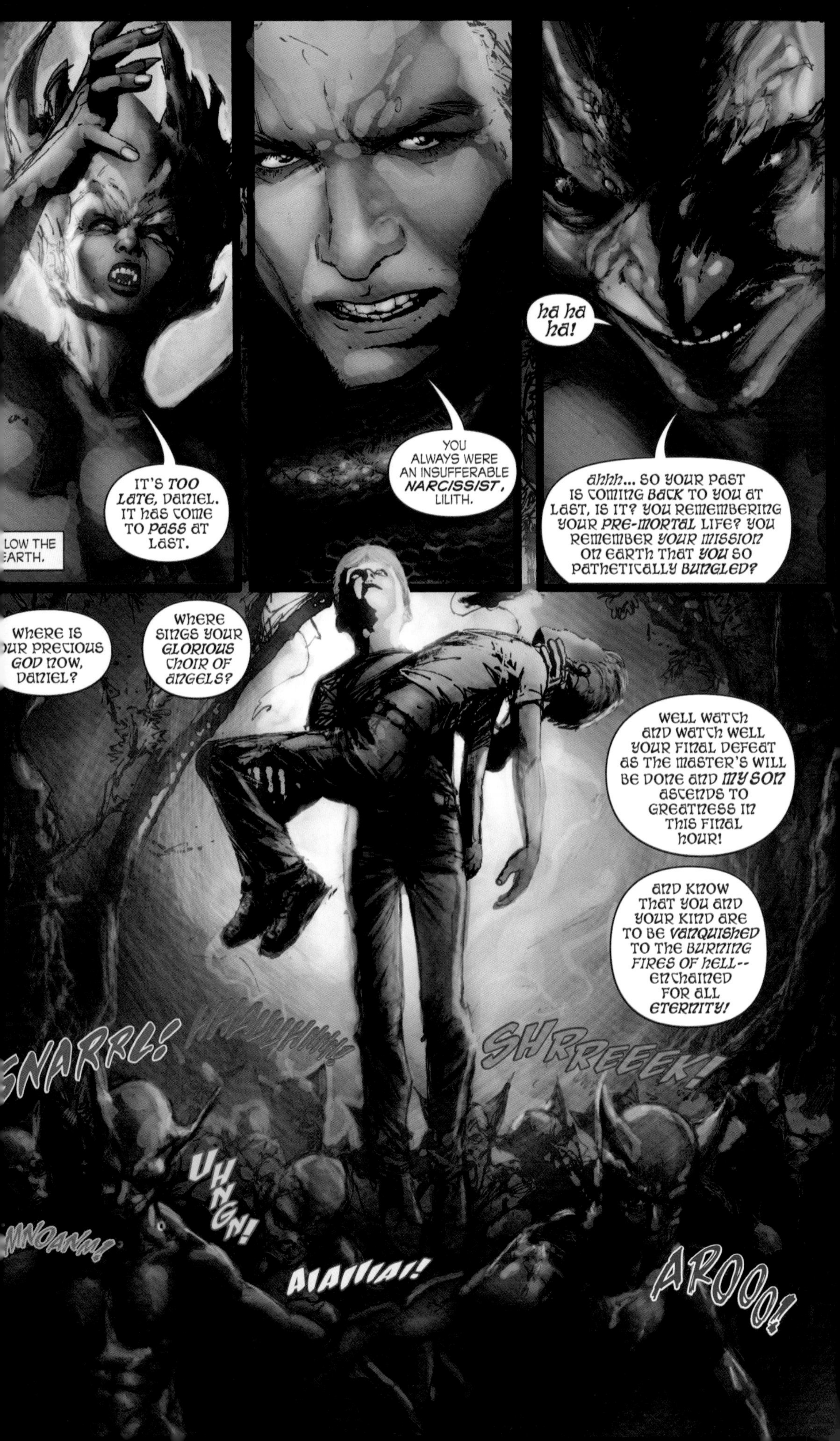
LOW THE
EARTH.
IT'S TOO LATE, DANIEL. IT HAS COME TO PASS AT LAST.
YOU ALWAYS WERE AN INSUFFERABLE NARCISSIST, LILITH.
ha ha ha!
AHHH... SO YOUR PAST IS COMING BACK TO YOU AT LAST, IS IT? YOU REMEMBERING YOUR PRE-MORTAL LIFE? YOU REMEMBER YOUR MISSION ON EARTH THAT YOU SO PATHETICALLY BUNGLED?
WHERE IS UR PRECIOUS GOD NOW, DANIEL?
WHERE SINGS YOUR GLORIOUS CHOIR OF ANGELS?
WELL WATCH AND WATCH WELL YOUR FINAL DEFEAT AS THE MASTER'S WILL BE DONE AND MY SON ASCENDS TO GREATNESS IN THIS FINAL HOUR!
AND KNOW THAT YOU AND YOUR KIND ARE TO BE VANQUISHED TO THE BURNING FIRES OF HELL--ENCHAINED FOR ALL ETERNITY!
SNARRL!
SHRREEEK!
UHNGN!
AIAIIIAI!
AROOOO!

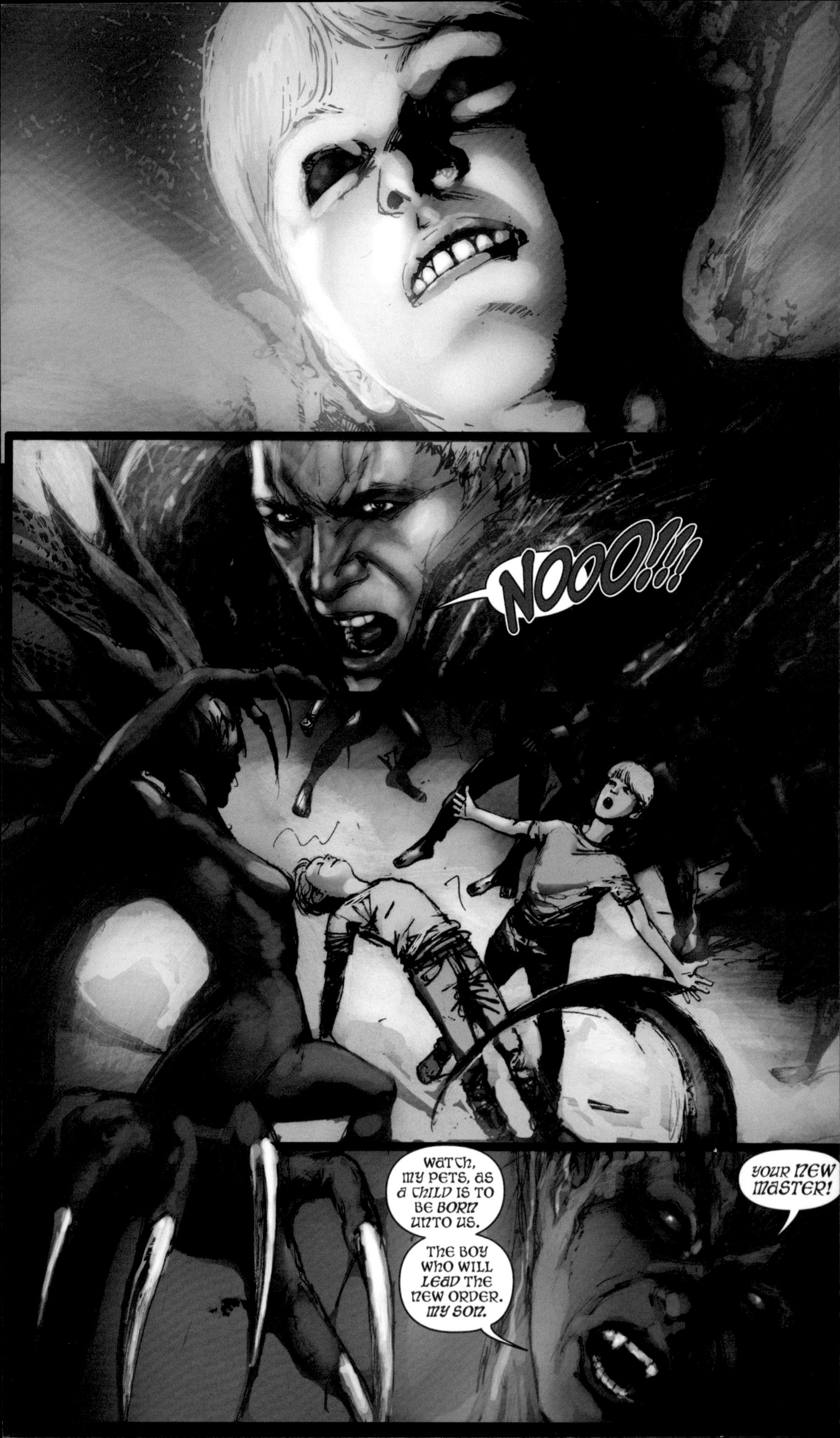
NOOO!!!
WATCH, MY PETS, AS A CHILD IS TO BE BORN UNTO US.
THE BOY WHO WILL LEAD THE NEW ORDER. MY SON.
YOUR NEW MASTER!

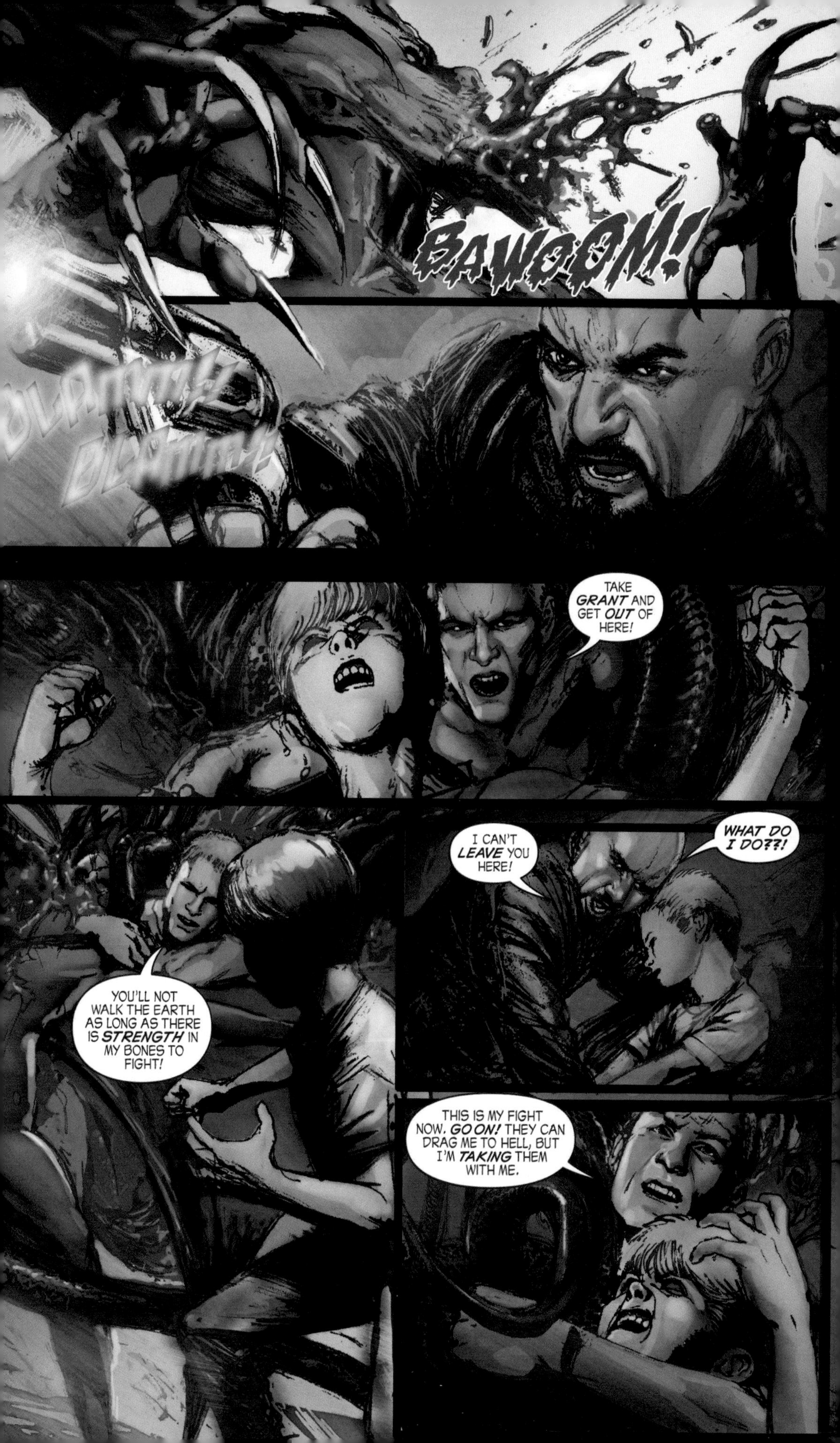
BAWOOM!
TAKE GRANT AND GET OUT OF HERE!
YOU'LL NOT WALK THE EARTH AS LONG AS THERE IS STRENGTH IN MY BONES TO FIGHT!
I CAN'T LEAVE YOU HERE!
WHAT DO I DO??!
THIS IS MY FIGHT NOW. GO ON! THEY CAN DRAG ME TO HELL, BUT I'M TAKING THEM WITH ME.

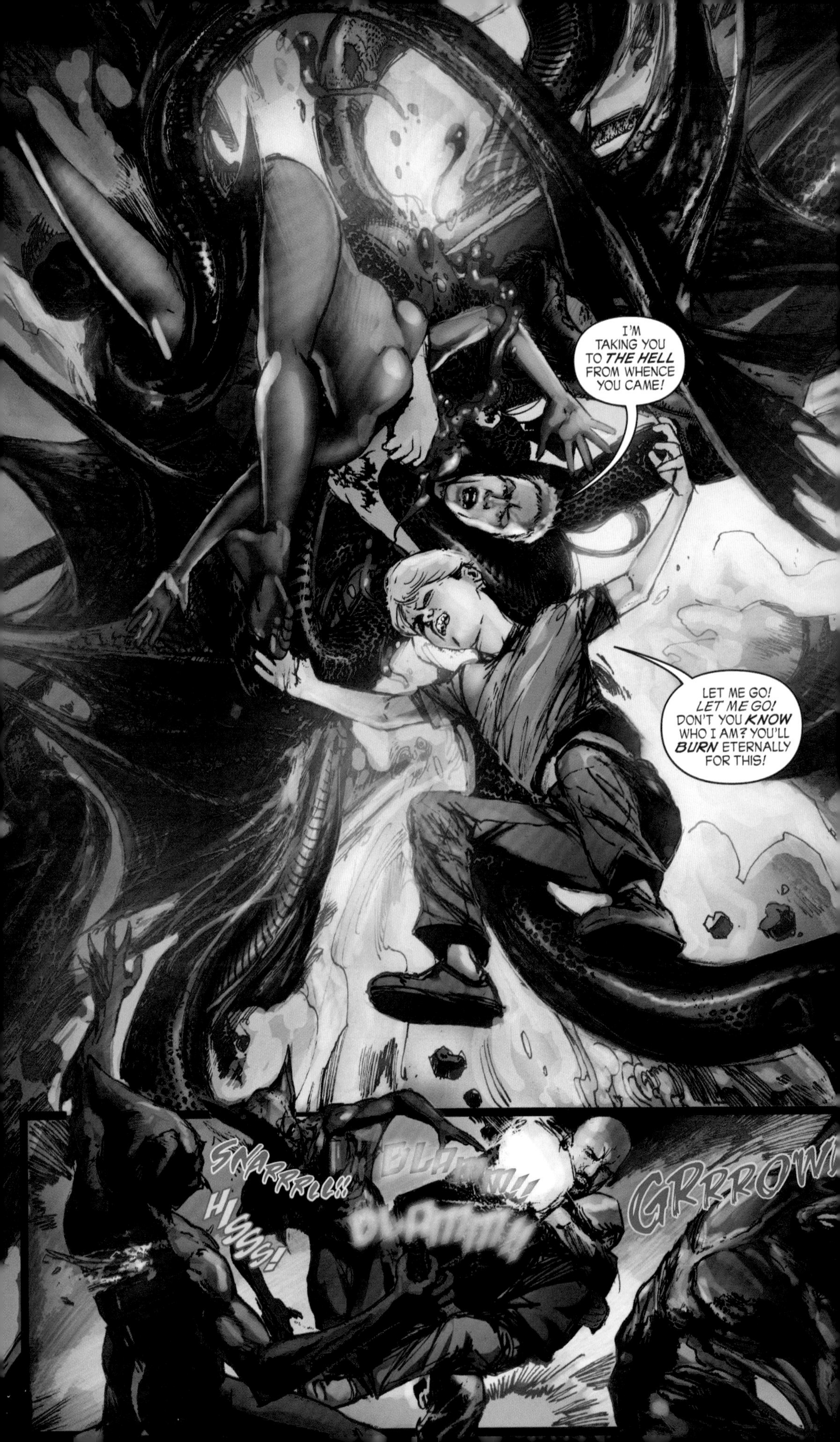
I'M TAKING YOU TO *THE HELL* FROM WHENCE YOU CAME!
LET ME GO! *LET ME GO!* DON'T YOU ***KNOW*** WHO I AM? YOU'LL ***BURN*** ETERNALLY FOR THIS!
SNARRRLL!!
HISSSS!
GRRROW

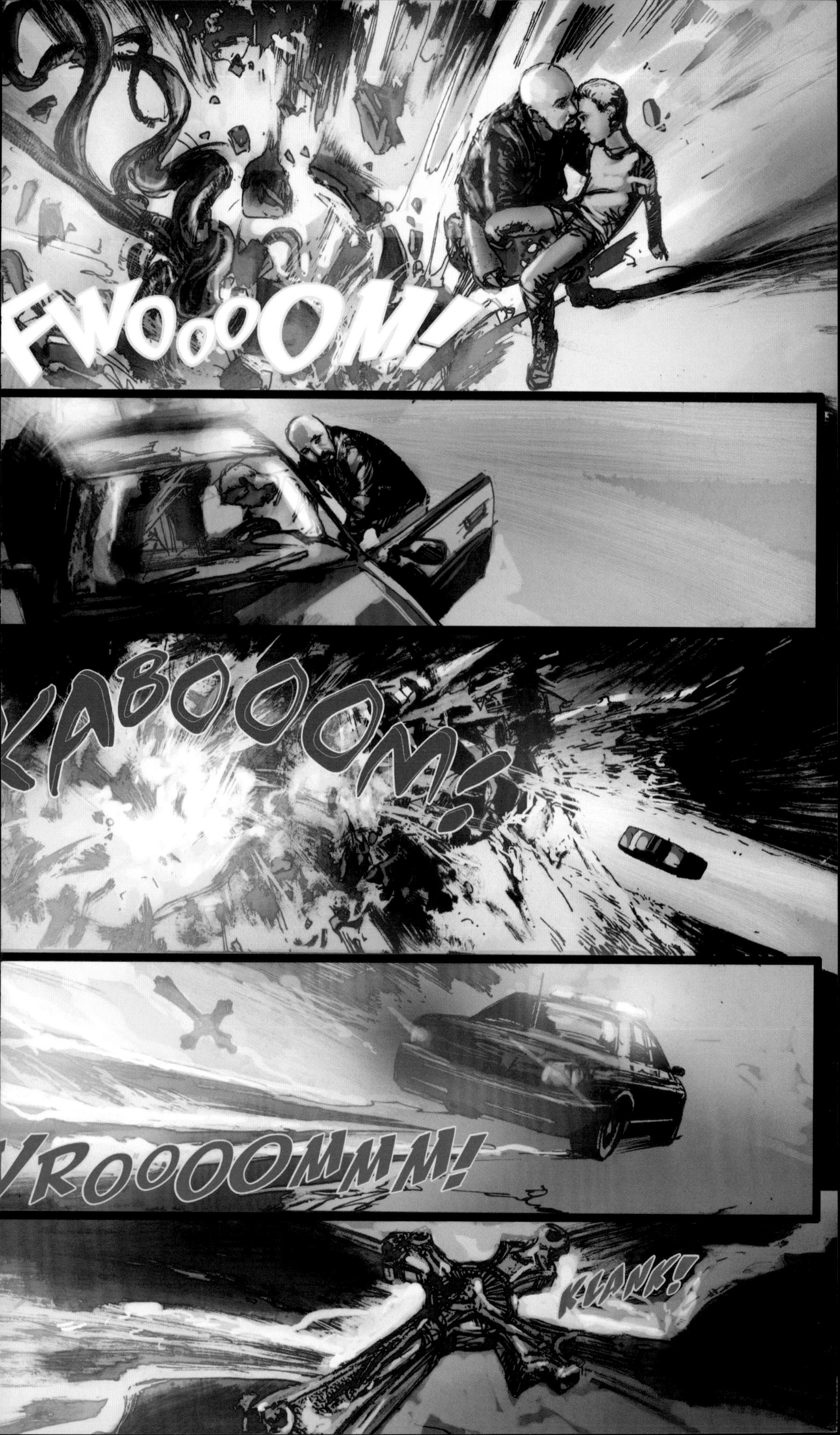
FWOoOOM!
KABOOOOM!
VROOOOMMM!
KLANK!

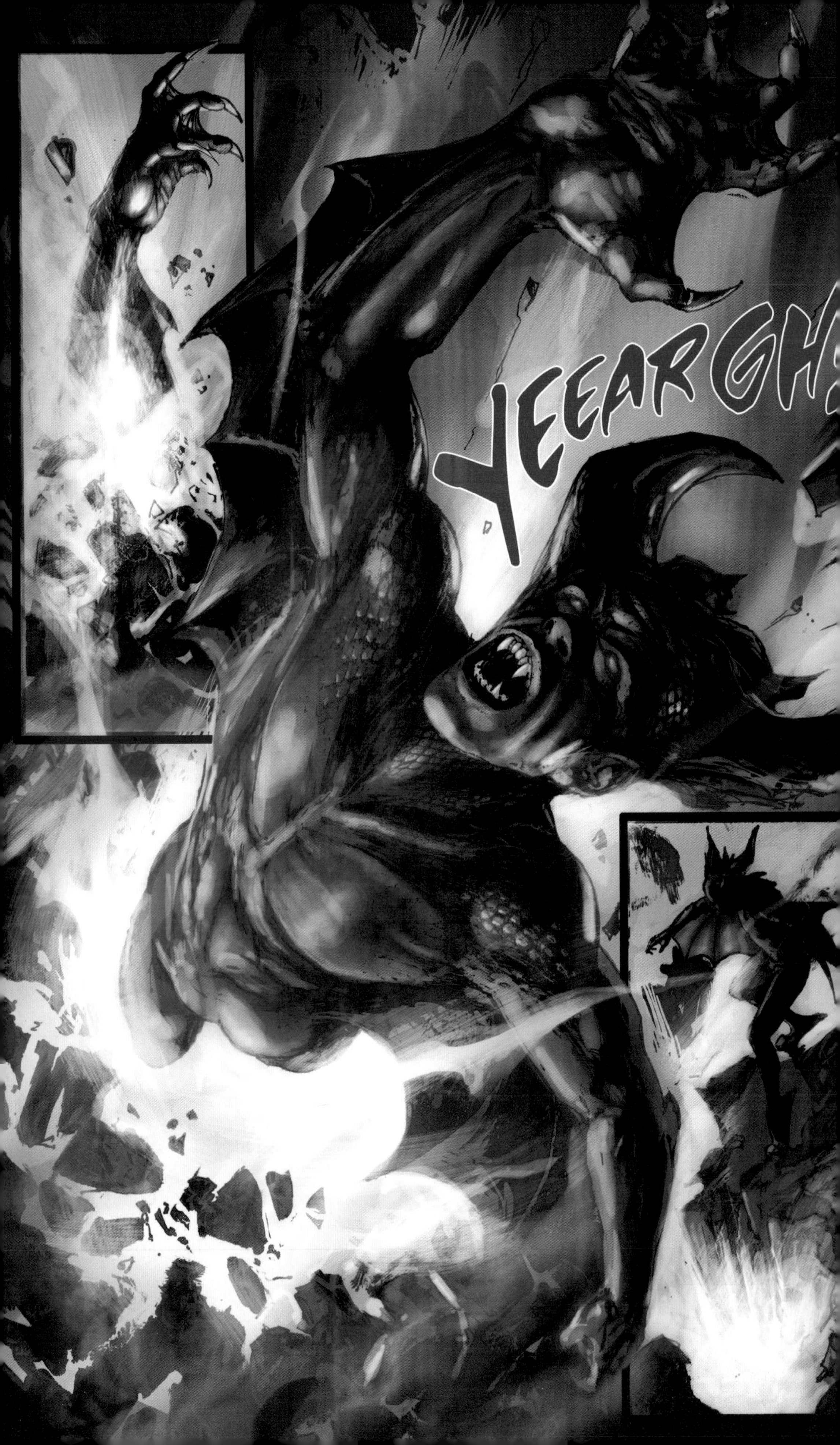
YEEARGH

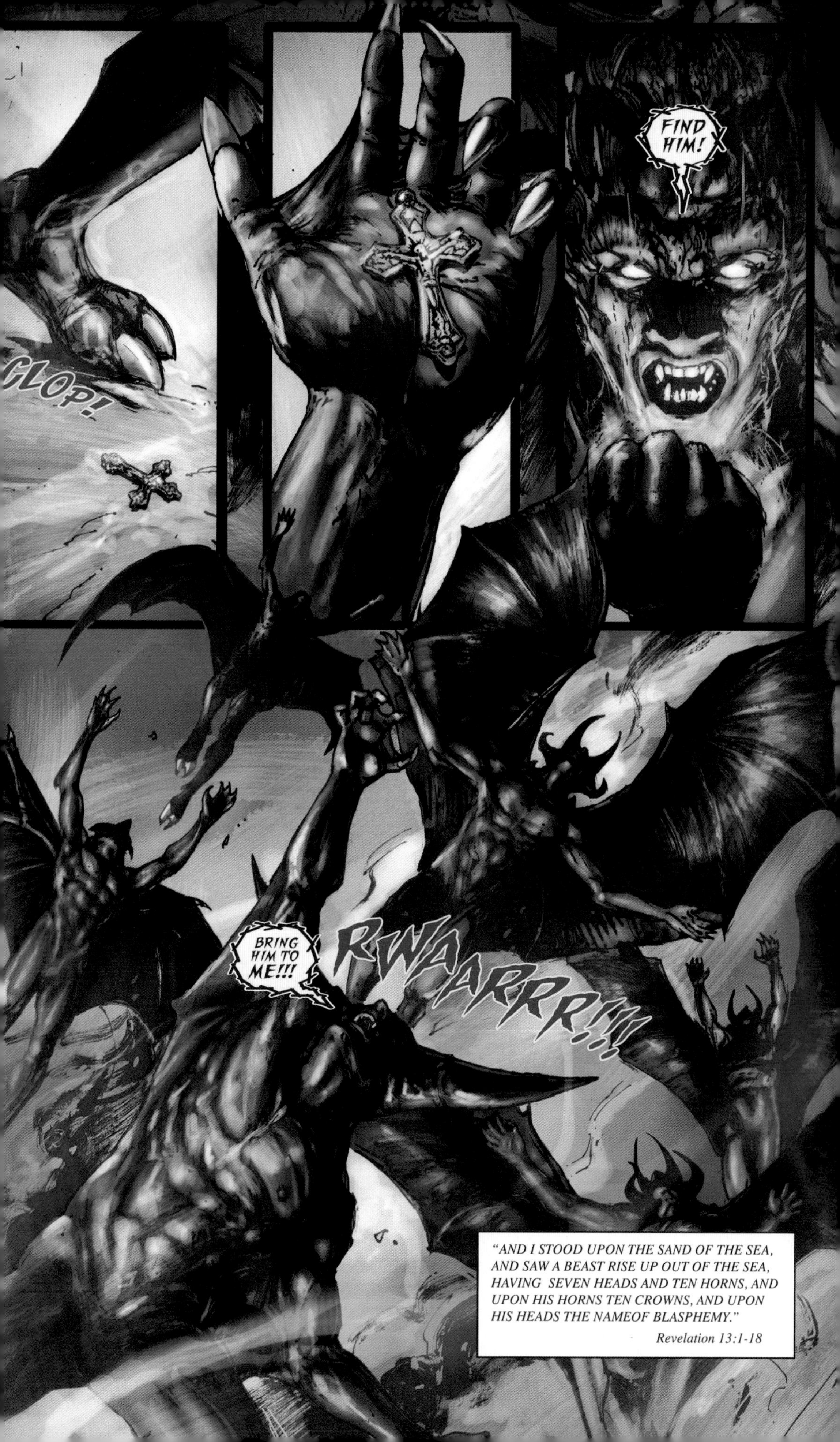
CLOP!
FIND HIM!
BRING HIM TO ME!!!
RWAARRR!!!
"AND I STOOD UPON THE SAND OF THE SEA, AND SAW A BEAST RISE UP OUT OF THE SEA, HAVING SEVEN HEADS AND TEN HORNS, AND UPON HIS HORNS TEN CROWNS, AND UPON HIS HEADS THE NAMEOF BLASPHEMY."
Revelation 13:1-18

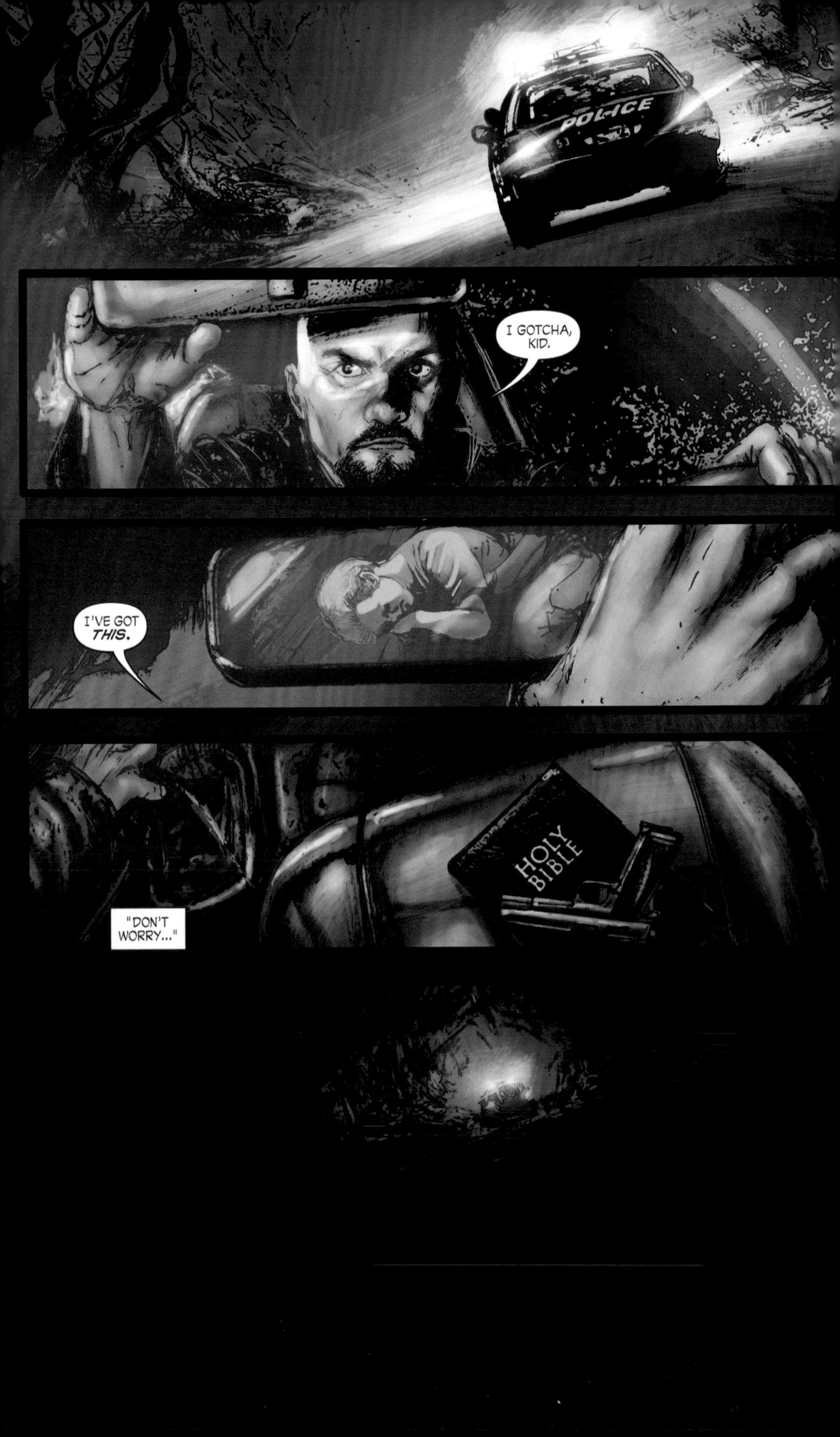
POLICE
I GOTCHA, KID.
I'VE GOT *THIS.*
HOLY BIBLE
"DON'T WORRY..."

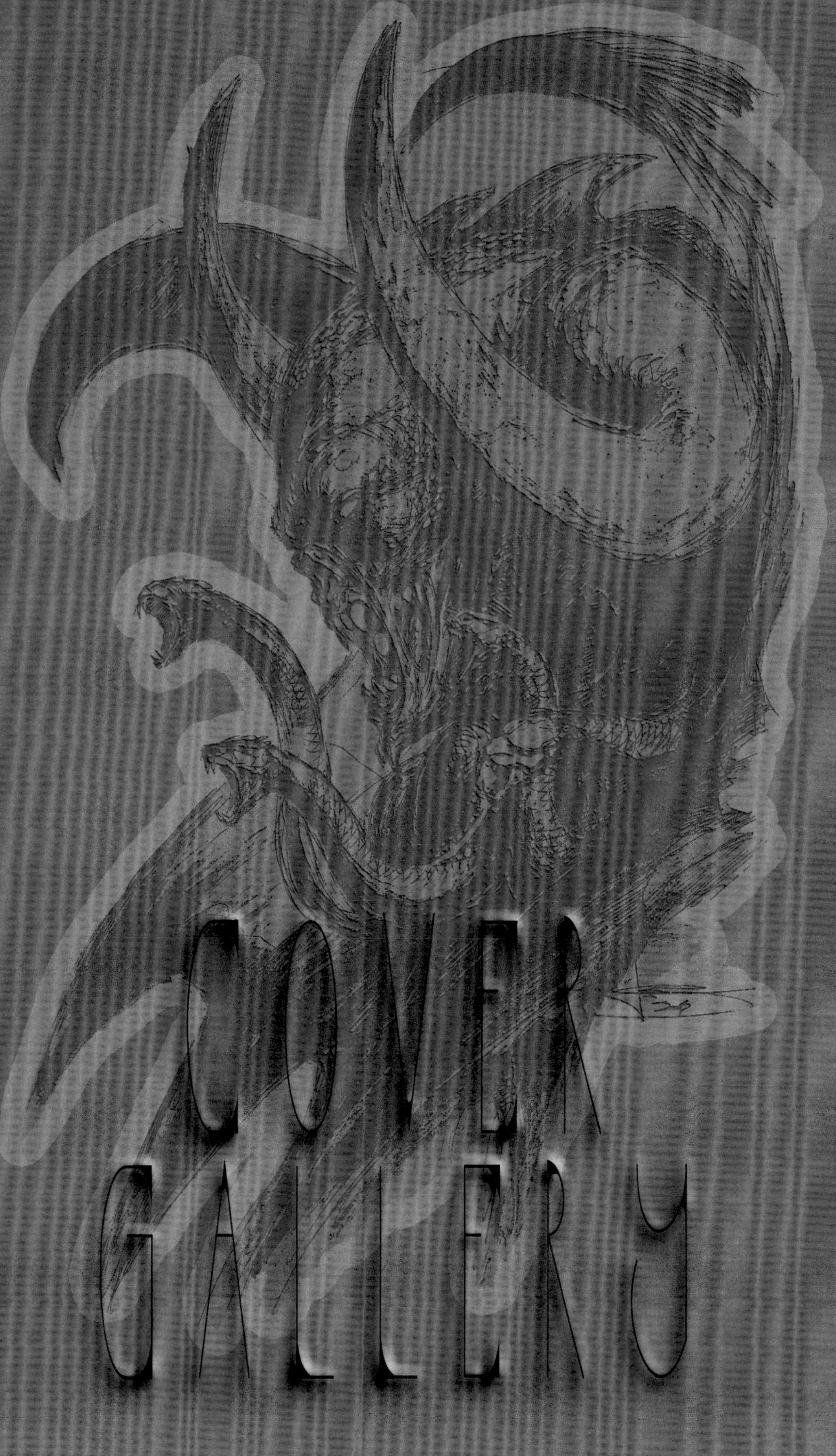
COVER
GALLERY

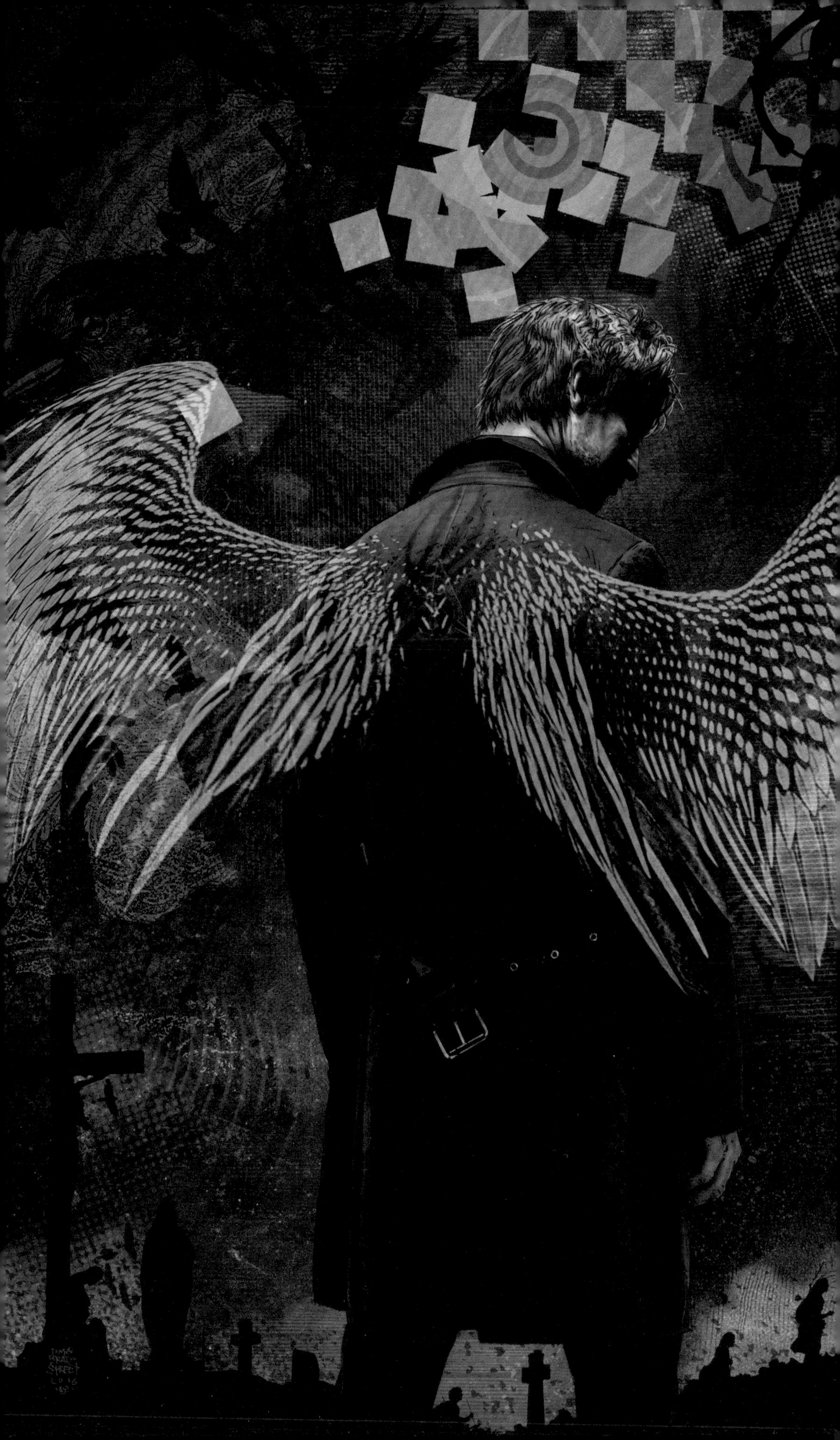

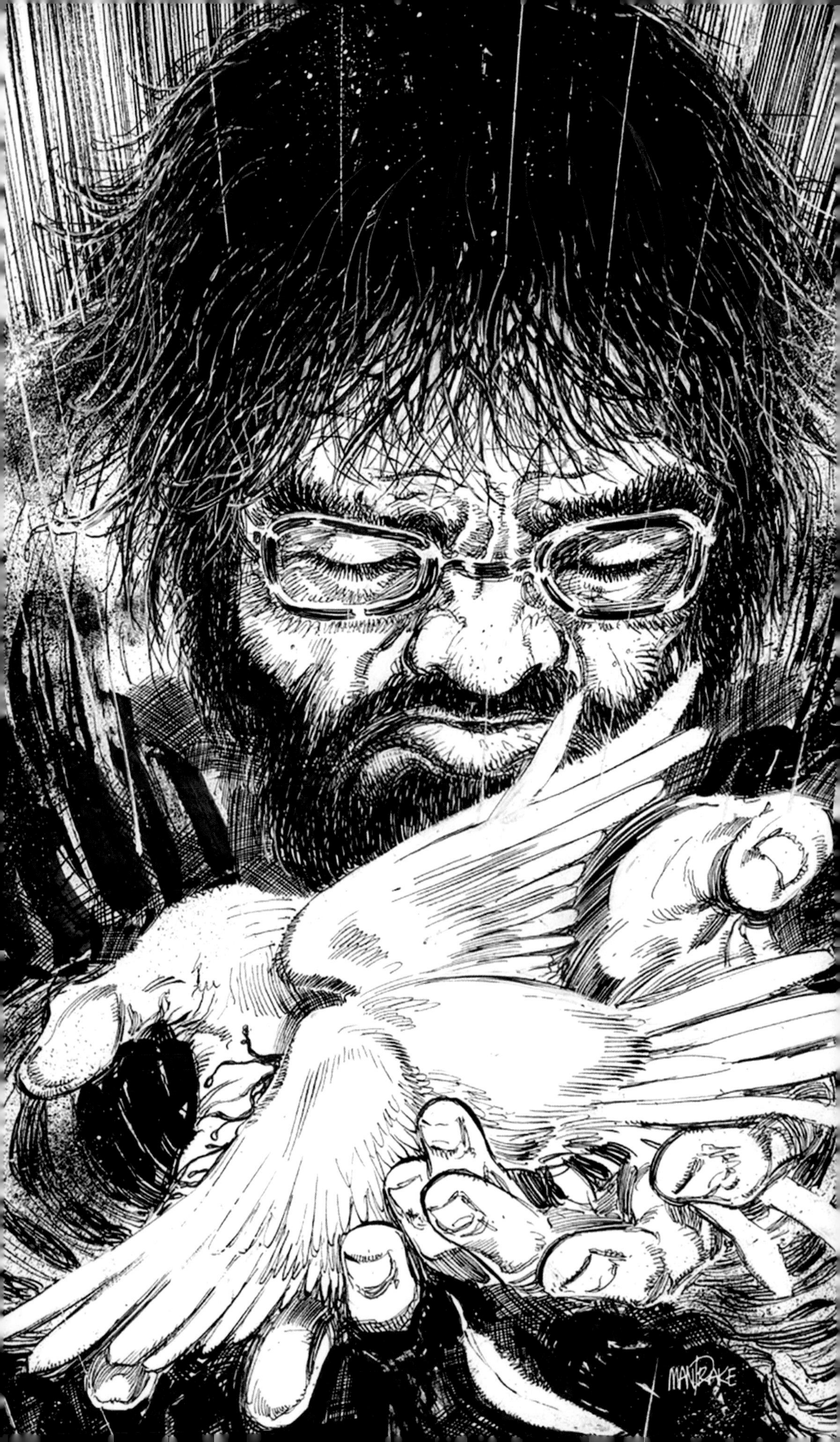
MANDRAKE

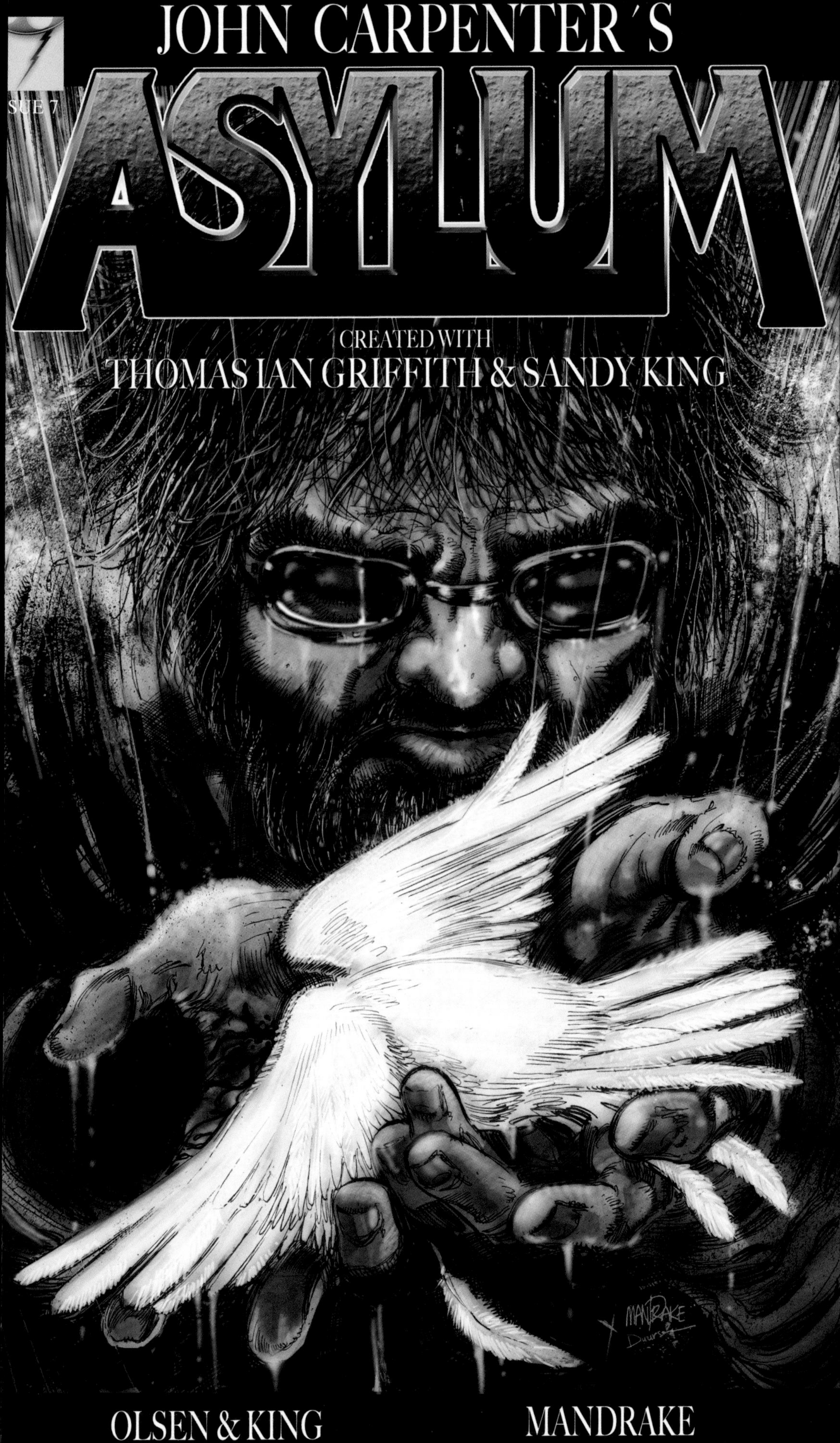
JOHN CARPENTER'S
SUE 7
ASYLUM
CREATED WITH
THOMAS IAN GRIFFITH & SANDY KING
MANDRAKE
OLSEN & KING
MANDRAKE

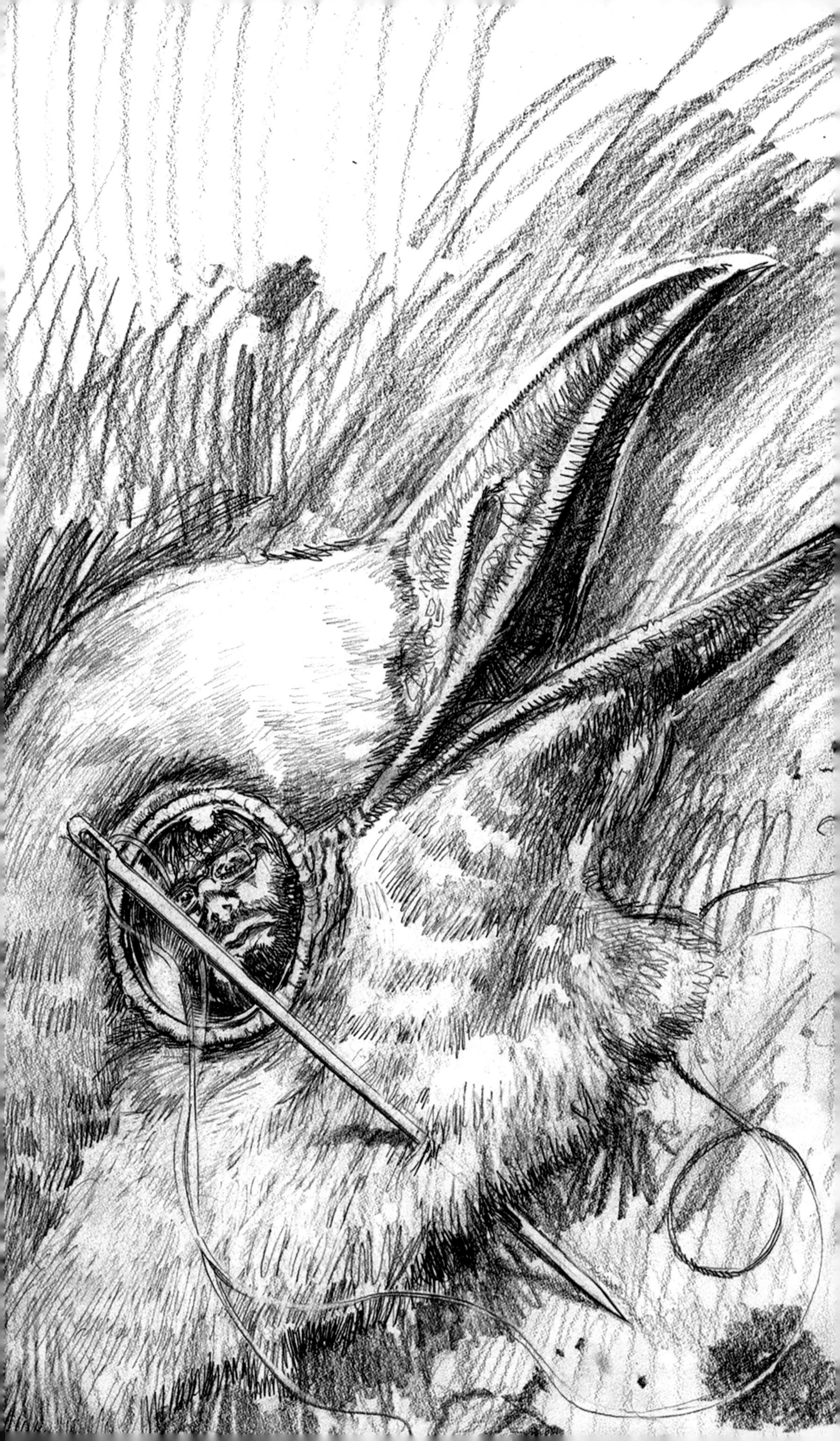

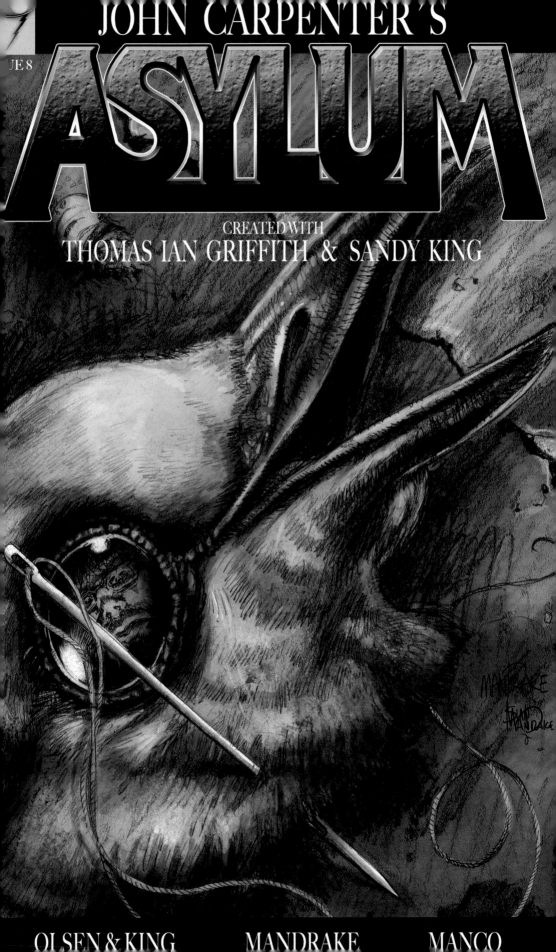

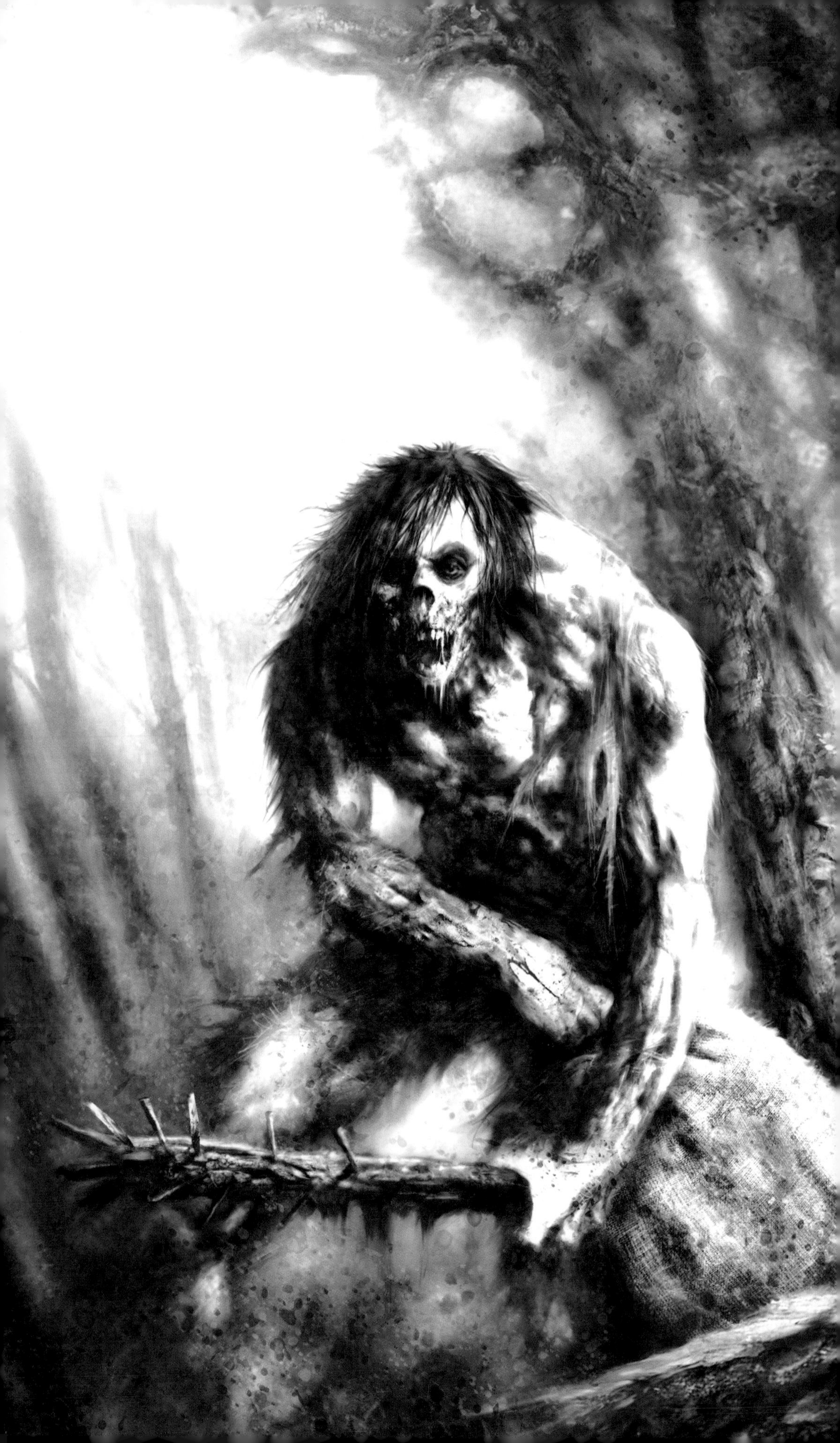

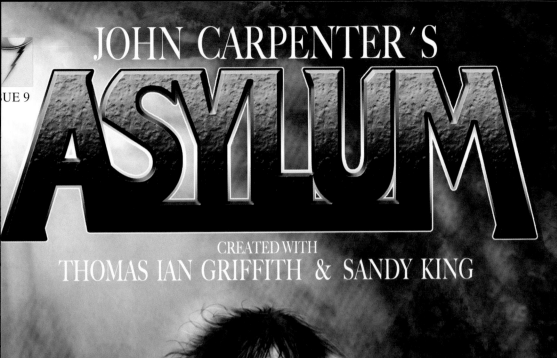

JOHN CARPENTER'S
ASYLUM

CREATED WITH
THOMAS IAN GRIFFITH & SANDY KING

OLSEN & KING   MANCO

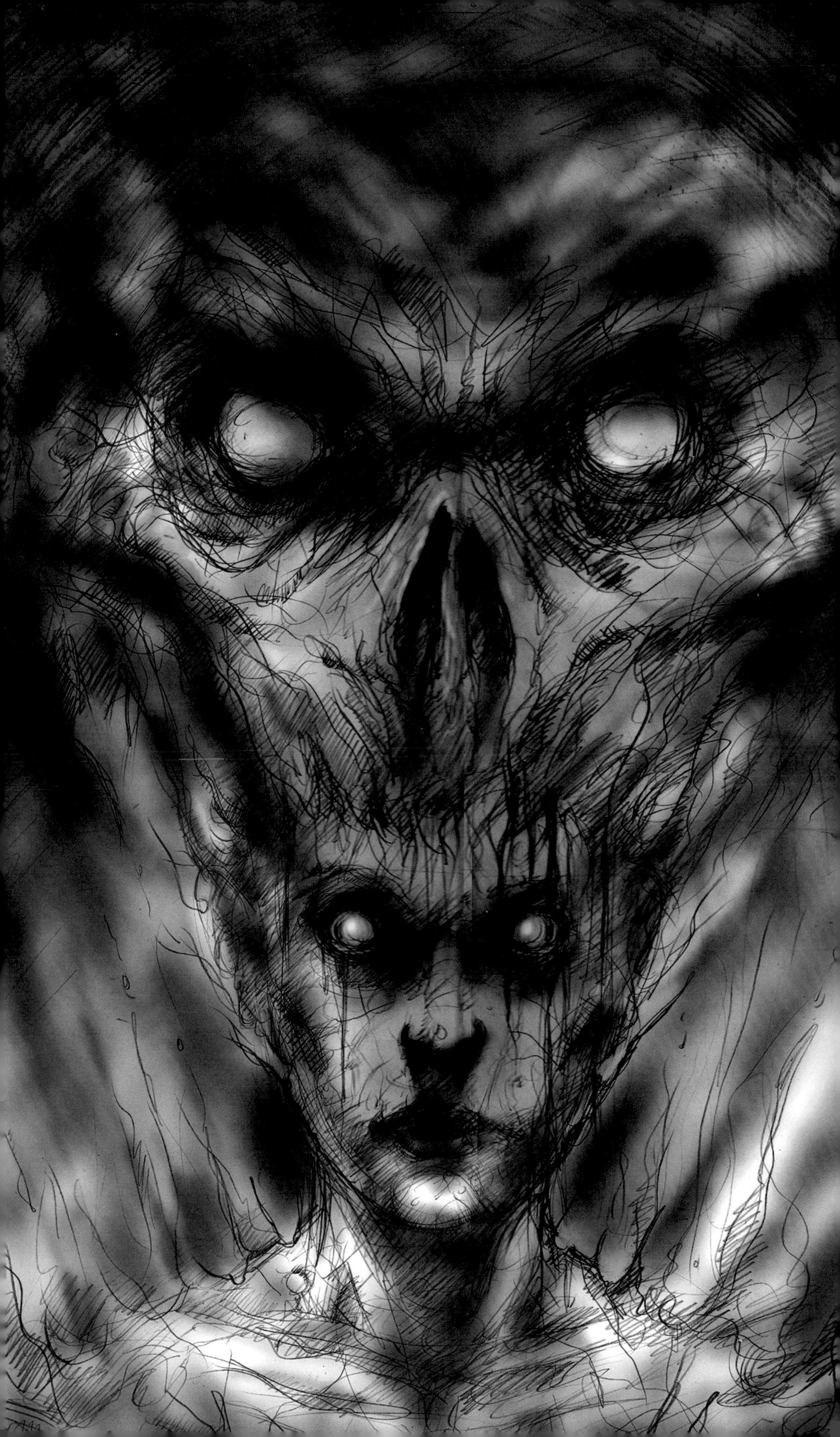

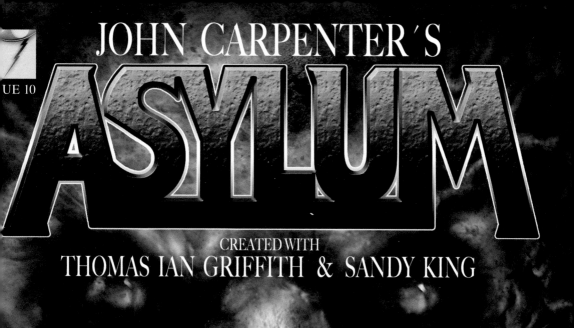

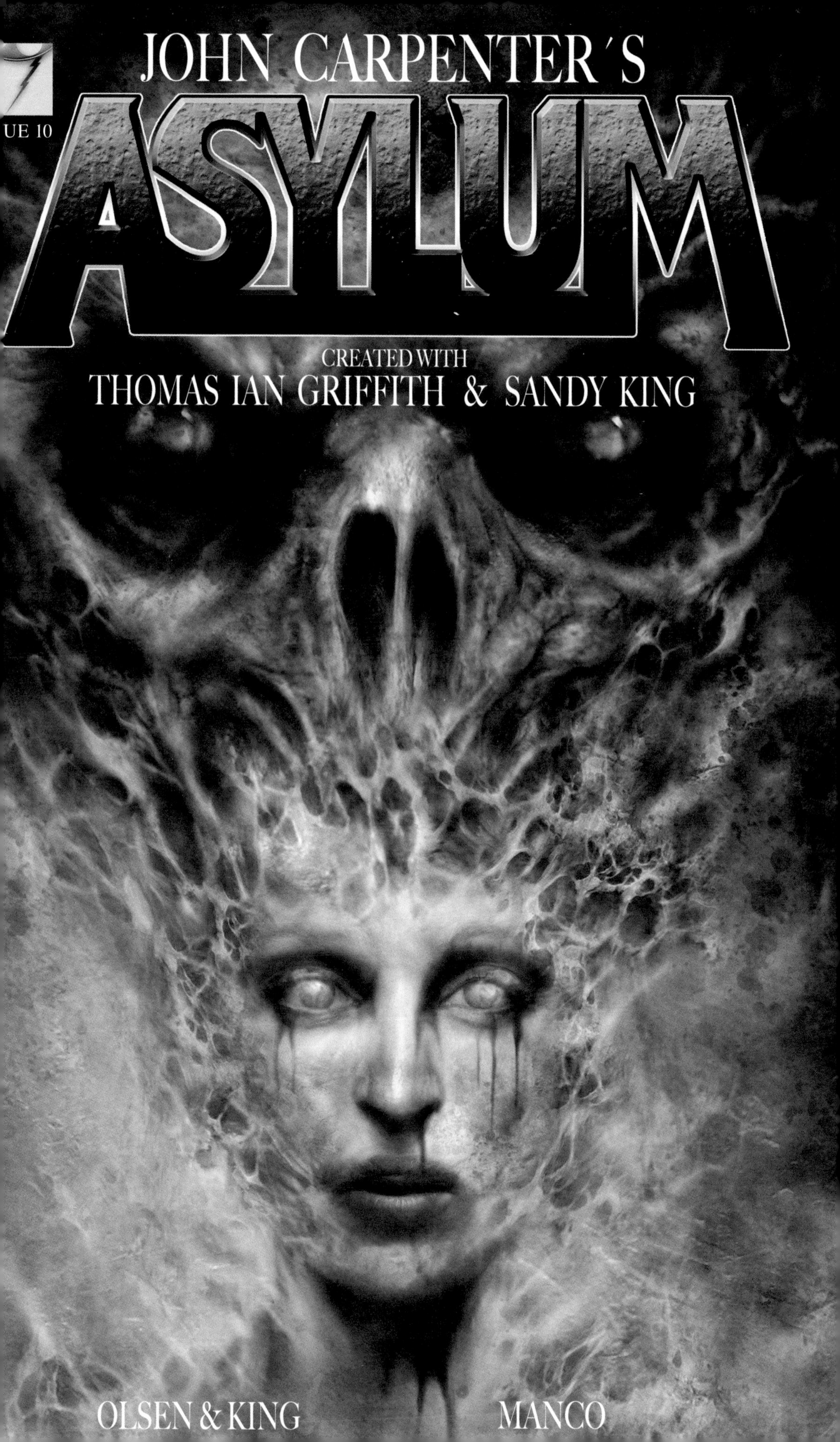

JOHN CARPENTER'S ASYLUM

UE 10

CREATED WITH
THOMAS IAN GRIFFITH & SANDY KING

OLSEN & KING   MANCO

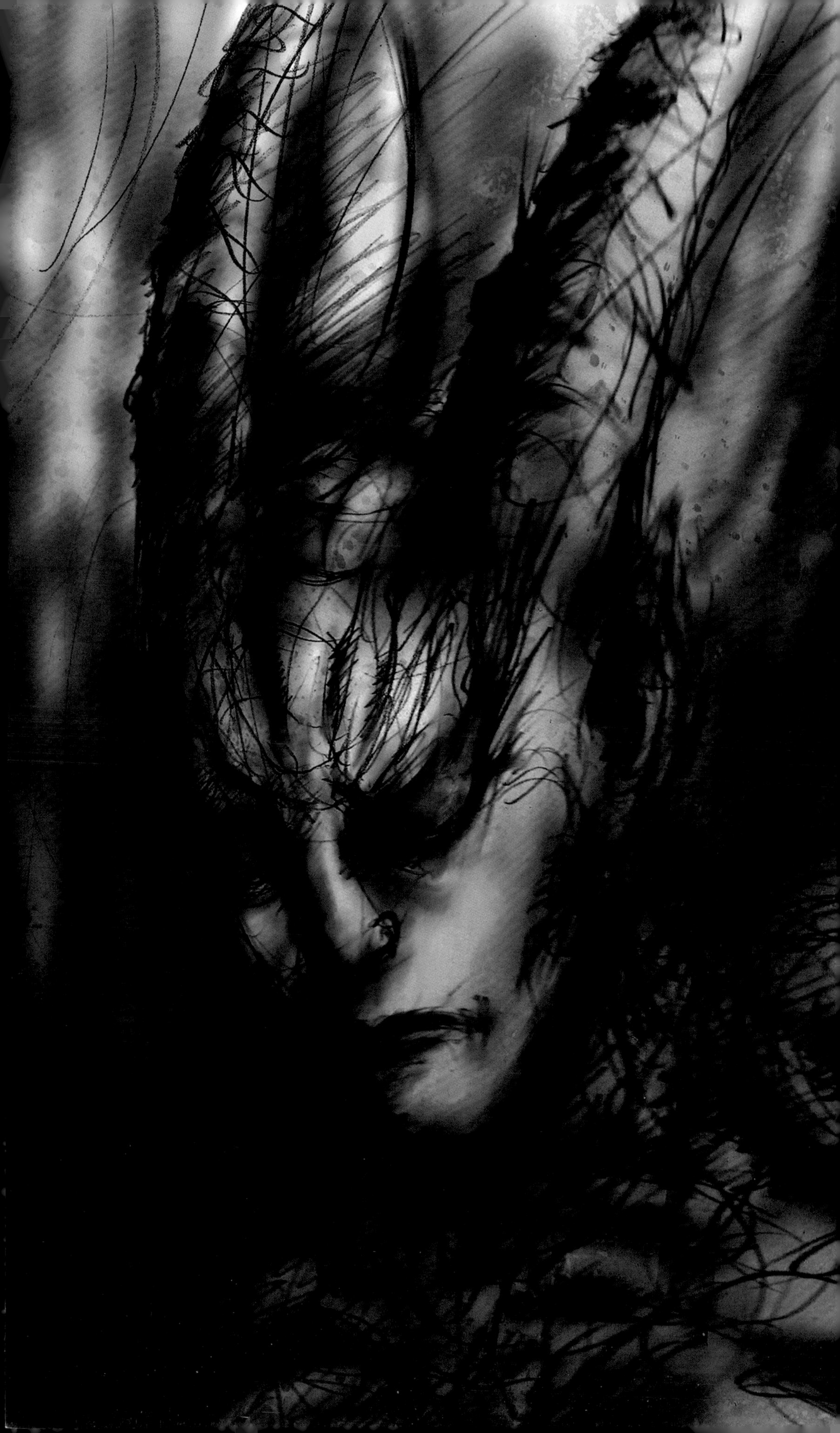

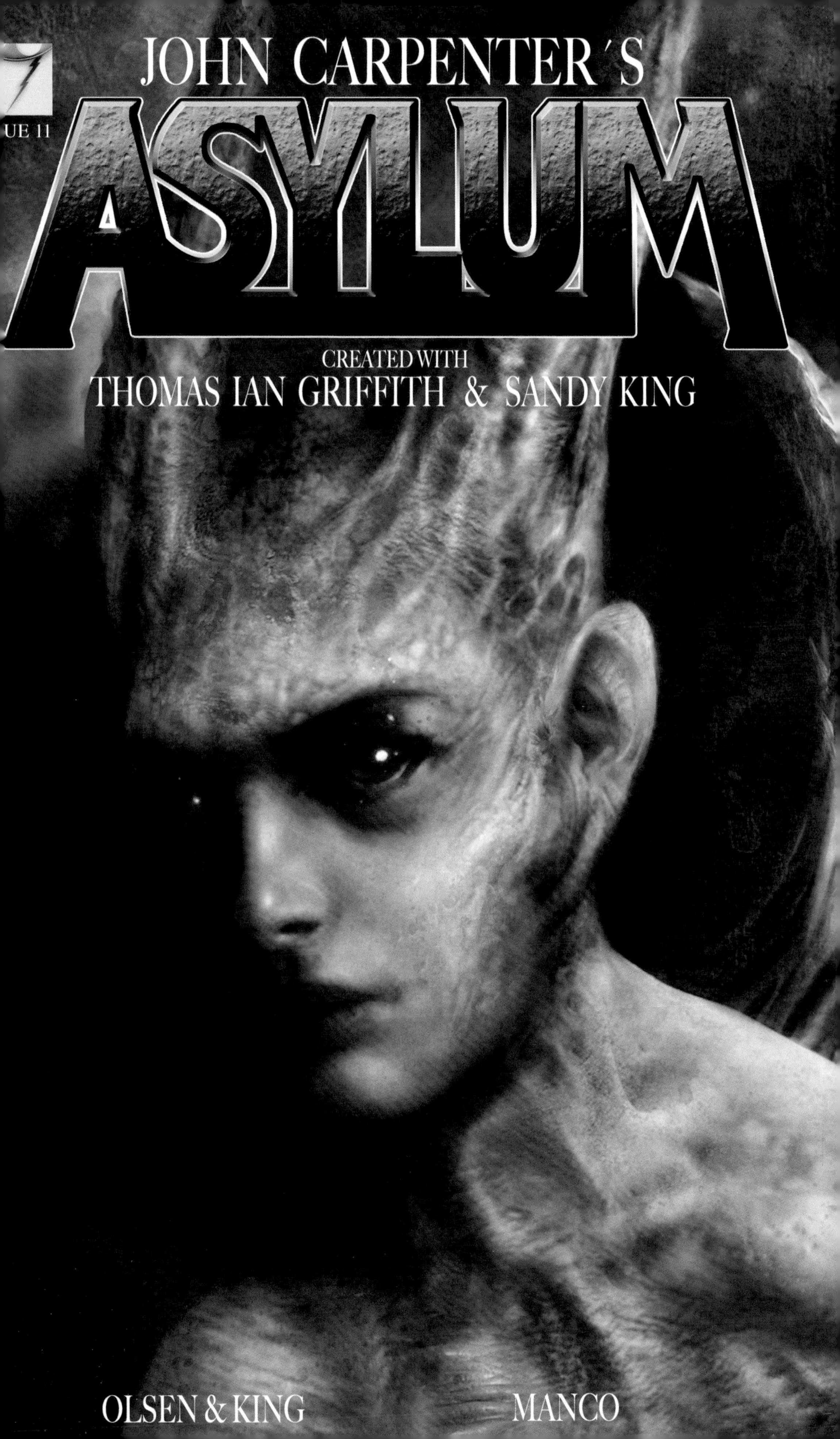
JOHN CARPENTER´S
UE 11
ASYLUM
CREATED WITH
THOMAS IAN GRIFFITH & SANDY KING
OLSEN & KING
MANCO

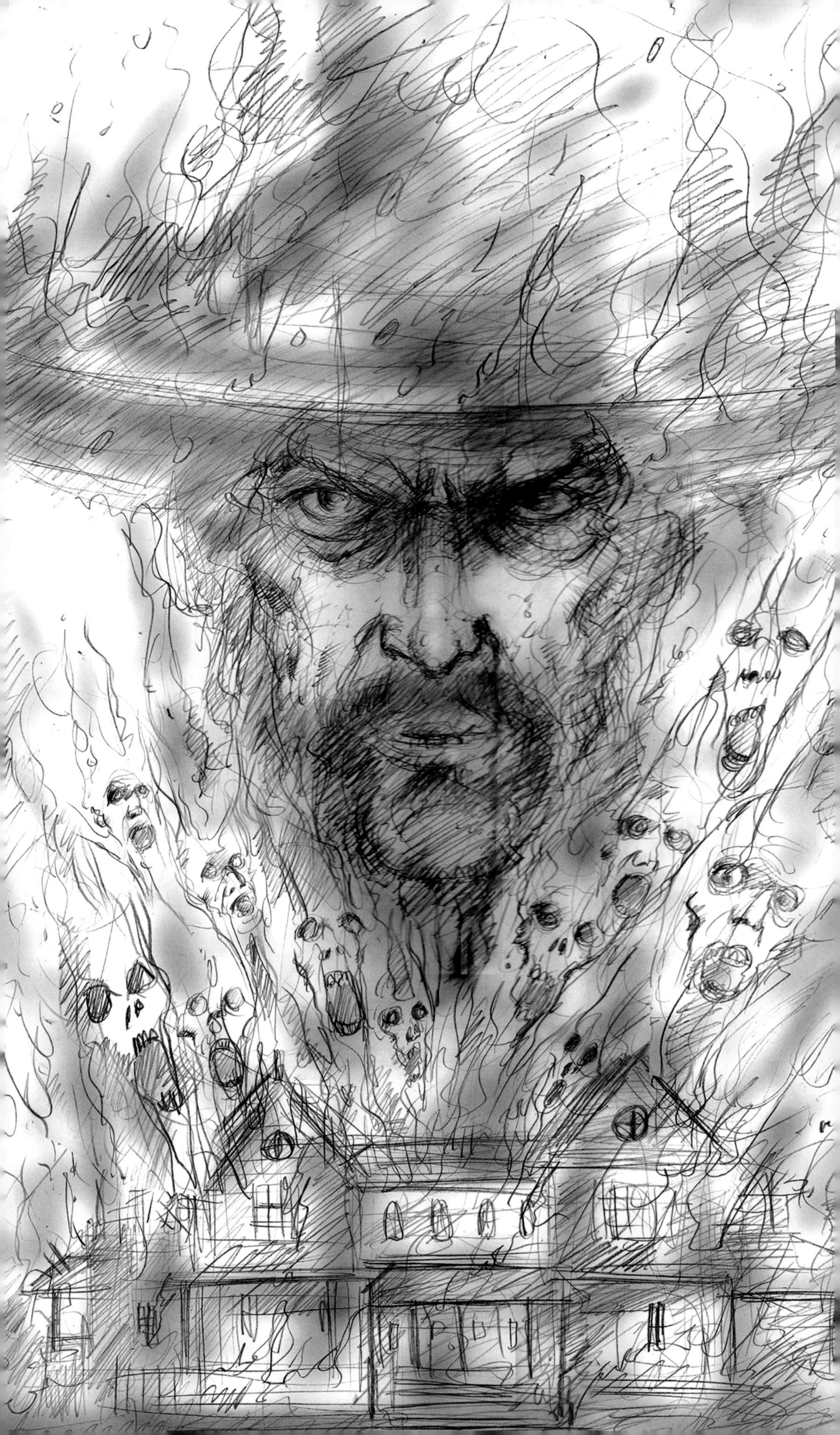

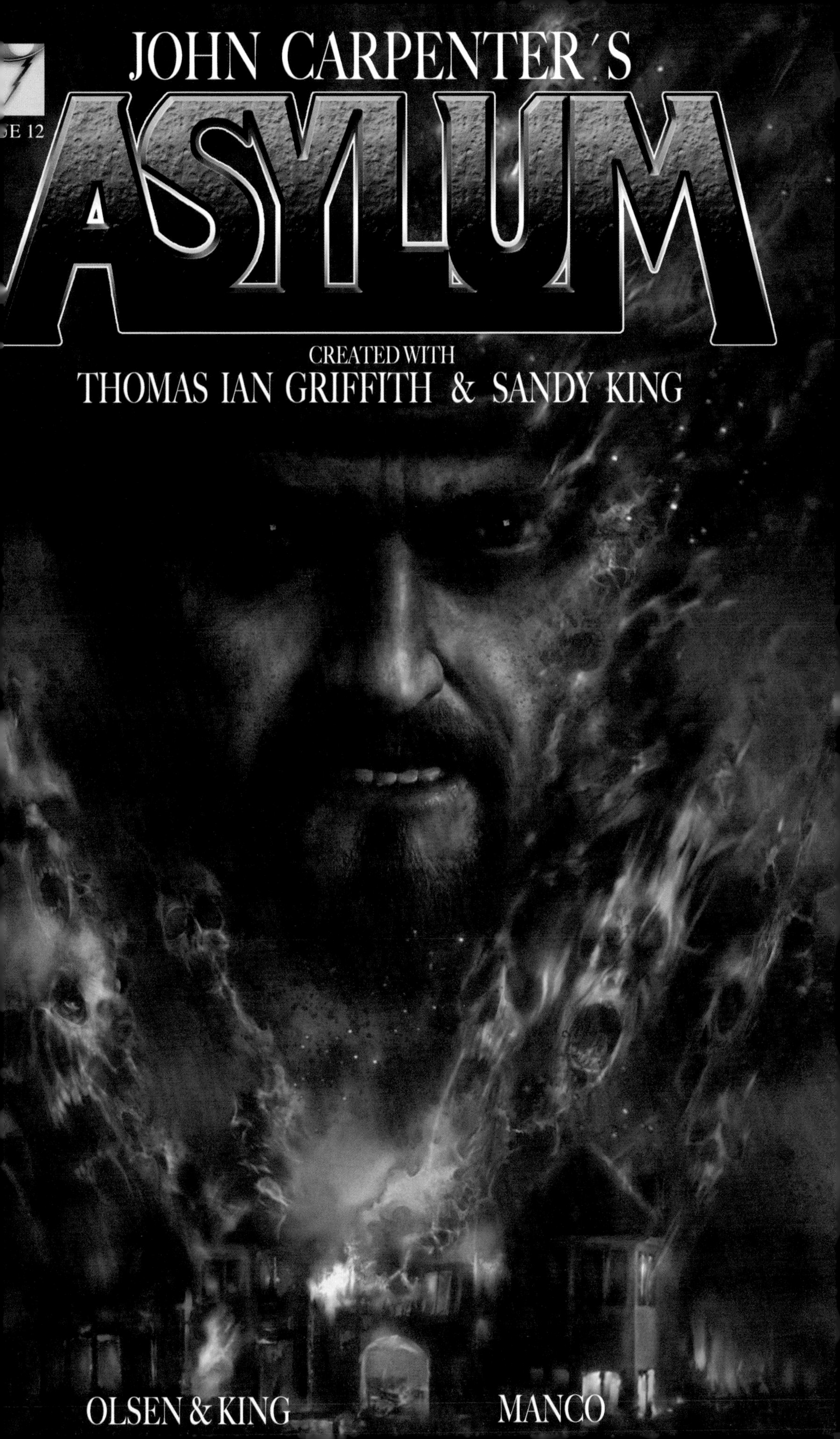
JOHN CARPENTER´S
ASYLUM
CREATED WITH
THOMAS IAN GRIFFITH & SANDY KING
OLSEN & KING
MANCO

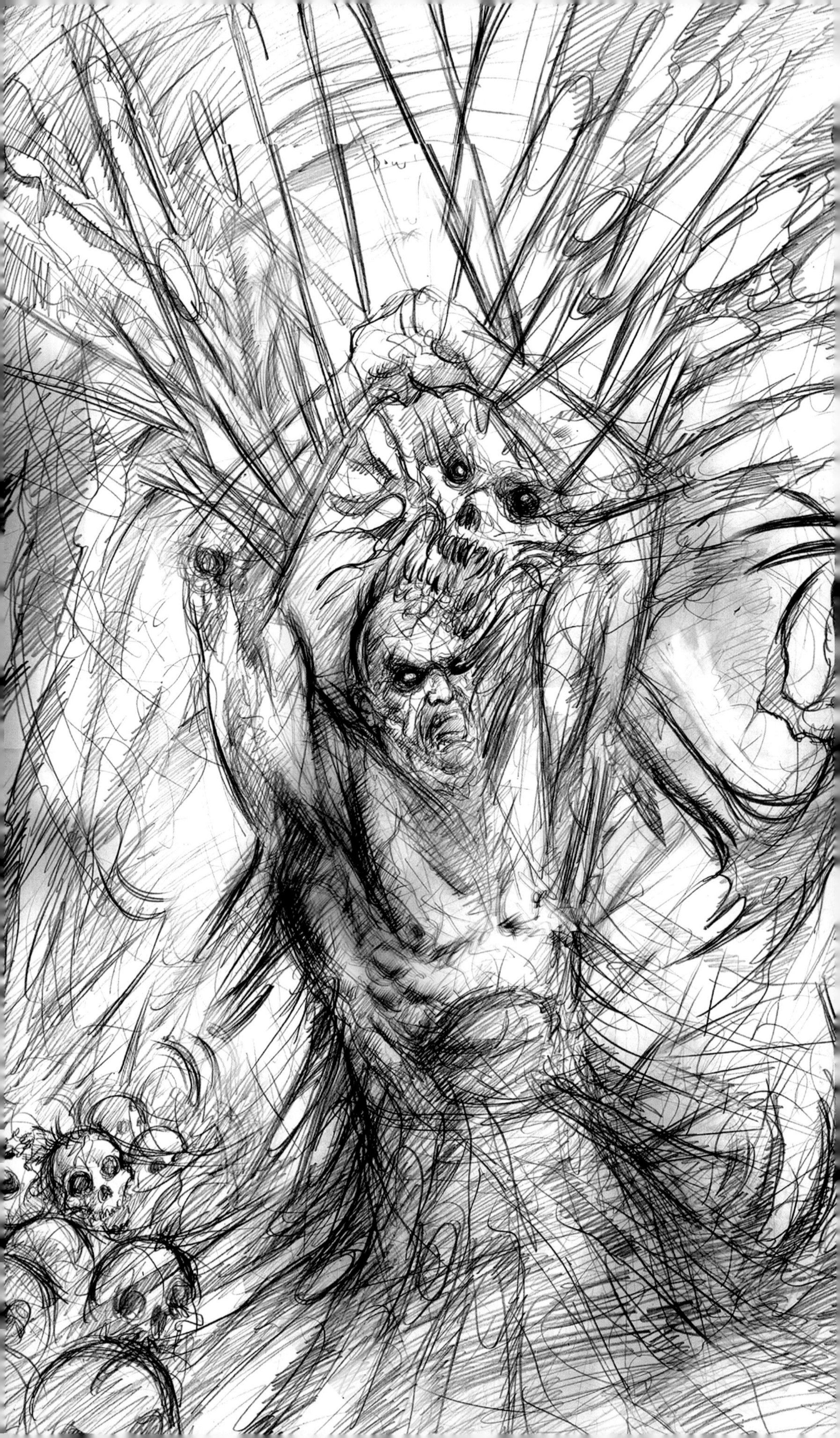

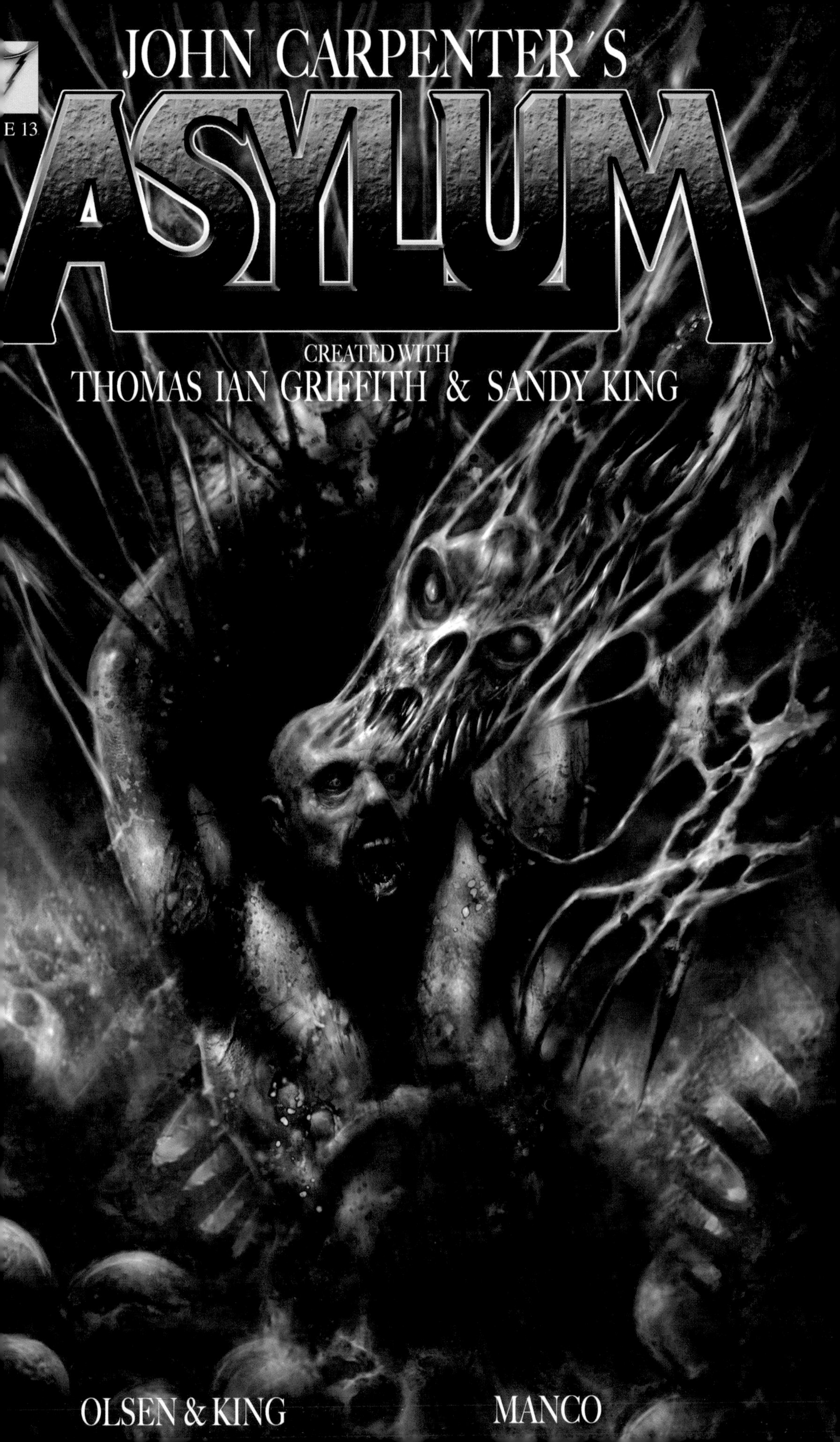
E 13
JOHN CARPENTER´S
ASYLUM
CREATED WITH
THOMAS IAN GRIFFITH & SANDY KING
OLSEN & KING
MANCO

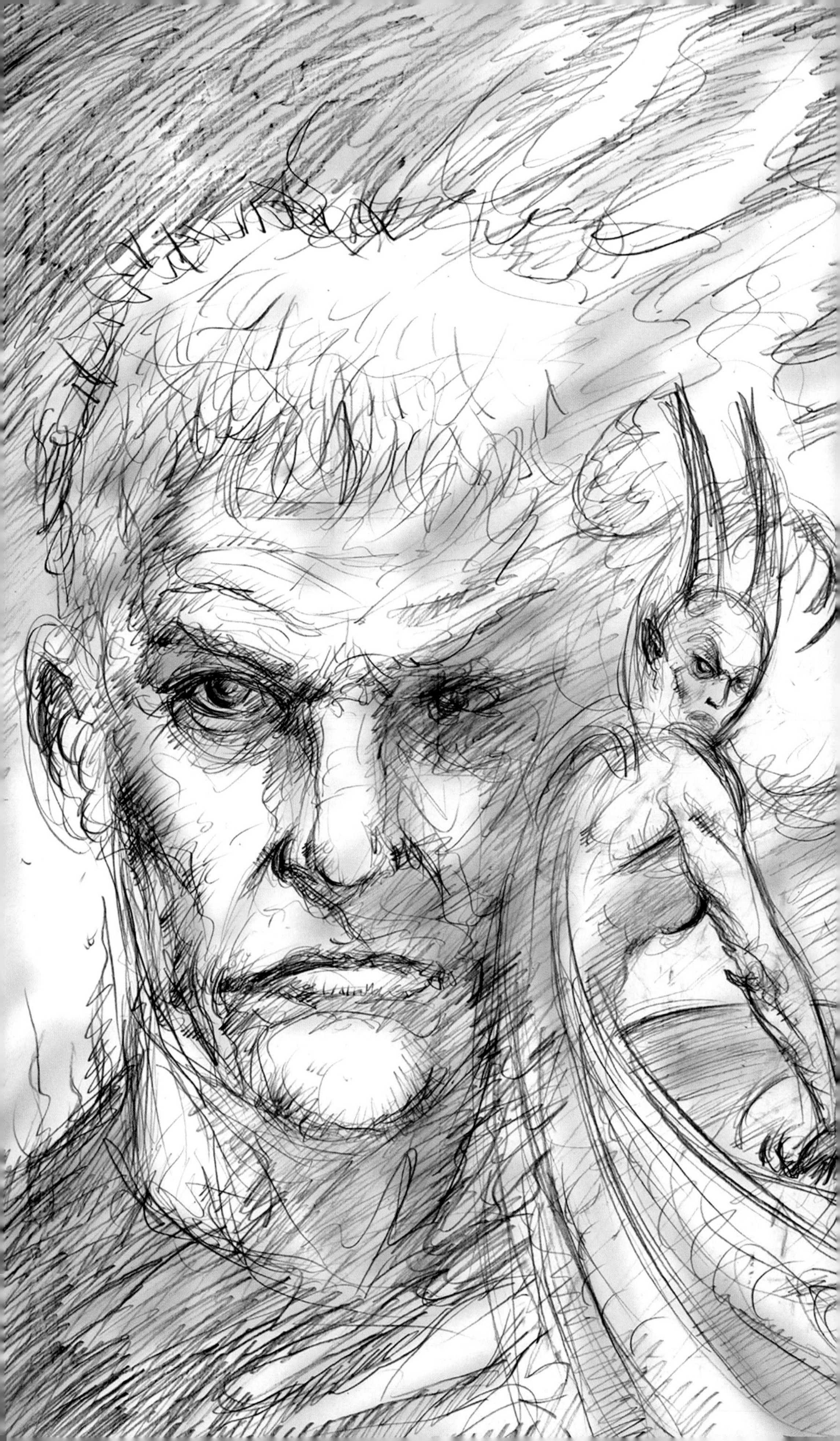

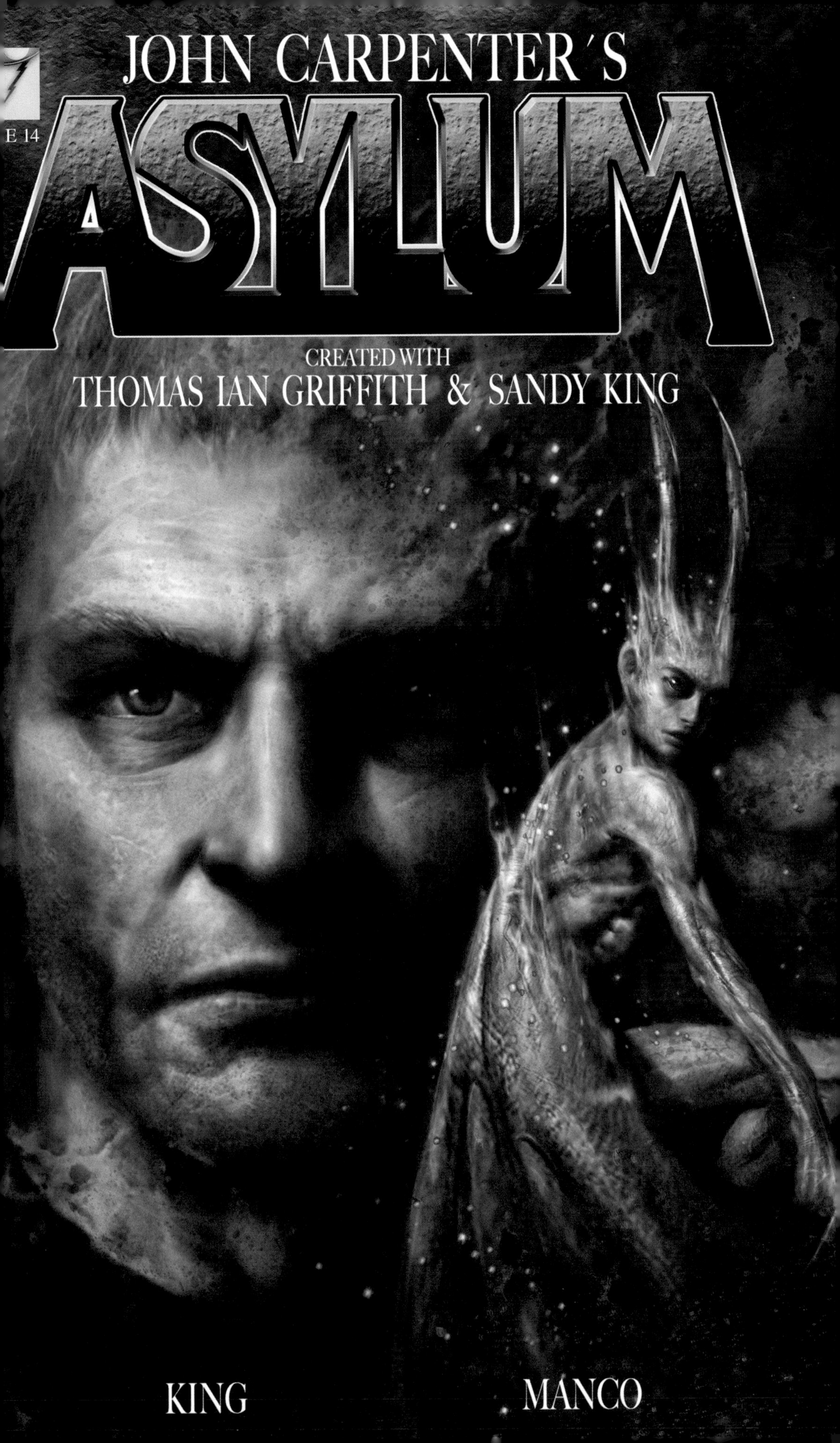
E 14
JOHN CARPENTER'S
ASYLUM
CREATED WITH
THOMAS IAN GRIFFITH & SANDY KING
KING
MANCO

BIOGRAPHIES

JOHN CARPENTER
Co-Creator

Director...writer...composer. The triple threat became a force to be reckoned with yet again as an award-winning comic book creator with *John Carpenter's Asylum, Volume 1*, followed by his multi-award-winning anthology, *John Carpenter's Tales for a HalloweeNight*.

Carpenter's breakthrough film was *Halloween*, the seminal horror movie, that made Michael Myers the best known boogey man in modern times. It was the most profitable independent movie of its day and launched the genre of the teen slasher film.

His movie, *The Thing*, remains a space alien classic which opened new frontiers in creature effects and suspense, while *Escape From New York* introduced the world to the iconic character of Snake Plissken, who along with *They Live*'s John Nada, epitomizes American cool.

John's two album's of non-soundtrack music, *Lost Themes* and *Lost Themes II*, have made the charts in both the U.S. and Europe, leading to a live appearance world tour in 2016 met by enthusiastic crowds from Los Angeles to Barcelona.

With this step into the comic book world, John Carpenter brings it all to the serial world he's loved since childhood. Supernatural horror with that twist of fate that only flawed mankind can provide.

SANDY KING
Co-Creator, Writer and Editor

Artist, writer, film producer and president of Storm King Productions.

With a background in art, photography and animation, Sandy King's filmmaking career has included working with John Cassavetes, Francis Ford Coppola, Michael Mann, Walter Hill, John Hughs and John Carpenter.

She has produced films ranging from public service announcements on Hunger Awareness to a documentary on astronaut/teacher Christa McAuliffe, and major theatrical hits like *John Carpenter's Vampires*. From working underwater with sharks in the Bahamas to converting 55 acres of New Mexican desert into the vast red planet of Mars, new challenges interest and excite her. The world of comic books is no exception. It allows her to bring her art and story telling experience to a new discipline with an expanded group of collaborators. She wrote the Harvey-nominated Womanthology: Space story *Dead Again*, and writes and edits the multiple award winning *John Carpenter's Asylum* comic book series and *John Carpenter's Tales for a*

THOMAS IAN GRIFFITH
Co-creator

Thomas Ian Griffith began his career as an actor on Broadway and in regional theatre. He moved to Los Angeles where he starred in numerous TV and feature films, including *John Carpenter's Vampires*, where he had the privilege of working with John Carpenter. His desire to continue to work with the horror master led to the creation of *Asylum*. As a writer, Griffith has several feature films to his credit and is a staff writer on the television series, *Grimm*. He currently resides in Los Angeles with his wife, actress Mary Page Keller.

TRENT OLSEN
Writer

A self-professed writer of wrongs, Trent Olsen found himself drawn to screenwriting from a young age. Although a departure from screenwriting, Trent excitedly dove headlong into another life passion - comic books! Influenced and inspired by his thirty thousand book collection, Trent happily tackled the world of *John Carpenter's Asylum*. With another book and two features in development, you can expect to see more of his work in the near future.

LEONARDO MANCO
Artist

Leonardo Manco is an Argentine comic book artist, who has a somewhat unique dark and gritty style. Perhaps best known for his work on Vertigo's *Hellblazer* title, he first started out in mainstream comics back in the mid 1990's, doing most of his work for Marvel and DC. His run on *Hellblazer* was a long one, and many consider him to have been 'THE HELLBLAZER ARTIST'. He practically illustrated all of Mike Carey's long run, and stuck with the book through Denise Mina's and Andy Diggle's runs. Books that he has worked on include: Marvel: *Doom, Deathlok, War Machine, Otherworld War, Druid, Werewolf by Night,* and *Hellstrom*. DC/Vertigo: *Hellblazer, Batman Gotham Knights* and *All Star Western*. BOOM: *28 Days Later* and *Hellraiser*. And, of course, Leo is producing the visually stunning artwork for Storm King Comics' John Carpenter's Asylum.

TOM MANDRAKE
Artist

Tom Mandrake is an American comic book artist of DC Comics' *JLA Destiny*, Marvel Comics' *Call of Duty: The Precinct*, and his creator-owned Image book, *Creeps*. He is perhaps best known for his collaborations with writer John Ostrander on several series, including *Grimjack* and *Firestorm*, the acclaimed five-year run on *The Spectre*, and *Martian Manhunter* from DC Comics. He is probably best known for his work in the horror genre and has a new Kickstarter-backed book coming out this year, *Kros: Hallowed Ground*.

MARIANA SANZONE
Colorist

Mariana Sanzone is an Argentinian comic book colorist who has previously done work for Marvel on books including *DOOM*, and is currently coloring the new DC comic *Wacky Raceland*. She lives in Uruguay.

SIAN MANDRAKE
Colorist

Sian Mandrake is an illustrator who has used her painting skills to add color to covers and interiors for *John Carpenter's Asylum*. Her other work includes pencils for the '7 Deadly Sinners', colors on *X-Files* and DC's *Convergence*. Sian is currently finishing up colors for Tom Mandrake and John Ostrander's *Kros: Hallowed Ground*. Horror is her happy place, and you can usually find her painting vampires and pet portraits in her creature filled studio.

JANICE CHIANG
Letter Artist

Janice Chiang is a professional comic letterer with four decades in the industry. She has a body of published work from Marvel, DC Comics, First Comics, Tundra, DarkHorse, Archie Comics, Harvey Comics, TokyoPop, Del Rey, CMX/Wildstorm, Papercutz, Pow! Entertainment, and Storm King Productions for all genres and readership. Janice has hand lettered on original art pages and is a digital letter artist on more recent projects. She enjoys working with mature talent as well as newly discovered creators. Everyday is a new adventure on 2D and 3D digital pages.

NICK PERCIVAL
Cover Artist

Nick is an award-winning Graphic Novelist also specializing in high-detail comic book artwork and concept/production designs for Film, Videogames and TV for such companies as Sony, EA, Microsoft Game Studios and Warner Bros. Well known for his horror themed art, Nick created artwork for Clive Barker's *Hellraiser* comic book series, as well as artwork for Marvel Comics, 2000AD, Judge Dredd, World of Warcraft and Magic the Gathering. Nick was the first artist to win the Rondo Hatton Horror Award (2014) for Best Cover Artwork for his Clive Barker, *Nightbreed* cover painting for FANGORIA. He is also the writer and illustrator of *Legends: The Enchanted* – winner of the HorrorNews award for 'Best Original Graphic Novel 2010' and was nominated for an Eagle Award for 'Favorite Single Story 2010'. *Legends* is now in development as a feature film.

TIM BRADSTREET
Cover Artist

Inkpot Award-winning and Eisner Award-nominated artist Tim Bradstreet has over 25 years of experience as an illustrator, graphic designer, lead artist, conceptual artist, production designer, and marketing strategist spanning the genre in the video game, comic book and film industries. Bradstreet is primarily known for his work on White Wolf's *Vampire: The Masquerade*, and as cover artist for *The Punisher,* and *John Constantine: Hellblazer.* His recent credits include *Clive Barker's Hellraiser* and *Escape From New York.* On the film side, Tim recently worked as an illustrator on AMC's *The Walking Dead.*

Afterword

Welcome back to **John Carpenter's Asylum!** What a long, strange trip it's been these last couple of years. We are grateful to those of you who have taken this journey along with us and traveled the demon-filled highways of our imaginations along with Beckett and Duran from Los Angeles into the Mid-West and now into the depths of the Barrens and Hell itself.

During this time our team has explored what personal salvation and damnation mean to us and possibly have challenged you as well in where you think your personal salvation might lie. And what denotes true innocence?

Does our purpose carry on beyond this mortal plane and what truths transcend the teachings of our childhood churches and temples? Is divinity only to be found from without or does it reside within each of us?

And has Beckett really been the angel he has always been looking for, or is he really just another fallen seraphim with mankind plunged into an eternal abyss?

If story tellers are truth seekers, then those who read and follow us illuminate the paths we draw. Story telling is within our DNA and we are having such a great time with you all exploring these tales.

So tell us:

Where do **you** look for your angels?

John Carpenter and Sandy King